Mental Health Problems in Old Age: A Reader

This Reader is one part of an Open University integrated teaching system and the selection is therefore related to other material available to students. It is designed to evoke the critical understanding of students. Opinions expressed in it are not necessarily those of the course team or of the University.

Mental Health Problems in Old Age:
A Reader

Edited by

Brian Gearing, Malcolm Johnson and Tom Heller
*Department of Health and Social Welfare, The Open University,
Milton Keynes, UK*

WITHDRAWN

*A Wiley Medical Publication
in association with
The Open University*

JOHN WILEY & SONS
Chichester • New York • Brisbane • Toronto • Singapore

British Library Cataloguing in Publication Data
Mental health problems in old age : a reader.
—— (Open University education for health
series).
1. Geriatric psychiatry
I. Gearing, Brian   II. Johnson, Malcolm
III. Heller, Tom   IV. Series
618.97′689   TC451.4.A5

ISBN 0 471 91871 7

Typeset by Photo·graphics, Honiton, Devon.
Printed and bound by Anchor Brendon Ltd., Tiptree, Colchester.

Contents list and author

Introduction

This Reader is intended as a sourcebook for workers with older people in the health and social services; for researchers in gerontology; and for a wider public interested in learning more about mental health issues in old age. The Reader stands as an independent publication, but it is also available as an integral part of the Open University course, also called *Mental Health Problems in Old Age**. The aims of the book and the course are the same. They are: to promote greater understanding about the nature of mental health and mental disorders found among older people living in the community; to increase knowledge of the needs of relatives and other lay supporters; to increase awareness of different kinds of treatment care and support; to encourage a critical awareness of the consequences of current community care policies; and to encourage a multidisciplinary and coordinated approach to working with mentally ill older people and their supporters.

These are broad aims which reflect the nature and size of the problems of mental health and illness in old age. The existing literature in this field, though diverse, does not adequately reflect the range of both the scientific research and the practical issues involved. The scientific literature tends to be very specialist, focusing narrowly on a very specific research problem or study and is of limited value to a general reader or a professional working in this field. The practitioner-based literature, on the other hand, can be found extensively in the professional journals but is frequently individualistic and case-oriented, offering few reliable lessons to other workers in different settings.

We have commissioned many of the articles in the Reader because we found surprising gaps in the literature in areas of central importance. A striking example was the absence of a comprehensive review of the main epidemiological findings concerning mental disorders among the elderly population in Britain. The article by Brayne and Ames, commissioned for the Reader, fills this gap. Similar difficulties were encountered in finding any coherent theoretical contribution to the understanding of positive mental health in later life. In other important areas, such as the mental health of older people from ethnic minority groups, a number of small-scale surveys and other local studies of different older ethnic minorities were available, but there was nothing about their mental health problems and no overview of the general situation of these minority old age groups in our society.

We have tackled these and other gaps and problems by commissioning new literature, specially for this volume, from experts in their particular fields. Thirteen of the twenty-six articles in the volume are original and have not been published elsewhere. Some of these are review articles, written in non-technical language, which provide an overview of the main issues and research findings in such areas as attitudes and stereotypes about ageing (Slater and Gearing), or 'risk' (Alison Norman). Others deal with the 'neglected' areas already referred to, such as concepts of mental health in old age (Peter Coleman), mental disorder and ethnic minority elders (Alison Norman), the subjective experience of the dementia sufferer (Alison Froggatt), and an alternative non-medical approach to understanding dementia (Tom Kitwood). We believe that these and the other specially commissioned articles which fill gaps in the existing literature should add to the usefulness of the volume. However, we would not claim that its coverage of issues is comprehensive. This partly reflects the need to supplement rather than duplicate areas covered elsewhere in the Open University course. Partly, too, it reflects the sheer absence of reliable research in some areas for which we have not been able to compensate.

*The Open University course *Mental Health Problems in Old Age (P577)* is the third of the three short courses developed as part of the *Education for Health* Project by the Department of Health and Social Welfare. Intending students can obtain further particulars from the Department of Health and Social Welfare, The Open University, Walton Hall, Milton Keynes MK7 6AA, UK.

What we do believe is that the breadth of coverage in the volume, its new material, and the high readability of almost all the contributions provide something new to help the growing group of students and practitioners working with older people. Our selection of articles gives emphasis to practitioner issues (as well as that distilling scientific/research literature and social policy analysis). This is reflected particularly in the last two sections of the book. A further influence on the selection has been our view that it is important to encourage identification with the older person who is the recipient of care. This is something which emerges particularly strongly in articles by Alison Froggatt, Malcolm Johnson, Alison Norman and Peter Coleman. Finally, this volume reflects a multidisciplinary and multioccupational orientation, both in the range of articles included and in the approach particular authors have taken in dealing with treatment and care issues and practices (e.g. Chris Cloke, Muir Gray and David Hunter).

With a view to assisting readers who may not be working through the book according to the plan suggested in the Open University course, we have grouped the individual articles in the Reader into sections, each dealing with a different topic. The first section deals with the broad societal and theoretical context for most of what follows. The second section deals with community needs and issues affecting older people as a social group, as well as the minority among them with serious mental health problems. The third section comprises articles which bring some very varied perspectives to bear on our understanding of a range of mental disorders. These include different conceptual approaches from Procter and Kitwood to explaining the root causes of dementia; Robert Slater's very readable review of the empirical research literature on memory; and Woods and Britton on cognitive loss in old age. The last two sections focus most directly on the world of practitioners. The fourth section covers the approaches of different disciplines to assessing the mental health problems of old people. The last section deals with issues and practices inherent in the treatment and care of older people, such as the organizational constraints on effective cooperative work (David Hunter); a newly commissioned review of recent projects and other practical approaches to meeting service needs (Christopher Cloke); the ethical and legal implications of treatment (Muir Gray); work with bereaved people (Lily Pincus); and reviews of specific therapies and treatments (Kinney *et al.,* Peter Coleman and Burns and Phillipson).

While the Editors must be held responsible for the final collation and selection of the articles in this Reader, and particularly for its deficiencies, some of the items included were recommended, commented upon and read by other members of the Open University team responsible for the production of the course. We gratefully acknowledge their collaboration:

Mike Church, Marjorie Gott, Janet Grant, Brian Lodge, Robert Slater, John Wattis, Ann Webber.

Caroline Malone has provided excellent administrative support.

We also owe thanks to Antonet Roberts for painstaking and highly efficient secretarial assistance.

Brian Gearing
Malcolm Johnson
Tom Heller
October, 1987

Section I

Mental health, ageing and society

An ageing Britain—what is its future?

MARGOT JEFFERYS

Chairman, Centre for Policy on Ageing, London

INTRODUCTION

What do we understand when we hear people talk or the newspapers write about 'an ageing Britain'? How has the age structure of Britain's population changed during this century, and how is it likely to change in its final years, and beyond? The even more important questions we must ask are what are the current and future implications of past changes and of those still to come? Are there grounds for the alarm—almost panic—which increased survival of so many more into their ninth and tenth decades appears to have evoked in some quarters? What are the real challenges to society of more octogenarians, nonagenarians and centenarians in its ranks? Can they be met, and at what price?

These are some of the questions posed for those concerned with older people.

FROM PYRAMID TO RECTANGULAR CUBE

Demographers, the social scientists who study the composition of human populations and trace changes over time in the patterns of fertility and family size, household groupings and so on, use a simple graphic device to illustrate the results of the great decennial count we have in this country—the Census. The graph in Figure 1 compares the age and sex structure of the population of Great Britain in 1901—the first Census of the century—with that of 1981.

In 1901, the graph has the shape of a pyramid—broad at the base and tapering to the top. The pyramidical shape in that year reflected the high mortality rates at all ages, and particularly among the very young. A

Reproduced with permission from the 1987 Annual CPA/NICCOL Lecture, Centre for Policy on Ageing, 1987 (edited). © Centre for Policy on Ageing.

comparatively small proportion of each birth cohort (i.e. of those born at a particular period) reached old age. In 1981, however, the graph is more rectangular. It sums up what has happened during the century. Although the birth rate has fluctuated from time to time—e.g. it was low in the inter-war years and high immediately after the Second World War—the proportion of survivors at each age—and especially in the youngest age groups—has increased. The result is that the proportion of the population which is over the age at which state pensions can be drawn has increased in 80 years from about one in twenty (5%) to over one in six (about 18%). There are clearly grounds, then, for talking about an ageing Britain, in the sense that a substantially greater proportion of all those born now advance to higher rungs on the human life span ladder. Surely, this is a matter for celebration? In simple life survival chances, the century has witnessed a massive change for the better.

MORE JOANS THAN DARBYS

It should be noted that both the pyramid and the cube in Figure 1 are a trifle lop-sided—the cube in particular. Males are to the left and females to the right. In 1901, as at present, rather more males than females were born. The ratio was about 105 or 106 males to every 100 females, but the former were most likely to die in all age bands. When mortality for both sexes was great, as it was at the beginning of the century, it did not take long for a cohort to advance up the age scale before females outnumbered males. In the 1980s, it is still true that males die more frequently than females at all ages, except possibly after reaching the age of 100 years (OPCS, 1987, p.5), but the number of all deaths in childhood and early adult life is now so small that it is not until individuals reach their late forties that women actually outnumber men. Thereafter,

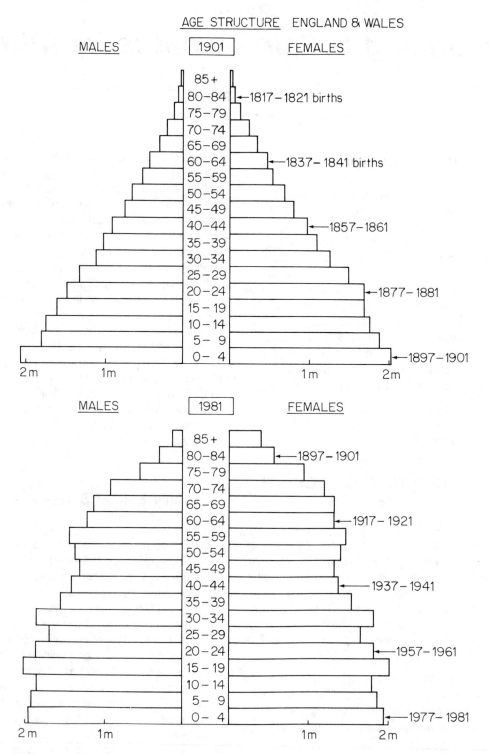

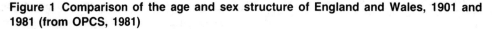

Figure 1 Comparison of the age and sex structure of England and Wales, 1901 and 1981 (from OPCS, 1981)

male mortality rates in the last decades of life have been so much greater than those for females that a significant disparity has developed in the numbers of men and women in the older age groups (Figure 2). Figure 2 indicates the extent to which death continues to discriminate between men and women in older age, leaving more and more women among the survivors.

The preponderance of women, especially among the over 85 year olds—a group which is becoming known as the oldest old—also leads to another interesting differentiating factor between the sexes at this age. While, not unnaturally, there are roughly comparable numbers of *still married* men and women in the population over 65, and even a slight excess of males because men generally marry women younger than themselves, widowers are greatly outnumbered by widows (Figure 3).

There are also fewer never married men than women. This, too, is due to the fact that single men at younger ages are more likely to die than single women. But it should also be said that women now 80 or more belong to a generation whose chances of ever marrying were reduced by the great loss of eligible young men in the First World War, 1914–18. In subsequent cohorts who reach the age of 80 and 90, there will be an even smaller proportion of never marrieds, especially among women.

WHAT ABOUT THE FUTURE?

Having introduced the idea that the future is likely to tell a different story about the number of people who remain single all their lives, it is time to ask what other predictions can legitimately be made about the shape of things to come. What is it going to be like in the first years of the twenty-first century? And can we look even further ahead?

There are no certainties in demography, but we can be fairly sure of the numbers of men and women over the statutory retirement pension age (60 for women and 65 for men) that there will be well into the twenty-first century—at least until the 2040s—because all of them are already born. Unless there are radical changes in migration to and from the British Isles, or in mortality rates in middle age, or an unprecedented natural disaster, the *numbers* can be confidently predicted (Table 1).

What is more difficult to predict into the middle of the next century is the *proportion* of the total population this older group will constitute, because that depends upon the birth rate, and that, if past experience is anything to go on, shifts unpredictably with transient social circumstances—such as the level of unemployment or whether or not there is a war—as well as with changing social attitudes to child-bearing and the age at which it is thought suitable for women to bear children.

Although the very long term future does play a part in present thinking (e.g. there is concern about the burden which present promises of pension levels may impose on future generations of working age) it is the shorter term prospects—from now until the end of the century—which should mainly concern policy makers. What that clearly involves (Table 2) is, first, a relatively stable number over statutory retirement pension age, but, second, a substantial increase in the number and proportion of that retirement-age population which is over 85 and a decrease in the number and proportion of 65 to 74 year olds who are now often described as 'the younger elderly'.

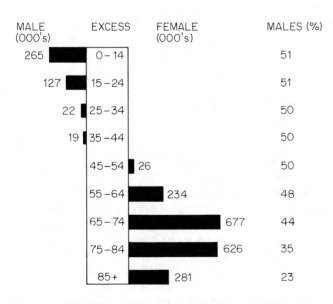

Figure 2 Mortality rates of men and women in the older age groups

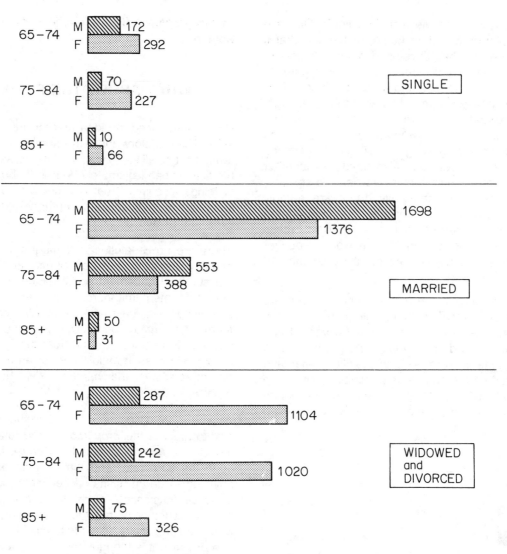

Figure 3 Marital status by age and sex (from OPCS, 1981)

WHAT ARE THE SOCIAL IMPLICATIONS OF THIS PREDICTED CHANGE?

There is no doubt that the shift in numbers towards the older section of the retired population has been viewed with alarm by some commentators as well as by some members of the professional groups whose work brings them closely into touch with the oldest old—the geriatricians, general practitioners, nurses, social workers, occupational therapists and physio-therapists and others (HAS, 1982). Particular worries have been expressed about the likely increase in the numbers of very frail individuals in need of constant attention and of those suffering from Alzheimer's disease and other forms of senile dementia for which there are as yet no known cures. One estimate suggests that one in five of those aged 85 and over now suffer from dementia (Norman, 1987a, p.2). If there are nearly a million over that age in 2001, then getting on for 200 000 will be afflicted by that time. A daunting prospect.

Table 1 Projected population, aged 65 and over (males) and 60 and over (females), 1991–2051

Year	Total (millions)	Percentage over 85
1991	10.4	8.7
2001	10.2	9.8
2011	10.9	12.1
2021	12.1	9.9
2031	13.7	10.2
2041	13.1	12.2
2051	12.3	15.5

Source: Government Actuary, *Population Projections*, 1986, p. 26.

Table 2 Actual and predicted numbers in three age bands, 1981 and 2001

Age band	1981 (millions)	2001 (millions)	Percentage increase (+) or decrease (−)
65–74	5.2	4.7	− 9
75–84	2.7	3.0	+11
85 +	0.6	1.0	+67
All 65 +	8.5	8.7	+ 2

Source: Government Actuary, Population Projection Series, No. 13.

Some official statistics serve to fuel the fire of alarm. For example, it is the population aged 80 and over which uses a whole gamut of health and social services more than do younger sections of the population. Very old people have high consultation rates with general practitioners, and have many more home visits from these doctors—the most expensive form of consultation (Central Statistical Office, 1987). They constitute the bulk—and an increasing bulk—of the caseload of district nurses (Central Statistical Office, 1987, p.131). The work of health visitors—traditionally and profitably with mothers and children—threatens to be 'undermined' by increasing requests from general practitioners that they take part in the home care of the very old (Central Statistical Office, 1987, p. 131).

The Home Help service—to all intents and purposes—is a service for the very old already (Central Statistical Office, 1987, p. 131). So too is the Meals-on-Wheels service (Central Statistical Office, 1987, p. 131). The number of residents of voluntary and private homes (and to a lesser extent of local authority homes) has increased, and the increase is almost entirely due to the numbers of very old entering such homes (Central Statistical Office, 1987, p. 133). An increasing proportion of all hospital beds—not only those in geriatric or psychogeriatric wards—are occupied by those well on into their seventies and eighties. (DHSS, 1987, pp. 117–18). Day hospitals have sprung up to assist the process of rehabilitation after acute illness which can herald the onset of chronic disability and handicap, and their patients are overwhelmingly the very old (Donaldson, Wright and Maynard, 1986). Local authorities, striving to fulfil the Government's policy of increasing community care, are facing increasing expenditure on house adaptations. These are designed to promote continuing self-care and autonomy for the very disabled among whom the elderly population is prominent.

Providing services of all these kinds—and in this way also helping to share the 'burden' which usually falls on unpaid relatives whose caring thus makes up for the lack of appropriate health and welfare services—can clearly not be done without resources, human and material (Abrams, 1978, p. 67). And the cost has to be borne in the main by central and local government, because, for one reason or another, most older people cannot meet the costs themselves.

It is the likelihood that those of working age will have to pay more in rates and taxes to ensure that adequate services are available for the expected increase in the numbers needing them which has given rise to the feeling in some quarters that old age, already a burden, threatens to be an even greater one in the future. It is a short step from such a view to 'blaming' older people themselves for the fiscal crisis—the heavy burden of taxation which is held, in some quarters, to be behind the late twentieth century failure of the British economy. This attachment of blame, incidentally, also occurs in countries other than Britain, because the ageing of the population is a world-wide phenomenon, especially in advanced, industrialised countries. Such attitudes are particularly rife in the United States of America where the youth cult has been and remains strong (Levin and Levin, 1980). Unfortunately, some of the older generation, despite a life-long contribution to the nation's well-being, have been heard to apologise for having lived so long (Norman, 1987b)! They have been made to feel guilty for surviving to an age where they need to call on more services than do younger people.

ARE THE RIGHT CONCLUSIONS BEING DRAWN?

If the statistics recited here are to be believed, does it not follow that there are serious grounds for alarm? If survivors into the ninth and tenth decade are to be adequately served, is it not clear that it will have to be at the expense of younger generations? Does not an ageing population inevitably imply a more impoverished nation, if not among elderly, among younger people?

There is little point in denying that if Britain is to enable the very old in the present as well as the future to live out their remaining years in dignity, more human and material resources will have to be devoted to their welfare. Older people need to be in hospital longer, to consult general practitioners more often and take more drugs, to have more home-based chiropody and nursing services and more personal social services than younger people (Central Statistical Office, 1987). They also require regular long-term financial support in the form of pensions which younger people do not receive unless they are chronically disabled or unemployed. The very young, of course, by reason of their educational needs and a societal commitment to support parenthood, are also more costly to the Exchequer than young adults, though not as costly as the very old. The question to be asked, therefore, is can the nation afford to increase the resources it already feels obliged to expend on the very old?

The answer should be an unequivocal 'yes'. It is our values and not our limited means which prevent us from recognising that our society possesses adequate resources for the task in hand. It is the way in which the public is presented with the facts, rather than the facts themselves, which almost guarantees that we panic at the size of the task ahead.

First, for example, take the matter of numbers (Table 3). In 1981, about 180 individuals in every 1000 were aged 65 or more. In 2001, there will be about the

Table 3 Estimated numbers in four age bands in every 1000 population, 1981–2001

Age band	1981	2001
Under 16	215	218
16–64	605	605
65 and over	180	177
(85 +)	(11)	(17)
All	1000	1000

Source: Government Actuary, Population Projections.

same number per 1000. This should not be a cause for alarm if a goodly portion of the 1000 is in work and willing to support all those—including the over 65s—who are not.

The second question is how far do those over pensionable age contribute currently to the gross national product of goods and services, and what proportion of that national product do they consume?

Here the answers are not straightforward. The balance between 'contribution' and 'outgoings' depends upon what is entered on each side of the balance sheet. One factor to which the prophets of doom draw attention and which is likely to increase the outgoings side of the balance sheet is the predicted change in the age distribution among pensioners, to which attention has already been drawn. The figures in Table 3 show that about 11 in every 1000 of the population in 1981 were over 85. In 2001, their number will have increased to about 17 in every 1000. These are the people likely to be most dependent on others.

These facts are usually presented in such a way as to frighten us out of our wits. For example, we are treated to the statistics of increased longevity as if they, in themselves, constitute a horrendous problem. A million over 85 by the beginning of the new century with no commensurate increase in the numbers between 18 and 64! Indeed, a 67% increase in this age group in a 20 year period and a decline in the number of the young old able to care for them! Is it not a gloomy forecast? It is possible, however, to look at the numbers in quite a different way. For example, even if every one of the predicted 17 in every 1000 were totally bedridden and/or demented (and clearly that is not the case), can it really be claimed that this would be an insuperable problem for a country which is as technologically innovative and as ingenious as ours? It is our political and social will which is at issue, not our capacity to cope had we the mind to.

Another item which will tend to weight the debit side of the balance sheet in future is the likely reduction in the numbers of people of pensionable age who will be earning currently and hence adding to the gross national product as that is at present calculated. At the beginning of the century, substantial numbers of the elderly population—especially men—continued to work, partly, no doubt, because they had no entitlement to a pension as of right and wished to avoid the fate of most survivors—an ignominious end in the dreaded parish workhouse (Parker, 1982, p. 177). In more recent years, not only has 60 for women and 65 for men tended to be the maximum age at which permanent retirement from the labour force takes place, earnings from current employment cease, and statutory and, in some case, occupational pensions are drawn; as a result of high levels of unemployment (and possibly also of the capacity of the most affluent to accumulate enough resources to enable them to retire early if they wish), the percentage of those in their late fifties and early sixties who regard themselves as retired has increased (GHS, 1986, p. 73).

The tendency to leave paid employment at or even before the age of eligibility for state pension may or may not continue into the future. Much depends upon the general level of employment, for when it is high, employers and government welcome the labour of older workers. When it is low, there is pressure from all sides for older workers to retire (Phillipson, 1982, p.167). When over 3 million of those between 16 and 64 are unemployed, there is certainly pressure for those in their late fifties and early sixties to leave the labour force and little encouragement for those over 65 to stay on. It should be noted, however, that if one million of the three million were back at work and not receiving support from Exchequer, there would be little difficulty in meeting the social security benefits for the million over 80 year olds.

Whether or not early retirement and high unemployment continue, however, they should not blind us to the need to consider other factors which influence our capacity to care for dependent populations. For example, the productivity of every hour of work, that is the volume of goods and services that can be produced in an hour, has immeasurably increased during the present century. For example, one calculation showed that while the occupied population increased by 35% between 1911 and 1966, the real value (at constant factor price) of the national income increased by over 150% (Bacon, Bain and Pimlott), pp. 64, 97). In future, given the microchip and other technological advances already certain, the trend will continue. Far fewer work hours will be required to produce goods and services to the level needed to meet all the basic requirements for food, shelter, leisure and health of the entire population, including the very old. An increase from 11 to 17 in the number of the latter should not throw us! It is because old age is presented as an intolerable burden falling on the shoulders of the young that we are persuaded to be pessimistic as to the outcome.

There is another assumption often made by the prophets of doom which needs challenging. It is that those who are not currently working for money make no contribution to the nation's gross national product—that they are consumers, not producers. For this reason, most of those over statutory retirement pension age are regarded as non-producers—as drones. This, however, must also be seen as a presentation of the lives of human beings which is useful perhaps for taxation purposes, but bears little resemblance to the real world. In this country, and indeed throughout the world, most of the productive tasks associated with sustaining day-to-day life and happiness, namely child-rearing, care of the sick and household management, are undertaken outside the field of paid employment (Stacey, 1981). They are basic to human life. Most of them are performed by women, and most women continue to perform them into their old age, whether or not they have had formal paid employment. If the performance was costed, the assumption that the retirement pension is not earned but an unreciprocated gift from the employed to the non-employed would be found to be untenable. In short, the older generation not only has given by its paid and unpaid labour in the past; it continues to give as well as take in the present.

Another 'prediction' frequently made is that there will be an increase in the extent of disability among the survivors into old age. It is beyond dispute that advances in medicine and improvements in living conditions have enabled individuals who at previous times would not have survived severe illness or chronic handicaps to live on, perhaps with some disability, into their seventh, eighth and ninth decades. No-one in this country, one hopes, would advocate the Nazi doctrine of exterminating the unfit. But those who see the longevity of disabled people as a threat also ignore other contemporary changes which will affect the future pattern of health among the elderly (Central Statistical Office, 1987, p. 136). Medical advances have not only enabled some very disabled to survive into old age: they have also reduced the dependency on others of very many elderly people. Hip replacements and coronary by-passes are the most spectacular examples of such advances. They increase mobility and enhance the quality of life. So too can the spread of knowledge about the behaviour patterns associated with fitness in old age which has resulted from epidemiological research.

We know, moreover, that the more affluent are more likely to feel that they enjoy good health and less likely to suffer from conditions which restrict their mobility and capacity to participate in a wide range of social and cultural activities than the least well-off (GHS, 1986, p. 126). There is encouraging evidence to suggest that the 'young old' today are generally both more affluent and in better physical and mental shape than their counterparts a generation ago were at the same age (GHS, 1986, p. 141). It is probable, therefore, that, as they age and become, in their turn, the 'older' and the 'oldest old', their health will be better than that experienced by the present generation of over 80 year olds.

Another reason for some optimism is the increase in personal possessions with which people enter the third age. At one time it was only an affluent few who owned their own houses or capital assets which they could invest to increase their incomes. The proportion who are owner-occupiers has grown substantially, and most of them have paid off their mortgages (Central Statistical Office, 1987, p. 140). Of course, this does not mean that accommodation problems for the old are solved for all time. Other statistics, for example, show that households with retired heads have fewer domestic amenities of most kinds than younger households (GHS, 1986, p. 61), and there is a serious shortage of sheltered housing at prices which older people can afford (Tinker, 1984, p. 86–8); but progress on all these scores is being made, and, if it is maintained into the 1990s, should help the oldest

individuals to maintain their independence—and their health—for longer periods of time.

THE CHALLENGES

In short, statistics relating to old people are presented in such a way as to spread a great deal of gloom about the future, not only for the old themselves but for society at large. If we examine these statistics critically and the social and economic context in which changes in the age structure of Britain are likely to occur in the future we can dispel much of that gloom. Policies and actions should not be dictated by widely held but largely unexamined preconceptions, since the distorted images which they can produce are to the detriment of ordinary people as they age.

Such a statement must not, of course, be taken to imply that the future for older people is assured if we sit back and let things take their course. Those who depend entirely for their income on the state pension, supplementary pensions and housing benefits are likely to be on the fringes of unacceptable poverty unless the level of benefits is increased. Moreover, we have to make sure that older people have increased opportunities for personal fulfilment. In order to do this, we need to challenge many popular perceptions of old age and ageing and of their impact upon society as a whole. We need also to identify opportunities for enrichment in older age, to promote these opportunities and to defend them if they are misguidedly under attack. We should remain concerned too with the welfare of that substantial minority of older people for whom (and for whose families) ageing has brought little joy.

One of the greatest challenges we face in these tasks is to convince ourselves and others that the lenses of the spectacles we are usually sold may seriously distort the picture we see. If they do not paralyse us altogether, they may make us too cautious about the steps we can take. We must make sure that the public generally is equipped in the future with spectacles which give it a clearer and more rounded view of the opportunities for all of an ageing Britain.

REFERENCES

Abrams, P. (1978). In J. Barnes and N. Connelly (eds.), *Social Care Research*, Bedford Square Press, London (quoted in Tinker, see below).

Bacon, R., Bain, G.S., and Pimlott, J. (1972). In A.H. Halsey (ed.), *Trends in British Society Since 1900*, Macmillan, London.

Central Statistical Office (1987). *Social Trends*, No. 17, HMSO, London.

DHSS (1987). *Health and Personal Social Services Statistics for England, 1987*, HMSO, London.

Donaldson, C., Wright, K., and Maynard, A. (1986). 'Determining value for money in day hospital care of the elderly', *Age and Ageing*, **15**, 1.7.

GHS (1986). *General Household Survey, 1984*, HMSO, London.

HAS (1982). *The Rising Tide. Developing Services for Mental Illness and Old Age*, National Health Service, Hospital Advisory Service, HMSO, London.

Levin, J. and Levin, W.C. (1980). *Ageism: Prejudice and Discrimination against the Elderly*, Wadsworth Publishing Co., Belmont, California.

Norman, A. (1987a). *Severe Dementia: The Provision of Long-stay Care,* Centre for Policy on Ageing, London.

Norman, A. (1987b). *Aspects of Ageism: A discussion paper,* Centre for Policy on Ageing, London.

OPCS (1981). *Census: Historical Tables*, Government Statistical Service, HMSO, London.

OPCS (1987). *Mortality Statistics for England and Wales*, No. 17, Government Statistical Service, HMSO, London.

Parker, S. (1982). *Work and Retirement*, Allen and Unwin, London.

Phillipson, C. (1982). *Capitalism and the Construction of Old Age*, Macmillan, London.

Stacey, M. (1981). 'The division of labour revisited or overcoming the two Adams'. In P. Abrams, R. Deem, J. Finch and P. Rock (eds.), *Practice and Progress: British Sociology 1950–1980*, Allen and Unwin, London.

Tinker, A. (1984). *The Elderly in Modern Society*, 2nd ed., Longman, London.

The epidemiology of mental disorders in old age

CAROLE BRAYNE* and DAVID AMES†

*MRC Fellow in Epidemiology at Addenbrookes Hospital, Cambridge;
†Research Fellow and Honorary Lecturer at the Royal Free Hospital School of Medicine

This article is a brief introduction to the epidemiology of mental disorders in old age. In order to make sense of epidemiological studies it is important to know some of the underlying concepts and general principles (which are also useful in interpreting other work). The first section therefore deals with some theoretical aspects of epidemiology, the second with dementia and cognitive function and the third with depression and other mental disorders of old age.

A. INTRODUCTION
Demography

In the past the number of people who reached 70 was a tiny proportion of the population. The decline in birth rates and infant mortality, the control of infectious diseases and improvements in nutrition and living standards have resulted in an increased life expectancy, an increase seen largely in the early half of this century in this country. This change in the proportion of the elderly to the rest of the population is seen in most countries, but is occurring more slowly in developing countries.

From the health perspective the population aged over 65 is separated into two groups, the young old and the old old, the latter group often being classified as those aged 75 and over. This is because of the great increase in many diseases with age. By the year 2000 there will be twice as many people aged over 80 in the world as there were in 1970.

One way of presenting this change in the proportion of the population surviving into old age is with a survival curve (see Figure 1). With improvements in average life expectancy the curve can be seen to become more angular, or rectangularized.

The concept of survival curves can be extended to morbidity and autonomy. This is the hypothetical curve representing the likelihood of surviving to a certain age without chronic disabling disease for the former or loss of independence for the latter. It has been suggested that people could live a disease-free, fully autonomous life until natural death from biological ageing occurs (Fries, 1980). It has also been argued that as the life span extends, a greater part of life is spent in poor health and dependence.

Epidemiology

Epidemiology is the study of the distribution and determinants of disease in human populations. In the past epidemiologists were primarily concerned with the infectious diseases, but because of the reasons outlined above the emphasis has now changed to the chronic disorders affecting the older age groups.

Why measure disease in populations?

1. To identify causes and contributory factors in the development of disease for the purpose of possible prevention and treatment.
2. To provide data essential to planning, implementation and evaluation of services for the prevention, control and treatment of disease, and to the setting up of priorities among these services.

The first can be seen to be a long term aim and the second more immediate.

What are the best ways to achieve these aims? The type of investigation needed varies according to the

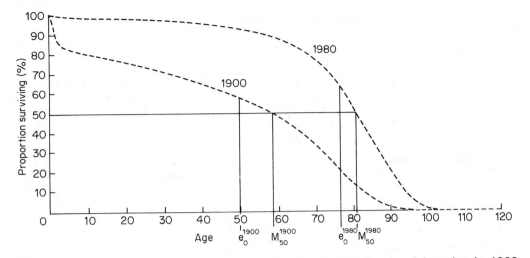

Figure 1 Survival curves for females born in the United States of America in 1900 and 1980. e_0^{1900} and e_0^{1980} are the life expectancies of birth for females in 1900 and 1980 respectively. M_{50}^{1900} is the age to which 50% of females subject to the mortality risks of 1900 could expect to survive and M_{50}^{1980} is the age to which 50% of females subject to the mortality risks of 1980 could expect to survive (from WHO, 1984).

purpose. The next section will deal with the specific approaches.

Epidemiological method There are several sources of information which can be used without having to set up new studies. These are the centrally collated statistics, summarized in Table 1. The mortality and routine morbidity statistics use internationally accepted coding systems for diagnoses—the International Classification of Disease (ICD). ICD also provides criteria for diagnoses. These are updated regularly to take into account new developments in diagnosis and understanding of disease. The version used at present is ICD9; ICD10 is in preparation.

Sources of information—surveys The data sources described in Table 1 do not provide much information on mental disorders of the elderly because these are not recognized as directly causing death, are often chronic and do not necessarily present to general practitioners. For a more accurate understanding of the disorders, more detailed investigations are necessary.

Surveys are required in order to measure how much of a particular disorder there is in a population. These can be conducted in any population, for example the community, institutions and hospitals.

Methods

The sampling technique If the survey is conducted in the community, the total population numbers to which the cases belong can be taken from the routinely collected statistics described in Table 1. This approach can be useful in hospital surveys, where the hospital may serve a specific geographic area. Often in epidemiological research in the United Kingdom the population from which the sample is chosen are the people registered with particular general practitioners. Another approach is to use the electoral register.

Case definition The medical model generally presents diseases or disorders as being clearly defined. When comparing hospital patients with healthy elderly people this apparent dichotomy is reinforced. However, when the whole population or a sample representative of it is studied, a whole spectrum from no abnormality to the full-blown disease is usually revealed, with varying proportions in a grey area on the edges of the disease. In the elderly the distinction between illness and normality is difficult to define. For example cognitive (i.e. mental) changes with age have been documented by many studies, and it has been suggested that dementia may represent an exaggeration of these changes. The debate becomes not 'has

Table 1   Routine sources of information in the United Kingdom

Type	Collected by	Information	Limitations	Uses
Census	OPCS—10 yearly	Sociodemographic variables on the whole population, e.g. age, sex, social class, migration	Questions change from census to census	Essential basic data on population
Mortality statistics	Registrar General OPCS	Causes of death for every death	Accuracy—especially in elderly	Time trends. Comparison with other areas and countries
Morbidity				
1. *Hospital*				
(a) Hospital in-patient enquiry	OPCS	Diagnoses of 1 in 10 discharges/deaths from hospital	Accuracy—especially in elderly. Numbers relate to events not people. Does not include mental health services.	Time trends. Planning and resource allocation
(b) Hospital activity analysis	Regional Health Authority	Every discharge/death		
(c) Mental health enquiry	OPCS	All admissions to psychiatric services		
2. *General practice*				
(a) National morbidity survey	Royal College of General Practitioners	Reasons for consultations with general practitioner groups throughout the country	Willing groups of general practitioners; therefore not necessarily representative	Regional variations and time trends

OPCS = Office of Population and Census Surveys.

he got it' but 'how much of it has he got' (Rose and Barker, 1984). Unless strict definitions for the presence of a certain disorder are laid down it is difficult to compare the results of different studies. The level of severity of cases will be determined by the needs of the study. Methods of case identification for mental disorders in the elderly include hospital diagnosis, full clinical interview in the community and lay interviewers administering short questionnaires. Such variation in techniques in studies can lead to differences in the cases identified. Early studies tended to rely on individual doctors' diagnoses whereas later studies used standard criteria for diagnosis. The internationally accepted criteria mentioned above (ICD) are being used increasingly in psychiatric research although there is a second system used extensively in the United States—DSM III (the third version of the *Diagnostic and Statistical Manual* of the American Psychiatric Association). More recently the questions themselves have been standardized, leading to either a clinical diagnosis using specified criteria or a computerized diagnosis (e.g. the Geriatric Mental Status Examination development in Liverpool by Professor Copeland and colleagues).

Quality control

Repeatability, variation in performance It is important to be aware that there can be considerable variation between different raters when assessing subjects–interrater reliability. This is usually consistent, producing a clear bias if present. Intrarater variation is the variation in one interviewer's performance, and is more likely to be random. Recently methods of training interviewers and standardizing techniques have been introduced throughout medical research, including psychiatry.

Gold standards In the field of mental disorders the standard—known as the gold standard—against which other methods (e.g. screening interviews by lay interviewers) are tested is usually a clinical interview by an experienced psychogeriatrician. The numbers of true cases and non-cases according to the gold standard is compared with those identified by the method under scrutiny.

Response rates If the refusal rate of a study is high there is a large proportion of the population about whom little is known. It is usually stated that those most likely to refuse are the older and sicker patients. This is a factor of great importance when considering mental health in the elderly age groups, since a high refusal rate could hide the very figures the research is aimed at measuring.

Types of survey

Cross-sectional population surveys In this sort of study, researchers define a population and then a sample of it to be surveyed. Information is provided on the amount of disease in a defined population (i.e. the prevalence) and its distribution within the population. Those with the disorder and those without can be compared for related factors. Surveys can be used as a screening process to identify undiagnosed cases.

This type of survey is appropriate for stable disorders such as dementia, but may not be for shorter lasting disorders such as mild depression. This form of investigation is also not very appropriate for looking at rare disorders, since the number of the non-cases seen will be disproportionate to the yield of cases. The smaller the sample size the less confidence one has in its results.

The statistic produced from cross-sectional studies is the proportion of the population studied suffering from the disorder measured; i.e.

$$\text{Prevalence} = \frac{\text{number of people with the disorder}}{\text{total population}}$$

The prevalence can be defined as the number of people with the disorder at one point in time (point prevalence), over a specified period extending up to the enquiry (period prevalence) and over an entire life span (life time prevalence). It is known that the further back in time questions extend the less likely the information is to be accurate. Point prevalence is the most frequently measured type, and is often shortened to prevalence.

Longitudinal population surveys Repeated observations on the same population, or a sample of it, permit the measurement of incidence, i.e. the rate of occurrence of new cases:

$$\text{Incidence} = \frac{\begin{array}{c}\text{number of new cases of a disorder}\\ \text{occurring in a given population during a}\\ \text{specific time period}\end{array}}{\text{population at risk during that time}}$$

These studies also provide information on natural history, outcome and the association between initial characteristics and the risk of future disease. There have been few longitudinal studies of representative community samples of the elderly, particularly in the United Kingdom. These studies are expensive and difficult to conduct with elderly populations because of high drop-out through death. The relationship between incidence, prevalence and recovery or death is shown in Figure 2.

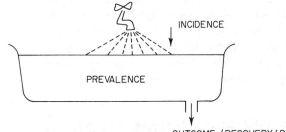

Figure 2 The bath analogy as an aid to understanding (1) the difference between incidence and prevalence and (2) the determination of prevalence

Comparison between studies

A difference in the age or gender structure of the population studied can lead to apparently different results if the disorder studied is age or sex dependent, even when the true result is actually the same. To avoid this problem it is possible to state the prevalence or incidence within small bands of ages (age-specific rates), or to adjust the figures to take account of these structure differences (standardization).

Having taken account of these differences and those in ascertainment of cases it is still possible to look for trends or patterns across studies. It can be seen whether there seems to be more illness in some communities than others, and for studies conducted at different times, whether there appears to be a change over time in the occurrence or existence of the disease in the population.

The search for causes

In all the above studies it is possible to examine the features of those with the disorder as compared to those without it. The first to be examined are usually age, sex and social status. If the samples are big enough other factors of interest can be examined, but with relatively uncommon disorders samples are rarely large enough for conclusions to be drawn. More detailed research into causation requires more intensive investigation and also actual hypotheses to test.

This is the area of research where case control studies are used. This is a much quicker and cheaper way of examining possible aetiological factors than large longitudinal studies. A group with the disorder—'cases'—and a group without the disorder—'controls'—are selected from hospitals and/or the community. These groups are usually matched for age and sex. This means that for each case there is one or more control who is the same sex and similar age. They are then compared for the presence or absence of factors of interest. These studies are rare in the elderly, particularly in the field of psychiatry.

B. ORGANIC MENTAL DISORDERS

Dementia is the main organic mental disorder in the elderly. It has been defined as the global impairment of higher mental function including memory, the capacity to solve the problems of day-to-day living, the performance of learned skills, the correct use of social skills and control of emotional reactions, without clouding of consciousness (Royal College of Physicians, 1981). It is often irreversible and progressive. As such it is a difficult disorder in which to standardize a diagnosis as it includes many facets of a person's life, some of which are culturally determined.

There are several types of dementia, the most common in the United Kingdom being senile dementia of the Alzheimer type (SDAT). This cannot be diagnosed with absolute certainty during life, but there are characteristic changes in the brain on examination at post mortem. These changes are also found in the brains of normal aged people in smaller numbers. The diagnosis is usually made by excluding the other causes of dementia. The next most common is multi infarct dementia (MID), a form of dementia caused by small strokes. In addition there are other causes such as dementia associated with Parkinson's disease, thyroid hormone disturbance, head injury, alcohol and many others. Table 2(a) and (b) shows the proportions of each type of dementia in series of hospital patients and from community-based samples. Follow up of subjects to validate the diagnosis by post mortem examination of the brain is difficult, but in those studies where it has been possible, the type of dementia is not always found to have been diagnosed accurately during life (particularly SDAT and MID).

Sometimes an apparently demented person is not in fact demented but suffering from a reversible cause of mental confusion (acute confusional state) or depression (pseudo dementia). Community studies cannot be as rigorous in differential diagnosis as hospital-based studies, but can probably improve their accuracy by asking other people who have known the subject for some time about the rate of progression of the mental changes. It does appear that these causes of an apparent dementing condition are extremely rare in the community, but are of much greater importance in the hospital setting. Most studies in the past did not attempt to differentiate between the different types of dementia or confusional states, but simply measured them all under one heading, e.g. organic brain syndrome.

Table 2   Types of dementia (%)

(a) In patients referred to hospital for diagnosis

	USA (Delaney, 1982)	UK (Gaspar, 1980)	USA (Larson, 1986)
Senile dementia of Alzheimer's type	49	38.6	74.5
Multi-infarct dementia	22	44.4	1.5
Parkinson's disease	5	1.3	—
Tumour	5	4.3	—
Toxic	4	—	9.5
Traumatic	3	—	—
Alcohol	3	1.7	4.0
Infection	3	—	—
Other—including metabolic	6	7.8	0.5

(b) In subjects identified during field surveys in community studies

	Newcastle, UK (Kay, Beamish and Roth, 1964)	Finland (Sulkava et al., 1985)	Japan (Hagesawa, Jomma and Imai, 1986)	California, USA (Pfeffer et al., 1987)
Senile dementia— Alzheimer's type	31.6	50.0	24.3	85.2
Multi-infarct dementia	49.0	39.0	41.4	6.2
Other	19.4	11.0	34.3	8.6
Including:				
Brain tumour		—		0.6
Parkinson's disease		1.4		1.2
Trauma		4.8		—
Infection		1.4		—
Alcohol/drugs		2.1		3.7
Miscellaneous/ unclassified		1.4		4.3

Note: Not all studies use same level or criteria of severity.

Prevalence of dementia

(a)   Community   The figures for the prevalence of moderate to severe organic syndromes are shown in Table 3. Also shown are the figures found for mild dementia, where measured. Figure 3 shows the differences between age groups. All the difficulties of diagnosis are greater when considering early forms of the disorder. There are major problems in differentiating cognitive impairment due to dementia, ageing, reversible illness or education-related poor performance. For this reason studies examining mild dementia have produced quite different figures. When the 'mildly demented' are followed over time, it is usually found

Table 3 Prevalence of severe and mild forms of organic brain syndrome in elderly populations from community samples in the United Kingdom

Author	Date published	Place	Age	Group number	Mild (%)	Moderate/ severely impaired (%)	Method	Response rate
Sheldon	1948	Wolverhampton Urban	65+	369	11.7	3.9	Psychiatric interview	
Kay, Beamish and Roth	1964	Newcastle Urban	65+	297	5.6	5.7	Psychiatric interview	98%
Williamson et al.	1964	Edinburgh Urban	65+	200	15.5	8.0	Psychiatric interview	81%
Parsons	1965	Swansea Urban	65+	228	24.9	14.0	Psychiatric interview	
Broe et al.	1976	Scotland	65+	808	4.3	3.8	Psychiatric interview	
Gilmore	1977	Scottish Borders Rural	65+	300	—	8.2	Psychiatric interview	
Clarke et al.	1984	Melton Mowbray Market town	75+	1073	—	2.5	Cognitive scale	95%
Morgan et al.	1987	Nottingham Urban	65+	1042	—	3.2	Screening and psychiatric interview	80%
Griffiths et al.	1987	Oxfordshire Rural	65+	200	—	10.0	Dementia scale	
Copeland et al.	1987	Liverpool Urban	65+	1070	—	5.2	Structured interview— computerized diagnosis	72%
Brayne et al.	Unpublished data collection 1986	Fen Area Rural	70–79	365	6.6	1.4	Structured interview	89%
Kemp	Unpublished data collection 1985	East Anglian sample Rural	75+	1000	—	6.0	Cognitive scale	95%

Table 4 Prevalence of organic brain syndrome in institutions in the United Kingdom

Author	Date	Place	Moderate/severely impaired (%)	Method
Kay, Beamish and Roth	1964	Newcastle	7.6	Interview
Mann et al.[a]	1984	London	31.0	Dementia scale
Clarke et al.	1984	Melton Mowbray	32.9	Cognitive scale
Ames[a]	1987	London	29.0	Dementia scale

[a] Part III homes only.

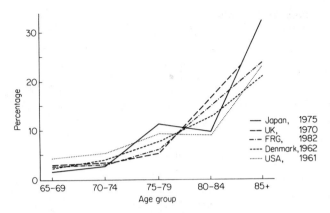

Figure 3 Age-specific prevalence of organic brain syndrome in five field surveys (point prevalence per 100 population in each age group). Included are all severe and moderately severe cases of dementia, delirium, confusional state and related conditions. The New York State study also includes some cases of functional psychosis. [Data derived from the following studies: New York State Department of Mental Hygiene, 1961 (USA); Nielsen, 1962 (Denmark); Kay et al., 1970 (UK); Kaneko, 1975 (Japan); Cooper and Sogna, 1983 (FRG).] (From Bergmann and Cooper, 1986)

that a substantial proportion become clearly demented, another group stay much the same and another group are better, i.e. were misclassified.

(b) Institutions Some prevalence studies have been carried out to estimate the proportion of people in institutions who are demented. As Table 4 shows, the prevalence in institutions is high. If the number of demented people admitted to institutions changes over time this can have a profound effect on the prevalence figures in a community sample from which institutionalized subjects are excluded. Unless these are known it is not possible to adjust the prevalence figures to look for true differences between populations.

The differences between these studies could be due to differences in methodology outlined in the section A. There has been speculation that there may be a decrease in the prevalence in the community in the United Kingdom over time. It is possible that there are regional differences, but as yet there have been no studies comparing different areas with the same methods.

International comparisons face the same problems of lack of uniformity of methods. Furthermore, even where the same diagnostic classification is used, there may be differences in interpretation which are culturally

determined. The only study which has examined two countries at the same time with the same techniques is the UK/US study (Gurland et al., 1983). Community samples of the elderly in London and New York were examined by trained interviewers. A considerably higher rate was found for dementia in New York than London (4.9% and 2.4% respectively). It is not clear whether this is a true difference or accounted for by differences in education and other sociodemographic factors. On the whole, studies from other countries show a similar range to those in Table 3.

Prevalence is affected by outcome and incidence. Recovery is not relevant in the case of dementia since it is usually considered to be irreversible. Duration of survival once the diagnosis has been made is of more importance. A recent follow-up of community residents seen in the prevalence study in Melton Mowbray shows a strong relationship between poor cognition measured on a short 12-point scale and survival (Jagger and Clarke, 1988). It appears that there is reduced survival according to the degree of the dementia, but this reduction may not be as great now as earlier studies found.

Incidence of dementia

Table 5 summarizes the studies conducted in the United Kingdom. Two methods of estimating incidence are shown. The first two studies count the number of cases presenting to services for the first time over a given period (tending to underestimate the true value); in the third a sample was interviewed at two points in time. There are several incidence studies currently in progress.

On the basis of studies in Scandinavia, it has been suggested that the incidence of dementia is decreasing, with the possible reason that experiences in early life could affect the individual's risk of developing dementia—a cohort effect. This is by no means proven.

Risk factors for dementia

Incidence studies of dementia are difficult to conduct, and the problems are compounded in the elderly. In order to study a group of 45 demented subjects, a population of 3000 would have to be followed for a year (using Bergmann's figures from Table 5). If the follow-up is extended the drop-out through death is

Table 5   Incidence studies of dementia

(a) Using first contact with hospital

Author	Date published	Place	Type of condition	Period of data collection	Sex	Incidence rate/1000 age 60+	Age groups		
							60–69	70–79	80+
Adelstein	1968	Salford	Senile organic disorders	5 year period	M	1.9 ± 0.45	1.1	2.4	6.9
					F	2.1 ± 0.37	0.8	2.8	6.7
Wing	1972	Camberwell	Dementia—any cause	5 year period	M	1.5 ± 0.45			
					F	3.0 ± 0.48			

(b) Field studies

Author	Date published	Place	Interview method	Follow-up period	Sex	Incidence rate/1000 age 60+
Bergmann	1971	Newcastle	Psychiatric interview	2½–4 years	M + F	15.0 ± 4.5

M = male.   F = female.

large. The case control method has been used to compare groups of SDAT and normals matched for age and sex for the presence or absence of possible aetiological factors. These studies have been conducted in the United States and Italy, and have found that age, family history of Alzheimer's disease, Down's syndrome, family history of Down's syndrome, head injury, thyroid abnormality and previous depression are more common in the cases than controls (Heyman *et al.*, 1984; French *et al.*, 1985; Amaducci *et al.*, 1986). It is difficult to interpret these findings at present for several reasons: uncertainty about the accuracy of diagnosis, choice of control—whether from hospital or community—and the difficulties introduced by having to ask a relative or other informant about past experience because the cases, by definition, cannot answer for themselves.

The finding that head injury appears to be associated with AD is an interesting one. This association is also found in studies of Parkinson's disease and other neurological disorders. It is possible that it is a recall bias which occurs in neurological patients. The association of Down's syndrome with dementia is also of interest and has led to speculation that the gene involved in Down's syndrome has some influence on the development of Alzheimer's disease in non-Down's subjects also. Other aetiological factors which have

been suggested but not proven include aluminium (because of the specific changes found in the brain).

In summary, therefore, it appears that dementia occurs more frequently with increasing age. Senile dementia of the Alzheimer type is thought to be the commonest form of dementia in the United Kingdom. SDAT may be more common in women than men, and MID more common in men than women. Taking all the prevalence figures into account there seems to be a rough consensus that dementia occurs in about 5% of the population aged over 65 and in up to 20% of the population aged over 80. The rate of new cases is about 1% per annum in those over 65, rising with increasing age. The rates for mild dementia are uncertain because of the difficulties in differentiating mild dementia from low performance due to other factors. Until more longitudinal studies are performed on this group the natural history of mild cognitive impairment will remain unclear. It is possible that there has been a decrease in incidence of dementia in the last decades, but differences in methodology could account for these differences.

Risk factors for AD (found by more than one study) appear to be family history of dementia or Down's syndrome, Down's syndrome itself and previous history of head injury.

Further work combining the detailed investigation of

demented subjects with the epidemiological approaches outlined in this article will lead to greater understanding of dementia in the future.

C. FUNCTIONAL DISORDERS
Introduction

Functional mental disorders are those for which no definite organic cause is yet established. These disorders cover a wide spectrum, from mild degrees of anxiety and depression to serious illnesses with severe symptoms such as hallucinations and delusions. Almost all these disorders are also encountered in younger adults, but the process of ageing often affects their incidence, prevalence, demographic distribution and presentation. For this reason the results of epidemiological studies which employ case finding procedures specially developed for use with the elderly are probably more reliable than those which use instruments designed for general use.

This section will consider the epidemiology of the important functional mental disorders of old age, concentrating on prevalence findings revealed in field surveys. Little information about the incidence of the disorders under consideration is available. Epidemiological findings from UK studies will be presented and contrasted with findings from overseas where relevant.

Depression

Depression is the commonest functional condition encountered in community surveys of elderly populations and in psychiatric practice with this age group. Attempts to produce a satisfactory definition of depression have not succeeded in producing criteria which are universally accepted. Depression as a term employed by psychiatrists and researchers working with the elderly is best understood as morbid sadness which is distinct from the sadness which normally accompanies loss. Depression is a broad syndrome whose central features include depressed mood, pessimistic thinking, reduced enjoyment and slowness. Because of the lack of consensus as to what constitutes a 'case' of depression, comparisons between methodologically different epidemiological studies are hazardous. A distinction can be made between the milder degrees of depressive neurosis which are commonly detected at rates of up to 20% or higher in community

surveys, and the more severe disorders variously labelled as manic depressive disorder, endogenous depression, affective psychosis or major depression (in the United States) which correspond more closely to the depressive disorders seen in routine psychiatric practice. Gurland (1976) has observed that when depression is defined on the basis of complaints in surveys the highest prevalence is encountered in those over 65, but that when it is diagnosed by psychiatrists milder ('neurotic') depression is commonest in the 35 to 45 age group and severe ('psychotic') depression is commonest between 55 and 65 with first episodes of depression becoming rarer with age. In those over 75 almost all episodes encountered are relapses rather than first attacks.

UK community studies The findings of the most important UK community studies are summarized in Table 6. In the now classic study of psychiatric disorders in the elderly of Newcastle upon Tyne conducted by Kay, Beamish and Roth (1964) depression and other neuroses were not considered separately, though it is likely that over half of these disorders were depressive in nature. Overall prevalence for affective illness and neurosis was 26%, but 16% of the cases were of only mild severity (more than twice as common in females), 10% moderate or severe (male to female ratio of 4:3), including 1.3% with the more serious diagnosis of 'endogenous affective illness'. Parsons (1965) examined 228 individuals over the age of 65 living in Swansea and reported an endogenous affective illness in 0.9%. Hare and Shaw (1965) found that 11% of 211 elderly in suburban London suffered from 'depressive symptoms'.

Gurland et al. (1983) in a rigorously designed cross-national study of elderly in New York and London used a structured interview (CARE) and a set of diagnostic criteria specifically designed for such a community population. The London sample consisted of 396 individuals over the age of 65 randomly drawn from the whole of greater London. Using criteria of varying stringency, up to just over a third of the sample could be regarded as having some evidence of depression, but the most important finding was that 12.4% could be classified as suffering from 'pervasive depression' (depression which pervades most aspects of life and warrants the attention of a mental health professional) including 1.3% with diagnosed manic depressive illness. Prevalence of pervasive depression

Table 6 Depression in UK community samples. (After Swartz and Blazer, 1986)

Study	Location and age	n	Instrument	Findings
Kay, Beamish and Roth, 1964	Newcastle 65+	505	Psychiatrist interview	26% affective illness and neurosis (inc. 1.3% endogenous affective illness)
Parsons, 1965	Swansea 65+	228	Psychiatrist interview	Endogenous depression 0.9% (lifetime prevalence ED 6%)
Hare and Shaw, 1965	London 65+	211	Interview	11% depressive symptoms
Gurland et al., 1983	London 63+	396	CARE	12.4% pervasive depression (inc. 1.3% manic depressive illness)
Maule et al., 1984	Edinburgh 62+	487	Psychiatrist interview	5.1% depression
Copeland et al., 1987	Liverpool 65+	1070	GMSA/AGECAT	11.3% depression (inc. 3.0% depressive psychosis)
Morgan et al., 1987	Nottingham 65+	1042	SAD	9.8% depression (4.9% met stricter clinical criteria)

declined steadily with age and rates were higher for females. In both sexes there was a strong and consistent association between depression and poor physical health. Copeland et al.'s (1987) recently published study of 1070 elderly in Liverpool interviewed with the AGECAT/GMS package (an interview designed for computerized diagnosis, sharing many items with Gurland's CARE schedule) reported a rate of 11.3% for depressive disorders despite using less strict diagnostic criteria than Gurland. The proportion of females with depression was almost twice that of males. Maule et al. (1984) also found depressive illness to be nearly twice as common in females in a North Edinburgh population aged over 62 and reported an annual incidence of 0.8% following reexamination of the cohort after five years. Morgan et al. (1987) used an instrument which had not been developed specially for the elderly. They found little difference in depression rates between those aged 65 to 74 and those aged over 75.

Community studies overseas The results of some important overseas studies of depression in elderly populations are presented in Table 7. The very high rates of depression reported by Zung (1967) and Stenback, Kumpulainen and Vauhkonen (1979) can

be attributed to the fact that the instruments they employed tend to overestimate depression in old age because they give heavy weight to the presence of certain physical symptoms which are often associated with depression in those under 65 but which are common and less likely to signify depression in the elderly.

In stark contrast to Zung, the Scandinavian studies of Essen-Moller and Hagnell (1961) and Bollerup (1975) found rates for psychiatrically diagnosed depression similar to those for endogenous and manic depressive disorders in the United Kingdom.

More recent North American studies have used instruments designed for the elderly. Blazer and Williams (1980) screened 497 elderly in Durham, North Carolina: 3.7% met DSM III criteria for major depression and a total of 14.7% of the overall sample were felt to have 'significant dysphoric symptoms' which were associated with poor health in 6.5%. The New York sample of elderly examined for the US/UK project (Gurland et al., 1983) had very similar rates for pervasive depression (13% vs 12.4%) to their London counterparts and twice the rate of manic depressive illness (2.5% vs 1.3%), but this difference was not given great emphasis as the diagnosis

Table 7 Overseas community studies of depression

Study	Location and age	n	Instrument	Findings
Essen-Moller and Hagnell, 1961	Scandinavia 60+	439	Psychiatrist interview	4.1% lifetime prevalence depression (inc. 0.9% 'psychotic')
Zung, 1967	SE USA 'community volunteers' 65+	169	Zung SDS	44% scored above general population cutpoint for 'case' of depression
Bollerup, 1975	Copenhagen 70	626	Psychiatric evaluation	0.6% depressive neurosis 0.3% endogenous depression 0.2% psychogenic depression
Blazer and Williams, 1980	SE USA 65+	497	OARS depression scale	14.7% sig. dysphoric symptoms (inc. 3.7% major depression)
Gurland et al., 1983	New York 65+	445	CARE	13% 'pervasive depression' (inc. 2.5% manic depressive illness)
Myers et al., 1984	4 sites in USA 65+	3350	DIS/DSM III	Major depression without bereavement 0%–0.5% men, 1.0–1.6% women Dysthymia 0.5%–1.8% men, 1.3%–3.1% women
Kay et al., 1985	Hobart, Australia 70+	158 (70–79) 115 (80+)	GMS6 comparing 3 different sets of criteria	DSM III major depression 6.3% (70–79), 15.5% (80+) DSM III 'dysphoric mood' 16.5% and 22.4% Pervasive depression 15.2% and 17.2% GMS6 psychiatric rating Mild depression 12.7% and 20.9% Moderate depression 12.0% and 13.0% Severe depression 1.9% and 0.9%

depended on the possibly unreliable report of past episodes from the subjects.

The most recent North American study of note is the NIMH-ECA programme. Preliminary data on 3350 elderly from four sites interviewed with a structured interview designed to permit psychiatric diagnosis by specific criteria (DSM III) were reported by Myers et al. (1984). Although there was an unexpectedly high degree of inter-site variation, overall rates for affective illness (mainly disorders of depressed mood) were lower among the elderly than the total population and females predominated at all ages. Rates for 'any affective disorder' in women over 65 varied from 3.1% to 5.0% between sites while those for men ranged from 0.5% to 2.2%.

An interesting exercise in comparative diagnosis was undertaken by Kay et al. (1985) who interviewed 274 non-institutionalized residents of Hobart, Australia, aged 70 and over, with a similar instrument (Canberra GMS-6) to that employed by Copeland's team in Liverpool. The information collected allowed the allocation of subjects to diagnostic categories using similar criteria to the NIMH/ECA investigators (major depression and 'dysphoric mood'—roughly equivalent to dysthymia), identical criteria to Gurland (pervasive depression, etc.) and a depression scale developed for the study. The report divides the sample into a group aged 70 to 79 and one aged 80 and over. For all three systems rates were higher in the older group, but there was considerable variation in rates between systems.

Depression in institutions About 2% of the UK population aged 65 and above live in residential homes run by local authorities. A survey of 12 homes in one London Borough (Mann *et al.*, 1984) found that 38% of assessable residents suffered from a 'significantly depressed state'. Overseas, Snowden and Donnelly (1986) reported that one-third of interviewable residents in nine Sydney nursing homes were depressed and Spagnoli *et al.* (1986) had very similar results in Milan. In general hospital populations of the elderly symptoms of depression are common and frequently unrecognized (Bergmann and Eastham, 1974).

Suicide

Although suicide is not strictly speaking a functional psychiatric disorder it is an important complication of depressive states. A recent study by Pierce (1987) reported that over 90% of elderly suicide attempters in Glamorgan were depressed, supporting the findings of earlier investigators.

The elderly represent only a small proportion of those who attempt suicide but are more likely to succeed in killing themselves than members of any other age group. In countries for which suicide statistics are available those over 65 represent between 25% and 30% of the total, although only 10% to 15% of these populations are elderly (Post, 1982). In those elderly who do attempt suicide a subsequent fatal attempt has been found to be twenty times more likely than in younger males (Shulman, 1978).

Mania

The main features of this disorder are mood elevation, increased activity and self-important ideas. Most patients who suffer from mania in old age have a past history of both manic and depressive episodes in earlier life. The precise incidence and prevalence of these disorders in the elderly is unknown. The NIMH/ECA programme in the United States failed to detect a single case of mania from a sample of 3350 elderly living in the community. Studies of admissions to psychiatric facilities yield a ratio varying from 6.5% to 19% of all admissions for both mania and depression worldwide (Post, 1982) and one (Shulman and Post, 1980) found a female to male ratio of 2.7:1.

Neuroses (see Table 8)

The term 'neurosis' refers to a wide range of disorders which have in common the absence of any organic brain disorder, the maintenance of contact with external reality and the lack of gross abnormalities in the personality of the sufferer. Some investigators have considered mild degrees of depression under this heading but recent work favours the classification of all forms of depression under a single rubric.

The epidemiology of neurotic disorders is an underresearched field. The huge disparity in rates for neurosis revealed by the three studies displayed in Table 8 is probably due to a lack of agreement about definitions. The high levels of disorder reported by Bergmann (1978) should be considered in the light of the information that only 18% of his neurotic subjects were significantly distressed by their symptoms. The NIMH findings may reflect methodological variations between sites. More work is needed to establish whether old people really suffer from phobic disorders (morbid fears of everyday situations and objects) in the numbers suggested by the findings in Baltimore where 14.2% of women over 65 were diagnosed as phobic.

Personality disorders (see Table 8)

These are conditions where lifelong characteristics of the individual cause suffering either to himself or society. The concept is controversial. There is a lack of knowledge about the epidemiology of personality disorders in all age groups but especially the old. Bergmann (1978) found that 6% of community sample of 300 elderly had 'long-standing personality deviations without super-added psychoneurotic symptomatology'. He described two general types of disorder, 'paranoid'

Table 8 Community data on other functional psychiatric disorders

Disorder	Study	Rate
Neurosis and anxiety states	Bergmann, 1971, 1978 (300 subjects)	45% of subjects without dementia or functional psychosis had at least 2 neurotic symptoms
	Myers et al., 1984 (NIMH/ECA, 3 sites) (2110 subjects)	Phobias 1.2%–7.6% men, 2.6%–14.2% women Panic 0% men, 0.1%–0.4% women Obsessive compulsive neurosis 0.2%–1.2% men, 0.4%–1.3% women
	Maule et al., 1984	12.3% anxiety state
Personality disorders	Bergmann, 1978 (300 subjects)	6% paranoid or inadequate
	Myers et al., 1984 (NIMH/ECA, 3 sites) (2110 subjects)	1.1% men at New Haven had antisocial PD No other cases
Schizophrenia	Kay, Beamish and Roth, 1964 (517 community and institutionalized subjects)	Schizophrenia (inc. paraphrenia) 1.1%
	Myers et al., 1984 (NIMH/ECA, 3 sites)	0% men, 0.9% women (includes schizophreniform disorder)
Alcoholism	Maule et al., 1984	0.9%
	Myers et al., 1984 (NIMH/ECA, 3 sites)	3.0%–3.7% men, 0%–0.7% women had alcohol abuse or dependence
Tranquillizer abuse	Williams, 1980	Approx 7% of men and 11% of women over 65 had taken a tranquilliser in the previous week

and 'inadequate'. The DSM III system has developed operationalized criteria for the diagnosis of personality disorders but the NIMH/ECA study detected only two elderly cases.

Schizophrenia and related disorders
(see Table 8)

Schizophrenia is a serious psychiatric condition with an estimated lifetime prevalence of about 0.9% (Shields and Slater, 1975). It usually presents in late adolescence or early adulthood and frequently becomes chronic. Features include 'positive' symptoms such as hallucinations, delusions and disordered thinking and 'negative' symptoms, particularly apathy, slowness, social withdrawal and lack of drive. Paraphrenia can be considered as a special type of schizophrenia with its onset in late life. Other forms of disorder with paranoia as the main feature also occur in old age.

Elderly patients with schizophrenia have often had the condition throughout adult life. In the United Kingdom many elderly sufferers live in mental hospitals and are therefore missed by community surveys. Kay, Beamish and Roth's Newcastle study examined both institutionalized and community residents and estimated the total prevalence of schizophrenia and paraphrenia combined to be 10.8 per 1000. Only one (institutionalized) paraphrenic was detected. Current US diagnostic criteria confine the term schizophrenia to disorders with their onset before age 45, and provide no category equivalent to paraphrenia. The NIMH study found low rates of schizophrenia in elderly women and no cases in elderly men.

Alcoholism and other addictive disorders (see Table 8)

Maule *et al.* found alcoholism in only 0.9% of their Edinburgh sample of 487 elderly, but the most convincing studies on the epidemiology of alcoholism in old age emanate from the United States where overall consumption of alcohol is higher than in the United Kingdom. Mishihara and Kastenbaum (1980) summarized investigations into alcohol use and abuse among the elderly and stated that the elderly drank less and included fewer heavy drinkers than younger age groups. They also tend to reduce their intake from the age of 50. Despite these facts a household survey in New York (Simon, 1980) found that one of the two peak ages of incidence for alcoholism was 65 to 75 (the other was 45 to 54). The NIMH/ECA study reported lower rates for alcohol abuse and dependence in the elderly than the young. Male rates were well in excess of female.

The only other important addictive disorders of old age concern the abuse of sedatives and minor tranquillizers for which fewer figures are available. Williams (1980) found that tranquillizer consumption increased with age and that women were heavier consumers than men.

Summary

Depression is by far the commonest functional mental disorder in old age and the only one for which good epidemiological data are available. The prevalence of severe depressive conditions is probably of the order of 1% to 3%. Significant depressions which interfere with functioning are often reported at rates exceeding 10% and mild symptoms of depression afflict up to a third of those over 65. Depression, especially of mild degree, is more commonly reported in women and is associated with poor physical health. The relationship of depression to age is not yet clear. Most other functional mental disorders are uncommon in the community although they represent a significant burden to psychiatric services. Further community studies are needed to establish the true levels of neurotic disorder and alcohol abuse in old age.

REFERENCES

Adelstein, A.M., Downham, D.Y., Stein, Z., and Susser, M. (1968). 'The epidemiology of mental illness in an English city', *Social Psychiatry*, **3**, 47–59.

Amaducci, L.A. Fratiglioni, L., Rocca W.A., Fieschi, C., Livrea P., Pedone, D., Bracco, L., Lippi, A., Gandolfo, C., Bino, G., *et al.* (1986). 'Risk factors for clinically diagnosed Alzheimer's disease: a case-control study of an Italian population', *Neurology*, **36** (7), 922–31.

Ames, D., Ashby, D.; Mann, A.H., and Graham, N. (1988). 'Psychiatric illness in elderly residents of Part III homes in one London borough: prognosis and review', *Age Ageing* (in press).

Barker, D.J.P., and Rose, G. (1984). *Epidemiology in Medical Practice*, Churchill Livingstone.

Bergmann, K. (1978). 'Neurosis and personality disorder in old age'. In A. Isaacs and F. Post (eds.), *Studies in Geriatric Psychiatry*, John Wiley, New York.

Bergmann, K., and Cooper, B. (1986). 'Epidemiological and public health aspects of senile dementia'. In A.N. Sorensen, F.E. Weinert and L.R. Sherrod (eds.), *Human Development and the Life Course: Multidisciplinary Perspectives*, Lawrence Erlbaum Associates.

Bergmann, K., and Eastham, E.J. (1974). 'Psychogeriatric ascertainment and assessment for treatment in an acute medical ward setting', *Age and Ageing*, **3**, 174–88.

Bergmann, K., Kay, D.W., McKechnie, A.A., Foster, E., and Roth, M. (1971). 'Follow-up study of randomly selected community residents to assess the effects of chronic brain syndrome', *Psychiatry* Part 2. Excerpta Medica *International Congress* (274), Amsterdam, Excerpta Medica.

Blazer, D.G., and Williams, C.D. (1980). 'The epidemiology of dysphoria and depression in an elderly population', *Am. J. Psychiatry*, **137**, 439–44.

Bollerup, T.R. (1975). 'Prevalence of mental illness among seventy year olds domiciled in nine Copenhagen suburbs:

the Glostrup study', *Acta Psychiatrica Scandinavica*, **51**, 327–39.

Brayne, C.E.G., *et al.* (1986). 'Cognitive function in an elderly female population' (in preparation).

Brayne, C., and Calloway, P. 'An epidemiological study of an elderly female population. Part I: diagnoses of dementia using CAMDEX and other instruments', unpublished article currently being submitted for publication.

Broe, G.A., Akhtar, A.J., Andrews, G.R., Caird, F.I., Gilmore, A.J., McLennan, W.J. (1976). 'Neurological disorders in the elderly at home', *J. Neurol. Neurosurg. Psychiatry*, **39**(4), 361–6.

Clarke, M., Clarke, S., Odell, A., and Jaggar, C. (1984). 'The elderly at home: health and social status', *Health Trends*, **1**(16), 3–7.

Cooper, B., and Sogna, U. (1983). 'Psychiatric disease in an elderly population. An epidemiologic field study in Mannheim', *Nervenarzt,* **54**(5), 239–49.

Copeland, J.R.M., Dewey, M.E., Wood, N., Searle, R., Davidson, I.A., and McWilliam, C. (1987). 'Range of mental illness among the elderly in the community. Prevalence in Liverpool using the GMS-AGECAT package', *Br. J. Psychiatry*, **150**, 815–23.

Delaney, P. (1982). 'Dementia: the search for treatable causes', *South Med. J., ***75**(6), 707–9.

Essen-Moller, G., and Hagnell, O. (1961). 'The frequency and risk in depression within a rural population group in Scandinavia', *Acta Psychiatrica Scandinavica Suppl.,* **162**, 28–32.

French, L.R., Schuman, L.M., Mortimer, J.A., and Boatman, R.A. (1985). 'A case-control study of dementia of the Alzheimer type'. *Am. J. Epidemiol.*, **121**(3), 414–21.

Fries, J.F. (1980). 'Aging, natural death and the compresison of morbidity', *NEJM*, 1930–5.

Gaspar, D. (1980). 'Hollymoor Hospital dementia service. Analysis of outcome of 230 consecutive referrals to a psychiatric-hospital dementia service', *Lancet*, **1** (8183), 1401–5.

Gilmore, A. (1977). 'Brain failure at home', *Age and Ageing Suppl.*, 56–60.

Griffiths, R.A., Good, W.R., Watson, N.P., O'Donnell, H.F., Fell, P.J., and Shakespeare, J.M. (1987). 'Depression, dementia and disability in the elderly', *Br. J. Psychiatry*, **150**, 482–93.

Gurland, B.J. (1976). 'The comparative frequency of depression in various adult age groups', *J. Gerontol.*, **31**, 283–392.

Gurland, B., Copeland, J., Kuriansky, J., Kelleher, M., Sharpe, L., and Dean, L.L. (1983). *The Mind and Mood of Ageing*, Croom Helm.

Hagesawa, K., Jomma, A., and Imai, Y. (1986). 'An epidemiological study of age-related dementia in the community', *Int. J. Geriatric Psychiatry,* **1**, 45–55.

Hare, E.H., and Shaw, G.K. (1965). *Mental Health on a New Housing Estate*, Maudsley Monograph 12, Oxford University Press, London.

Heyman, A., Wilkinson, W.E., Stafford, J.A., Helms, M.J., Syman, A.H., Weinberg, T. (1984). 'Alzheimer's disease: a study of epidemiologic aspects', *Ann. Neurol.*, **15**, 335–41.

Jagger, C., and Clarke, M. (1988). 'Mortality risks in the elderly: five year follow-up of a total population,' *Int. J. Epidemiol.* (in press).

Kaneko, Z., (1975). 'Care in Japan'. In J.G. Howells (ed.), *Modern Perspectives in the Psychiatry of Old Age*, Brunner Mazell, New York, pp. 519–39.

Kay, D.W.K., Beamish, P., and Roth, M. (1964). 'Old age mental disorders in Newcastle upon Type. Pt. 1. A study of prevalence', *Br. J. Psychiatry*, **110**, 146–58.

Kay, D.W.K., Henderson, A.S., Scott, R., Wilson, J., Rickwood, D., and Grayson, D.A. (1985). 'Dementia and depression among the elderly living in the Hobart community: the effect of the diagnostic criteria on the prevalence rates', *Psychological Med.*, **15**, 771–88.

Kemp, F. (1985). 'The elderly at home', Report for the East Anglian Health Authority (unpublished).

Larson, E.D., Reisler, B.V., Sumi, S.M., Canfield, E.G., and Chinn, N.M. (1986). 'A prospective study of 200 elderly out-patients', *Archives of Internal Medicine*, **146**, 1917–1922.

Larsson, T., Sjogren, T., and Jacobson, G. (1963). 'Senile dementia. A clinical, socio-medical and genetic study', *Acta Psychiatrica Scandinavica Suppl.*, **167**(39), 1–259.

Mann, A.H., Graham, N., and Ashby, D. (1984). 'Psychiatric illness in residential homes for the elderly: a survey in one London borough', *Age Ageing*, **13**, 257–65.

Maule, M.M., Milne, J.S., and Williamson, J. (1984). 'Mental illness and physical health in older people,' *Age Ageing*, **13**, 349–56.

Mishihara, B.L., and Kastenbaum, R. (1980). *Alcohol and Old Age*, Grune and Stratton, New York.

Morgan, K., Dallosso, H.M., Arie, T., Byrne, E.J., Jones, R., and Waite, J. (1987). 'Mental health and psychological well-being among the old and very old living at home', *Br. J. Psychiatry,* **150**, 801–7.

Myers, J.K., Weissmann, M.M., Tischler, G.L., Holzer, C.E., Leaf, P.J., Orvaschel, H., Anthony, J.C., Boyd, J.H., Burke, J.D., Kramer, M., and Stoltzman, R. (1984). 'Six-month prevalence of psychiatric disorders in three communities,' *Arch. Gen. Psychiatry*, **41**, 959–67.

New York State Department of Mental Hygiene (1961) *A Mental Health Survey of Older People*, State Hospital's Press, Utica, NY.

Nielsen, J. (1962). 'Geronto-psychiatric period-prevalence investigation in a geographically delimited population', *Acta Psychiatrica Scandinavica*, **38**(4), 307–30.

Parsons, P.L. (1965). 'Mental health of Swansea's old folk', *Br. J. Prevent. Soc. Med.*, **19**, 43–7.

Pfeffer, R.I., Afifi, A.A., and Chance, J.M. (1987). 'Prevalence of Alzheimer's disease in a retirement community', *Am. J. Epidemiol.,* **125**(3), 420–36.

Pierce, D. (1987). 'Deliberate self-harm in the elderly', *Int. J. Geriatric Psychiatry,* **2,** 105–110.

Post, F. (1982). 'Functional disorders. 1. Description, incidence and recognition', In R. Levy and F. Post (eds.), *The Psychiatry of Late Life,* Blackwell, Oxford.

Sheldon, J.H. (1948). *The Social Medicine of Old Age,* Oxford University Press for the Nuffield Foundation, London.

Shields, J., and Slater, E. (1975). 'Genetic aspects of schizophrenia'. In J. Silverstone and B. Barraclough (eds.), *Contemporary Psychiatry,* British Journal of Psychiatry Special Publication 9.

Shulman, K. (1978). 'Suicide and parasuicide in old age: a review', *Age and Ageing,* **7,** 201–9.

Shulman, K., and Post, F. (1980). 'Biopolar affective disorder in old age', *Br. J. Psychiatry,* **136,** 26–32.

Simon, A. (1980). 'The neuroses, personality disorders, alcoholism, drug use and misuse, and crime in the aged'. In J. Birren and R. Sloane (eds.), *Handbook of Mental Health and Aging,* Prentice-Hall, Englewood Cliffs, N.J.

Snowden, J., and Donnelly, (1986). 'A study of depression in nursing homes,' *J. Psychiatric Res.,* **20,** 327–33.

Spagnoli, A., Foresti, G., MacDonald, A., and Williams, P. (1986). 'Dementia and depression in Italian geriatric institutions', *Int. J. Geriatric Psychiatry,* **1,** 15–23.

Stenback, A., Kumpulainen, M., and Vauhkonen, M.L. (1979). 'A field study of old age depression'. In H. Orimo (ed.), *Recent Advances in Gerontology,* International Congress Series 469, Excerpta Medica, Amsterdam.

Sulkava, R., Wikstrom, J., Aromaa, A., Raitasalo, R., Lehtinen, V., Lahtela, K., and Palo, J. (1985). 'Prevalence of severe dementia in Finland', *Neurology,* **35**(7), 1025–9.

Swartz, M.S., and Blazer, D.G. (1986). 'The distribution of affective disorders in old age'. In E. Murphy (ed.), *Affective Disorders in the Elderly,* Churchill Livingstone, Edinburgh.

WHO (1984). 'The uses of epidemiology in the study of the elderly', Technical Report Series 706.

Williams, P. (1980). 'Prescribing antidepressants, hypnotics, tranquillisers', *Geriatric Med.,* **10,** 50–5.

Williamson, J., Stokoe, I.H., Gray, S., Fisher, M., Smith, A., McGher, A., and Stephenson, E. (1964). 'Old people at home: their unreported needs', *Lancet,* **i,** 1117–20.

Wing, J.K., Hailey, A., Bransby, E.R., and Friers, T. (1972). 'The statistical context: comparisons with national and local statistics'. In J.K. Wing and A. Hailey, (eds.), *Evaluating a community mental health service. The Camberwell Register 1964–71,* New York & Oxford.

Zung, W.W.K. (1967). 'Depression in the normal aged', *Psychosomatics,* **8,** 287–92.

Paper 3

Attitudes, stereotypes and prejudice about ageing

ROBERT SLATER* and BRIAN GEARING†

*Lecturer in Psychology, University of Wales Institute of Science and Technology, Cardiff;
†Lecturer in Health and Social Welfare, The Open University

GETTING AT THE TRUTH

What is 'the truth' about normal mental changes in old age? *Is* there a 'true' picture of normal ageing, or do we just act on our implicit assumptions about what we think the 'true' picture is? Ideally the 'true picture' is established, where possible, through scientific procedures. If we had the time (and the inclination!) to read all the information on almost any scientific topic we might (assuming we understand it) be a little closer to 'the truth', but often we have neither the time nor the inclination. Yet we still have beliefs: about the 'basic' differences between men and women; between whites and blacks; Jews and Gentiles; young and old; about all sorts of things. Miller (1982) has edited a useful set of papers on this topic. In the context of the organization of our beliefs on such matters, we now label certain beliefs as indicative of a sexist or racialist *attitude—of a settled mode of thinking.*

PROCESSES

Many of our attitudes involve *stereotypes*—sometimes defined as a set of widely shared generalizations about the characteristics of a group or class of people, which may be simplistic and overgeneralized. Neither you nor I can examine all the 'scientific evidence' there is to be read concerning all the decisions we have to make, and a lot of the time we just have to go on what we can, which may be our own more or less limited experience, or what someone else (who is credible in our eyes) tells us. But in the process of stereotyping there are activities that at first appear to

help clarify the situation—one is *sharpening* and the other is *levelling*. We tend to sharpen or accentuate differences between groups of people and level or de-emphasize differences within groups of people. The racialist sees less variation within the group—'whites are all the same'—and more *difference* between, often 'them' and 'us'. The male sexist sees all women as more homogeneous than they are and emphasizes the perceived differences between men and women.

Analogously, with respect to age and to mental illness, all older people may be seen as more or less the same and pretty different from us 'younger ones', and all mentally ill people may tend to be seen as more or less the same, i.e. 'mad', and certainly different from the likes of you and me—the normal ones.

Also at play in the process of stereotyping is the tendency to overgeneralize, so our experiences of a few older persons, in the absence of contradictory evidence, lead us to expectations about other old people, and expectations can colour subsequent perceptions as well as help elicit the expected behaviour (Jones, 1982). For example, Rosenhan (1973), in an intriguing study in which eight 'normal' people were accepted as patients in twelve mental hospitals, and behaved normally in them, found that these 'pseudo-patients' were never discovered by the professional staff to be normal. He remarks that:

Whenever the ratio of what is known to what needs to be known approaches zero, we tend to invent 'knowledge' and assume that we understand more than we actually do. We seem unable to acknowledge that we simply don't know. The needs for diagnosis and remediation of behavioural and emotional problems are enormous. But rather than acknowledge that we are just embarking on understanding, we continue to label patients 'schizophrenic', 'manic-depressive', and 'insane', as if in those words we had captured the essence of understanding. The facts of the matter are that we have known for a long time that diagnoses are often not useful or reliable, but we have nevertheless continued to use them (p. 257).

One consequence of these stereotyping processes is that they reduce our need for further explanations and mental effort. 'It's your age' or 'What do you expect at your age?' is an explanation which appears to require little consequential action. And better still, so to speak, for the overworked GP (in the short term) having patients who say to themselves 'Well what else can I expect at my age', who don't bother to go to their GP because they 'know' there is nothing she or he can do about it, whatever 'it' is. Partly also at play here is what psychologists call the fundamental attribution error—the tendency to underestimate the power of situational constraints on behaviour and to overestimate the role of personal dispositional factors (Jones, 1982).

The easy mental option—but a 'cop-out'— is to believe all older people *are* more alike and hence different from us; to see 'ageing' as *the* explanation for all the differences we see between older and younger people around us. (The other extreme, of course—and another cop-out—is to say that there is no such thing as 'ageing'.)

Perhaps the point about difficulties in diagnosing things as being due to 'age' is even more dramatically made when one considers what one might conceive of as more straightforward *physical* diagnoses. Bloor (1976) reports studies of children who had *all* cleared a screening for tonsillectomy surgery by one group of doctors who were then—in 46% of cases—recommended for it by another group of doctors. Of the children *not* recommended for tonsillectomy by this second group of doctors, 44% were recommended for it by a third group of doctors.

LABELS

Townsend (1979) argues not only that the layman 'naturally' overgeneralizes and oversimplifies, but that mental health professionals, especially psychiatrists, may do it even more readily. Although his article concerns the diagnosis of mental illness in general and psychosis in particular, rather than mental health

and illness matters related to ageing, the thrust of the argument is the same. There is a temptation to jump to a diagnostic category and then 'make the symptoms fit', rather than proceeding the other way around. In the context of mental illness in old age, the diagnostic category that might too readily spring to the layman's and professional's mind alike is 'senile'. The following extract illustrates the problem:

Cross-national studies of diagnosis support the notion that American psychiatrists have relatively broad criteria for the recognition of psychosis. Kendell *et al.* (1971) had matched groups of British and American psychiatrists view videotapes of patient interviews. Agreement was good in the major diagnoses of patients who exhibit classic, 'textbook' symptoms. In contrast, more British than American psychiatrists diagnosed 'affective psychosis' in those patients with mixed schizo-affective symptoms, but the authors noted that this was an anticipated and 'manageable' difference. Those tapes, however, which were chosen specifically to represent non-psychotic disorders caused serious disagreement. The American audience tended predominantly to diagnose schizophrenia (69–85%) while the British shunned this category (2–7%). This glaring difference was not due to semantics but rather to *psychiatrists actually perceiving* different symptoms in the patients' behavior. One patient, for example, was rated by a majority of the Americans as showing delusions, passivity, and thought disorder. Only about seven percent of the British gave similar responses. The authors concluded that the diagnosis 'schizophrenia' is used so freely in America as to be virtually meaningless. They noted, however, that diagnosis of 'affective disorders' was gaining popularity due to the introduction of lithium salts as an antipsychotic medication.

The results of these comparisons are not merely of academic interest. Such diagnostic differences carry weighty implications. A person labelled 'psychotic' is much more likely than a non-psychotic to be: (1) involuntarily committed: (2) treated with major tranquilizers and shock therapy (ECT): (3) have their normal rights and duties suspended. The Americans' response to those tapes representing non-psychotic disorders also raises serious questions as to whether virtually anyone could be perceived as psychotic in America. The following study suggests that this is a possibility.

Temerlin (1968) had a professional actor portray an ideal, normal man in an audiotaped, clinical interview. Before hearing the tape, each group of experimental subjects heard a prestigious confederate remark that the man appeared neurotic but was really psychotic. Control subjects heard that the man was perfectly healthy. Of the experimental subjects 60 percent of the psychiatrists, 28 percent of the psychologists, and 11 percent of the graduate students diagnosed psychosis. In contrast, all control subjects agreed unanimously that the man was not psychotic. Thus, the psychiatrists in particular seemed to have a perceptual set to retain a labelled 'out-grouper' in the out-group, and the broadness of their criteria allowed them to do so. Like the experiments in ethnic stereotyping (Secord, 1959; Razran, 1950), the label attached to a person played a more important role in determining what qualities were attributed to that person than the person's actual appearance or behavior (Townsend, 1979, pp. 212–13).

Such evidence need not imply that the diagnostic category is unreal, and diagnostic reliability among American psychiatrists has no doubt tightened up since Townsend's study. A consultant psychiatrist told the authors of this article that he spent most of his time persuading the people referred to him that they were no more mad than himself. But wait, you must be 'mad' by definition to have been referred to a consultant psychiatrist—surely? Of course you don't have to be, but people tend to overgeneralize from one facet of a person—his or her illness—sometimes to the extent that people ' become' their illness, 'the loonies', 'the veggies', 'the mentally handicapped', 'the elderly', 'the dements', as if this one facet was the only thing one needed to know about them. Then, given the cognitively convenient peg—the label—on which to hang things, we may henceforth (or in retrospect) be tempted to see other bits of their behaviour as indicative or supportive of the label given.

A recent study of ageism among psychiatrists in the United States found that they generally held negative attitudes towards older patients, viewing them as less than ideal as prospective patients and as having poorer prognoses than other age groups (Ray, Raciti and Ford, 1985). This echoes earlier US research findings that when elderly patients are seen by psychiatrists in private practice, they most frequently receive consultation concerning institutionalization rather than psychotherapy (Ford and Sbordone, 1980). A common thread linking the attitudes of American psychiatrists and British social workers to older people would seem to be their mutual pessimism about achieving personality change and greater mental health—more optimal living—among this age group. Until fairly recently, social work training in Britain was influenced by Freudian psychoanalytic theory. An interesting finding in the study of US psychiatrists was that it was the psychoanalytically oriented psychiatrists who demonstrated the most substantial prejudices against older patients. Ray, Raciti and Ford (1985) point out that 'this is consistent with and may reflect an attitude historically evolving out of Freud's view that psychoanalysis is generally not applicable to persons near or above the age of 50'. Herr and Weakland (1979) also comment on the slow development of psychotherapy for older people.

AGEISM

Townsend's (1979) in this context would suggest that the step from perceiving, for example, the memory 'to be going' to inferring senility is likely to be too readily made, and that once the *label* 'senility' is suggested, there is a strong likelihood that other aspects of behaviour will be *perceived* as confirmatory symptoms.

This is what Samuel Johnson (1709–84) probably had in mind when he wrote:

There is a wicked inclination in most people to suppose an old man decayed in his intellects. If a young or middle-aged man, when leaving a company, does not recollect where he laid his hat, it is nothing; but if the same inattention is discovered in an old man, people will shrug up their shoulders, and say, 'His memory is going'.

In *The Concise Oxford Dictionary senile* is described as 'Showing the feebleness etc of, incident to, old age (senile apathy, decay, garrulity, etc)' (Sykes, 1976).

People in later life can sometimes be disadvantaged by dictionary definitions—are old people naturally apathetic and garrulous?—and frequently by the attitudes of others. For example, a physician may fail to fully investigate the possible physical causes of 'confusion' in an older person which might appear suddenly after an illness or an accident. This is a consequence of professional *ageism*. Because professionals tend only to see the older people who *do* have problems, they may be in the least likely position to have any negative preconceptions about older people in general disconfirmed.

There are also instances of other, possibly less obvious, negative attitudes and beliefs about ageing. For example, there are sometimes 'well-meaning' neighbours, relations and others who appear to think that someone who is old and mentally ill does not have similar needs and feelings in most respects to 'normal' people. When an older person gets labelled mentally ill, there may well be an assumption by neighbours that the individual must need *continuous* protection from the everyday risks which are inherent in living with some degree of independence in the community. Such paternalism, though probably well-intentioned, may be excessive and too restricting of freedom. Environmental deprivations often put up with by older people—a barely adequate pension, poor housing and access to transport (OPCS, 1984)—can also be conceptualized as a covert form of ageism by society. Hendricks and Hendricks (1985) suggest that *ageism* 'refer(s) to the *pejorative* image of someone who is old simply because of his or her age'.

The view underlying most of these negative attitudes is that old age is *inevitably* a time of decline, when you must expect mental and physical ill-health, and where poverty and a poor environment are the natural order of things. When such a view of old age is widespread in a society, despite the evidence to the contrary (see, for example, Tinker, 1984), it can have a pernicious effect on individuals, sometimes producing the very effect it purports to describe (the 'self-fulfilling prophecy' (Lehr, 1977)) and which Rosow (1974) persuasively argues is part of a much wider process of socialization to old age.

Shonfield (1982) has argued that ignorance or misconceptions by the public about older people can be equated neither with age prejudice nor with stereotyping. Indeed, Shonfield notes that gerontologists may be oversensitive to stereotypes of old age, anticipating them where they may not in fact exist, and one might infer that 'many gerontologists are guilty of stereotyping "society"' (p. 267). Shonfield suggests that vested interests in the area probably exert some influence on gerontologists' attitudes and that 'there is a religious flavor in the manner in which writers rebuke their readers for their prejudices towards the aged, and religious faith can lead to blindness to counterarguments' (p. 271). Shonfield's warnings illustrate the general point that gerontologists are human too—as prone to overgeneralizing as the rest of us. Shonfield's conclusion after reviewing several research studies is that there is insufficient evidence to justify the generalization that ours *is* an ageist society—he

suggests there is ample evidence to contradict that generalization. With Shonfield's strictures in mind it is interesting to note that the journal article following his, by Nuessel (1982), points out how 'the language used to depict the elderly is overwhelmingly negative in scope' (p. 273) and argues that 'such deprecatory language is a linguistic mirror of the pervasive and institutional ageism in our society' (p. 273). Norman (1987) warns that it is a mistake to assume that ageism is necessarily simply the result of irrational prejudice and that we must examine our real ambivalence about old age and the real conflicts of interests between the fit and the frail.

It does, however, seem likely that some of the negative expectations of old age demonstrated in the 'Harris Poll' study (NCOA, 1975) and revealed in Table 1 stem in part from myths and prejudices which are held in contemporary Western culture.

The Harris Poll authors go on to write:

As concluded earlier in this report, it is not the young alone who have negative expectations of old age. The older public themselves have bought the stereotypes and myths of old age, and, recognizing that life is not so terrible for them, consider themselves the exception to the rule.

In fact, for many older people, life has turned out better than they expected it to be. For every older person who feels that his or her own life is worse now than what he/she thought it would be, there are three who say that life is better now than they expected. In fact, as many people under 65 feel that their current lives fall short of earlier expectations as those 65 and over (NCOA, 1975, p. 111).

Such expectations often find expression in a well-meaning but ultimately harmful presentation of old age as *necessarily* a problem state. Problems which affect *some* older people—often a small minority—are presented in an 'overdrawn' picture of inevitable decline seen in the necessary accompaniment of old age which affects *all* old people. This has been called the 'Inevitability Myth' (Saul, 1974). In the long run, such images which are often intended to generate concern about the very real and serious problems of some old people (e.g. as in much charity advertising) can have a negative effect. The general public, professional workers and older people themselves may come to expect old age to be characterized by an impoverished, restricted and dependent life-style.

Table 1 Differences between personal experiences of Americans 65 and over and expectations held by other adults about those experiences

	Very serious problems experienced by the elderly themselves (%)	Very serious problems the public expects the elderly to experience (%)	Net difference
Fear of crime	23	50	+27
Poor health	21	51	+30
Not having enough money to live on	15	62	+47
Loneliness	12	60	+48
Not having enough medical care	10	44	+34
Not having enough education	8	20	+12
Not feeling needed	7	54	+47
Not having enough to do to keep busy	6	37	+31
Not having enough friends	5	28	+23
Not having enough job opportunities	5	45	+40
Poor housing	4	35	+31
Not having enough clothing	3	16	+13

Source: L. Harris and Associates, *The Myth and Reality of Aging in America* (The National Council on the Aging, Inc., Washington, D.C., 1975), p. 31.

This affects not only how we treat older people but also influences the kind of behaviour they expect of us and themselves. Examples would include the too ready conclusion that *any* perceived mental problem is indicative of dementia, or that the first response to mental or physical vulnerability must be to protect an older person from the normal risks of everyday life.

Branco and Williamson (1982) in reviewing studies related to stereotyping and the life cycle with particular reference to views of ageing and the aged introduce the topic thus:

A few years ago a youth of 17 was fortunate enough to reach the finals of his home-town tennis tournament. It was the summer after his high school graduation, and he felt strong, quick, and confident, qualities he identified as exclusively those of young people. His opponent was 58, and upon learning of the competitor's 'advanced age', the youth's confidence grew. The local newspaper saw an opportunity for combining a human interest story with a sports story, and headlined an article on the match 'Age and Experience Versus Youth and Ambition'. Even though the older man was known to be a good player, the youth was convinced that he would triumph rather easily. 'After all', he thought, 'it's a hot summer afternoon and we're going to play on a hard asphalt court'. His strategy was clear: 'Make the old man run'. He believed that all he had to do was keep hitting the ball first to one side of the court and then to the other. The hot sun and the hard court would do the rest. He was sure that no one of his opponent's age could continue that pace through an entire match.

He was wrong. The older man ran continuously for the two hours they were on the court. He also kept the youth running after shots that were so well placed that it was all the youth could do just to hit the ball. He hit many of them out of the court, into the net, or right back to the older man, who won rather easily.

The youth learned an important lesson. As a result of this experience he became much more cautious when it came to making generalizations about older people. Many of our readers, no doubt, have had experiences with older persons that violated their conceptions of what it means to be old. Unfortunately, these experiences are often discounted or forgotten. We say, 'That's an exception', and the stereotype lives on (pp. 364–5).

Among other ageing-related stereotypes they examine are: that biological ageing takes place at a uniform rate; that to be old is to be unhealthy; that behaviour that violates 'normal' expectations is due to 'senility'; along with other stereotypes concerning intellectual and sexual decline, poverty, social isolation and voting behaviour. Branco and Williamson (1982) also consider the theoretical perspectives used to suggest why such stereotypes are maintained.

But how widely held are such stereotypical beliefs? In the NCOA survey it was found that younger adults expected the problems identified with growing older 'to be far more serious than they are for the elderly who actually experience them' and it is not unreasonable to suggest that some of the negative expectations of both the general public and of older people themselves stem from stereotypes and negative views about ageing which have been embedded deeply in American and perhaps to a somewhat lesser extent in British culture.

OTHER PEOPLE'S ATTITUDES

There has been no major survey in Britain of the attitudes of the public or of old people towards ageing since a survey by Abrams (1978). Perhaps this in itself is an indication of our neglect or relative lack of interest in older people. Abrams reported that, on the whole, retired people were more satisfied with their lot than younger people, despite the fact that they were generally financially far worse off than the latter. Abrams' 1978 survey covered 1600 people aged 65 and over drawn from four socially different urban areas. The survey report drew attention to those over

75 whose earlier lives 'were lived against a background of abject poverty, hard work, danger and wretched housing'. The modest expectations derived from this background, combined with recent improvements in their material standards of living, caused old people to feel satisfied with their position, even though they had gained much less than most younger people (Abrams, 1978).

Whilst it is likely that this general comment would also apply to some extent to today's very old people (such as those over 80) who were born in the same era of relatively harsh deprivation, it would be unwise to use such previous survey data to draw firm conclusions about the present. First, relative satisfaction with old age may have been modified by reductions in social service provision and access to medical care in some parts of the United Kingdom during the 1980s (Baldock, 1986). But more significant than this is what might be called the 'age cohort effect'. In the early 1980s a generation born immediately after the First World War reached retirement age. They grew up in a different kind of society and, in middle age, will have enjoyed some of the affluence of the 1950s and 1960s. More of them will have retired with good pensions. It seems unlikely that the remainder will be as satisfied with relative and real deprivation in retirement as were their predecessors.

ATTITUDES OF PROFESSIONALS TO OLD PEOPLE: PROFESSIONAL STEREOTYPES

The problem is not just that old people and the public have inappropriate beliefs and attitudes; many professionals also hold beliefs that are inaccurate in the light of modern research, and have attitudes that are unduly pessimistic and negative. This was clearly demonstrated in a study of attitudes to exercise conducted in England by Jean McHeath (1983). She found that 82 per cent of her sample of elderly people believed that exercise was 'what is wanted and needed' by old people and that it was 'important, necessary and good', whereas only 62 per cent of the professional staff had these positive attitudes. Secondly, she found that the proportion of elderly people who believed that professional staff should talk to old people about the benefits of exercise was higher than the proportion found among those staff.

Of particular concern is the fact that 14 per cent of rehabilitative staff felt that talking to old people about exercise was a waste of time or unimportant.

These findings pose a serious challenge to those responsible for professional education, as the problem is not simply one of ignorance but of prejudice. Not only is professional training failing to teach professionals the facts about health in old age, it is failing to change, and sometimes reinforcing, the popular prejudices about old age (Gray, 1985, pp. 219, 221).

In the 1970s a series of studies of social workers' attitudes to different client groups, and of the ways in which new referrals were allocated between trained and untrained staff, demonstrated that older people received much lower status and priority than children and younger families. Stevenson and Parsloe (1978), commenting on the findings of their major research project (funded by the Department of Health and Social Security) into the social work task in over thirty social work teams throughout the United Kingdom, wrote 'work with the elderly was perceived in a stereotyped way as tasks which only require practical services and routine visiting'. The following statement from a social worker illustrates this attitude:

The family have their whole life in front of them and an elderly person has fewer years and it doesn't have as big an effect on an old person going into an old people's home as it does on a child going into a children's home'.

The assumption that older people's needs were straightforward and practical in nature led them to be allocated to untrained and less experienced workers. Similarly a study of social work in practice by Goldberg and Warburton (1979) demonstrated that work with old people was largely confined to meeting practical and material needs and that social workers were not trying to achieve environmental and personal change. This passive acceptance of old people's problems has been compared with the fatalistic attitude adopted by other professionals and some older people themselves, summed up in the comment 'it's your age' (Tinker et al., 1983). It exists despite evidence that skilled social work can make a considerable difference to the quality of life enjoyed by older clients by achieving improvements in their material circumstance and helping them with social and psychological difficulties (see, for example, Goldberg et al., 1970).

Whilst the report of the 1982 'Barclay Inquiry' into the tasks of social workers echoed the earlier findings concerning the low priority given to old people by social workers, some more recent evidence suggests that, in some parts of the country, the potential for social work with old people is now more widely recognized and attempts are being made to apply the skills of assessment, counselling and the appropriate use of resources to this client group (Tinker et al., 1983). Unfortunately for the practical realization of this growing awareness, social work has had to operate in a context of resource shortages and media alarm over child-abuse cases—which have reinforced existing tendencies to concentrate on statutory child care work.

It would be wrong to imply that social work is more culpable of a kind of professional stereotyping and relative neglect of old people than are other caring professions. Although 96% of elderly people live in the community, and GPs are the professional group with whom they are most likely to seek contact, many older people experience problems in obtaining satisfactory GP services and some GPs are reluctant to treat them. A recent review paper from Age Concern England about GPs and the needs of older people suggested two main reasons why some GPs do not give work with older patients a higher priority: 'negative or pessimistic attitudes to ageing' and 'deficiencies in undergraduate education which does not always recognize that treating elderly people can be professionally rewarding' (Age Concern England, 1985). Norman (1987) catalogues other examples of professional stereotyping.

There is, though, encouraging evidence that district nurses, who already spend three-quarters of their patient-time with people over the age of 65, are one professional group which would like to spend more time with elderly people (Johnson et al., 1983). On the other hand, an Office of Population Censuses and Surveys study reported that only 9% of health visitors' time—viewable as more 'positive' and preventative—was spent with this age group (Dunnell and Hobbs, 1982).

What, then, are the implications of the pessimism found among some professionals about older people's capacity to change? There are several likely consequences of such views for work with mentally ill older people. There may be failure to carry out a full diagnosis or assessment which attends to the *strengths* of the older patient or client and considers which problems are remediable, or there may be a failure to provide treatment aimed at improving the mental and social functioning of the older person. Perhaps there might be less commitment to arranging activities and creating an environment which offers mental stimulation. 'Therapeutic pessimism' might also lead to a 'warehousing' approach to the needs of old people, whereby only their basic survival needs are considered. Also, when such an attitude is widespread, work itself with older people loses prestige, and consequently the professions may not attract good and well-motivated recruits.

A CHANGE IN ATTITUDES?

Can attitudes be changed? Some American literature (see Ray, Raciti and Ford, 1985) suggests that when practitioners are actively involved with elderly patients —both the infirm and the healthy—they develop more realistic and optimistic attitudes to this age group. In other words, exposure to actual older people (rather than to the cultural stereotypes) helps to promote a non-ageist outlook.

In this country, a recent study by Peach and Pathy (1982) assessed an attempt to influence the career preferences of doctors in their second pre-registration post. Attitudes of those randomly allocated to geriatric and to general medical firms were compared. Attachment to a geriatric firm for two years appeared to influence favourably nine out of sixteen selected attitudes towards the elderly patient. It also appeared to have some effect on career plans in that 13% of the students attached to a geriatric firm 'were prepared to give "high" or "very high" consideration" to a hospital career in geriatric medicine and 20% to a career in general medicine with a particular interest in the elderly'. Similarly, Wattis, Smith and Binns (1986) report an investigation into medical students' career preferences and attitudes to old people. They suggest that a medical school which attaches sufficient importance to health care of the elderly to create a special department, and puts students through a month-long course, could generate—*independently of this special course*—a more favourable attitude to old people

in trainee doctors than a school without such a department.

Such studies suggest something which is corroborated by anecdotal accounts: that positive imagery can help foster positive attitudes and that when professional workers, including some of those with negative preconceptions, have personal contact with older people, they are frequently surprised to find the work interesting and professionally rewarding. Perhaps more thought should be given by service planners to finding acceptable ways of making this happen more systematically.

REFERENCES

Abrams, M. (1978). *Beyond Three Score and Ten*, Mitcham, Age Concern England.

Age Concern England (1985). *General Practitioners and the Needs of Older People—A Policy Paper*, Age Concern England, Mitcham, Surrey.

Baldock, J. (1986). 'How to do more while spending less: social work's search for the holy grail of the 1980s'. In *The Year Book of Social Policy in Britain 1985–6*, Chap. 10, Routledge and Kegan Paul, London.

Bloor, M. (1976). 'Bishop Berkely and the adenotonselfectomy enigma: an exploration of variation in the social construction of medical disposals', *Sociology*, **10**(1), 43–60.

Branco, K.J., and Williamson, J.B. (1982). 'Stereotyping and the life cycle: views of aging and the aged'. In A.G. Miller (ed.), *In the Eye of the Beholder: Contemporary Issues in Stereotyping*, Praeger, New York, Chap. 8, pp. 364–410.

Dunnell, K., and Hobbs, J. (1982). 'Nurses working in the community', OPCS, London, reported in Johnson *et al.* (1983).

Ford, C.V., and Sbordone, A.I. (1980). 'Attitudes of psychiatrists towards elderly patients', *American Journal of Psychiatry*, **187**, 151–5.

Goldberg, E.M., and Warburton, R.W. (1979). *Ends and Means in Social Work*, George Allen and Unwin, London.

Goldberg, E.M., with Mortimer, A., and William, B.T. (1970). *Helping the Aged, a Field Experiment in Social Work*, George Allen and Unwin, London.

Gray, J.A.M. (1985). 'Education for health in old age'. In J.A.M. Gray (ed.), *Prevention of Disease in the Elderly*, Churchill Livingstone, London, pp. 214–25.

Hendricks, J., and Hendricks, C.D. (1985). *Ageing in Mass Society: Myths and Realities*, 2nd ed., Winthrop, Cambridge, Mass.

Herr, J.J., and Weakland, J.H. (1979). *Counselling Elders and Their Families. Practical Techniques for Applied Gerontology*, Springer, New York.

Johnson, M., and Challis, D., with collaboration from Power, P., and Wade, B. (1983). 'The realities and potential of community care'. In DHSS (eds.), *Elderly People in the Community: Their Service Needs*, HMSO, London.

Jones, R.A. (1982). 'Perceiving other people: stereotyping as a process of social cognition'. In A.G. Miller (ed.), *In the Eye of the Beholder: Contemporary Issues in Stereotyping*, Praeger, New York, Chap. 2, pp. 41–91.

Kendell, R.E., Cooper, J., Gourley, A., and Copeland, J. (1971). 'Diagnostic criteria of British and American psychiatrists', *Archives of General Psychiatry*, **25**, 123–30.

Lehr, U. (1977). 'Stereotypes of ageing and age norms', unpublished paper presented at *Ageing: A Challenge for Science and Social Policy,* a conference organized by the Institut de la Vie, held at Vichy, April 1977.

McHeath, J.A. (1983). *Activity, Health and Fitness in Old Age*, Croom Helm, London.

Miller, A.G. (ed.) (1982). *In the Eye of the Beholder: Contemporary Issues in Stereotyping*, Praeger, New York.

NCOA (1975). *The Myth and Reality of Ageing in America*, The National Council on the Ageing, Washington, D.C.

Norman, A. (1987). *Aspects of Ageism: A Discussion Paper*, Centre for Policy on Ageing, London.

Nuessel, F.H., Jr. (1982). 'The language of ageism', *The Gerontologist*, **22**(3), 273–6

OPCS (1984). *Britain's Elderly Population: Census Guide 1*, HMSO, London.

Peach, J., and Pathy, M.S. (1982). 'Attitudes towards the care of the aged and to a career with elderly patients among students attached to a geriatric and general medical firm', *Age and Ageing*, **11**, 196–202.

Ray, D.C., Raciti, M.A., and Ford, C.V. (1985). 'Ageism in psychiatrists: associations with gender, certification and theoretical orientation', *The Gerontologist*, **24**(5), 496–500.

Razran, G. (1950). 'Ethnic dislike in stereotypes', *Journal of Abnormal and Social Psychology*, **45**, 7–27.

Rosenhan, D. (1973). 'On being sane in insane places', *Science*, **179**, 250–8.

Rosow, I. (1974). *Socialization to Old Age*, University of California Press, Berkeley.

Saul, S. (1974). *Ageing: An Album of People Growing Old*, John Wiley and Sons, New York.

Secord, P. (1959). 'Stereotyping and favourableness in the perception of negro faces', *Journal of Abnormal and Social Psychology*, **59**, 309–15.

Shonfield, D. (1982). 'Who is stereotyping whom and why', *The Gerontologist*, **22**(3), 267–72.

Stevenson, O., Parsloe P. (1978). *Social Services Teams: The Practitioner's View*, HMSO, London.

Sykes, J.B. (ed.) (1976). *The Concise Oxford Dictionary*, The Clarendon Press, Oxford.

Temerlin, M.K. (1968). 'Suggestion effects in psychiatric diagnosis', *Journal of Nervous and Mental Disease*, **147**, 349–353.

Tinker, A. (1984). *The Elderly in Modern Society*, Longman, Harlow, Essex.

Tinker, A., with collaboration from Abrams, M., Gray, J.M., and Rowlings, C. (1983). 'Improving the quality of life and promoting independence of elderly people'. In DHSS (eds.), *Elderly People in the Community: Their Service Needs*, HMSO, London.

Tounsend, J.M. (1979). 'Stereotypes of mental illness; a comparison with ethnic stereotypes', *Culture, Medicine and Psychiatry*, **3**, 205–229.

Wattis, J.P., Smith, C.W., and Binns, V. (1986). 'Medical students' attitudes to old people and career preference: a comparison of two universities', *Medical Education*, **20**, 498–501.

Paper 4

Mental health in old age

PETER COLEMAN

Senior Lecturer in Social Gerontology, University of Southampton

THE SIGNIFICANCE OF OLD AGE FOR MENTAL HEALTH

Adjustment, adaptation, morale, life satisfaction and the various other expressions that are used to refer to the individual's sense of well-being are some of the most commonly used terms in social and psychological studies of ageing. Such is the frequency of their use in British and American research that an external observer would be likely to conclude that ageing was a particularly problematic period of life. The same impression is conveyed in other ways as well. For example, the very first British government discussion document on policy for older people, issued in 1978, was entitled *A Happier Old Age*. This in itself suggests that old age is often not a happy period of life, certainly not as happy as younger periods of life.

This impression is strengthened by the evidence from epidemiological surveys that there is a very high prevalence of depression among older people, affecting one in seven of all people over the age of 65. Indeed, depression has been called an 'epidemic' condition in old age. It is then not so surprising that within the study of ageing, adjustment and mental health should be such major foci of interest.

Yet it is worth stopping to reflect whether the current emphasis on 'problems' is justified. Might this negative orientation not just be another of the ways in which we unjustly stigmatize old age? Do we give sufficient weight to the positive elements in late life? Policy makers do tend to look at old age with blinkers which make them recognize sickness, poverty and mental deterioration, but not the pleasures and achievements. Depression is very prevalent in later life, but the evidence also shows it to be as common in other periods of life as well. Brown and Harris in their study of young women in London, for example, showed a comparably high rate of depression (Brown and Harris, 1978).

It has to be acknowledged, too, that older people display much higher rates of expressed satisfaction with their lives than younger people. The most recent British national survey, *The Elderly at Home* (Hunt, 1978), points out that the over-sixties age group expressed a greater degree of life satisfaction than any other age group with all aspects of life, apart from health. The same findings have emerged from American studies (e.g. Palmore and Kivett, 1977). These findings are often seen as paradoxical when set beside the evidence on high rates of depression in late life. Certainly they may reflect the particular characteristics of recent generations of older people, stoical and acceptant, and future generations may be much more complaining. But they also suggest that we should consider more carefully the preconceptions that we may have about old age as a difficult time of life which threatens mental health.

I think that we can best keep the subject of adjustment and ageing in a proper perspective if we remember that adjustment is a constant issue throughout life. Every change that occurs in the life course requires adjustment. Taking up an adult role, beginning work, marriage and child birth particularly require major adjustments, often in close proximity to each other early on in adult life. If old age has a special character in this regard it is the likelihood of unwanted changes occurring, sometimes also in close proximity and often unprepared for: loss of work role, loss of spouse, decreased income and increased physical frailty.

Loss is a common element in many old people's lives. Indeed, from this perspective the rates of depression observed in later life are not remarkably high but remarkably low. Older people cope well with loss. Often indeed it seems that depression occurs when the losses of old age reawaken earlier losses that

36

have never been properly healed. The results of large studies on life satisfaction and living circumstances (Abrams, 1978) and on adjustment to bereavement (Bowling and Cartwright, 1982) show how well many older people do adjust to loss, but this is often not the message that is read from them. The focus is on the minority who show signs of maladjustment and depression.

IMAGES OF AGEING

It is a pity we have little systematic knowledge about how people manage the last parts of their lives as successfully as they do. What we do possess are certain 'images', positive and negative, about how people cope with problems in this period. Stereotyped views, for example of stoic acceptance of hardship on the one hand and crippling loneliness and misery on the other, play a large part in people's thinking about being old. These images affect our own everyday and working attitudes, perhaps more than we imagine. There is thankfully now a growing number of popular books, like Alex Comfort's *A Good Age* and Mary Stott's *Ageing for Beginners* (Comfort, 1977; Stott, 1981), which address the subject of attitudes to ageing and propose more positive ones to those commonly expressed. They challenge such popular prejudices as that older people are stuck in their ways, that they are self-centred and will not listen to others or that they are obsessed with their own physical ailments.

Within the academic study of the sociology and psychology of ageing there is a suspicion of general models or theories about human ageing. This is in large part ascribable to the experiences with 'disengagement theory' in the 1960s which followed the publication of the results of a large study of older people living in Kansas City in the United States (Cumming and Henry, 1961). The authors could not resist the temptation to formulate a general theory on the basis of their observations that the more aged the people in their sample the lower was the level of investment they showed in major social roles. A large part of gerontological research in the ensuing ten years was taken up with 'disproving' disengagement theory—demonstrating that decreased activity was neither inevitable nor necessarily desired. Indeed, retirement in later life may provide the opportunity for new activities and interests.

The theory of disengagement was particularly harmful because of its potential for becoming a self-fulfilling prophecy. If we expect and demand less of people because they are old, they are likely to conform to this expectation. This experience made gerontologists wary of embracing too eagerly any kind of generalization about how older people do or should behave. Such generalizations might not reflect on old age itself, but on the limitations of the research setting, for example the particular culture or subgroup studied or even the particular generation of old people interviewed. They might have a quite different background of education, perspective and life expectations than the younger people with whom they were to be compared. How could one know that this younger generation might not age quite differently, or even in another cultural setting show radically different characteristics?

However, lack of theory can be as detrimental as overemphasis of a particular theory. Absence of constructive ideas breeds the kinds of stereotypes and prejudices already mentioned which can be equally as damaging as disengagement theory. It is certainly striking how people in professional training for work with older people seek out the few accounts of ageing which do exist in the literature that present an ideal model for growing old. There are a number of such 'theories' which provide interesting suggestions on what the crucial ingredients of positive mental health in old age may be.

ERIK ERIKSON'S STAGES OF LIFE

The most obvious starting point for surveying positive ideas on mental health in old age are the writings of the American psychotherapist Erik Erikson. This is not because he wrote much about ageing in itself—at least not until recently when he reached an advanced age himself—but because he formulated a stage theory of human development that did not end with the onset of adulthood but went on into old age.

Briefly set out in his book *Childhood and Society* (Erikson, 1950) he describes the child's or rather baby's first psychological task in life as developing a sense of trust rather than a sense of mustrust. The ensuing childhood stages are characterized in terms of 'autonomy', 'initiative' and 'industry'. In adolescence the issue is the development of 'ego identity' versus 'identity diffusion' and in early adulthood the development of 'intimacy' versus a sense of 'isolation'.

In middle age the issue becomes one of 'generativity', again a word coined by Erikson himself. He describes it as 'primarily the interest in establishing and guiding the next generation'. The task of the last stage of life, old age, for Erikson is to attain 'ego integrity', an assured sense of meaning and order in one's life and in the universe, as against despair and disgust. Successful resolution of the developmental task of late life should include 'acceptance of one's one and only life cycle as something that had to be and that, by necessity, permitted of no substitutions'. Despair may be expressed in a feeling that one has failed and does not have the time to attempt another life or an alternative road to integrity, and also in disgust with other people, especially the young.

Discussion of the relevance of Erikson's theory to ageing often focuses on the last stage of 'integrity', which is a pity. His theory is in fact much more sophisticated than brief presentations often imply. It is not the case that at each stage the crisis is either left unresolved or resolved, thus allowing the way forward to further development. A solution may be only relatively successful, and this will have repercussions on all subsequent stages. Thus major unresolved residues of earlier crises can play a salient part in late life, and make the issues somewhat different for each individual according to his or her own past experience.

Erikson's ideas can be seen as a precursor to what is now called a 'lifespan' approach to ageing. In order to understand people in late life it is necessary to see them in the context of their whole life history with the problems both successfully and unsuccessfully resolved from earlier periods in life. This is a challenge above all to professions working with older people and Erikson's writing can be illuminating and provide new horizons precisely in those settings where work with older people often seems so dull, as in long-stay hospitals. Lesley Archer, for example, provides a telling account of how she came to find added meaning in working with mentally infirm older people on a British hospital ward, through a consideration of each of Erikson's stages of development (Archer, 1982).

The notion of 'integrity', the last task of life, is only sketchily worked out in Erikson's early writing. In more recent years he has attempted to develop it further (e.g. Erikson, Erikson and Kivnick, 1986). Other writers have elaborated similar ideas (Peck, 1968; Butler, 1963). At the same time the stage theory as a whole has been criticized for being too idealistic (Clayton, 1975). Certainly it would be foolish to pretend that Erikson offers a worked-out theory of positive adjustment in later life. His value I believe is that he points to key elements that have to be taken into account in any consideration of mental health in old age, some of which have often been neglected by gerontologists.

Death, for example, must be central to the study of old age. Much gerontological writing, on the contrary, almost gives the impression that death is an avoidable rather than inevitable conclusion to old age. But the old know well enough that life is nearing an end. As those researchers who have investigated attitudes to death readily acknowledge, older people do not generally share the same hesitancy and reluctance to discuss death (Lieberman and Tobin, 1983). They talk about it openly and in personal terms. Coming to terms with one's 'finitude' is a key feature of adjustment to old age (Munnichs, 1966). This is manifested in a number of ways, one being the process of 'tidying up'. Concern with what will happen to property, and attempts to distribute some of it to children, friends and others, represent a recognition of mortality and a wish to leave the world with some orderly distribution of the products of a life well lived.

People also are generally concerned with what will happen to their society after they die. Yet if society is to be so different from the one one has known, if it appears likely to overthrow or indeed already has overthrown the values that were so important in guiding one's own life, it can be hard to accept. Living in a fast changing society can make adjustment to ageing more difficult. It needs courage and imagination to see through the different manifestations of human interests and activities and to perceive an underlying constancy. Erikson refers to the 'comradeship with the ordering ways of distant times and different pursuits. . . . Although aware of the relativity of all the various life styles which have given meaning to human striving, the possessor of integrity is ready to defend the dignity of his own style against all physical and economic threats' (Erikson, 1965, p. 260). It is not to deny that there are differences. It is to be confident enough about one's own life to defend the course it has taken, yet be able at the same time to tolerate other ways as well. Self-acceptance and acceptance of others go hand in hand.

Judgements on the value of one's own past life do become inevitable in old age as new opportunities diminish. It may appear too late to start again or to make amends for wrongs done. A sense of fulfilment or at least a sense of progress does appear crucial to happiness in late life. The 'life review' has been described by the American psychiatrist Robert Butler as a naturally occurring phenomenon in late life in which people survey the courses their lives have taken (Butler, 1963). On occasions the help of professional therapists may be needed in assisting them to face painful truths about themselves. The role of ministers of religion with those with a religious faith must also be considered since all the major religions recognize the importance of seeking reconciliation.

SELF-PERCEPTION

'Integrity' as defined by Erikson describes an ideal end state to the life course, a state of wholeness in oneself and at the same time of relatedness to the rest of humanity. Some of those who have criticized the excessively idealistic elements in Erikson's and similar writings have proposed more limited and what they would regard as more realistic goals for mental health in late life. Lieberman and Tobin (1983), for example, in their investigations into the adjustment of older people moving into institutions in the United States, examined the notion of the life review. But in their view such objective truth seeking about one's life course was not common. Rather reminiscence was used to bolster a positive view of the individual in the face of difficult circumstances. They, like others, have stressed a positive view of oneself and high self-esteem as the 'linchpin' of quality of life in old age (Coleman, 1984).

Theorizing on the importance of self-esteem has a long history. One of the early psychoanalysts, Alfred Adler, who broke away from Sigmund Freud to found his own school, stressed that a prime motivating force in all people's lives is a feeling of inferiority. All individuals have this feeling to some extent because of the inferior position they once occupied as children where power and privilege were exerted by adults.

Some feel this more strongly than others, for example as a result of physical defects or heavy handed parenting. Adler saw subsequent developments of an individual's lifestyle as a means of compensating for feelings of inferiority. There are psychotherapists, notably Brink (1979), who see particular relevance in Adler's thinking for old age, because feelings of inferiority and loss of self-esteem can become major issues again in late life, as a result of physical decline, loss of relationships, status and other favourable attributes. In Adlerian terms rigid, rejecting attitudes on the part of older people and even disengagement can be seen as problems resulting from a fear of inferiority. The perspective of an Adlerian approach to therapy is essentially constructive. Inferiority feelings and neurotic lifestyles are overcome by helping the individual to develop a wider interest in others and cultivate a sense of belonging.

One very important form of self-perception is the perception of being in control of events. It is clear that loss of perceived control is damaging both to morale and eventually to physical health (Rodin, 1986). A number of recent experiments have shown that it is possible for older people to regain a greater sense of personal responsibility, often in unpromising circum-stances such as institutional care. These studies emphasize the gains in mental alertness and general morale to be expected from shifting people from a passive state of mindlessness to an active state of mindfulness (Langer, 1983).

MEANING IN LIFE

The use of the term 'self-esteem' conceals an important distinction between what can be termed 'self-evalu-tion' and 'self-worth' (Freden, 1982). High self-evalu-ation refers to the ascription of positive qualities to oneself, implicitly by comparison with others or at least by reference to some standard which indicates that one is intelligent, beautiful and so forth. But self-worth is less involved in measurement and assessment and more concerned with perception of absolute value. A person has self-worth if he(she) values him(her)self and sees his(her) life as meaningful.

This distinction is very important for the study of mental health in old age. We may be mistaken to overemphasize the self-evaluation component of self-esteem, as in perceptions of being attractive and capable, and neglecting the cultivation of self-worth, such as perceiving and feeling there is meaning to one's life, having a sense of purpose and having hope. Meaning is not an abstruse issue. It is a vital question whether people find meaning in their lives and how they do so. Some find it in the course of their ordinary everyday pursuits, whereas others do not. Some lose it with their partner, with their job or with their health. In old age the issue of meaning often becomes more acute because previously given meanings disappear that have been contained in the tasks that society requires of individuals in growing up, working, raising a family and so on.

It is no accident that many great writers have chosen old age as their theme when it comes to raising issues of the meaning of existence. It is as if an old person, freed from the strait-jacket of societal pressures and suffering losses in ability to exercise previous functions in society, is somehow let free to question life. Gerontologists have only begun tentatively to approach these issues. Of course there is a lot of interest in the writings of those theorists who have stressed the importance to mental health of perception of meaning and coherence throughout life (e.g. Frankl, 1963; Antonovsky, 1979), but there also appear to be developmental issues special to late life.

Of particular value are the work of those theorists who have taken a broad cross-cultural view of ageing. Carl Jung, for example, another colleague of Sigmund Freud in the original band of psychoanalysts who eventually broke away to develop a quite distinct approach to human development, possessed a remarkable understanding of the variety of human culture and history. Placing less emphasis on childhood experience as a determinant of adult development, he drew attention to a set of special tasks that he saw as characterizing the second half of life. For him mid-life was the crucial turning point when the individual was provided with opportunities for new developments. These were less to do with involvement in the outside world and more with interior processes that he referred to with the term 'individuation'. His knowledge of different cultures and religions led him to propose certain common features in societies which promoted mental health in the second part of life (Jung, 1934).

The major goal for Jung is the achievement of harmony between the individual's consciousness and what he

described as the 'collective unconscious', a residue of the experience of the whole human race which is shared by each individual. The manner of relating to the collective unconscious is largely through symbolic experience, and the practices of the various religions which cultivated the power of symbols Jung saw as healthy and essential features of human life. Indeed, Jung was fond of saying of his patients that they had become ill because they had lost touch with religion and become 'whole' again by experiencing the more intimate contact with the world around them that religious practice provided. Certainly the importance of religion to older people has been surprisingly neglected by researchers in Britain, despite the fact that older people make up such a large proportion of church congregations and audiences of religious services on the radio and television.

The more recent work of David Gutmann, an American psychologist who has done much work on the experience of ageing in other societies especially in Central America and the Middle East, has also pointed to developmental processes in late life which are neglected in Western society (Gutmann, 1987). Older people in traditional societies do 'disengage' from the world of pragmatic action, but they do so to become tenders of the values of their culture. Both older men and older women come to personify the moral norms that underpin their extended families and the larger public world. Their detachment from ordinary affairs frees them to make this advance so that they represent the abstract but vital elements underlying their culture. In so doing they gain new meaning in their own eyes and in the eyes of others.

Although comparable possibilities do exist for older people in Western society—one of Gutmann's favourite examples is the courage of the old lawyers who more than their younger colleagues were determined to prosecute President Nixon because he had offended against the fundamental ideals of the American constitution—the bases of Western civilization have been diluted in the rapid social changes of the last two hundred years and more. The pathological behaviour shown by some older people, the regression into self-absorption and self-pity, are for Gutmann the signs of loss of stability in a culture. They have lost their vital role in renewing and strengthening the basis of their culture. As Erikson also stressed, realization of psychological potentials at all ages of life depends on suitable social circumstances which promote their development. A shifting, changing society appears to pose a threat to the realization of integrity. A coherent culture, argues Gutmann, with well-defined traditions is the necessary context for the development of characteristics of wisdom and self-transcendence which give old age its special meaning.

CONCLUSION

I hope that this brief survey has been enough to show the richness of the range of ideas that exist about the constituents of mental health in late life. They are not exclusive to old age of course. Indeed, they parallel the various approaches to positive mental health outlined by Marie Jahoda in her analytical account of the literature thirty years ago (Jahoda, 1958). Six major categories of concepts emerged: attitudes of an individual towards his own self; growth, development or self-actualization; integration; autonomy; perception of reality; and environmental mastery. All are reflected in the literature on ageing: in the importance of maintaining self-esteem; in the development of potentials ranging from the realization of talents neglected earlier in life to the defence of one's culture; the achievement of integrity and the perception of meaning in life; a sense of control; the search for a truthful assessment of one's achievements and limitations; and a sense of belonging, purpose and hope in relationship to the world around.

It should not be surprising if depictions of an ideal old age appear to represent a peak for mental health throughout life. A consideration of the meaning of old age does raise fundamental questions about the meaning of the whole life course that has preceded it. Far from being an anti-climax, old age serves as a beacon illuminating childhood and adulthood, love, work and leisure.

REFERENCES

Abrams, M. (1978). *Beyond Three-Score and Ten. A First Report on a Survey of the Elderly*, Age Concern England, Mitcham, Surrey.

Antonovsky, A. (1979). *Health, Stress and Coping*, Jossey-Bass, London.

Archer, J.L. (1982). 'Discovering a philosophy for working with the elderly mentally infirm', Social Work Service, Department of Health and Social Security, Summer 1982, pp. 43–9.

Bowling, A., and Cartwright, A. (1982). *Life after a Death: A Study of the Elderly Widowed*. Tavistock, London.

Brink, T.L. (1979). *Geriatric Psychotherapy*, Human Sciences Press, New York.

Brown, G.W., and Harris, T. (1978). *Social Origins of Depression: A Study of Psychiatric Disorder in Women*, Tavistock, London.

Butler, R.M. (1963). 'The life review: an interpretation of reminiscence in the aged', *Psychiatry*, **26**, 65–76.

Clayton, V. (1975). 'Erikson's theory of human development as it applies to the aged: wisdom as contradictive cognition', *Human Development*, **18**, 119–28.

Coleman, P.G. (1984). 'Assessing self esteem and its sources in elderly people', *Ageing and Society*, **4**, 117–35.

Comfort, A. (1977). *A Good Age*, Mitchell Beazley, London.

Cumming, E., and Henry, W. (1961). *Growing Old: The Process of Disengagement*, Basic Books, New York.

Erikson, E.H. (1950). *Childhood and Society*, Norton, New York, republished 1965, Penguin, London.

Erikson, E.H., Erikson, J.M., and Kivnick, H.Q. (1986). *Vital Involvement in Old Age: The Experience of Old Age in Our Time*, Norton, New York.

Frankl, V.E. (1963). *Man's Search for Meaning: An Introduction to Logotherapy*, Pocket Books, New York.

Freden, L. (1982). *Psychosocial Aspects of Depression: No Way Out?*, Wiley, Chichester, Sussex.

Gutmann, D.L. (1987). *Reclaimed Powers: Towards a New Psychology of Men and Women in Later Life*, Basic Books, New York.

Hunt, A. (1978). *The Elderly at Home*, HMSO, London.

Jahoda, M. (1958). *Current Concepts of Positive Mental Health*, Basic Books, New York.

Jung, C.G. (1934). *The Integration of the Personality*, Routledge and Kegan Paul, London.

Langer, E.J. (1983). *The Psychology of Control*, Sage, Beverly Hills, California.

Lieberman, M.A., and Tobin, S.S. (1983). *The Experience of Old Age: Stress, Coping and Survival*, Basic Books, New York.

Munnichs, J.M.A. (1966). *Old Age and Finitude*, Karger, Basle.

Palmore, E., and Kivett, V. (1977). 'Change in life satisfaction: a longitudinal study of persons aged 46–70', *Journal of Gerontology*, **32**, 311–16.

Peck, R.C. (1968). 'Psychological developments in the second half of life'. In B.L. Neugarten (ed.), *Middle Age and Aging*, University of Chicago Press, Chicago, Chap. 9, pp. 88–92.

Rodin, J. (1986). 'Aging and health: effects of the sense of control', *Science*, **233**, 1271–6.

Stott, M. (1981). *Ageing for Beginners*, Blackwell, Oxford.

Approaches to the study of ageing

CHRISTINA VICTOR

Director of Community Medicine and Nursing Research Unit, St Mary's Hospital, London

Social gerontology does not possess an extensive theoretical framework in its own right. The systematic development of theory, and its subsequent application, are activities which have been absent from many social scientific studies of ageing. Frequently, researchers have been content simply to describe aspects of behaviour in later life, or the characteristics of various sub-groups of the elderly population, without trying to organise the findings into a coherent theory of social ageing.

As Fisher (1978, p. 194–5) wrote:

Social gerontology has not succeeded in creating a body of theory. . . . Probably, gerontology will never be a theoretical discipline in its own right, but rather a consumer of theory from other sciences. Its major function seems to be that of an applied social science. . . . Its major role, perhaps, has been to destroy the myths which so thickly encrust the study of ageing, to oppose the age prejudice which has grown so strong. . . .

This failure to formulate a systematic theory of social ageing is perhaps not surprising, given the complexity of the field and its relatively recent development as a substantive area of study. However, social gerontology has not been immune from the broader sociological paradigms such as social interactionism, social exchange theory and functionalism. In the rest of this chapter we shall summarise the main sociological theories and frameworks which have been used to study ageing. [. . .]

DISENGAGEMENT THEORY

One of the earliest theoretical perspectives used by gerontologists was disengagement, which was

originally formulated by Cumming and Henry (1961). Expressed in its simplest form, this perspective states that, independent of other factors such as poor health or poverty, ageing involves a gradual but inevitable withdrawal or disengagement from interaction between the individual and their social context. This withdrawal is undertaken in preparation for the ultimate act of disengagement, the death of the individual. By disengaging from activity, the individual prepares herself for death. At the same time, society also prepares the individual for the later phases of life, by withdrawing the pressure to interact. Whether this process is initiated by the individual, or others in her social system, the end result is that the elderly person plays fewer social roles and experiences a deterioration in both the quality and quantity of her relationships.

Disengagement therefore implies a triple loss for the individual: a loss of roles, a restriction of social contacts and relationships, and a reduced commitment to social mores and values. Successful ageing, from the viewpoint of disengagement theory, implies a reduction in activity levels and a decrease in involvement, until the individual withdraws from all previous activities and becomes preoccupied with self and ultimate death. At the heart of this theory is the loss of the major life role. For males this is implicity seen as employment, whilst the major female role loss is in the sphere of the family. For males the role loss is seen as more problematic, because it is usually much more abrupt than changes in family structure.

Central to this theory is the assumption that both the individual and the wider society benefit from the process. Withdrawal for the individual may mean a release from social pressures which stress productivity, competition and continued achievement. For society, the withdrawal of older members permits younger, more energetic individuals to take over the roles which need to be filled. Disengagement therefore is seen as a way of permitting an orderly transfer of power between generations. The mutual withdrawal of the individual and society from each other is presented as a necessary condition for both successful ageing and the orderly continuation of society. [. . .]

The empirical evaluation of disengagement as a theory of ageing must address three core aspects of the theory. First, disengagement is a life-long process; for most individuals, it takes place over a period of time rather than suddenly. Throughout the life course the individual is continually acquiring and dropping particular social roles. Second, there is an implicit statement that disengagement is inevitable because death and biological decline are inevitable. Third, disengagement is seen as adaptive for both society and the individual.

There is some empirical evidence to support disengagement theory although not all of the aspects noted above have been subject to investigation. Clearly, older people do experience a loss of roles with ageing, whether through retirement, the death of a spouse or the departure of older children from home. However, most of the evidence is, at best, ambiguous. Insufficient attention has been paid to the strategies of substitution and compensation used by the elderly to compensate for losses of role. Widowers might remarry, or the elderly may replace a widespread and loose-knit pattern of interaction with more intense, locally based networks.

There is little good empirical evidence to support the assertion that the withdrawal of the elderly from employment and other roles is socially adaptive. It could be just as convincingly argued that it is bad, since some of the most knowledgeable and experienced members of society are being removed, either by voluntary or mandatory methods, and are replaced with less competent younger people.

There have been several other criticisms of this approach. One has been its relative simplicity. It seems highly likely that disengagement, if it exists, will require a much more complex and sophisticated explanation, including many aspects of psychology and biology. Another difficulty is the assumption that, at the individual level, the desire for disengagement encounters no competition from desires which seek to prolong engagement. This seems to be very improbable given the complex nature of human behaviour. Central to the theory is the notion that, if an individual withdraws from a particular interaction

then behavioural norms will wither away. This seems unlikely. Research evidence indicates that once a norm has been internalised, more than the mere absence of interaction is required to make it wither away. A further difficulty with this theory is the implicit value judgement that disengagement is 'a good thing' for both society and the individual. Blau (1973, p.152) argues that disengagement theory has been used to 'avoid confronting and dealing with the issue of older people's marginality in American society'. The presumed inevitability of the process, with its basis in the biomedical and sickness model of ageing, has also been subject to considerable criticism. Whilst disengagement theory has been highly influential upon the development of social gerontology, empirical testing and debate have exposed its essential frailty.

Estes, Swan and Gerard (1982) consider that the popularity of disengagement theory has had a marked influence upon the formulation of policy for the elderly in the United States. They argue that this conceptualisation of old age prescribes either no policy response to ageing or interventions which achieve the separation of the older person from society. Disengagement theory has formed the intellectual basis for age-segregated policies and the separation of the elderly from other forms of welfare development. The notion of disengagement has been used to legitimise policies which have sought to exclude the elderly. Fisk (1986) suggests that the existence of disengagement theory has enabled professionals dealing with the elderly to rationalise their often negative stereotypes. This theory has further enabled the erection of 'barriers' between the elderly and other social groups and the professionals dealing with them.

ACTIVITY THEORY

Diametrically opposed to the notion of disengagement is activity theory developed by Havighurst (1963). This perspective maintains that normal and successful ageing involves preserving, for as long as possible, the attitudes and activities of middle age. Thus, to compensate for the activities and roles the individual surrenders with ageing, substitutes should be found.

Activity theory assumes that the relationship between the social system and the ageing individual remains stable. The norms for old age are seen as being the same as those for middle age. Therefore older persons should be rated in terms of a middle age set of values. Ageing is conceptualised as a continuous struggle to remain middle aged. According to exponents of this view, any behaviour exhibited by older people which would not be appropriate for the middle aged should be considered as maladjustment. Given the way that many older people reject the label 'old', and rate themselves as middle aged, it would appear that the old consider middle-aged behaviour patterns as appropriate to themselves.

Lemon, Bengtson and Peterson (1972) isolate the two central assumptions of activity theory as:

(1) Morale and life satisfaction are related to social integration and high involvement with social networks.
(2) Role losses such as widowhood or retirement are inversely correlated with life satisfaction.

To date, the empirical evidence in support of these assumptions has been ambiguous. Lemon *et al.* (1972), in their study of a retirement community, found no evidence to support these assumptions. However, Palmore (1965) demonstrated a relationship between morale, activity and personal adjustment.

A further difficulty with this approach is that it says nothing about those who lose the battle to remain middle aged. Again, one may question the value judgements inherent in the theory that activity in old age is a 'good thing'. The social policy implications of this perspective are rather more positive than disengagement theory, for it argues for the integration of the elderly as full members of society.

DEVELOPMENT THEORY

Dissatisfaction with both these approaches to the study of ageing has led to the search for other ways of theorising about ageing. Some gerontologists have stated that an understanding of later life requires a knowledge and understanding of what happened to the individual at earlier phases in the life cycle. Gerontologists have turned to the theories of Freud, Buhler, Jung and Erikson to try and understand ageing.

Of the various developmental theories, that of Erikson (1950) is the most complete. He describes life as

being composed of eight phases: early infancy, late infancy, early childhood, late childhood, adolescence, late adolescence, the productive years and late life. The function of each of these stages is, according to development theorists, to master developmental tasks which will be required in the next phase.

Developmental theorists have concentrated upon youth and early infancy. However their work identifies three key issues for the ageing individual. First, old age is seen as a time of summing up of the individual's life. It is a stage in the life cycle when she must come to terms with what she has achieved (and not achieved) during her life. Second, old age is seen primarily as a time of adjustment during which the individual must come to terms with new social realities such as retirement or widowhood. Third, and related to this, the individual must adjust to being cut off from familiar roles, identities and relationships because of retirement, widowhood or the death of friends.

These theories offer the gerontologist a way of looking at the adaptation of individuals to the later phases of life. In particular, they encourage the researcher to explain the older person's current life style in terms of their earlier history. Later life is viewed as a progression from earlier phases. This approach does not outline a 'desired' or 'right' way of ageing as with disengagement or activity theories. Rather, a diversity of approaches and adaptations to the problem of ageing will be displayed, depending upon the history of the older person. Development theories see old age as a time of challenge which poses new possibilities for the individual. The response to these new circumstances may be either positive or negative.

Whilst offering a stimulating perspective upon ageing, these theories are not yet well developed and there are disadvantages to the approach. First, these theories are highly abstract in their approach. Second, they say very little about those who have arrived at the later phases of life without mastering the tasks of the earlier stages. They are also rather deterministic. The approach implies that if the individual has made a mistake in one of the earlier phases there is little, or nothing, she can do to correct it and put her life back into order. A particular problem is the difficulty of generalising across the population, as the experience of ageing will vary widely between males and females, or between Asians and whites. A further limitation of this approach is that it is culturally and historically specific. Thus, whilst these approaches offer an innovative way of looking at ageing, they are very difficult to test empirically.

CONTINUITY THEORY

Developmental approaches to the study of ageing have largely been utilised by gerontologists interested in the psychological dimensions of later life. Sociologically inclined gerontologists have turned to continuity theory. Sociologists have argued that the experiences an individual has at a particular stage are preparatory for the roles and functions to be assumed at the next phase of the life cycle. This is the well-established sociological tradition of the continuity of socialisation. For example, both formal and informal child rearing patterns are seen as contributing to the socialisation process which prepares children for the assumption of adult roles. Life cycles, therefore, are seen to have patterns in which there is considerable continuity from one phase to the next.

Continuity theory holds that, in the course of growing older, the individual will attempt to maintain stability in the lifestyle she has developed over the years. This approach implies that ageing can only be properly understood by examining the relationship between biological, social and psychological changes in the individual's lifestyle and previous behaviour patterns. Continuity theory suggests that in the process of ageing, the person will strive to preserve the habits, preferences and lifestyle acquired over a lifetime. Ageing is, therefore, a constant battle to preserve favoured lifestyles.

This perspective clearly identifies retirement as being problematic for the individual, as nothing in their previous experience will have prepared them for retirement. Career and job skills become redundant, work is replaced by leisure and the constant drive for achievement and success no longer dominates life. Major role changes, such as widowhood or children leaving home, are also perceived as being problematic because of the lack of anticipatory socialisation.

Both disengagement and activity theory suggest that successful ageing is achieved by movement in a single direction. Continuity theory, in contrast, starts from the premise that the individual will try to preserve her favoured lifestyle for as long as possible. It then suggests that adaptation may occur in several directions according to how the individual perceives her changing status. The theory does not assert that one must disengage, or become active, in order to cope with ageing. Rather, the decision regarding which roles are to be disregarded and which maintained will be determined by the individual's past and preferred lifestyle. Unlike activity theory, this approach does not assume that lost roles need to be replaced.

Continuity theory, therefore, has the advantage of offering a variety of adjustment patterns from which the individual can choose. The disadvantage is the problem of trying to test it empirically. Each individual's pattern of adjustment in old age or retirement becomes a case study in which the researcher attempts to determine how successfully the individual was able to continue in her previous lifestyle. Building a generally applicable theory from this basis is, therefore, difficult. [. . .]

AGEING AS EXCHANGE

[. . .] Exchange theory provides a detailed explanation of why individuals behave as they do in particular situations. The notion of social behaviour as exchange can be traced back to the anthropological work of Mauss (1954). He considered that interaction constituted an exchange of material and non-material goods and services. The sociological studies of Homans (1961) and Blau (1964) have also studied the exchange relationship.

The centrality of exchange in the relationships of older people has been recognised since the writings of Simmons (1945) who argued that the ability of the older person to maintain reciprocal relationships was the key to the status of the aged. It is, however, only fairly recently that Dowd (1980) has proposed an explicit theory of ageing as social exchange, which seeks to explain the decreased social interaction of later life. The basic premises of exchange theory are as follows:

(1) Society consists of social actors pursuing common goals.
(2) In pursuit of these goals actors enter into social relationships with other actors. Participating in such interactions entails costs such as time or effort.

(3) In order to achieve their goals actors will pay these costs.

(4) Actors seek to minimise costs and maximise gains.

(5) Only interactions which are economic will be preserved.

From this perspective Dowd (1980) interprets interaction between groups or individuals as an attempt to maximise rewards and minimise costs. Interaction is sustained because, and only as long as, it is profitable for the participating actors. Power derives from the imbalance of the exchange, i.e. when one actor values the rewards to be gained from interaction more than the other. Thus one participant achieves power through the inability of the other to reciprocate.

As the power of older persons, relative to their social environment, is gradually diminished, so interaction declines until all that is left of their stock of power and prestige is the ability to comply. Dowd (1980) considers that the only social currency the older person can bring to the exchange relationship is esteem and compliance. Thus where the worker was once able to exchange skill and knowledge in return for wages she has to comply with statutory retirement in return for a subsistence welfare income. The older worker has to cope with the outdating of her skills. This too can bring imbalance to the exchange relationship. The difficulty for the older person is that this unbalanced power relationship becomes institutionalised and then becomes the norm for future exchanges.

This theory explicitly rejects the functionalist notion of reciprocity between individual and society, in which both sides benefit from interacting. Rather, the exchange theory approach calls for an explicit analysis of both sides of each social transaction (or exchange) to determine who benefits most and why. The great value of an exchange model study of ageing is the multidisciplinary origin of the model, its dynamic nature, and its ability to incorporate processes of both role and resource allocation. As yet there have been few empirical applications of this theory because of its relatively recent formulation. However, this may prove to be one of the more fruitful areas in the development of social gerontology theory in the future. [. . .]

THE ELDERLY AS A MINORITY GROUP

Some sociologists argue that the most appropriate way to study the elderly is as a minority group experiencing all the problems characteristic of groups which are discriminated against. Here the term minority group does not refer to their numerical size, but to their marginality to society as a whole. The elderly, like other minority groups such as Asians or Afro-Caribbeans, are distinct from the wider society because of a common biological trait. Palmore and Whittington (1971) propose this perspective by indicating the negative stereotypes of, and discrimination which accompanies, old age. Breen (1960) argues that the elderly show the characteristics typical of a minority group such as low income, unequal opportunity and an inferior status. As with racial minorities, discrimination against the old is promoted by the relative ease with which the undesirable trait can be observed.

Whilst not describing older people as a minority group, Rose and Peterson (1965) argued that the elderly comprise a specific sub-culture. They consider that a sub-culture emerges when members of a group interact more with each other than with other members of society. This tendency for a group to interact mainly with itself is brought about by the operation of two social processes. First, the existence of common problems, such as poor housing, interests or concerns, may encourage the group to interact more with each other than with those outside the group. Second, they may be excluded, either formally or informally, from interaction with the wider society. To varying degrees, both of these pressures operate upon older adults in modern Western industrial societies. Features such as the exclusion of older people from the employment market, their dependence upon others for their income and marginality to the mainstream of life have been used to support the viewpoint that the elderly constitute a specific sub-culture.

The obvious weakness of this view is that the theory does not apply universally, for the elderly are a highly diverse group. Some older people are ascribed considerable power and prestige in areas such as the law and politics. Additionally, though poverty is common in old age, not all the elderly are poor (Walker, 1980). Neither are the elderly characterised by residence in age-segregated communities, or by patterns of social interaction confined within their own age groups. Thus, given the heterogeneous nature of the elderly population, this perspective is of only limited utility as a conceptual framework.

AGE STRATIFICATION THEORY

Society is often conceptualised as being stratified, or divided, along a number of dimensions, such as social class or ethnic status. Age stratification theory uses chronological age as the defining variable (Riley, 1971; Riley, Johnson and Foner, 1972). Thus the elderly, teenagers and the middle-aged are seen as distinctive status groups. Every society divides individuals into age groups or strata and this stratification reflects and creates age-related differences in capacities, roles, rights and privileges.

Three basic issues dominate age stratification theory. The first is the meaning of age and the position of age groups within any particular social context. Second, there are the transitions which individuals experience over the life cycle because of these social definitions of age. Third, there are the mechanisms for the allocation of roles between individuals.

Age stratification models are obviously flexible. This approach may be used to look at a variety of age groups, not just the elderly. However we must remember that, whilst all societies can be characterised by age stratification, the social meaning that individual societies ascribe to different age groups will vary. These models are both culturally and historically specific.

Age stratification theory is related to theories of social class stratification. However, unlike class stratification, mobility across the strata in the age-stratification model is inevitable, universal and irreversible because of the natural progression of time. Social mobility, the class stratification corollary of age mobility, is not inevitable. Linked to this demographic aspect are the age-related differences in roles and behaviour which constitute the structural elements of the model. Thus individuals of varying ages behave differently, have different abilities, hold different values and may be motivated by different attitudes.

The model of age stratification has two distinct elements: structure and process. The structural component relates to the way that roles and behavioural expectations are age-graded. The process dimension of the model is concerned with the mechanism of allocation whereby people are matched with roles. [. . .]

The age-grading of roles within a stratification system creates age differences and inequalities. Each age group is evaluated, both by itself and others in the society, in terms of the dominant social values. This differential evaluation of roles will produce an unequal distribution of power and prestige across the age groups. Thus when societies value the accumulated experience and wisdom of the old, and allow them to undertake roles which capitalise upon this experience, then the aged will be accorded a position of respect.

Age stratification suggests that the role transitions which we experience are timetabled by age norms rather than being selected by us. To understand these transitions we have to have a knowledge of the process of socialisation by which individuals learn to accept specific roles and role transitions. Age stratification makes socialisation a life-long process as people move between a sequence of roles as they age.

The value of this approach is that it allows the gerontologist to look at any age group in terms of its demographic characteristics and its relationships with other groups. However the system of age stratification in any society is complex and dynamic and linked in with other systems of stratification such as class or ethnicity. Thus the task of understanding the effects of age stratification is complicated by these interactions. This is very much a macro-scale approach to the study of ageing for, whilst it tells us about the attributes of different cohorts, it is of limited value in explaining individual behaviour. This approach can often be seen as being deterministic and allowing little freedom of action for the individual social actor.

CONCLUSION

Theoretical formulations in the social sciences display a marked variation in terms of complexity and sophistication. This chapter has indicated that the theories used by social gerontologists reflect these varying levels of sophistication and complexity. We have also indicated that most of the theory used by gerontologists to inform their work has been derived from other disciplines such as sociology or psychology. Thus there are sometimes difficulties in applying the concepts involved across disciplinary boundaries. It is important for the European reader to remember that the majority of these theoretical approaches have been developed in North America which may limit their utility and explanatory power when applied elsewhere.

The earliest formulations in social gerontology such as activity and disengagement theory, although not derived from other academic disciplines, were simplistic in approach. Considerable empirical evaluation of these two theories indicates that neither is sufficient to explain the experience of ageing. Indeed these perspectives seem to be as much, if not more, philosophical than theoretical. Both activity and disengagement theory appear to be prescriptive recommendations about how to live in the later years of life, rather than theories attempting to explain human behaviour. However, these two theories have had considerable impact upon the development of gerontology and the formulation of social and medical policies for later life. In particular, disengagement theory has been used to justify the age segregated policies for the elderly which characterise many modern industrial societies.

The utility of a particular theory in explaining old age requires considerable empirical investigation. Of the theories described in this chapter, continuity theory is probably the hardest to evaluate because it does not readily lend itself to empirical study. Hypotheses about ageing suggested by this theory require the researcher to have extensive knowledge about the subject's previous lifestyle. [. . .]

REFERENCES

Blau, P.M. (1964). *Exchange and Power in Social Life*, John Wiley, New York.

Blaue, Z.S. (1973). *Old Age in a Changing Society*, Franklin Watts, New York.

Breen, L.Z. (1960). 'The aging individual'. In C. Tibbitts (ed.), *Handbook of Social Gerontology*, University of Chicago Press, Chicago, pp. 145–62.

Cumming, E., and Henry, W.E. (1961). *Growing Old*, Basic Books, New York.

Dowd, J (1980). *Stratification amongst the Aged*, Brooks-Cole, Monterey, California.

Erikson, E. (1950). *Childhood and Society*, W.W. Norton, New York.

Estes, C.L., Swan, J.S., and Gerard, L.E. (1982). 'Dominant and competing paradigms in gerontology', *Ageing and Society*, **2**, 151–64.

Fisher, D.H. (1978). *Growing Old in America*, Oxford University Press, New York.

Fisk, M.J. (1986). *Independence and the Elderly*. Croom Helm, London.

Havighurst, A. (1963). 'Successful ageing'. In R.H. Williams, C. Tibbitts, W. Donahoe (eds.), *Process of Ageing*, Vol. 1, University of Chicago Press, Chicago, pp. 311–15.

Homans, C.G. (1961). *Social Behaviour: Its Elementary Forms,* Harcourt, Brace and Wald, New York.

Lemon, B.W., Bengtson, V.L., and Peterson, J.A. (1972). 'Activity types and life satisfaction in a retirement community', *Journal of Gerontology,* 27(4), 511–23.

Mauss, M. (1954). *The Gift*, Free Press, Glencoe, New York.

Palmore, E. (1965). 'Differences in the retirement patterns of men and women', *The Gerontologist*, **5**, 4–8.

Palmore, E., and Whittington, F. (1971). 'Trends in the relative status of the elderly', *Social Forces*, **50**, 84–91.

Riley, M. (1971). 'Age strata in social systems'. In R. Binstock and E. Shanas (eds.), *Handbook of Aging and Social Sciences*, Van Nostrand, Reinhold, New York, pp. 189–217.

Riley, M., Johnson, M., and Foner, A. (1972). *Aging and Society*, Vol. 3, *A Sociology of Age Stratification*, Russell Sage, New York.

Rose, A.M., and Peterson, W.H. (1965). *Old People and Their Social World*, F.A. Davis, Philadelphia.

Simmons, L. (1945). *The Role of the Aged in Primitive Society*, Yale University Press, New Haven, Connecticut.

Walker, A. (1980). 'The social creation of poverty and dependency in old age', *Journal of Social Policy*, **9**, 49–75.

Mental disorder and elderly members of ethnic minority groups

ALISON NORMAN

Former Deputy Director of the Centre for Policy on Ageing, London

Awareness of, and treatment for, psychiatric disorder is still extremely patchy and in many cases grossly inadequate for *all* elderly people in Britain.[1] However for people who came to this country as adults, having grown up in another culture, the risk of psychiatric disorder in old age is even greater and the likelihood of having it recognized and competently treated is very much less.

We are not talking about small numbers. As Table 1 shows, there are already nearly 400 000 people of pensionable age in the United Kingdom who were born overseas (excluding 'the old Commonwealth') and by the end of the century the figure will be close to 1 million. Moreover, many of these members of the 'immigrant generation' are, and will remain, highly concentrated in inner-city areas.

Why are elderly settlers especially vulnerable to mental disorder? Philip Rack in his study *Race, Culture and Mental Disorder*[2] (from which much of this article is derived) lists a number of causes of mental ill-being to which anyone in the same circumstances would be vulnerable but which are particularly likely to affect people who are racially and culturally distinct from the indigenous population. These causes, it must be remembered, are in *addition* to the stresses of living in inner-city areas where the quality of housing and all public services and amenities are at their lowest; where unemployment is at its worst and the quality of health care at its poorest. They are also in addition to the stress from racism and its associated physical violence, abuse, rejection and stigma which members of ethnic minority groups encounter every day of their lives.[3]

CAUSES OF MENTAL VULNERABILITY
Culture shock

The psychological effects of going to live in an utterly different environment were first identified as a syndrome in relation to the problems experienced by American Peace Corps Volunteers and technologists working in 'Third World' countries in the 1950s. The concept is, however, almost equally applicable to travel in the opposite direction. The symptoms (in the case of the Peace Corps Volunteer) were found to include excessive preoccupation with the purity of food and drink, fear of physical contact with natives, great concern with minor pains and skin eruptions, excessive anger over trivial frustrations, a paranoid belief that one is being cheated, feelings of helplessness and inadequacy combined with refusal to learn the local language, desire for the company of ones own 'kind' and:

. . . that terrible longing to be back home, to be able to have a good cup of coffee and a piece of apple pie, to walk into that corner drugstore, to visit one's relatives, and in general to talk to people who really make sense.

The effects of this 'dislocation' gradually wear off as the new language is learned and adaptation to local customs is achieved, but this may be extremely difficult for newcomers (especially women) who have received little or no education in childhood, who may be illiterate in their mother tongue and whose social norms may reinforce their natural desire to withdraw into a 'cultural enclave' of their fellow-countrymen so that the effect of culture shock is minimized (as many British people did in India). Women who do not go out to work may thus remain insulated for many years, but when changes in housing, family circumstances or health do thrust them into contact with the alien environment

Table 1   Older immigrants by country of birth ('000s)

	45–pensionable age	Of pensionable age
East Africa	14.7	1.6
Caribbean	101.3	16.2
Bangladesh	9.4	3.8
India	104.0	44.1
Far East	12.5	3.9
Mediterranean	9.4	3.7
Pakistan	33.7	4.8
Irish Republic	233.0	132.0
European Community	104.0	41.8
Other foreign	183.5	113.5
Total born abroad (excluding 'old Commonwealth')	828.700	374.5

Source: Census 1981, *Country of Birth: Great Britain*, HMSO, 1981, Tables 2 and 3.

the effect can be devastating—and made even worse by old age. Also, even individuals who appear to have made a successful adjustment to the new environment may have feelings of loss, despair, homesickness and anger reactivated by a new stimulus such as worrying news from home, conflict with the younger generation or a particularly distressing experience of racial harassment.

Loss of role identity

The use of personal skills in a familiar role is a basic means of affirming identity. Many of the skills of immigrants, however, are likely to be unusable or unused in this country and accustomed roles may change drastically. As Rack puts it:

In an Indian family the elders have patriarchal (and in some respects matriarchal) authority. The head of the household enacts a particular role which will descend on his death to his eldest son. He has responsibility for arranging marriages, apportioning land or other family property, approving the plans and ambitions of children and grandchildren, and applying corrective discipline to any youngster who steps out of line and places the family honour in jeopardy. People come to him for advice and value his wisdom. But in Britain

such a man may discover that his wisdom is scorned, his judgement disregarded. His daughter or grand-daughter objects to his marriage plans; his son manages his affairs with the aid of solicitors and accountants; when domestic discords erupt into violence, a social worker appears on the scene. His social role is eroded. Similarly a West Indian matron offers support to her young daughter or grand-daughter who has just had a baby. The old lady puts herself out to help the young mother and to teach her from her own experience. But here comes a health visitor with different ideas—and the old lady is disregarded.

Rack goes on to compare the effect of losing role identity in this way to the apathy and inertia experienced by people living in institutions. *'What am I for?'*, he says, leads easily to *'What am I?'*

Loss of caring relationships

Traditional modes of caring for elderly people inevitably tend to break down under the impact of a changed environment, cramped housing in a cold climate and the radically different cultural experience of British-born children and grandchildren. Thus a Social Work Service study of the problems of Asians in a Midlands town reports that:

Although health visitors had very few elderly on their case load, they had nevertheless picked up from young mothers with elderly people in the house that, in some instances, there was great unhappiness on both sides. Whilst some middle-aged couples were as a matter of course caring for their elderly parents, they did not expect to be cared for to the same extent by their own children, and could see problems intensifying in the future. And, in spite of the stated norm that elderly people should be cared for by their own family, there were increasing numbers of elderly Asians, perhaps already as many as 100, living alone.

Similarly, a survey of older Afro-Caribbean people in Nottingham asked respondents what they felt to be the difference between the treatment of older people in England and the West Indies and the authors of the report comment:

A strong sense of loss pervades the replies recorded to this question—the loss of close family and community ties, and of respect for the older person. Whether the characterisation of life in the West Indies was true at the time these people left, or is true today, is less important than the *belief* that it is so. The replies also carried a strong indication that the community spirit of the West Indies could not be created in this country.

Examples of such responses are:

Back home family will look after you when you are old, but here they are too busy because they all go out to work.

In England, when you reach 60 or 65 years old, you become a social problem. No-one cares about you . . . if you ill, that makes it worse. In the West Indies you don't finish at 60 or 65—you are respected. The older you are, the more respected you are.

You get very lonely here . . . the social life is very poor for a West Indian.

In England the government looks after you, but in the West Indies everybody cares for each other, whether relatives, friends or neighbours.[5]

And Philip Rack says of the plight of elderly Polish and Ukranian widows:

Many of them married within their own national group, and they have children who are now grown up. Usually the husband learned to speak English in the course of his employment, but the wife did not always become completely fluent or confident. Women tend to outlive men, there are now a growing number of widows in the community, many of them living in conditions of social isolation. This isolation is bound to increase as friends die and members of the next generation become increasingly preoccupied with their own families.[6]

The refugee experience

For refugees who have fled from political, racial or religious persecution there is an added dimension of loss and fear. People who have lived through terror and torture and barely escaped with their lives are likely to be scarred for life. They may have successfully established homes and careers and families in their new homeland, but in old age all too often the past reasserts itself and elderly ex-refugees may experience psychic flashbacks to their traumatic experiences. They may also fear, not so much death itself, as having their bodies treated like those in the casual dehumanized holocausts they witnessed in Hitler's concentration camps, or Amin's massacres, or the horrors of Indochina. Furthermore, attempts at psychiatric intervention and treatment can trigger memories of past interrogation and imprisonment with which the present experience may be indentified and if a severe organic dementia develops the individual concerned may be literally living in that terrifying past. These ex-refugees may need a very special kind of understanding and support in their old age which neither health nor social services are at present geared to provide.[7]

DIAGNOSIS OF MENTAL DISORDER

In view of this list of possible additional causes of psychological stress there must surely be a massive weight of unrecorded and untreated mental suffering amongst elderly members of ethnic minorities (though the extent to which this can be counted 'illness' rather than a normal reaction to an intolerable situation is debatable). Certainly severe depression, apathy, anxiety, paranoid fear, alchoholism and acute confusional states are reported anecdotally and, although few of the groups concerned have as yet a population which is old enough to have a high incidence of dementia, organic brain cell loss arising from strokes and Alzheimer's disease must be increasingly common. Difficulties in communication offer a formidable barrier to accurate diagnosis and effective treatment. It is not enough for a therapist to use an interpreter, however skilled (and most 'interpreters' are simply people who happen to be on hand), if the vocabularies of the two languages concerned simply do not coincide. All cultures develop language which reflects their environment and meets their needs (Laplanders are said to have over twenty different words for snow and most African languages have a vocabulary to define family relationships which is infinitely more rich and precise than the English equivalent). English, however, has a wealth of words to describe states of mind (Roget's *Thesaurus* lists a full page of synonyms for 'dejection') while many non-European languages have very few such words. For example, Rack says that in Yoruba one word suffices for 'angry' and 'sad' and in Ghana three words cover all shades of unpleasant emotion. Other problems may arise in the diagnosis of dementia because current methods of testing memory and intellect are designed for the indigenous population and may not be appropriate for someone with different experience and background. Furthermore, people of various cultures have various ways in which they conceptualize their malaise. Rack says that depressed Indian and Pakistani patients are likely to describe their symptoms in somatic terms, complaining of pain, weakness, an ache throughout the body, discomfort in the chest or abdomen or a general loss of strength; psychological symptoms of depression may only be elicited by direct questioning or may not be elicited at all. A depressed English patient, on the other hand, will usually refer first to disorders of mood and later mention diffuse muscular aches and pains or a sense of general weariness and lassitude. Conversely Afro-Caribbeans may complain of 'low feelings' when referring to physical illness and not a state of mind. There are varied causes of 'somatization'. It may be a simple metaphor, comparable to English phrases such as being 'heartbroken' or having a 'a lump in one's throat'. It may be a response to the patient's perception of a doctor's role as being the treatment of physical illness so that illness has to be expressed in physical terms. Or it may be that physical symptoms are the only ones acceptable to the patient—'mental illness' being associated with 'madness' and carrying an intolerable stigma. Sensitivity to all the possibilities is therefore of great importance and it is dangerous to dismiss or ignore complaints of physical pain for which no physical cause can be found.

ACCESS TO HEALTH SERVICES

Maggie Pearson, director of the Centre for Ethnic Minority Health Studies in Bradford, says of the National Health Service:

... its policies and practices have understandably evolved in response to the needs of the white British population, as perceived by professionals and planners. This has entailed the development of culture-bound and 'colour-blind' policies which do not consider that established practice might be inappropriate for ethnic minority users, and are insensitive to their beliefs and way of life. ...

The overwhelming majority of health problems faced by ethnic minorities in Britain are different in degree, but not in kind from those experienced by the rest of the population. Social factors contributing to ill-health, and the general health-care experience of the NHS are often intensified for the ethnic minority users by racism and racial prejudice, cultural insensitivity and language differences.[8]

If this is true of health care in general it is doubly so in relation to elderly people from the ethnic minorities and trebly so in relation to psychiatric provision. The height of the barriers to obtaining psychiatric help are well indicated by the difficulties of access encountered in making use of non-psychiatric health services. For example, although most people of all ethnic groups are registered with a GP, only Asians are likely to find it relatively easy to make contact with a GP who speaks their language. The Cypriot and Chinese communities report particular difficulties in this regard but the hundreds of smaller groupings have even greater problems. Even when there is a common language, as for most people from the Caribbean, mutual comprehension may be difficult to achieve and apart from this a sense of pressure in doctor's surgeries, the brevity of consultations and a lack of confidence in GPs' knowledge of tropical diseases, such as sickle-cell anaemia and yaws, often cause people of Afro-Caribbean origin to pay privately for a second opinion. Patients from the Asian communities may also consult Hakims who practise traditional Unani or Ayurvedic systems of holistic medicine which consider the importance of temperament and the balance of humours, diet and lifestyle in the causation and treatment of ailments. Such Hakims may be highly trained and qualified but Western-trained GPs, including in many cases Asians, seem to be largely unaware of their work and there is a real danger of serious side effects if the patient is receiving Western and traditional treatment at the same time.

People of Asian origin make less use of hospital-based services than would be expected from their numbers and their high level of health risk.[9] This probably reflects the special difficulties which many Asians have in using the service as it is provided at present. Hospitals are frightening and confusing places for elderly people from any background but much more so if the staff cannot understand what you are saying and cannot make themselves understood, if you cannot eat the food provided, and if your body is exposed and handled in a way which you find shaming and distressing. Much can be done, as a checklist on *Providing effective health care in a multi-racial society*[10] sets out, to make hospital-based services more accessible. Much-needed measures include the provision of: multilingual signs and directions; flexible and appropriate catering arrangements; varied provision for personal hygiene; visiting arrangements which take cultural norms into account; the availability of interpreters and bilingual staff; and greatly improved staff training in sensitivity and knowledge, including the training of receptionists, records staff and ward clerks who frequently cause chaos by their ignorance of Asian nomenclature.

However, such measures will, at best, be only partly successful in allaying fears, particularly in relation to psychiatric treatment. This is because there is a very deep, and largely well-justified, suspicion amongst the black communities about the way in which psychiatric service personnel treat black people. This suspicion (and a much stronger word could be used) was graphically demonstrated at a Conference on the subject in April 1987 which was organized by the Mental Health Act Commission.[11] Research has now proved that Afro-Caribbean patients, particularly if young and male, are disproportionately likely to be labelled as schizophrenic, to receive medical rather than psychotherapeutic treatment and to find themselves processed by the rougher, more coercive end of the mental health care services. Young black men also account for an unusually high proportion of people receiving compulsory treatment. Thus the stigma which mental illness carries for most ethnic communities (including Anglo-Saxons) is reinforced by a deep fear of, and antagonism to, psychiatry and psychiatrists which is bound to affect the attitude of the immigrant generation as well as that of younger people.

SO WHAT CAN BE DONE?

The first step is to recognize that the vulnerability to mental ill-being and the barriers to receiving help which were sketched above are common to elderly people of all ethnic backgrounds and that many indigenous people, especially in our inner cities, suffer them with almost equal severity. We need to make all our health and social services much more aware of this fact and much more sensitive to it. All too often the professionals reach for the prescription pad and dole out tranquillizers and sleeping pills without trying to discover the underlying reason for the malaise. All too often, also, even where the patient is English-born, there is no real verbal communication and common understanding. Frequently, the assumption

is 'what can you expect at your age and in your situation? There is nothing to be done'. And so no-one tries to do anything or even to find out what the patient or client is really asking for. On a more specifically 'ethnic' level we need much more education of front-line health care workers, and particularly GPs, along the lines of Bradford's transcultural psychiatry unit. Here a team runs meetings and seminars which are designed to enhance the 'cultural competence' of practitioners from all over the region while its direct work brings together the skills of community psychiatric nurses, social workers, GPs, consultants and interpreters (the interpreters have the title and function of 'communication assistants' and are specially trained to work in this field). We need also the development of accessible health counselling services and community-based mental health centres, such as those planned in Haringey, set up in close association with the relevant community groups. Pioneer organizations already working along these lines are the Nafsyat centre in north London, the black mental health project on the Stonebridge Estate in Brent, two SSD mental health day centres for Asians, also in Brent, and the Fanon project in Brixton. These initiatives are, however, a drop in the ocean and they are very largely directed at younger people. Moreover, they are in addition to, and not a substitute for, obtaining an equality of employment opportunity within health and social services which would greatly increase the range of cultures represented in staff at all levels. Unfortunately, radical improvement in the quality and sensitivity of formal psychiatric or other health service provision is bound to be slow, and elderly people in distress need help *now* or they will not live to get help at all. There is therefore an urgent need to deepen the understanding of the religious and community leaders about the nature of mental stress and illness in the immigrant generation and to train members of the communities concerned to offer front-line help. There is also an urgent need to increase the availability of day centres and clubs which are specifically geared to the needs of particular groups—clubs in which elderly immigrants can relax, enjoy themselves, feel at home, make friends and forget their troubles. Such clubs and centres also provide an opportunity for people to learn English, become literate in the mother tongue, acquire new skills and use old ones, obtain trustworthy information and advice, eat palatable and nourishing food, go on trips and outings and make contact with supporters who will then also be trusted to give help in the home if this should be needed; they can be combined with appropriate sheltered housing and they offer a base from which culture shock, home sickness, social isolation, family breakdown and loss of role can be combatted. They therefore become not only a means of treating mental ill-being but also a source of mental health.[12]

REFERENCES

1. Alison Norman, *Mental Illness in Old Age: Meeting the Challenge*, Centre for Policy on Ageing, London, 1982.
2. Philip Rack, *Race, Culture and Mental Disorder*, Tavistock Publications, London, 1982. (Chapters 5–10 have been used as a general source for the material in this article and are attributable unless other sources are quoted.)
3. Alison Norman, *Triple Jeopardy; Growing Old in a Second Homeland*, Centre for Policy on Ageing, London, 1985. (This provides a general review of the situation of ethnic minority elders and their access to health and social services. Where other sources are cited followed by (TJ) the findings are summarized in this report.)
4. Unpublished DHSS Social Work Service Report, 1984 (TJ).
5. Steward Berry, Mike Lee and Sue Griffiths, *Report on a Survey of West Indian Pensioners in Nottingham*, Nottingham County Council Social Services Department Research Section, 1981 (TJ).
6. P. Rack, *Race, Culture and Mental Disorder*, Tavistock Publications, London, 1982, p. 85.
7. Ron Baker (ed.), *The Psychosocial Problems of Refugees*, British Refugee Council and the European Consultation on Refugees and Exiles, London, 1983.
8. Maggie Pearson, 'An insensitive service', in Anthony Harrison and John Gretton (eds.), *Health Care UK 1984: An Economic, Social and Policy Audit*, Chartered Institute of Public Finance and Accountancy, London, 1984.
9. Summary of data provided in 'Health needs and health service', *Triple Jeopardy* (Ref. 3), pp. 60–78.
10. Health Education Council and National Extension College for Training in Health and Race, *Providing Effective Health Care in a Multi-racial, Society: a Checklist for Looking at Local Issues*, HEC and NEC London, 1984 (TJ).
11. Boyd Tonkin, 'Black and blue', *Community Care*, 14 May 1987.
12. See *Triple Jeopardy* (Ref. 3) for a description of 33 such centres and a discussion of the issues relating to their establishment and management.

Section II

Community needs
and issues

Paper 7

The demographic and social circumstances of elderly people

MALCOLM WICKS and MELANIE HENWOOD

Directors of Family Policy Studies Centre, London

INTRODUCTION

'Care *in* the community must increasingly mean care *by* the community.' So stated the 1981 White Paper *Growing Older*,[1] establishing firmly the cornerstone of contemporary social policy towards elderly people in Britain. As a broad policy aspiration, 'community care' is of long standing, and enjoys a remarkable degree of support. Since the Second World War a general shift away from institutions has been advocated for all the main client groups.

The slow transition from policy to practice has, however, been repeatedly highlighted over the years. Throughout the 1960s and 1970s (and beyond) a rush of government enquiries and reports into institutional neglect and abuse was paralleled by a similar burst of interest in the academic and research communities. Townsend's *The Last Refuge*; Goffman's *Asylums*; and Meacher's *Taken For a Ride* are just three of the early landmarks of social criticism.[2] The initial popularity of community care solutions thus reflected a widespread reaction against the excesses and indignities of institutional life. More positively, community care has been inspired by the ideals of social integration and civil liberties. From the early 1970s a new spirit of optimism was evident in policies which spoke of better services and improved priority for those needing care.

Recent criticisms of policy and practices have been less concerned with the evils of institutions than with the paucity of much statutory service development *in the community*. The 1986 report by the independent Audit Commission (*Making a Reality of Community Care*)[3] added its voice to a chorus of criticism and provided a particularly damning indictment of lack of progress. The Commission called for radical change in the strategic organization and funding of community care, without which 'the community care initiative will largely have failed'.

The arguable failure may be seen to reflect tensions and conflicts between what Titmuss described as '. . . the practice, as distinct from the theory, of community care'.[4] These tensions are of long standing but have intensified over recent years. One particularly important reason for this is the ageing of the population. In numerical terms at least, elderly people represent the main challenge to community care policies and aspirations.

Public expenditure is also a crucial consideration. The combined cost of health and social services per person in 1984–5 was £325 for all ages. For children from 0 to 4 years the cost was £320, falling to £215 for each child aged 5 to 15. However, for persons aged 65 to 74 it was £575, and for those aged 75+, £1420. In the light of such pressures the present form of community care policy which emphasizes the central importance of non-statutory sources of care (in particular, the family, the voluntary sector and the private market) may be better understood. Here we consider the future prospects for community care, examining both the demand and supply questions, and the significance of family trends.

DEMOGRAPHIC AND SOCIAL CIRCUMSTANCES

An ageing population

Viewed historically the ageing of the population is striking (see Table 1). In Britain the number of people

Table 1   The elderly population of Great Britain: past, present and future

000's	1901	1931	1981	2001	2021
65+	1734	3316	7985	8546	10005
75+	507	920	3052	4006	4355
85+	57	108	552	1029	1202
% of total population					
65+	4.7	7.4	15.0	15.2	17.6
75+	1.4	2.1	5.7	7.1	7.7
85+	0.15	0.24	1.03	1.8	2.1

Source: OPCS Census 1971 and 1981, and population projections by the Government Actuary Mid 1983 based principal projections 1983, 2023, OPCS PP2, No. 13.

aged 65 and over was less than 2 million in 1901. By the time of the 1981 Census this had risen to almost 8 million. The increase has not only been numerical, but proportionate: comprising less than 5% of the total population in 1901, the total 65+ group constituted some 15% in 1981. These are dramatic trends by any measure, but it is not so much the increases in the elderly population overall which are important, but rather its changing composition and, in particular, the growing numbers of the very elderly. Over the same period the older cohorts (those aged 75+ and 85+) increased even more markedly. The numbers aged 75+ rose from half a million to more than three million, and those aged 85+ increased almost tenfold from 57000 to well over half a million.[5]

The composition of the elderly population *is* vital and has different implications for various areas of policy. There is a general correlation between advancing years and increasing disability on a number of measures, with frailty and incapacity greatest amongst the very aged.

Future trends

The *total* elderly population is expected to downturn after 1991 before beginning to rise once again—but at a much reduced rate. By the turn of the twenty-first century gross numbers are expected to only be 7% higher than in 1981. By comparison, between 1951 and 1971 numbers rose by 34%. The slowing or reduction in overall numbers reflects the low birth rates of the 1920s and 1930s. After the turn of the century the impact of the post-war 'baby boom' will begin to take effect (between 2001 and 2021 the total over 65 population is expected to increase by 17%). Meanwhile the 'older elderly' are expected to continue increasing. The ageing of the elderly population itself is now a characteristic feature of demography throughout the advanced world, with both numbers—and proportions of the oldest and potentially most frail—increasing fastest. Between 1981 and 2001 the number of people aged 75+ is expected to rise by 30% (from 3 052 000 to 4 006 000), while those aged 85 or over who numbered around half a million in 1981 will virtually double.[5]

Geographical variation

Geographically the elderly population is unevenly distributed. Higher proportions of the resident population are elderly along the south coasts of England and in other traditional 'retirement' areas. Above average proportions are also to be found in inner city areas, particularly in the North and North West of England. At the time of the 1981 Census the highest concentration of persons of pensionable age was recorded for the constituency of Bexhill and Battle at 36.2%. Indeed, East Sussex overall is reputed to have the highest proportion of elderly persons *in Europe*. In more than one-sixth of *all* parliamentary constituencies in 1981 persons of pensionable age represented at least 20% of the population.

The ethnic dimension

A further important dimension is the ethnic one. There is a dearth of research data on older people in ethnic minorities in Britain. Much of the work which *has* been completed has concentrated on a few geographical studies and been concerned mainly with black and South Asian respondents.

The 1981 Census found just under 1% of all persons of pensionable age in Britain had been born in the new Commonwealth or Pakistan (NCWP). Persons of this age make up a far smaller proportion of the NCWP population (5.8%) than of the indigenous population. Other than refugees and the parents of early migrants, most immigrants came to Britain in the early part of their working lives during the 1940s and 1950s. Most are therefore still well below retirement age, although over the next 20 to 30 years many more will reach this stage.

Not all members of ethnic minorities share similar characteristics. There are some significant variations. The sex ratio, for example, is more heavily skewed towards males among those of African and Asian origins (because many men came to Britain alone) than among West Indians.

At the time of the 1971 Census two-thirds of persons of pensionable age born in the New Commonwealth or Pakistan and living in Britain were to be found in London. By 1981 this had fallen to 37%—comprising 5% of London's elderly people. Most others are concentrated in and around other big cities: almost 80% of the NCWP population is concentrated in 10% of Census enumeration districts, and many of these are areas of low quality and overcrowded housing.

Men and women

The majority of old people are women, and this imbalance becomes increasingly pronounced with advancing age. Life expectancy at birth has increased by an average 22 years this century. Female life expectancy, however, has improved more than male, and indeed the differential is widening. Upon reaching 60 men can—on average—expect to live another 16 years; women another 21. The skewed age structure of the present elderly population, however, also reflects the impact of two world wars and the loss of men in action. It is estimated that in Britain in 1986

women represented 61% of all those aged 65 or over, but 67% of those over 75 and 77% of those aged 85+. By the turn of the century it is expected that elderly women will outnumber men one and a half times, but among those aged 85 and over the ratio will be around 2.7 to 1.

This imbalance also means that higher proportions of elderly men are married, but they are more likely to die before their wives. Consequently elderly women are particularly likely to be widowed. This also reflects the tendency of women to marry men—on average—a few years older than themselves. The 1981 Census found 44.3% of all women aged 65+ were married, compared to 72.9% men of this age. Some 42.3% of the women were widowed (but only 17.4% of men). Among the oldest people, only 7.2% of women aged 85+ are still married (and 76.3% widowed). Men in this age group also experience widowhood (53.7%), but they are more than five times as likely to be married (38.6%). Marital status is particularly significant in its consequences for the household composition of elderly persons.

Household composition

At the time of the 1981 Census almost one-third of elderly persons in private households in Britain were living alone. This indicated a dramatic increase on earlier decades: in 1961 less than 19% of all elderly persons lived alone, and in 1971 just over 25% did. The high incidence of widowhood among very elderly women (aged 80 and over) leads to an increased likelihood of either living alone (61%) or with children/children in law, siblings, or other relatives (26% compared to just 12% of all aged 65 and over).[6] The experience of widowhood may often trigger a move towards shared households.

Marriage and divorce

Some elderly people have never been married. In 1981, among people aged 65 and over, this was true of 8% of males and 11.2% of females. Consequently, for many elderly people, the vital 'ties of kinship' upon which community care policy is heavily reliant simply do not exist. Significant numbers of elderly people have either never had children or now have none surviving: a 1978 study by Mark Abrams found 30%

of those aged 75 and over had never had children and 7.5% had outlived them.[7]

Current projections of marital status of elderly persons up to the year 2019 anticipate a continued increase in the likelihood of widowhood among women aged 65 and over, but a slight decline among elderly men. However, if male life expectancy improves—as comparisons with other countries suggest it may do—the experience of widowhood among elderly women may change: with a greater similarity of life expectancy widowhood should be less of a characteristic of women's old age (or it should occupy a briefer period than is often the case).

Both sexes are expected in future years to be less likely to remain single, but more likely to experience divorce. In general the divorce rate declines with age, and the proportion of elderly divorcees is low. This is, nevertheless, a growing minority. In 1981, 1.6% of elderly males were divorced, and this is expected to rise to 3.6% by 2019. For women the proportions are higher: 2.2% in 1981 rising to 7.2%. At all ages the remarriage rate is higher for men than for women. The net effect of such changes is to increase the likelihood in future years of being alone, particularly for women.

Housing

Housing is a crucial determinant of living conditions among elderly people, influencing both the ability of elderly people to care for themselves and determining the extent to which others are able to support elderly people in their own homes.

Amenities

Housing circumstances vary, but in general elderly people are poorer housed than younger households. A small but significant minority of elderly people lives in inadequate housing. Elderly people have shared in the trend towards owner occupation, but are still slightly less likely to be home owners than are younger households. Elderly households are *more* likely than others to live in local authority accommodation or in privately rented unfurnished rooms. The last includes part of the housing stock with the most inadequate amenities. Private households which include elderly persons are more likely than those without elderly members to lack some basic amenity. In the 1981 Census 6% of all people of pensionable age lacked exclusive use of a bath or inside toilet, compared to 1% of younger households. Among older people the proportion was even higher: 9% of people aged 75+ and 11% of lone female householders of that age. Some 345 000 people of pensionable age (30 000 of them aged 85+) had no indoor toilet.[8]

Central heating is taken for granted by many people—certainly warm homes should be an essential part of community care. Elderly people are less likely to have adequate heating and more likely to have older homes which are hard to heat: 44% of elderly persons (60+) living alone in 1984 had no central heating. For couples where one or both were elderly this was true of 37%. For *all* households the comparable figure was 34%. The lack of adequate insulation among many elderly and other low income households is a major waste of energy resources and a significant factor in fuel poverty.[8] What these figures indicate overall is that although the majority of older people *do* have adequate housing, nonetheless conditions for disproportionate numbers are still below the standards enjoyed by most other people today.

Unsuitable homes

In addition to basic housing standards questions need also to be asked about the *appropriateness* of accommodation. Many elderly people living in apparently good housing may face problems of too much space and too many rooms to heat. The position of elderly homeowners is increasingly significant. Many find themselves coping with large, unsuitable and hard to heat homes, with attendant problems of repairs, improvements, maintenance and adaptations.

Poverty

The experience of old age varies from individual to individual; however, a general association has long existed between old age and poverty. The position of people in old age reflects prior socioeconomic position and social class, as well as sex and marital status. Inequalities which exist during the working life are perpetuated and amplified in retirement. Married couples are generally better off than the unmarried; men better off than women; younger elderly better off than the oldest; and spinsters better off than widows. This hierarchy reflects differentials in work experience and earnings earlier on.

Early retirement has grown in parallel with the emergence of mass unemployment. The exclusion of older people from the labour market and from earned income means that most are heavily reliant on the State for financial support. Retirement brings a sudden and dramatic fall in income, and for many represents the beginning of years of declining resources and living standards.

While there are inequalities *within* old age, nonetheless *as a group* elderly people are generally financially disadvantaged, many living in, or on the margins of, poverty. The basic State pension is below what might be viewed as a subsistence level (below levels of supplementary and housing benefits). The importance of the basic pension as a main source of income, and its relatively low level, is reflected in the large numbers additionally reliant upon supplementary benefit.

In 1984, 1.7 million persons over pensionable age (around one in six) were receiving SB. Additionally, some 870 000 were eligible for this further support but failed to claim it.

Occupational pensions have expanded considerably in recent years, particularly benefiting the younger retired. In 1981 they represented 15% of total pensioners' income. By 1984–5 this had risen to 22%. Men are better served in this respect than women (who are more likely to be forced into reliance on SB). By the turn of the century 80% of men of retirement age are expected to receive some form of occupational pension. This is likely to apply to about 20% of women (in their own right), but this represents a doubling of the 1975 proportion.

Ageing and incapacity

We have already remarked on the general association between advancing years and increasing disability and frailty. This is the main significance of the ageing population to social policy. Severe incapacity increases markedly beyond about 70 years, so the growth in the very elderly population is especially important.

In much discussion the elderly population is presented as a 'burden of dependency'. How accurate is this view? Alan Walker has suggested that British society is generally ageist and 'has helped to foster and legitimate a caricature of elderly people, which is at best limited and at worst downright degrading, as a burden on the community'.[9]

The *majority* of elderly people are fit, healthy and able to lead independent lives. Precise up-to-date information on the amount of disability and incapacity is not available (an OPCS Survey on disablement should be published in 1988). A 1976 Survey by Audrey Hunt found 0.3% of the elderly population permanently bedfast and 4.2% housebound.[10] In 1985 a report by the Audit Commission on managing social services for the elderly suggested that around 18 per 1000 elderly people comprise a 'small but significant' proportion who are very severely physically incapacitated.[11] Information from the General Household Survey adds to this picture.

It is a *minority* of elderly people who experience the extreme dependency of old age characterized by senility, incontinence and physical incapacity. Nonetheless, they are a numerically significant (and growing) minority, at the extreme end of a continuum of many variants of dependency and need for assistance with everyday living. The application of *The Elderly at Home* findings to current populations, for example, indicates 1 100 000 *severely* disabled elderly people (1 in 8 of all aged 65+). This is an increase of more than 100 000 since 1976. A further 2 million people aged over 65 are moderately disabled.[12]

It is often assumed that the elderly of today are very much fitter and more independent than their forebears. Is there any evidence to support this suggestion that the need for care will not increase at the same pace as the increase in the elderly population itself?

A study which compared survey findings from 1962, 1966 and 1976 concluded that virtually no change had occurred in the amount of severe incapacity among the elderly in the community. However, a marked increase was noted in the numbers of moderately disabled, and lower proportions were judged 'fully functional'.[13]

One reason for this is that both the average age and dependency of those admitted to residential care has risen; this means that elderly people remaining in the community will have more intensive needs for support than previously.

What assumptions can be made about future needs? In addition to the ageing of the population, other trends are relevant. The success of medical intervention at all stages of life means that very many more individuals will survive into old age, even if profoundly mentally or physically handicapped. This is a unique phenomenon of the twentieth century; never before have people with such conditions as Down's syndrome, spina bifida, or hydrocephalus approached adulthood— —let alone old age. While very disabled and frail individuals may thus survive where in the past they would certainly have died, a counter-trend of medical interventions may mean that improved ante-natal screening will reduce the incidence of handicap in future generations.

Elderly people are over-represented in the incidence of various forms of handicap. They comprise around two-thirds of all mentally and physically handicapped people. Mental illness is also significant. In particular, senile dementia affects some 6% of all people aged over 65, but among the very elderly (80+) the incidence is widespread at 22%. Around 25% of all referrals to psychiatric departments are of patients aged 65 and over.

If it is assumed that in future years the same proportions of the elderly population will have particular characteristics as is currently so, a 'guesstimate' of future needs may be made. Indicators of personal mobility and of self-care capacity provide vivid illustrations of the practical difficulties facing many elderly people, and their likely needs for support. Certainly the association between increasing age and the loss of some independence is evident. For example, while only 9% of all elderly people are unable to bath/shower or wash all over without help, this is true of 15% aged 80–84 and of more than one-third (34%) of those aged 85 and over. Elderly women appear less able to manage independently than men at all ages. Given the preponderance of females in the elderly population this is especially significant.

A number of features may be highlighted:[14]

1. Between 1981 and 1991 the number of elderly people unable to bath, shower or wash all over alone could increase by 122 000 (88 000 of whom will be aged 85 or over).
2. Between 1981 and 2001 the numbers of elderly people living alone are likely to increase by 270 000.

3. In the 30 years between 1981 and 2001 an extra 64 000 elderly people may be unable to get in or out of bed without help.
4. Over the same period a 30% increase is expected in the numbers unable to manage stairs unaided (an additional 206 000 people).

WHO CARES?

We have presented some of the facts and figures which detail the reality of need for care and for various packages of support, both now and in the future. We began this chapter by quoting the 1981 White Paper *Growing Older*. That paper clearly stated the view that

Whatever level of public expenditure proves practicable, and however it is distributed, the primary sources of support and care are informal and voluntary. These spring from the personal ties of kinship, friendship and neighbourhood. They are irreplaceable.[15]

The research evidence—from the 1976 *Elderly at Home* Survey, through to more recent exercises—has consistently found that the reality of community care is largely care by families, which in turn mainly means care by women.

It is often said that 'the family no longer cares'. In fact the evidence shows quite the reverse. Information on the social contacts of elderly people underlines the importance of the family. The 1980 General Household Survey found 32% of elderly people saw a relative or friend every day or nearly every day, 29% two or three times a week, and overall 85% reported contact at least once a week. A similar picture is true for those living alone, and 30% have a relative living nearby. As we have seen, many of the oldest elderly people actually live with relatives (e.g. of women aged 80+, 21% live with their children or children-in-law, 3% with brothers or sisters, and 2% with other relatives).[6]

The proportion of elderly people living in institutions or residential care (around 5%) is no higher now than at the turn of the century. Yet we have seen that there are many more elderly people around today who need care.

Family care

No reliable national data exists about the numbers of carers in Britain (the 1985 volume of the General

Household Survey expected in late 1987 should provide a more complete picture). Nonetheless numerous small-scale studies *have* been conducted. One 'conservative' estimate suggests there are probably at least 1.3 million carers in Britain today providing crucial support in daily living tasks (and 'worth' an annual £5.1–7.3 billion). If the results of the Women and Employment Survey[16] are applied to all women a figure of 3.25 million carers is suggested. The majority of these are caring for an elderly dependent. Predominantly these carers are women (most surveys find around three-quarters of carers are women), and typically they are the daughters and daughters-in-law of the person being cared for. Many carers are far from young themselves. Given the demographic changes we have outlined, many 'younger elderly' people will have very aged parents still living.

The caring task is often an onerous one with social, financial, and psychological costs. Many carers are isolated and lack support. The evidence suggests that despite much rhetoric about the need to 'care for the carers', very often the presence of a carer (especially a woman) prejudices the likelihood of receiving statutory services.[17] Mainstream services have failed to keep pace with the growing elderly population (and some have declined in absolute terms). Nonetheless the evidence shows that rationing services where carers are present is shortsighted: carers who do receive support are more likely to continue caring than those who do not.

In recent times special services intended to support carers have been the focus of much interest (e.g. respite care, care assistant schemes, 'sitters', etc.). Many valuable schemes *have* emerged, but much supposed good practice has arisen incrementally, with no clear strategy or critical evaluation. Development has also been ad hoc and patchy. Overall it is unclear what all the schemes add up to, how comprehensive is their coverage or how appropriate their service. There is also a possible tension between services which are focused on carers and those which concentrate on those they care for; often any benefit to carers has been incidental or unintentional. The respective rights of each party are now being increasingly debated.

We have so far focused on what might be viewed as the 'demand' side of the community care equation. We have seen that on demographic grounds alone the elderly population represents a major social challenge. How viable is the policy of community care for elderly and other dependent people in future years? We turn now to consider other broader trends which may influence the likely *supply* of care.

The supply of care

As in other fields, underlying assumptions about the family within community care policy do not match the reality of family trends. As has been noted by Rossiter and Wicks:

The notion of 'family care' often assumes a particular model of family life. It is rarely specific, but is implicit in policy statements from government. It includes all or many of the following characteristics: an elderly relative either living with or near her family; a stable 'nuclear' family; and an able-bodied woman at home supported financially by her husband at work.[18]

Several trends now challenge this family model.

One of the most significant trends of recent times has been the increase in women's employment, particularly among married women. In 1921 fewer than 10% of married women were active in the formal labour market. Today over half of all married women are in paid employment; they are not all 'at home ready and waiting to undertake the role of carer'. Changes in roles and expectations may, in the future, increasingly question women's 'cultural designation as carers'.[19] There is a potential discord between the interests of women and the pursuit of community care policies. While women today may have achieved considerable emancipation relative to previous decades, the thrust of current policies could undermine such advances by emphasizing the domestic unit and the supply of personal care as women's lot.

The recent Women and Employment Survey[16] shed some light on the impact of caring on women's employment. The survey found 13% of women had caring responsibilities for sick or elderly dependents. Most of these (68%) were caring for aged parents or parents-in-law, and this was reflected in the age of the carers themselves: two-thirds were aged 40 or over. Indeed, one in five women aged 40 to 59 was undertaking such care. It is married women who are most likely to care for dependents. Only 13% of those providing care were working (compared to 69% of all women).

The relationship between employment and caring responsibilities is complex. Such responsibilities may influence the opportunity to work at all, or may restrict the number of hours. The survey found 29% of non-working carers, and 12% of those working, felt their employment had been affected by caring responsibilit-ies, and 'for some the amount of care they undertook was quite considerable and for a sizeable minority affected whether they could undertake paid work at all or the kind of work they could do'.[16]

Other trends need also to be considered. The move towards smaller and more mobile families may mean potentially fewer people—especially women—'available' to provide support and care for elderly relatives in the future.

Developments in divorce and remarriage may also be significant. We have noted the likely increase of divorce among elderly people themselves. Some evidence suggests that divorced elderly people are more isolated than others. Moreover, it is increasingly likely that elderly people will be members of extended families disrupted by divorce. Divorce is now a major social trend. Between 1971 and 1981 the total number of annual divorces granted in England and Wales virtually doubled, reaching 157 000, and giving one of the highest divorce rates in Europe.[20] Numbers are still rising (175 000 in 1985) and if current trends continue, one in three marriages might be expected to end in divorce. The consequences of the break-up and re-constitution of families for the care of elderly dependents are uncertain:

The reconstitution of families has, as yet, unpredictable consequences for the supply of informal tending. On the one hand, it may widen the network of kinship by the addition of step-relatives. On the other hand, the sense of obligation of dependent step-kin may be weak, thereby reducing the tending available.[21]

Equally, divorce may necessitate changes in employ-ment or in the number of hours worked (especially for women) which may leave less time for caring; div-orcees may be obliged to move to smaller, cheaper accommodation; re-marriage prospects may be blighted by the presence of dependent relatives; and the additional financial expense of caring may be unaffordable—especially for those who have further responsibilities for dependent children.[18]

Attitudes to care

The future is clearly uncertain, not least in terms of attitudes. Recent attitudinal data are of interest here. Future community care may well depend on adjust-ments in gender roles. If greater sexual equality is to be achieved, this will involve a new division of labour within the home, including caring responsibilities (both for children and for other dependents). The pages of some journals and newspapers are currently scattered with the pundits' discovery of the species 'New Man'. A re-definition of masculinity and a rejection of traditional images of 'macho man' is allegedly taking place. Economic, social and political forces have all been viewed as contributory factors: the legacy of the women's movement, for example, and the economic recession which has introduced—for some—the new experience of women as the major breadwinners.[22]

The British Social Attitudes Survey, however, places such punditry in realistic context: this found the division of household responsibilities between husbands and wives to be rarely equal. It suggested that little change had occurred: 'It is also probably similar to the pattern that would have been produced if we had asked the same questions in Britain at any time during the past thirty years or so.'[23] However, some interesting results concerned questions of responsibility for elderly parents:

The most consistent (and surprising) difference that emerges is between men and women—rather than between old and young—in children's obligations towards their parents. Men in all age groups are more likely than women to support the statement (that children have an obligation to care for elderly parents).[24]

The recent Britons Observed Research conducted by Harris for The Observer[25] reached very similar conclusions. About one person in five thought that elderly people who did not need hospital care, but who were not entirely able to look after themselves, should live with younger members of their families. However, while 25% of men agreed with this, only 15% of women did so, and only 14% of elderly people themselves. The following question was also posed:

'If you were working, would you be prepared to give up your job to look after an elderly parent if the only alternative was their going into a home?' Fifty-one per cent of the whole sample said they would, and 32% of male respondents.

Is there any evidence to suggest that men *are* taking a greater part in the practice of caring, rather than merely agreeing with the principle? Recent research data from the EOC found (in common with previous research) that most carers are women, but found an unusually high 41% of the sample were men.[26] Nonetheless, the experience of caring was typically different for the two. Male carers were most likely to care for an elderly spouse or, if caring for another relative, were much less likely than female carers to live in the same household. Those elderly persons sharing a home with their carers were typically much more dependent than those living apart. There were also very significant differences in patterns of help received by male and female carers. The allocation of support was seen to reflect a number of expectations 'which assume that it is appropraite for women to undertake a heavier burden of care than might be expected of men'.

It would seem that equality in care has a long way to go, and certainly lags behind trends which are both arguably increasing the need for care and diminishing its traditional supply.

Prospects for community care

Beneath the consensus around the concept of community care, there are in fact very different views about the substance of such policy, and these are associated with wider debates about the role of the state and the nature of any 'mixed economy' of welfare. While some see community care policy as a major challenge to government itself, and hence an area within which ideas for social planning should develop, others see the opportunity for less state intervention. Both interpretations, however, are based fundamentally on notions about the family and its caring role.

A number of factors and trends have been identified that raise serious doubts about conventional community care thinking. The family is experiencing change, and these changes may undermine its capacity to provide care, at the very time when the

need for such care is increasing substantially. The position of women within the extended family network is particularly significant. Historically, declining birth rates and changing attitudes have enabled more women to work in the formal labour market. Female economic activity rates are high, not least among those age groups which traditionally provide many carers. In practice, many such women still become carers, despite the social, personal and economic costs involved. The continued viability of community care may depend upon a broader view of responsibilities—both within the family and 'the community' more generally.

A wider policy agenda

The role of the personal social services and of the many active voluntary bodies in supporting community care is crucial. But it could be argued that a more comprehensive and positive policy approach is also now needed. There are clear implications for different central government departments, and various parts of local government. Education and transport have a role to play, as do the health services, social security and taxation policies, housing and employment.

REFERENCES

1. DHSS, *Growing Older*, Cmnd 8173, HMSO, 1981.
2. P. Townsend, *The Last refuge*, Routledge and Kegan Paul, 1962.
   E. Goffman, *Asylums*, Doubleday, 1968.
   M. Meacher, *Taken for a Ride*, Longman, 1972.
3. The Audit Commission, *Making a Reality of Community Care*, HMSO, 1986.
4. R.M. Titmuss, *Commitment to Welfare*, Allen and Unwin, 1968, p. 105.
5. *An Ageing Population*, Fact Sheet, Family Policy Studies Centre, 1986.
6. General Household Survey, 1985, Table 2.8 in *Social Trends 17*, Central Statistical Office, HMSO, 1987.
7. M. Abrams, *Beyond Three Score and Ten*, A second report on a survey of the elderly, Age Concern, 1978.
8. Rose Wheeler, 'Housing policy and elderly people', in Chris Phillipson and Alan Walker (eds.), *Ageing and Social Policy*, Gower, 1986.
9. A. Walker, in C. Phillipson and A. Walker (eds.), *Ageing and Social Policy*, Gower, 1986, p. 9.

10. A. Hunt, *The Elderly at Home*, OPCS, HMSO, 1978.
11. The Audit Commission, *Managing Social Services for the Elderly More Effectively*, HMSO, 1985.
12. A. Walker, in C. Phillipson and A. Walker (eds.), *Ageing and Social Policy*, Gower, 1986, p 6.
13. A. Bebbington, 'Changes in the provision of social services to the elderly in the community over 14 years', *Social Policy and Administration*, **13**, 111–23, (1979).
14. Melanie Henwood and Malcolm Wicks, 'Community care, family trends and social change', *The Quarterly Journal of Social Affairs*, **1**(4), 357–71 (1985).
15. DHSS, *Growing Older*, Cmnd 8173, HMSO, 1981, p. 3.
16. J. Martin and C. Roberts, *Women and Employment: A Lifetime Perspective*, Department of Employment/Office of Population Censuses and Surveys, HMSO, 1984.
17. Melanie Henwood and Malcolm Wicks, *Forgotten Army*, Family Care and Elderly People Briefing Paper, Family Policy Studies Centre, 1984.
18. Chris Rossiter and Malcolm Wicks, *Crisis or Challenge? Family Care, Elderly People and Social Policy*, Study Commission on the Family, 1982, p. 63.
19. J. Finch and D. Groves, 'Community care and the family: a case for equal opportunities?', *Journal of Social Policy*, **9**(4), 487–511 (1980).
20. *The Family Today: Continuity and Change*, Fact Sheet, Family Policy Studies Centre, 1985.
21. R. Parker, 'Tending and social policy' in E.M. Goldberg and S. Hatch (eds.), *A New Look at the Personal Social Services*, Policy Studies Institute, 1981.
22. Melanie Henwood, Lesley Rimmer and Malcolm Wicks, *Inside the Family: Changing Roles of Men and Women*, Occasional Paper, Family Policy Studies Centre, 1987.
23. R. Jowell and C. Airey (eds.), *British Social Attitudes*, Gower, 1984.
24. *Ibid*, p. 95.
25. Harris Research Centre, 'Britons observed', *The Observer Colour Supplement*, 16 September – 21 October 1984.
26. A. Charlesworth, D. Wilkin and A. Durie, *Carers and Services: A Comparison of Men and Women Caring for Dependent Elderly People*, Equal Opportunities Commission, 1984.

Prevention of depression and suicide

ELAINE MURPHY

Professor in Psychogeriatrics, United Medical and Dental Schools of Guy's and St Thomas's Hospitals, London

Depression in old age is commonly regarded as a predictable, understandable, though sad response to the losses and declines of the last period of life. [. . .] However, we know now that the majority of elderly people do not feel depressed, unhappy or unfulfilled and that the fear and hopelessness which many young people feel about their future years is mainly a result of stereotyped misconceptions. For every older person who feels life in old age is worse than they expected in their youth, there are three others who believe life has turned out better than they expected. Nevertheless, significant and severe depression is common in old age. Sufferers endure a particularly distressing misery which not only blights their own lives but has far-reaching consequences for the morale of those around them. [. . .]

Depression is unfortunately a word in common currency. The lay person's view of being 'depressed' is simply being 'sad', 'fed up' or 'bored'. Psychiatrists, on the other hand, talk confidently of 'depressive illness', a syndrome in which persistently lowered mood is accompanied by physiological symptoms such as weight loss, insomnia, psychomotor retardation and subjective loss of concentration. For the psychiatrist, depressive illness becomes 'depressive psychosis' when guilt feelings, delusional ideas and severe hypochondriasis complicate the picture. At the milder end of the spectrum, depression is indistinguishable from the sadness and demoralisation which most individuals go through at some stage of their lives in response to unhappy circumstances; at the other end, depressive psychosis may be a life-threatening and disabling illness. [. . .] The majority of depressions in old age however fall in the middle range of the spectrum and are not easily 'pigeonholed' into a category of 'illness' or 'not illness'. [. . .]

Depression is such a commonly used term that it is as well to be reminded of the suffering and hardship endured by those afflicted. Patients often describe their feelings as 'a sense of being trapped', 'the future seems hopeless', 'a blank darkness ahead'. Emotions seem empty and shallow. The depressed subject finds it impossible to take an interest in children and grandchildren who were previously the focus of their lives. There is often and all-pervading feeling of desolation and irremediable emptiness. It is hard for relatives and friends to understand the self-preoccupation, withdrawal from social gatherings, the lethargy of hours wasted in purposeless inactivity while household chores are neglected. The sufferer often feels quite unable to participate in normal social interaction and, while clinging to the reassuring company of relatives, may yet drive them away by irritating and self-centred behaviour. Family and friends often feel neglected and rejected and begin to visit less frequently, finally leaving the patient feeling more socially isolated than ever. A depressed person is a depressing companion, and families need maximum help and support if they are to carry on caring for the patient. [. . .]

PREVENTABILITY

There is little concrete evidence that successful preventive measures have been found. The child guidance movement started in the United States at the turn of the century with the expressed belief that many mental disorders of adulthood had their origins in faulty personality development arising from the mismanagement of children. Sadly, this early enthusiasm has not paid off in terms of preventing adult mental illness. Preventability depends on a thorough understanding of the aetiology, and we are not yet in that position with depression at any age. However, there are three groups of factors which appear to be

From *Prevention of Disease in the Elderly*, J.A. Muir Gray (ed.), Churchill Livingstone, London, 1985. Reprinted with permission.

of importance, and a thorough understanding of the mechanisms of interaction of these factors may ultimately lead to a coherent policy for primary prevention. The three groups of causal factors are, firstly, biological cerebral factors, secondly, physical health factors and, lastly, psychosocial factors.

Biological factors

Major affective psychoses at all ages occur in those who are genetically predisposed. However, the evidence for a strong genetic component is greatest in young people with bipolar manic depressive illness. In general, the older the patient at first onset of depression, the less likelihood there is of a positive family history. This may be due in part to the difficulty of obtaining a reliable history about parents' and grandparents' mental illnesses from an older subject. Mendlewicz (1976), reviewing evidence from a variety of studies, concluded that the genetic component was small for depression in old age.

There are, however, biological changes in the ageing brain which might make elderly people more vulnerable to depression. It has been known for many years that severe depression is associated with a depletion of biogenic amines in the brain. It has also been shown that catecholamines are lowered in the hindbrains of ageing animals and, postmortem, in patients who have died as a result of a range of illnesses. It has been tempting to assume that healthy subjects also have an age-related reduction of catecholamines in the brain. This reduction is hypothesised to cause a functional depletion of biogenic amines and thus predispose to depression. The case is, however, unproven. [. . .]

It is possible that the more severe forms of depression in old age are linked with cerebral pathology related to the ageing process but which is of a different nature from that occurring in dementia (Grauer, 1977; Hendrickson, Levy and Post, 1979; Jacoby *et al.*, 1983). Unfortunately, in our current state of knowledge, prevention of these biological changes is impossible. We must therefore look to other aetiological factors to institute preventive measures.

Physical illness

At all ages, physical ill health and depression are closely linked, but the relationship is especially marked in old age. This association has been demonstrated by many authors, notably Roth and Kay (1956), Kay and Bergmann (1966) and Post (1969). The nature of the relationship was examined further by Murphy (1982) in a study comparing a wide range of possible aetiological factors in depressed patients with a comparison group of elderly people in the general population judged to be psychiatrically normal. [. . .]

The health of depressed patients was rated for a period of a year before first onset of depression and rated for the year before interview for the normal elderly. Twenty-six per cent of normal elderly had chronically poor physical health, compared with 39 per cent of depressed patients receiving psychiatric treatment. However, of depressed elderly subjects discovered during the course of the general population survey, no fewer than 63 per cent had severe chronic physical health problems. Turning to adverse physical health events during the preceding year, only 6 per cent of normal subjects reported such an event, whereas 28 per cent of depressed subjects had experienced a major setback in their health. Depressed subjects of course complain more about their physical health than normal subjects, even when there are no objective signs of organic physical disease, so the judgements in this study were made on objective evidence where possible and not simply on the subjects' opinions of their health. [. . .]

Prevention of physical illness and alleviation of accompanying handicaps might make a substantial impact on the occurrence of depression in the elderly. It is particularly tempting to hope that measures aimed at reducing the prevalence of cerebrovascular disease in middle-aged and elderly people may lead to a reduction in the severer forms of depression. However, the wide range of illnesses found in depression suggests that physical illness acts largely through its meaning for the individual rather than through biological mechanisms. A loss of mobility so often requires the sufferer to become more dependent on others to maintain social relationships. The implications of imminent future mortality of a stroke or heart attack are known to everyone. It is likely that the anxiety provoked by serious illness compounded by the irritation and frustration of chronic pain or handicap predispose to depression in the susceptible individual.

The sensitive management of elderly patients with physical illness by the primary care team opens up the possibility of preventive mental health work in a variety of ways. Firstly, considerable improvements in the quality of life can be made by the provision of appropriate aids in the home to assist with tasks of daily living. Domiciliary occupational therapists and physiotherapists give specialist advice on such aids and also give guidance on appropriate furniture, mobility aids and special clothing. More traditionally, district nurses and care attendants considerably lighten the load of a family caring for a sick person by providing a 'getting up' and 'putting to bed' service, regular baths and supervision of medication.

Physically ill patients hate being a burden to their relatives, and the patients' morale can be lifted by the provision of help to the carers. Simply offering practical help may be enough to prevent a loss of morale. However, it is also possible that there is a role for someone to talk over the implications of the illness or handicap with the patients and their families. Some diseases having frightening connotations: 'stroke', 'coronary', 'diabetes' and 'cancer' are words that may have devastating implications for the patient which may be quite innaccurate. It is this author's personal view that good nurses and remedial therapists do explore these issues with patients in the course of their daily work, and that 'psychological help' is very often more acceptable when provided at the same time as practical assistance. Perhaps more time should be spent in training therapists to 'talk as they work'. [. . .]

Psychosocial causes

Depressed patients naturally seek to understand their illness by discovering reasonable explanations in terms of the events of their lives. Old age is a time of loss, of bereavement of family and friends, of loss of income and status with retirement and of loss of health. As a group, elderly people are poorer financially and more likely to be living alone and in poor housing than any other age group. Even so, psychiatrists have been reluctant to view these social changes as anything other than 'triggers', firing off a depression in a previously susceptible person who would sooner or later develop depression anyway. [. . .]

There have been several studies demonstrating that depressed patients experience more severely adverse life events of all kinds before the onset of depression

(Paykel *et al.*, 1969; Brown, Harris and Peto, 1973). Brown and his team at Bedford College, London, have taken the argument further and have suggested that all depression is primarily caused by psychosocial factors. The evidence that this is the cause in the vast majority of minor episodes of depression in younger people is striking. [. . .]

But what of depression in old age?

Murphy's study used Brown's method to compare the rates of life events in the year before onset in 100 elderly depressed subjects and in a group of 168 normal elderly. The same period of one year before interview was also used in the case of normal subjects. Depression in old age was found to be closely associated with adversity. Events involving loss, such as bereavement, separation and so on, were implicated just as in younger subjects. Often the loss was irretrievable; the older we are, the less we can expect to reverse the circumstances which arise as the outcome of severe events.

Severe events of certain kinds—financial loss, forced change of residence, family trouble with police, adverse health events—were related to social class. In general, the more prosperous social classes are protected from a good many adverse experiences. [. . .]

In the study there was often a background of social disadvantage in the depressed subjects. Major housing problems and financial hardship, for example, were commonplace, although rarely complained about by the subjects directly. [. . .]

It might be thought that the milder 'reactive' or 'neurotic' depressions are most likely to follow adverse life events, but this is not the case, and in Murphy's study similar proportions of 'neurotic' depressions and 'psychotic' depressions followed severe life events. Post (1972) also commented on the apparently 'reactive' nature of many of the classic psychotic depressions, pointing out the misuse of the term 'endogenous' as applied to severe depression where physiological symptoms predominate.

Having said that poor physical health and adverse social circumstances precede the onset of depression, it is also clear that the majority of elderly people remain remarkably cheerful. It is only those who are vulnerable in some way that react to adverse circumstances with depression. Lowenthal (1965) demonstrated that the presence of an intimate confidant was associated with good morale and positive mental health. Further, she showed that it is not those who are lifelong isolates by choice who adapt badly to old age stresses, but those who had tried to establish good relationships, sought the intimacy of others but had failed to establish an intimate tie, who were most at risk. Those who had previously had a good relationship but were now without one fared relatively better. These findings were borne out by Murphy's community study in which 30 per cent of elderly subjects who reported a lack of a confiding relationship were found to be depressed. Conversely, 39 per cent of depressed patients attending psychiatric treatment reported a lack of confidant. Two-thirds of those without a confidant reported that they had never had a confiding relationship. [. . .]

It is hard to judge the relevance of findings about the importance of psychosocial factors to the primary prevention of depression. An improvement in the financial status of the elderly would certainly reduce the frequency of some class-related events. Financial security brings with it a sense of control over options for the future. The ability to choose whether to move house, whether to take a holiday, whether to employ private domestic help in the home—all these are real options for a middle-class property-owning elderly person, disabled or not. A sense of mastery over future options is one component of hope, and it is the possibility of renewal of hope that prevents depression from becoming chronic.

The question remains whether it is possible to provide alternative effective social supports for those with no close relatives but who retain the capacity for making close ties. Day centres for elderly people, luncheon clubs and the many hundreds of informal clubs all exist to foster supportive relationships and, it is anticipated, improve general morale. The popularity of these clubs suggests that they do indeed provide a good deal of friendship and a sense of 'belonging' for those who attend regularly. Whether or not such clubs can provide sufficient support to prevent depression in those faced with a severe adverse life event obviously depends on the quality of the relationships established.

If we take at face value the finding that approximately a third of elderly people who lack a confiding relationship report that at some time in their lives they felt close

to someone, there is surely the possibility of stretching that capacity for intimacy and establishing a supportive relationship. However, the provision of formal clubs and social gatherings is probably of less importance than the overall social environment of a neighbourhood. Coordinated planning of housing and social services and thoughtful development by town planners can have a vital impact on the social life of the elderly. The provision of cheap and convenient transport, architectural schemes which encourage neighbours to meet, the provision of local food markets which provide a focus for daily activity—these may well be more preventive of social isolation than the hopeful provision of residents' lounges in sheltered housing schemes and special clubs, both of which tend to be patronised by the habitual extrovert.

An alternative approach to prevention of depression is to tackle the immediate precipitating cause—the serious adverse life event. Life events are after all the stuff of life—bereavement, separations, illness occur to all of us at some stage of our lives. It has been suggested that intervention by prophylactic counselling after an event has occurred may reduce distress and thereby prevent depression developing in vulnerable individuals. Bereavement counselling schemes have been started on just such tenets of faith. [. . .]

The question remains as to whether those who are willing to be 'counselled' are the ones at risk of developing depressive illness. Subjects accepting such a service have already recognised their need to talk of their bereavement and believe in the value of support from others in a crisis. It is those who are ill at ease in interpersonal discussion who may be most at risk of breakdown and yet are likeliest to refuse help. [. . .]

More valuable perhaps would be an improvement of primary health care. Greater attention to the physical health and mobility of elderly people as mentioned above and more active intervention by GPs at an earlier stage of disability may be one of the few practical measures which will reduce the numbers of depressed elderly.

In conclusion, current knowledge of the causes of depression suggests that there are no known primary measures of prevention which are, realistically, likely to be effective on their own. A general raising of living standards in the elderly population and an improvement in health care services are the two major changes which at present offer the greatest hope of prevention. [. . .]

SECONDARY PREVENTION

The early identification of cases and appropriate treatment by GPs requires a raising of their vigilance and an anticipatory approach to those at greatest risk.[. . .] On the whole, 'unrecognised' depressions are at the milder end of the spectrum. However, a good deal of controversy surrounds the question of whether the majority of patients with depression in the community can be treated effectively by medical or other means. Recently, however, there has been renewed interest in a technique known as 'cognitive therapy', a brief structured psychotherapy derived partly from dynamic psychotherapy and partly from behaviour therapy. Cognitive therapy for depression is founded on the idea that abnormality of mood is a consequence of primary abnormalities of cognition, that is in judging, reasoning and remembering. A depressed person may have irrational beliefs about himself and his worthlessness, may make arbitrary incorrect assumptions about himself and those around him.[. . .]

It is very early to draw any conclusions about the efficacy of cognitive therapy without a far greater number of clinical trials, and there remains the practical issue of who would acquire the technical skills and offer a service to patients in general practice if it does prove to be a useful treatment. One hope is that it could lead to a more rational approach to the prescribing of antidepressant drugs, since it would offer a constructive alternative in the family doctor's treatment options.

PREVENTION OF HANDICAP IN DEPRESSION

The natural history of severe depression in old age is unknown. The expansion of the elderly population has coincided with pharmaceutical advances in the treatment of depression and the widespread use of ECT for major depressive illness. The recognition of the treatability of depression at all ages ensures that, once depression is diagnosed, the patient will almost certainly receive some form of active treatment, usually

psychotropic medication. One of the major problems of this willingness to prescribe psychotropic drugs is that patients often receive drugs over a prolonged period of months and years, often far beyond the need for medication. Both in general practice and in hospital outpatients there is a need for more regular review of medication than is generally carried out. If relapse occurs following withdrawal of medication, it is an easy matter to institute treatment again if patients are kept under surveillance. In spite of advances in physical treatments, outcome studies suggest that, over a prolonged period, depression in old age pursues a relapsing, chronic course in the majority of cases. It is probable that currently used regimes of treatment do not prevent relapse or discourage the development of chronic social impairment. [. . .]

The sad fact remains that in current clinical practice a good deal of effort must be directed towards minimising the social handicaps of patients with continuing chronic depressive illness. The major aim is to help the patient and her (or his) family to lead as normal a life as possible, given her special disabilities. Day care facilities, whether day hospitals run by health service professionals or day centres run by social services or voluntary agencies, provide diversion for the self-preoccupied and a convenient way for professionals to detect relapse and remission. They also play a valuable role in relieving a caring relative of a few hours' contact with a permanently gloomy elderly person living in the house.

The patient and her family may also be helped by regular support from a professional worker such as a visiting community nurse, social worker or doctor, but at present the role of supportive psychotherapy of this kind in maintaining hope in the chronically depressed elderly patient is unknown. [. . .]

SUICIDE

Suicide rates are higher for elderly people than for any other age group. The rate for elderly men over 65 years is approximately 20 per 100 000 in the United Kingdom. This represents a rate three times as high as that for men between 15 and 24 years old. The rate is substantially lower in women throughout life, reaching a peak of about 11 per 100 000 in middle age and remaining at this level throughout the sixties, seventies and eighties (OPCS, 1977).

Interestingly, the suicide rate for men has dropped dramatically since the early 1960s. In 1961 the UK rate for male suicides over 65 years of age was 35 per 100 000.

[. . .] On the whole, elderly people who attempt suicide intend to kill themselves and use serious means. Elderly men in Britain frequently hang themselves, use car exhaust fumes or suffocate themselves with polythene bags. The majority of women, however, choose overdose by drugs, or poison. The fatal intent of elderly suicide attempts is in marked contrast to younger people, where the majority of attempts fall into the 'parasuicide' category, where intent is less clearly formulated and the attempt is a way of registering distress. Failed suicide attempts in the elderly are usually 'bungled' jobs and the risk of future suicide remains high. Kreitman (1976) found that 8 per cent of older males who survived a suicide attempt later killed themselves.

Unfortunately there is a tendency in society to consider suicide in old age, but not at any other age, as, somehow, normal. It is commonplace to hear comments that suicide in the old is the rational response to a hopeless, irreversible decline and that suicide should not necessarily be discouraged but accepted as a proper existentialist stance. This view gains credence from the finding that in many studies of suicide and attempted suicide, between 35 and 85 per cent of subjects were suffering from serious physical illness (Sainsbury, 1972; Barraclough, 1971). This argument ignores the findings on the rate of treatable mental illness in those who kill themselves. It also ignores the serious impact that suicide has on the immediate relatives. Suicide is the most potent demonstration of desolation and brings home to the family in the most wounding and frequently catastrophic fashion their inability to console or help someone close to them. The stigma of a parent's suicide can remain for ever on the conscience of the children.

In recent years it has become clear that suicide in the elderly usually occurs with a background of depressive illness. Barraclough's (1971) study of 80 elderly suicides rated 87 per cent suffering from affective disorder, a judgement based on interviews with close relatives and information from medical records. Key symptoms of depression which were recorded for these suicides and which appear to be signs of grave risk were persistent insomnia, weight loss, hypochondriasis, difficulty in concentration, severe anxiety and delusional ideas of guilt and illness. A history of alcohol abuse adds further risk in the elderly, as at all ages. Depressive illness, however, is the key factor for suicide and, as has been noted earlier, depression is very closely associated with physical illness. This is possibly the reason why so many suicides have a history of grave physical illness. [. . .]

Living alone and recent bereavement are also important ancillary factors underlying the decision for suicide. The background theme for the decision is a personal sense of desolation and loss. There may be some rational suicides among isolated physically ill elderly who know there will be no improvement in the future, but it is likely that the majority are depressed and that a substantial but important minority have a major depressive psychosis.

The role of the doctor in prevention

Suicide is theoretically preventable. If it is true that a substantial proportion of those who kill themselves have a treatable depressive illness, then early detection and treatment should be effective prevention. Unfortunately, as noted earlier, GPs are reluctant to diagnose depression in the elderly and, even where it is recognised, they are less likely to refer them to psychiatrists than younger patients (Kessel and Shepherd, 1962). Furthermore, suicide victims have normally seen their doctors quite recently: 50 per cent of Barraclough's elderly suicides had seen their GP within the week before the suicide, 90 per cent within the previous three months. They had consulted for physical symptoms, and presumably the doctors had failed to spot the depression lurking behind the reported physical illness.

The opportunities for intervention are potentially much improved if GPs learn to be vigilant with those at risk. Having recognised that an elderly person is depressed, the GP should always enquire about suicidal thoughts and plans. Even if thoughts are fleeting, the doctor should never unwittingly provide an easy means of suicide by prescribing antidepressant drugs to an unsupervised depressed patient with suicidal ideas. Once the doctor has spotted the problem, a speedily available psychiatric service should, ideally, provide the necessary back-up of treatment opportunities. [. . .]

Public health measures

The easy availability of the means of suicide might be considered a good target for intervention. Hudgens (1983) pointed out that an effective method of preventing suicide is to make it harder to do; no one now jumps off the Empire State Building since the authorities put a fence round the observation platform! Similarly, very few people shoot themselves in the United Kingdom because firearms are not generally available. Again, the numbers of suicides from coal gas poisoning dropped from 1350 in 1967 to 8 in 1977. Quite small changes in policy can have a marked effect on methods used. For example, the decision of a large British chain of retail chemists to stop the sale of aspirin in large containers was a direct consequence of the publicity arising from Kessel's study of self-poisoning among young people and his highlighting of the ease with which large quantities of aspirin could be purchased (Kessel, 1965).

In the United Kingdom, drugs are the main means of suicide in the elderly, especially psychotropic drugs. Barbiturates used to be the main culprits, but this hazard has diminished since benzodiazepines have now replaced them as the most popular prescribed hypnotics. However, tricyclic antidepressants remain lethal. A relatively small dose may kill an elderly person, and tricyclics should never be left with a depressed person living alone who is known to be at risk. An expensive but potentially efficacious method of preventing drugs being consumed on impulse is to prescribe drugs in 'blister packs' where determination to take an overdose has to be maintained over the course of several minutes. This may prove a surprisingly effective 'brake' on the suicidal impulse. Another helpful influence may be the development of antidepressant drugs which are not lethal when taken in large quantities. The efficacy of the newer safer antidepressants is unfortunately unproven at present.

REFERENCES

Barraclough, B.M. (1971). 'Suicide in the elderly'. In D.W.K. Kay and A. Walk. (eds.), *Recent Developments in Psychogeriatrics*, Headley, London.

Brown, G.W., Harris, T.O., and Peto, J. (1973). 'Life events and psychiatric disorder. Part 2. Nature of the causal link', *Psychological Medicine*, **3**, 159–76.

Grauer, H. (1977). 'Depression in the aged: theoretical concepts', *Journal of the American Geriatrics Society*, **25**, 447–9.

Hendrickson, E., Levy, R., and Post, F. (1979). 'Average evoked responses in relation to cognitive and affective state of elderly psychiatric patients', *British Journal of Psychiatry*, **134**, 494–501.

Hudgens, R. (1983). 'Preventing suicide. Editorial comment', *New England Journal of Medicine*, **308**, 897–8.

Jacoby, R., Dolan, R.J., Levy, R., and Baldy, R. (1983). 'Quantitative computed tomography in elderly depressed patients', *British Journal of Psychiatry*, **143**, 124–7.

Kay, D.W.K., and Bergmann, K. (1966). 'Physical disability and mental health in old age', *Journal of Psychosomatic Research*, **10**, 3–12.

Kessel, N (1965). 'Self-poisoning', *British Medical Journal*, **ii**, 1265–70, and **ii**, 1336–40.

Kessel, N., and Shepherd, M. (1962). 'Neurosis in hospital and general practice', *Journal of Mental Science*, **108**, 159–66.

Kreitman, N. (1976). 'Age and parasuicide "attempted suicide"', *Psychological Medicine*, **6**, 113–21.

Lowenthal, M.F. (1965). 'Antecedents of isolation and mental illness in old age', *Archives of General Psychiatry*, **12**, 245–54.

Mendlewicz, J. (1976). 'The age factor in depressive illness: some genetic considerations', *Journal of Gerontology*, **31**, 300–3.

Murphy, E., (1982). 'Social origins of depression in old age', *British Journal of Psychiatry*, **141**, 135–42.

Office of Population Censuses and Surveys, (1977). *Mortality Statistics*, HMSO, London.

Paykel, E.S., Myers, J.K., Dienelt, M.N., Klerman, G., Lindenthal, J.J., and Pepper, M.P. (1969). 'Life events and depression: a controlled study', *Archives of General Psychiatry*, **21**, 753–60.

Post, F. (1969). 'The relationship to physical health of the affective illnesses in the elderly', *8th International Congress of Gerontology Proceedings*, Washington, D.C.

Post, F. (1972). 'The management and nature of depressive illnesses in late life: a follow-through study', *British Journal of Psychiatry*, **121**, 393–404.

Roth, M., and Kay, D.W.K. (1956). 'Affective disorder arising in the senium. II. Physical disability as an aetiological factor', *Journal of Mental Science*, **102**, 141–50.

Sainsbury, P. (1962). 'Suicide in late life', *Gerontologia Clinica*, **4**, 161.

The supporters of confused elderly persons at home

ENID LEVIN, IAN SINCLAIR and PETER GORBACH
Research Unit, National Institute for Social Work, London

1. AIMS OF RESEARCH

The research reported here was commissioned by the Department of Health and Social Security and undertaken by a team at the Research Unit of the National Institute for Social Work (NISW) between 1979 and 1983.

The research team were asked to study as wide a variety of supporters as possible, subject to the constraint that the supporters or the elderly persons should be in touch with services. In order to sharpen the focus of the research yet further, it was decided to exclude from the study supporters who were paid to provide support (e.g. home helps) and neighbours and friends who provide support to persons to whom they are not related. It was then agreed that the research should have the following aims:

1. To identify the specific practical, social and emotional problems experienced by the principal supporters of confused elderly persons, to describe the ways they are handled, the perceived relevance of various services, and assess which problems are more and which are less stressful.
2. To describe factors which are associated with the supporters' willingness and ability to continue to support confused elderly relatives at home and those which precipitate contact with the health and personal social services.
3. To assess the implications of these findings for service delivery, the supporters themselves, and for future experimental work.

From Extract from the Main Report, 1983. For a full account see E. Levin, I. Sinclair and P. Gorbach, *Families, Services and Confusion in Old Age*, Gower, Aldershot, 1988.

In broad outline the research methods used were:

1. An initial survey of confused elderly persons in touch with health and social services in three local authority areas.
2. Assessment of the mental and physical state of a sample of 150 elderly persons identified in the initial survey by one of the two research psychiatrists at home and, unless death intervened, reassessment at least a year later.
3. Two intensive structured interviews with the main supporting relatives of the elderly persons, with an interval of about a year between them.

In accordance with its aims, their work has provided:

1. A very detailed account of the specific problems experienced in the practical, behavioural, inter-personal and social dimensions of caring and of the ways in which these were handled.
2. Analyses of the associations between these problems and:
   (a) stress in the supporters;
   (b) outcomes for the elderly persons and for the supporters on follow-up after one year.
3. An evaluation of the effectiveness of the standard services provided to the supporters by doctors, nurses, social workers, home helps, day care, relief care, other services, forms of help and cash benefits.
4. A list of the kinds of help which supporters require.

2. THE CASE FOR 'SUPPORTING THE SUPPORTERS'

Evidence from previous studies

For the past 30 years, researchers and practitioners have been drawing attention to the problems of elderly persons who are confused in the sense of suffering from dementing illnesses. Two streams of research have produced relevant evidence: first, the seminal community surveys of mental disorder in old age from Professor Roth's group in Newcastle-upon-Tyne and, second, beginning with Sheldon's classic study in the 1940s, the studies by various groups of researchers into the effects of caring for mentally ill relatives upon their families.[1-12] In relation to dementia, these two kinds of research have pointed to:

The extent of the problem It is estimated that about 6% of the population aged 65 and over, and 22% of the population aged 80 and over have moderate or severe dementing illnesses.

The community base of the problem At least four in five elderly persons with dementia are cared for at home.

The dependency of these elderly persons Those at home in whom the degree of dementia is severe are as seriously ill as those in residential care. Persons with dementia are also likely to be afflicted with other mental and physical illnesses. The combination of impaired mental state and physical illness renders elderly persons totally or partially unable to look after themselves and so dependent for prolonged periods of time on relatives and others for survival in their own homes.

Their use of services Elderly persons with dementia make particularly heavy use of places in residential care and of domiciliary social services. Yet many of those already in receipt of community services require additional support and many others do not receive relevant services and appear to require them.

The strain on caring relatives Living with dementia can impose severe strain and a lot of hard work on the main supporters. However willingly borne, it can affect health, family life, work, leisure and finances.

Evidence from this study

In our view, our findings both confirm and strengthen the case already made for 'supporting the supporters'. They confirm it by providing additional evidence of the chronic ill-health and dependency of elderly persons with dementia at home and of the increasing demands which they are likely to make on residential and community services. They strengthen the case by providing additional data on the supporters, their activities and problems and the effectiveness of services.

1. The elderly persons Relevant findings include:

- **Age relatedness of confusion** The 900 elderly persons identified as confused in the initial survey of service providers were on average very old (mean age: 80.4 years). The use of services amongst confused elderly persons aged 85 and over was far greater, relative to their numbers in the population, than that amongst those aged 65–74. This finding has resource implications in view of the projected increase in the numbers of very old persons in the next two decades.

- **Mental state** In the main survey the research psychiatrists found evidence of dementia in almost four in five of 150 elderly persons identified as confused. The degree of dementia was severe in two in five of those with dementia. The diagnosis of dementia and usually its degree was associated with such problems as falls, incontinence, repetition, restlessness, mistaking the supporters for others, unsafe acts, lack of purposeful activity, hitting out at the supporters, disturbing the supporters' sleep and inability to carry on normal everyday conversations.

- **Multiple health problems** As well as dementia, the psychiatrists identified a wide range of other psychiatric conditions, physical illnesses and disabilities. About half the elderly persons had physical illnesses grave enough to impede the performance of daily living activities. The most common problems were related to mobility, including arthritis and balance difficulties.

- **Use of community services** All the elderly persons were in touch with one or more of the different services and the majority received practical help from at least one source. However, a considerable proportion of the supporters and their elderly relatives were not receiving services relevant to their problems, had not been offered them and would have accepted them if offered. For example, almost half the elderly persons who were incontinent were not visited by community nurses; four in five supporters whose relatives had not been admitted to relief care had never been offered such a break; one in three of those whose relatives did not attend day care would have accepted this service if offered.

- **Use of residential care** Elderly persons in the main survey who had dementing illnesses were far more likely to be in permanent residential care within one year of initial interview than those who were not dementing. Moreover, the follow-up of the sub-sample of those identified in the initial services' survey suggested that the need for residential care for this group has to be met somehow; there was no significant difference in the proportion of persons who had been placed in residential care in each of the three areas; however the likelihood that they had entered hospitals or homes did vary by area. It seemed that when care could not be provided by the health services sector, then the elderly persons were deflected into the social services sector and vice versa.

2. Supporters   Relevant findings include:

- **Number and availability of helping relatives** In the initial services' survey about three in four elderly persons identified as confused either lived with others, almost invariably relatives, or lived alone and had a helping relative nearby.

- **Key contribution** All the elderly persons in the main survey had regular help with household routines and the great majority had help with personal care. The supporters commonly provided far more practical help and supervision than other members of the family, friends, neighbours or services. This was particularly the case where the elderly persons required regular help at frequent intervals, for example with eating and drinking or going to the toilet. These relatives then seemed central to the success of the policy of community care. Moreover attributes of the supporters, including their own health, their feelings about the elderly persons and their attitude to residential care for them had a major influence on whether or not their relatives were at home or in residential care on follow-up.

- **Willingness to care** Although the variety amongst supporters was striking, their wish to care grew out of a pattern of life which was long-established and

was reinforced by bonds of affection and obligation. About two in five supporters were wives or husbands of the elderly persons and just over two in five were their daughters or sons. Where the elderly persons and the supporters lived together, this arrangement had been established, on average, for 36 years. Most supporters still felt close to their relatives, got satisfaction from helping them and still had good times with them. The great majority wanted to keep their relatives at home. On initial interview, only 13 per cent of supporters would definitely have accepted permanent residential care for their relatives whereas 57 per cent of them would definitely not have accepted it.

- **Strain** However willing the supporters, there was evidence, as previous researchers have suggested, that the strain on some supporters was great. The mean age of supporters was 61 years. One-quarter of them said that their health had not been good in the year prior to initial interview and about half of them had disabilities which limited their activities. Many had other family responsibilities and one in three supporters combined caring with paid employment. As their relatives' illnesses persisted over years rather than months, they had made considerable changes in their own lives.

The supporters faced problems in four main areas:

(a) **Practical** Giving the elderly persons regular help with household and personal care, for example doing housework, getting them up, washed and dressed, taking them to the toilet and making sure that they ate.
(b) **Behaviour of the elderly persons** For example incontinence, repetitive questions, aggression, wandering, unsafe acts, night disturbance.
(c) **Inter-personal** For example sadness at the change in their relatives, losing their tempers with them and tension in their households.
(d) **Social** For example restrictions on getting out, seeing family and friends, having a holiday or going out to work.

Although their reactions to particular problems varied, the majority had difficulties in helping and they were very specific about the practical tasks of which they would like to be relieved.

In such contexts, the provision of regular help and supervision to chronically ill, dependent relatives, day after day, week after week, created strain. On initial interview, three-quarters of the supporters expressed distress about the circumstances arising from their relatives' condition. When they completed the General Health Questionnaire (GHQ), about one-third of the supporters reported a number of symptoms of acute stress sufficient to suggest a need for psychiatric attention.[13]

Strain in the supporters, as measured by GHQ scores, was associated with a number of the precise problems which they faced in looking after their relatives. These included incontinence, disturbance during the night, having to cope with a lot of trying behaviours, lack of normal conversation, and a lot of major behavioural and inter-personal problems, restrictions on their own leisure activities and on time with friends and family. This was consistent with the distress expressed by the supporters about specific difficulties encountered. On the whole, the supporters were particularly likely to express distress about behavioural and inter-personal difficulties.

About a year after initial interview, one in five elderly persons were dead, and of the survivors three in ten were in permanent residential care. The level of stress in supporters on first interview, as measured by GHQ score, was associated with whether surviving elderly persons were at home or in residential care on follow-up. Not surprisingly, problems associated with stress in the supporters on initial interview were also commonly associated with placement of the elderly persons in residential care. For example, incontinence, trying behaviours, lack of normal conversation, and social restrictions affected the likelihood of entry into residential care. This suggests that if elderly persons with dementia are to survive at home, the problem of stress in the supporters and the precise problems producing it will have to be tackled.

Sadly, one in five supporters who would not have accepted residential care on initial interview, had allowed their relatives to enter homes or hospitals within the year. Despite their willingness to care, others were gradually worn down by the stress which this imposed. On follow-up, whereas the psychological health of supporters whose relatives were dead or in residential care showed, on average, signs of improvement, the psychological health of those who continued to care showed, on average, no such signs of improvement.

3. Effectiveness of services The most encouraging and perhaps the most important findings of this study were those which suggested that mainstream community services were relevant to the supporters' problems, appreciated where received and could reduce the adverse effects of caring on the supporters' psychological health.

Relevance Services were relevant to some but not all of the problems faced by supporters in the practical, behavioural, inter-personal and social dimensions. For example:

- Home helps made the routine workload of the supporters of elderly persons living alone and of spouses who were themselves frail and elderly more manageable.

- District nurses helped with personal care routines such as bathing, getting in and out of bed, dressings and injections, and addressed the major problem of incontinence by providing advice and supplies.

- Community psychiatric nurses provided advice on the management of persistent, difficult behaviours.

- Day care gave the supporters some time to get on and get out without anxiety, provided a regular break from help with personal care and from trying behaviours and enabled some supporters to remain in paid employment.

- Relief care in homes or hospitals gave the supporters a break from caring day after day and enabled them to go on holiday, have a rest, devote some time to other members of the family or get out in the evening or at weekends.

Appreciation: Most supporters placed a high value on the particular services they received and many would have liked them more often. The interviewers and the psychiatrists were in no doubt that the services promoted the capacity of the supporters to continue to care.

Statistical evidence This was consistent with the supporters' view of the beneficial effects of community services. Thus:

- Amongst supporters whose relatives were still at home on follow-up, the ones who at first interview had been receiving the services of home helps or community nurses or day care or relief care or attendance allowance manifested less build-up of strain than those who had not.

- Amongst supporters whose relatives were in permanent residential care on follow-up, there was, on average, a marked improvement in their psychological health. This apparent improvement in psychological health was generally even greater for those who had not been in receipt of services on first interview.

- Elderly persons looked after by men who had the services of home helps on first interview were less likely to be in permanent care on follow-up than those looked after by men who did not have the services of home helps.

Overall case for supporting

The number of persistently confused elderly persons is increasing and most will have to continue to be cared for in the community. They are a very old, chronically sick group and their mental state combined with other illnesses renders them totally or partially unable to look after themselves. They make heavy use of community and residential services. Potentially their demand on these facilities could be massive.

On our evidence relatives are central to any policy of community care for elderly persons with dementing illnesses. Amongst those in touch with services, relatives are often available, willing and able to make the key contribution. Yet, the cost of the policy to those upon whom its success depends is high and relatives are gradually worn down by the care they provide. On our evidence, services are effective in reducing the build-up of strain in supporting relatives. In our view, action should be taken to channel these services to those who want to continue to care before they are exhausted.

3. SERVICES: THE SUPPORTERS' REQUIREMENTS

The study provided a detailed picture of the supporters' strengths, problems and limitations and of the way in which services and benefits can promote their capacity to care. On this basis, it is possible to identify the kinds of services, benefits and other forms of organised help required by supporters. We ourselves suggest that in developing a comprehensive system of services,

attention should be paid to ten key requirements for confused elderly persons and their supporters at home:

1. **Early identification** As we have shown, the strain of caring wears the supporters down. Services can apparently prevent or reduce this process. To do so they need to be linked up with the elderly persons early in the course of the dementing illness rather than when supporters are already exhausted.

2. **Comprehensive medical and social assessments** No single branch of the services can usually meet the combination of medical and social needs which arise from dementing illnesses. Assessments therefore should cover all the main problems which the elderly persons and their supporters face. The precise content of these assessments will differ depending on whether or not the assessor is a doctor, a social worker or other professional, but many elements are common to all. In our research we found that assessors were commended by the supporters and interviewers if:

- they arranged interviews promptly,
- made it clear who they were, where they came from and why they were visiting,
- showed sensitivity in their dealings with the elderly persons,
- were willing to listen to the supporters and showed concern about their well-being,
- gave clear explanations
- understood the possible causes of confusion,
- where a diagnosis of dementia was made, through careful questioning, established the precise problems which its management posed,
- agreed and promptly implemented a clear plan of action.

The general practitioners have a key role in ensuring that assessments are initiated, for it is to them that families first turn, and where they played this role, the families appreciated it.

3. **Timely referrals** We have pointed to the wide range of referrals for assessment and help from other services which had been made by the general practitioners, hospital consultants and social workers who participated in the initial services' survey. The supporters in the main survey often defined these professionals as helpful precisely because their referrals had resulted in practical help, advice or treatment from another service which the referring

service itself was not set up to provide. These referrals need to be made at a point when there is a possibility of beneficial intervention rather than when the supporters have already reached breaking point.

4. **Continuing back-up and reviews** The supporters were providing a lot of practical help and supervision over a prolonged period of time to relatives whose behaviour could be very trying and who had no prospect of getting better. Moreover, the majority of the elderly persons were said on first interview to have deteriorated since a change was first noticed in their mental state and again, on follow-up, the majority were said to have deteriorated between interviews. There were often changes too in the supporters' health, in the level of stress they experienced and in their family circumstances.

Not surprisingly, the supporters often referred appreciatively to the continuing involvement of professionals who were knowledgeable about the problems and strains. It was reassuring to them that the professionals knew of their relatives' condition and the care they themselves provided, were interested in the supporters' well-being, could be called upon at times of difficulty, reviewed their progress at regular intervals and where necessary suggested help to match the changing problems. General practitioners, psychiatrists, geriatricians, social workers, community nurses and day centre staff were all mentioned as fostering supporters' confidence in this way.

5. **Active medical treatment** The supporters were coping with chronically ill old persons at home, some of whom were as severely impaired as those to be found in residential care, requiring basic nursing care and supervision throughout 24 hours. They appreciated the regular involvement of doctors and nurses who were readily available, who treated acute episodes of illness and other remediable conditions, who prescribed and supervised the use of medication and who monitored the progress of the dementing illness. They commented favourably, for example, on specialist attention at day centres which led to referral back to the general practitioners and on district nurses who took on skilled nursing procedures which the supporters did not have the expertise to undertake themselves.

6. **Information, advice and counselling** The supporters made it very clear that they required information, advice and counselling. They liked to know what help was available locally, how to go about getting it, what the particular services could and could not offer, and what benefits they were eligible for. They also liked clear explanations of their elderly relatives' health problems, of the likely course of the illness and what to expect. They wanted straight-forward advice on routine care-giving activities and problems: for example, how to lift; how to reduce restlessness, disturbance during the night and repetitious questioning; and how to manage incontinence, for example which techniques, pads, sheets and clothing were most appropriate.

They gave high praise to doctors, social workers and nurses who gave them the opportunity to express their feelings about their experience, who recognised what they did for their relatives and who helped them to come to terms with the changes in their elderly relatives and the associated feelings of sadness and loneliness and, at times, anger, resentment and frustration.

7. **Regular help with household and personal care tasks** The supporters were heavily involved in providing regular practical help to their relatives and found services which reduced their workload very helpful. There is statistical evidence that the home help service can postpone or prevent admission to residential care of those looked after by men and that the home helps and community nurses appear to tackle the problem of strain, thus benefitting the supporters' psychological health. We found that incontinence in the elderly persons generated a great deal of work for the supporters and was associated with high levels of strain and with entry into permanent residential care. The district nursing service and for the few supporters who received it, laundry service, were very relevant to this problem.

8. **Regular breaks** The supporters were faced with providing care week after week to elderly persons who could be very difficult to live with and very difficult to leave. Other members of the family, friends and neighbours gave some help but had rarely relieved the supporters for 24 hours or more in the preceding year. Day care and short-stay

admissions to homes and hospitals were rated by the majority of the supporters receiving them as very helpful. They freed the supporters for a limited period from social restrictions, gave them time to get on or get out, and a respite from giving practical help and supervision, and from anxiety and exposure to trying behaviours. Moreover, day care was seen to be helpful to the elderly persons themselves and relief care was said to have had adverse effects on only a minority of those receiving it. Statistical evidence suggests that both day care and relief admissions reduced the build-up of stress in the supporters.

9. **Regular financial support** Extra expenses and reduced income were amongst the consequences of these elderly persons' illnesses. Some supporters incurred heavy bills in keeping the home warm for elderly persons who had difficulties in moving about, were inactive and rarely went out or in dealing with the extra washing and a need to replace clothing or furnishings because of incontinence. Some supporters had given up paid jobs or were unable to go out to work because of their relative's illness and others could not afford to pay market rates for private help. The relevant benefits were attendance allowance and, to a lesser extent, invalid care allowance, and where successfully claimed, these were a boon in offsetting expenses. They were also seen as official recognition of the heavy dependency brought about by illness.

10. **Permanent residential care** In this study the supporters were wives and husbands, sons and daughters and a very small number were sisters, brothers, daughters-in-law and other younger relatives. Most wanted to keep their relatives at home and this attitude was related to outcome on follow-up. The majority of surviving elderly persons with moderate or severe dementia whose relatives on initial interview would not have accepted permanent care for them were at home on follow-up whilst the majority of those similarly afflicted whose relatives would have accepted it were in residential care on follow-up. Furthermore, placement in permanent care relieved the strain on most supporters and this effect was particularly marked if they had not been receiving practical services prior to admission.

Permanent residential care will continue to be required by many confused elderly persons who have no relatives available or willing to look after them. It will also be required by those whose relatives become exhausted. Attempts by one sector, for example the health services, to switch its resources to care in the community is, on the evidence of the follow-up of the initial services' survey, likely to deflect those requiring permanent care into establishments run by other sectors, for example local authority homes.

4. FINAL NOTE

Something can be done to alleviate most of the problems which these supporters face. Community services which are adequate in resources and standards of practice can make a major contribution to the policy of home-based care for the majority of old people with dementia by promoting the well-being of relatives who actually put the policy into practice.

REFERENCES

1. K. Bergmann, E.M. Foster, A.W. Justice and V. Matthews, 'Management of the demented elderly patient in the community', British Journal of Psychiatry, **132**, 441–9 (1978).
2. G.W. Brown, M. Bone, B. Dallison and J.K. Wing, Schizophrenia and Social Care, Oxford University Press, London, 1966.
3. C. Creer and J.K. Wing, Schizophrenia at Home, Institute of Psychiatry, London, 1974.
4. E.M. Foster, D.W.K. Kay and K. Bergmann, 'Characteristics of old people receiving and needing domiciliary services: the relevance of psychiatric diagnosis', Age and Ageing, **5**, 245–55 (1976).
5. J. Grad and P. Sainsbury, 'The effects that patients have on their families in a community care and a control psychiatric service—a two year follow-up', British Journal of Psychiatry, **114**, 265–78 (1968).
6. J. Hoenig and M.W. Hamilton, The De-segregation of the mentally ill, Routledge and Kegan Paul, London, 1969.
7. B. Isaacs, M. Livingstone and Y. Neville, Survival of the Unfittest, Routledge and Kegan Paul, London, 1972.
8. D.W.K. Kay, P. Beamish and M. Roth, 'Old age mental disorders in Newcastle upon Tyne. Part 1: A study of

prevalence', *British Journal of Psychiatry*, **110**, 146–58 (1964).

9. D.W.K. Kay, P. Beamish and M. Roth 'Old age mental disorders in Newcastle upon Tyne. Part 2: A study of possible social and medical causes', *British Journal of Psychiatry*, **110**, 668–82 (1964).

10. D.W.K. Kay, K. Bergmann, E.M. Foster, A.A. McKechnie and M. Roth, 'Mental illness and hospital usage in the elderly: a random sample followed up', *Comprehensive Psychiatry*, **11**, 26–35 (1970).

11. J.R.A. Sanford, 'Tolerance of debility in elderly dependents by supporters at home: its significance for hospital practice', *British Medical Journal*, **3**, 471–3 (1975).

12. J.H. Sheldon, *The Social Medicine of Old age*, Oxford University Press, London, 1948.

13. D. Goldberg, *Manual of the General Health Questionnaire*, NFER Publishing Company, Windsor, 1978.

Risk

ALISON NORMAN

Former Deputy Director of Centre for Policy on Ageing, London

When dealing with emotive words like 'risk' and 'danger' it sometimes aids clear thinking to go back to the dictionary and find out what they really mean. For example 'danger', which is often used as if it is synonymous with 'risk', has a double-edged definition. It can mean 'the state of being *vulnerable* to injury, loss or evil'[1] but it can also mean a person or thing which may *cause* injury or pain to others. The second meaning was in fact the original one since the word derives from the Latin for the 'ownership' or 'mastery' which gives the power to inflict injury. 'Safe' is similarly double-edged. It can mean 'affording security or protection from harm' but it can also mean a person or thing who has been rendered harmless. A criminal is 'safe' behind bars. Moreover, the primary meaning of its Latin origin *salus* is 'a sound or whole condition, health, welfare, prosperity' which means that a proper consideration of a person's safety includes their whole well-being, not just protection from physical harm. It follows that in analysing any risky situation we need first to ask 'Who is causing the danger?', 'Who requires protection?' and 'What kind of danger are we talking about?', 'What kind of safety are we talking about?'. It is all too easy to act in the name of protecting a vulnerable elderly person from physical harm when what one is really doing (perhaps quite justifiably) is protecting the relatives from guilt or the GP from being bothered or health and social services from having to provide intensive domiciliary care. And it is also all too easy to increase someone's physical safety while greatly endangering their psychological well-being.

'Risk' is also an interesting word. As I have said elsewhere[2] it is not, as it is often taken to be, an evil in itself. We all take risks every moment of our waking lives, weighing the likely danger of a course of action against the likely gain. Most of the time this is of course a purely unconscious process. We do not normally worry whether we will choke on a breadcrumb if we eat toast for breakfast or whether we will be run over by a bus on the way to work. But if circumstances increase the likelihood of harm from some course of action, or make it less rewarding, we may well take extra precautions or look for ways of making the danger more worth while. The same principle applies when we have the responsibility of weighing other peoples' risk, whether as parents or social workers or in any other role, and as Paul Brearley has pointed out in detail[3] it is also the basis of commercial insurance. To take a risk, therefore, is to take a gamble and while we may lengthen or shorten the odds in any particular situation there is no way in which we can avoid risk altogether—to try and do so would be to run into other and worse dangers. Indeed, it would be hard to think of any course of action which would be more dangerous in terms of mental and physical health than to stay tucked up in bed all day and every day. This inevitability of risk is well illustrated by the origin of the word. It derives from *rhiza*—Greek for 'cliff'—and refers to the hazards of sailing along a rocky coast; the voyage could not be accomplished without incurring the danger.

Another factor in weighing risk is the image which society has of old age and old people as being pathetic, powerless, mentally incompetent and objects of charity. This image is a social construct which has little to do with the ageing process and much to do with the comparative longevity of women, life-long occupational status, inadequate income and society's failure to provide proper services. Indeed, it has been suggested that ageism has the same roots as sexism and racism—all three spring from stereotyping, prejudice, discrimination and minority group status.[4] As I have illustrated in detail elsewhere[5] the consequence of this derogatory social image of old age is that elderly people are seen as having a reduced right to liberty, choice and self-determination.

Society imposes on elderly people forms of care and treatment which are the fruit of social perception, social anxiety, convenience or custom rather than inescapable necessity. Old people are taken from their homes when domiciliary support and physical care might enable them to stay there: they are subjected in longstay hospitals and homes to regimes which deprive them of many basic human dignities; and they are often not properly consulted about the care and treatment to which they are subjected.

This *general* social image of old people as being less than human beings with less than human rights rubs off on the way in which we treat and think about elderly people with mental disability. The mental 'set' is already there and so we look at the dangers, problems and conflicts of interest in any particular situation through ageist glasses. Thus, for example, an elderly person with dementia who is living in squalor is likely to be perceived quite differently from, say, a drug-addicted young person living in similar squalor. Indeed Section 47 of the National Assistance Act is commonly seen as only applying to old people although it allows for the compulsory removal of *any* persons who 'are suffering from grave chronic disease or being aged, infirm or physically incapacitated, are living in insanitary conditions and are unable to devote to themselves, and are not receiving from other persons, proper care and attention'. Similarly, an elderly person who is 'found dead' or is homeless, or is refusing medical treatment or living in a chronic alcoholic haze, arouses quite different emotions in the popular press or the individual professional conscience from a young person in the same situation. So if we are to deal fairly with people who are themselves in danger or are endangering the well-being of others and who are not responsible for their actions, we must first try to come to terms with our own ageist perceptions.

Another aspect of ageism is a tendency to allow decision-making to be dictated by emergency situations simply because a person is old. When an elderly person is bereaved, or has an accident or illness, or leaves a tap on and floods the flat or the house is burgled, suddenly the person concerned is seen as being unable to manage alone—and indeed may see herself in the same light. Clearly, emergency action may be needed to deal with the immediate situation, as would be the case for someone of any age, but all too often the emergency action becomes the permanent solution without any proper consideration of its drawbacks or the possible alternatives. Very many people give up their homes to go and live with relatives after some such event—a course of action which is so socially acceptable that no-one stops to think that the resulting loss of independence, self-determination, personal possessions and social network may be nearly as great and sometimes greater than that occasioned by entering institutional care. Hard thought and perceptive counselling is necessary before making *any* irrevocable decisions on the grounds of 'risk'.

'Well', the reader may say, 'that is all very well when the person concerned is able to appreciate the danger which they are in and choose to accept it. But what about those who are genuinely not capable of exercising sound judgement?' As Professor Tom Arie graphically puts it:

. . . a paralysed polio victim who can only twitch one eyelid but is of sound mind can call for help when he needs it; he is his own monitor. A demented person, on the other hand, far from being her own monitor is the agent of her own undoing. It is she who leaves the gas on, she who wanders inappropriately in the street, she who neglects to feed herself or keep herself warm, she who persistently disturbs the family or the neighbours to the point that their spirit breaks and they reject her.[6]

In such situations, decisions, whether social or legal, negative or positive, do have to be made on the person's behalf. Social workers and others who by temperament or training are reluctant to exercise such authority may try to justify their actions by making a distinction between protecting people from the consequences of their behaviour and forcing them to do things which they do not want to do. This distinction does not hold water in practice. Protection from harm always demands some form of positive deprivation or restraint. People may be refused access to sharp knives or electric kettles or have their gas turned off at the main; they may not be allowed to bath in private or to go in and out as they wish; or they may be kept in bed by the use of cotsides or confined in geriatric chairs—all in the name of protecting them from the consequences of their own actions. There is no real difference between such negative controls and the use of oral commands, enforced institutional routine, tranquillizing drugs and legal compulsion to try and ensure compliance. It is also important to remember that people who have been conditioned to respect authority or accept professional advice, whether in the 'community' or in an institution, may well do what they are told without protest, but it does not follow that that is what they want to do. The proper exercise of authority on behalf of people who cannot themselves make informed decisions certainly demands that expressed wishes should be taken into account but it is important that *whether the client protests or not*, the professionals concerned should defend dignity, independence and self-determination as far as they possibly can. The key issue is of course what one means by 'possible'. The extent to which risk will be tolerated depends not only on the likelihood and seriousness of the danger to the person concerned but also on the degree of responsibility felt by the carer and the threat which the situation poses to the convenience, comfort or physical safety of others. In general much greater risk is tolerated when someone is living independently than when they are living in close association with others, especially if they are in some form of institutional care. Or, to put it another way, the less any one individual feels responsible for preventing danger, the greater the risk which society is prepared to tolerate. Thus, at one extreme, elderly homeless people live in constant danger and everyone turns a blind eye, while at the other extreme nurses in a psychogeriatric ward are likely to see 'keeping people safe' as their highest priority and believe that their own professional reputation is in danger if they fail to do so.

Another factor in the tolerable/intolerable balance sheet is the amount and the availability of the resources which would be required to reduce the danger effectively without using some form of restraint. Nurses and care assistants often say that they simply cannot spare the staff to provide the close supervision which a person with dementia may need if locked doors and sedation are to be avoided, while satisfactory care in the community is likely to require a very high level (in both quality and quantity) of domiciliary support. Thus we come back full-circle to 'ageism'. How much are we, as a society, prepared to spend in order to minimize danger while at the same time maximizing independence?

Finally, it is essential to emphasize again that no action which is taken to promote safety can itself be risk free. To move someone with dementia from a familiar environment carries with it a high risk of increased disorientation, loss of remaining self-care skills, anger, apathy and premature death. It also has very serious implications for the physical and mental well-being of those living in the new environment, especially if it is someone else's home. Similarly locked doors, cotsides, geriatric chairs and sedative drugs may well do more harm than the danger they are intended to prevent. In any risky situation the decision-makers have to weigh the dangers of the status quo against the dangers of possible action.

To try and illustrate some of these points let us take as an example an imaginary lady called Mrs Jones.[2] She lives on the ground floor of a block of council flats and is a widow with one daughter who lives a complicated bus journey away. The daughter is the breadwinner for her own household and has a husband who is long-term sick and is unemployed. Her only child has left home, so she has a spare room. Mrs Jones is suffering from a long-standing and increasingly severe dementia with consequent serious neglect of herself and her flat and some nuisance to her neighbours. She is reluctant to accept the help of anyone except her daughter and will not eat meals-on-wheels though she seems to keep quite healthy on a diet of bread, cheese and tea. A small fire which was caused by airing her clothes too close to the heater has brought the neighbours up in arms saying that *Something must be done!* Mrs Jones is fiercely independent and does not want to leave her home but she retains a deep respect for the authority of officialdom and would not actively resist being moved. The choices are:

1. To keep her at home and make a real effort to provide supportive services.
2. To tell her she must go and live with her daughter and put moral pressure on the daughter to accept this.
3. To take her into residential care.

One might (in very simplified terms) weigh up the situation like this:

STAYING AT HOME

Danger to Mrs Jones	Advantages to Mrs Jones
Painful death by fire or accident	No traumatic change
Slow death by malnutrition and neglect	Stays in a familiar place
Increasing mental isolation and bewilderment at inability to understand and control environment	Minimal loss of identity
Development of paranoid fears	Wishes respected
Antagonism from neighbours	

Danger to daughter	Advantages to daughter
Guilt	Does not have to share her home
Increased strain and cost from travelling to give care in a deteriorating situation	May transfer guilt by blaming SSD for the decision
Repercussions of this on the family	Can still give help—as opposed to an institutional situation
Possible blame from family members for 'not taking mother to live with her'	

Danger to social services	Advantages to social services
Extensive domiciliary services will be needed	Respects self-determination and independence
Pressure from neighbours, GP, etc.	Other solutions possible later
Possible fire or accident with resultant bad publicity	Residential care place available for another client

MOVE TO DAUGHTER

Danger to Mrs Jones	Advantages to Mrs Jones
Anger at forced move	Increased physical safety
Disorientation	More social contact
Loss of independence and self-care	Better diet, warmth, etc.
Possible antagonism from family members	

Danger to daughter and family	Advantages to daughter and family
Lost earning power	Relief from guilt and anxiety
Lost privacy and freedom	Less travelling
Marital relationships might suffer	

Potentially very long-term responsibility of increasing severity

Danger to social services	Advantages to social services
Possibility of breakdown in daughter's care, with institutional care then the only solution left	Socially acceptable, cheap solution (at least in the short term)
Cost of giving the daughter appropriate support	

MOVE TO RESIDENTIAL CARE

Danger to Mrs Jones	Advantages to Mrs Jones
Anger	Safety
Disorientation	Social contact (if it is a good home)
Loss of self-care skills	Warmth and diet
Reduced family contact	'Not being a burden'
Possible antagonism from residents	No conflict with family/ neighbours

Danger to daughter	Advantages to daughter
Guilt	Home and lifestyle unchanged
Resulting family conflict	No anxiety about safety
Little opportunity to give personal care	
Possible dissatisfaction with home	

Danger to social services	Advantages to social services
Residential care place used up	Safety
Self-determination not respected	Flat freed
Home may be reluctant to go on coping	Resources not used on domiciliary care
	Neighbours happy

Of course, in any of these possible scenarios the nature and quality of the resources available have to be taken into account. It will be much more possible to maintain Mrs Jones at home, at least for a time, if an intensive support scheme and flexible 'care packaging' can be provided. The previous relationship between Mrs Jones and her daughter, the daughter's own view of her responsibilities, her own mental and physical health and the attitude of her husband will be key factors in assessing the possible dangers and advantages of a move to the daughter's care. The availability, cost and quality of residential care also need to be taken into account. Above all, the process of decision-making needs to be honest and open, involving a fair discussion of the risks to, and the rights of, everyone concerned and taking into account psychological as well as physical danger. Is such a model of 'risk weighing' too much to ask?

Finally, I would suggest that, as professionals, we have a duty to stand beside dementia sufferers in the decision-making process and try to judge as we would wish people to judge for us if we were the sick person. Most people, in their right minds, would not wish to drive their closest relatives to physical and mental breakdown, or endanger the lives of their neighbours or make the existence of their fellow-residents a misery. Also, I believe that when domiciliary care, family care or 'ordinary' residential care is no longer sufficient, society has a responsibility to offer specialist long-stay care which is well staffed, highly skilled and fully adapted to the needs of those whose minds have deserted them. We know how this can be done[7] but

so far such care is very much the exception. Until we can offer it as a right to everyone who really needs it, we are blackmailing care-givers and care-receivers into enduring the unendurable.

REFERENCES

1. Definitions are taken from *Collins Dictionary of the English Language*, Patrick Hanks (ed.), Collins, London, 1979.
2. Alison Norman, *Aspects of Ageism*, Centre for Policy on Ageing, London, 1987.
3. C. Paul Brearley, *Risk in Social Work* and *Risk and Ageing*, both published by Routledge and Kegan Paul, 1982.
4. J. Levin and W.C. Levin, *Ageism: Prejudice and Discrimination against the Elderly*, Wadsworth Publishing Company, Belmont, California, 1980.
5. Alison Norman, *Rights and Risk*, Centre for Policy on Ageing, London, 1980.
6. Tom Arie, *Psychogeriatrics: how and why?*, Fotheringham Lectures in the University of Toronto, 1979 (unpublished).
7. Alison Norman, *Severe Dementia: Provision of Longstay Care*, Centre for Policy on Ageing, London, 1987.

Section III

Understanding mental
health problems

Memory in later life: an introduction to the basics of theory and practice

ROBERT SLATER

Lecturer in Psychology, University of Wales Institute of Science and Technology, Cardiff

RECEIVED WISDOM

Everyone complains of his memory, but no one complains of his judgment

> Duc de la Rochefoucauld, 1613–18—*Les Maximes*

Memory, the Warder of the brain

> Shakespeare, 1564–1616—*Macbeth*

Remember thee!
Ay, thou poor ghost, while memory holds a seat
In this distracted globe. Remember thee!
Yea, from the table of my memory
I'll wipe away all trivial fond records,
All saws of books, all forms, all pressures past,
That youth and observation copied there

> Shakespeare—*Hamlet*

'But the iniquity of oblivion blindly scattereth her poppy, and deals with the memory of men without distinction to merit of perpetuity'

> Sir Thomas Browne, 1605–82—*Urn Burial*

'It's a poor sort of memory that only works backwards', the Queen remarked

> Lewis Carroll, 1832–98—*Through the Looking-Glass*

Most people would probably agree with some general statement to the effect that 'One of the things that goes first when you get old is your memory'. Indeed memory for people's names, for example, does seem to decline from a relatively early age. Baddeley (1983)—an expert on memory—notes:

I recall a conversation with an older colleague who pointed out that one's ability to retrieve names at the appropriate moment deteriorated at a depressingly young age. However, he comfortingly pointed out that one does soon develop strategies to cope with the problem. I was 36 years old at the time of this conversation, and listened with interest; I still had no difficulty at all in pulling out from my memory information from journal articles that I had read years before, together with the name of the author and a pretty good guess at the date and place of publication. Depressingly soon after this conversation, however, I began to discover that he was right, at least about recalling names, or rather retrieving them at the crucial moment. I find it particularly difficult to retrieve rapidly the names of even quite close friends and colleagues whom I have known for many years, particularly when introducing them to visitors. This is a terrible confession for someone who is writing a book on memory to make. The best strategy I usually manage on the spur of the moment is to use the name of whichever of the two I can remember, saying to the other 'This is Dr Bloggs', and hoping the person will reply with his own name (p. 139).

Many older people (and their relatives) would also be worried if they thought their memory was 'going' that this was the first sign of something more sinister—the first sign of senility. More of an ultimate problem for the health and caring professions is if the older person and her or his relatives then decide, whether its 'just old age' or 'the start of senility', that nothing can be done about it.

RESEARCH EVIDENCE

Kausler (1985) introduces *episodic memory research*, i.e. memory for personally experienced events and activities, in an accessible manner, thus:

'Sorry, I forgot—what's your name again?' 'Who won the 1980 World Series?' 'Has the Jack of Spades been played yet?' 'Did I take the roast out of the freezer this morning?'

'Where did I leave my keys?' 'Did I really say that?' 'Did you remember to mail that letter on your way to work this morning?'

The fact that we often ask ourselves and others such questions is testimony to both the breadth and the imperfections of human memory. Our reference is to episodic memory—that is, memory for personally experienced events and activities (Tulving, 1972). The importance of episodic memory in mediating everyday performance is readily apparent. Imagine, if you can, what a single day in your life would be like without its normal operations. There would be no record of your activities and accomplishments, no record of your interactions with other people, no record of television shows watched, no record of events read about in the newspaper, and so on. In effect, that day would not exist. Equally apparent is the importance of determining the extent to which the imperfections of episodic memory increase during late adulthood and of understanding the reasons for whatever increases do occur. Hopefully, our understanding of the adverse changes in episodic memory that accompany human aging will lead eventually to means of modifying those changes or to means of circumventing their negative effects on various aspects of human performance in the everyday world.

In general, elderly people themselves do believe that their episodic memory proficiency 'isn't what it used to be'. When surveyed regarding the obstacles they encounter in their everyday living, elderly people frequently cite 'memory problems' as being among the foremost obstacles they face in everyday living (e.g. Lowenthal et al., 1967). It is conceivable, however, that many normally aging people simply forget how imperfect episodic memory is even for young adults (Cavanaugh and Perlmutter, 1979). Many elderly people may perceive the perpetuation of memory's imperfections into old age as a sign of their own expected decline in cognitive competence, rather than the continuation of what had actually been present throughout their lives. Such perception may be greatly abetted by the knowledge that abnormal aging, as in senile dementia, is indeed accompanied by a severe increment in the imperfections of episodic memory. That is, concern with the normalcy of one's own aging process may well result in an emotionally tinged exaggeration of episodic memory's imperfections, imperfections that have actually existed, perhaps largely unaltered, over the full course of the adult lifespan.

Self-reports of memory proficiency are of uncertain validity for young adults as well as for elderly adults. While some investigators have reported modest correlations between the severity of self-perceived memory problems and performance scores on standard laboratory memory tasks (Sunderland et al., 1983; Zelinski et al., 1980), other investigators have found an absence of a correlation (Lowenthal et al., 1967; Kahn et al., 1975; Zarit et al.; 1981) (p. 102).

Kausler (1985) goes on to point out that a vast amount of research on memory has examined intentional memory for lists of one sort or another. He contends that such an ability is only one contributor to the everyday memory operations of most elderly people—and probably a minor one at that. Furthermore, the learning of list-like information is likely to be a major contributor to the learning activities of college students—the young adults who commonly provide the comparison groups for adult age differences in memory proficiency! This illustrates that relevance and practice may be factors affecting the outcome of research apparently examining changes in memory ability with age. This is one reason why forms of memory assessment that seem more relevant and acceptable to the people being tested have been developed. For example, the Rivermead Behavioural Memory Test (Wilson, 1987) involves remembering a name, a hidden belonging, an appointment, a picture, some prose, a short route, an errand, as well as learning a new skill, recognizing faces and checking on orientation for time and place. Wilson argues that list-learning forms of memory assessment often do not relate directly to the problems individuals encounter in their everyday lives, even if they are reasonably good indicators of the site of neurological changes.

Of equal significance in highlighting the difficulties in generalizing from laboratory-based research data is the fact that memory for a lot of everyday episodic events takes place without conscious intent to commit those events to memory, whereas most research involves intentional remembering. You may have needed a reminder to put the rubbish bin out this morning, but you probably didn't instruct yourself to remember doing it!

MODELS AND COMPONENTS

Memorizing is itself a complex process, and researchers tend to conceive of different models and facets of memory and investigate how these might change with age—so any general statement about 'memory decline with age' being 'normal' immediately oversimplifies the issue. Researchers with a 'dual-store' model often talk about primary memory and secondary memory, while others also refer to working memory, and sometimes tertiary memory. Let us consider these in turn, while bearing in mind the factors influencing the generalizability of laboratory study findings to everyday behaviour.

Primary (short-term) memory

This relates to immediate recall. For example, read the following string of numbers out loud once, then close your eyes and try to recall them. 1–4–2–7–4–8–5–2–5–7. You probably couldn't, since there seems to be a ceiling to how much information presented in this way can be recalled immediately. If the amount is within the range, say 1–4–2–7–4–6, like a local telephone number, then there is little evidence in decline of this facet of memory with normal ageing. Another example would be being told the name of someone at a party and being able to *immediately* tell it to someone else.

Secondary (quasi long-term) memory

This requires some effort being given to rehearse information in primary memory so that it can be retrieved after a short time rather than immediately. For example, you look up someone's phone number in the telephone directory, but have to remember it while you answer questions about how that someone is these days. Or at the party you try and recall the name of the first person you were introduced to after you've been introduced to five others. According to Kermis (1984), memory research indicates that old people suffer from age-related decreases in secondary memory. Can you now remember, without looking back, the six-digit number in the previous paragraph?

Working memory

Charness (1985) gives a nice illustration of working memory. Try to multiply 8×78 mentally. Depending on how calculator-independent you've become, suggests Charness, you can probably strain a bit and do the task successfully. Now try to multiply 78×78 mentally. Having difficulty? Operations such as 8×8, 8×7, 7×8, 7×7, are probably quite easy to carry out in isolation, but Charness remarks that where you get bogged down is in remembering the results of previous operations or subgoals so that you can retrieve them to arrive at later ones—you run out of 'working memory'. Another example would be trying to repeat the following string of digits *backwards* after having

read them once forwards—3–7–2–8–5–4–6. Charness concludes from the laboratory research evidence that there are probably pronounced age effects on working memory capacity. One possible explanation put forward for the apparent decline in working memory capacity with age is that information in short-term memory decays if it is not attended to or rehearsed. If older people carry out operations more slowly, then when they return to previously processed material it may have decayed further than the material available to younger people who return to it more quickly. But can working memory capacity be improved? As Charness (1985) points out, there are people whom he calls 'mental calculators' who can multiply 78×78 easily because they devise strategies that override working memory problems, and these have been taught to university students. Perhaps they could be taught to older people as well?

A working memory model conceived by Baddeley (1986) has three components: a 'central executive' and two slave systems, one which specializes in handling language material and the other visual-spatial material. One of the assumed functions of this (theoretical) central executive—rather like the 'job controller' software on the central processor hardware in a computer—is to schedule the time-sharing operations necessary to carry out more than one task at the same time. Baddeley (1986) suggests that the central executive might be characterized in terms of its total processing capacity and its flexibility. He suggests that normal ageing may produce a drop in overall processing capacity, whereas over and above that senile dementia may involve defects in the central executive's control processes. Much of this, however, is admittedly speculative.

A major alternative to the dual-store model is a 'levels-of-processing' model (Kausler, 1982). Here older people are considered to generate less durable memory traces because the coding of the incoming information is done at a less 'deep' level. For example, the stimulus 11 may be processed as two straight lines, as a number that rhymes with another number, as a number between 10 and 12, or as the only two-digit prime number with both integers the same. Each level here represents a deeper, more abstract analysis than the preceding one. According to most contemporary analyses of information processing, the greater the depth to which a stimulus is processed the more likely it will be stored in memory for later recall (Reber, 1985).

Tertiary (remote long-term) memory

Is an 80 year old's memory for events in his or her sixties likely to be inferior to a 40 year old's memory for events in his or her twenties? Kermis (1984) considers that the research evidence suggests not. One's ability to recall memories from the far past—those that have gone firmly into the long-term memory store—doesn't seem to change much with age.

REHEARSAL, MEMORY AIDS AND REHABILITATION

The 'problem' in memory changes with age seems linked to lack of rehearsal or acting upon material in short-term primary memory. It needs to be rehearsed in order to be laid down in secondary memory and distractions, attention to other tasks, may preempt rehearsal. What, then, might be done to alleviate the problem? The following extract from a chapter by Welford (1985) entitled 'Changes of performance with age: an overview' gives some suggestions:

Suggestions about how to deal with deficient memory fall into two classes. One seeks to reduce the load on memory by using notes, establishing routines, and adopting systematic procedures and habits. The other attempts to improve memory itself. The principles that have been enunciated here suggest three ways in which this can be done. First is by allowing more time for data to register ('sink in') before diverting attention elsewhere. The habit of repeating the name of someone to whom one has been introduced can be regarded as sound strategy in this respect, in that it holds attention on the name for a few seconds longer than it would otherwise be. The speaking of the name is also in line with a second way of improving memory: as mentioned earlier, we remember not what impinges on our senses but our response to it. This principle appears also to lie behind the 'discovery' method of training, which we have seen to have been highly successful with older people. A third method of improving memory has been in encouraging the use of mnemonics. These provide and emphasize schemata within which individual items can be organized. Younger people tend to use mnemonics spontaneously more than do older, but older people have been found able to

use them to advantage if given suitable training. One further suggestion arises from the seeming fact that in sensory-motor tasks, skills mastered when young tend to remain high in old age, although they are then difficult to acquire. A broad training in youth, not only in driving a car and riding a bicycle and, perhaps, a horse, but also in using a variety of tools, knitting and sewing, could equip older people for a wider range of leisure activities than many of them are now able to pursue (pp. 359–60).

Let us try and put some of Welford's ideas into a GP consultation setting. As the patient you should arrive with all your questions written out, and tick them off as they get answered, and be prepared to make notes there and then of anything you want to remember. (How many of us have been asked 'Did you remember to ask the doctor if . . . ?' and have had to answer 'No, I forgot!') As the GP you would write notes down for your patient or preferably encourage them to. You would ensure you took time for instructions to 'sink in', and ask patients to repeat them to you so you know they have 'sunk in'. If the pills need to be taken after meals you could invent a mnemonic. Pills for PAM: *P*ills *A*fter *M*eals. (Pills for Pam might be ambiguous: it could mean Pills A.M.,—i.e. in the morning!) Or you could invent a visual mnemonic—get the patient to draw a plate with knife and fork in the middle (a finished meal position) and a pill to one side. Other suggestions arise from an article by Cohen and Faulkner (1986), namely that repetition, slow speech rate, short words and sentences, reiterating important information at the *end* of an utterance, enhancing intonation and stress, and maintaining attention by physical contact, can all aid comprehension of instructions. Memory aids in general can be many and varied, and one might pick and choose from the nineteen that Baddeley (1983) lists:

1 **Shopping lists**
2 **First-letter memory aids** For example, the first letters of 'Richard of York Gave Battle In Vain' give the first letters of the colours of the rainbow.
3 **Diary**
4 **Rhymes** For example, 'In fourteen hundred and ninety-two Columbus sailed the ocean blue' helps you to remember the date 1492.
5 **The place method** Items to be remembered are imagined in a series of familiar places. When recall is required one 'looks' at the familiar places.

6 **Writing on hand** (or any other part of your anatomy or clothing).

7 **The story method** Making up a story which connects items to be remembered in the correct order.

8 **Mentally retracing a sequence of events or actions** in order to jog your memory; useful for remembering where you lost or left something, or at what stage something significant happened.

9 **Alarm clock** (or other alarm device) for waking up only.

10 **Cooker timer with alarm** for cooking only.

11 **Alarm clock** (or other alarm devices such as watches, radios, timers, telephones, calculators) used for purposes other than waking up or cooking.

12 **The pegword method** 'One is a bun, two is a shoe, three is a tree', etc., as a method of remembering lists of items in correct order.

13 **Turning numbers into letters** For remembering telephone numbers, for example.

14 **Memos** For example, writing notes and 'To do' lists for yourself.

15 **Face-name associations** Changing people's names into something meaningful and matching them with something unusual about their face. For example, red-bearded Mr Hiles might be imagined with hills growing out of his beard.

16 **Alphabetical searching** Going through the alphabet letter by letter to find the initial letter of a name. For example, does a particular person's name begin with A . . . B . . . ah yes, C! C for Clark . . . .

17 **Calendars: wall charts: year planners: display boards, etc.**

18 **Asking other people to remember things for you**

19 **Leaving objects in special or unusual places** so that they act as reminders.

As well as using memory aids, one can stimulate and exercise memory processing, although as Wilson and Moffat (1984) point out, the therapeutic effects are often unclear. Even if games like Pelmanism (trying to remember the places of card pairs from many lying jumbled face down) or Kim's game (trying to remember objects on a tray briefly revealed) can't be shown to have much efficacy, they can't do any harm and can be enjoyable.

AVOIDING NEGATIVE STEREOTYPES

'Memory' is a very complex construct, and the delineation of normal changes in memory with age is quite problematical. Perhaps the most important conclusion is that with memory, as with all other elements of mental functioning, there are large individual differences between older people (Baddeley, 1986). Furthermore, the variability in performance between individuals may increase, not decrease, with age, i.e. individuals may become less, not more, alike, so stereotyping a person's memory or intellectual capacities becomes more prejudicial and inaccurate the older he or she is.

The individual's subjective perceptions of memory changes can be markedly influenced by one other factor in particular than by actual performance, and that factor is depression. This is succinctly described by Kermis (1984) thus:

Memory impairment, especially if severe, is often a behavioral symptom of depression or senile dementia. Given the common social stereotype that 'senility' is inevitable, many old people believe that any change in memory indicates the presence of 'senility'. Old people typically complain about their memory, even though research indicates that such complaints are often not accompanied by any decrease in memory function (LaRue, 1978). A partial explanation of this phenomenon is that affective status and memory are interrelated and that there is a relation between depression and memory performance (Kahn and Miller, 1978). Old persons who suffer from depression may complain that they are losing their memory when in reality they only perceive they are losing it because of their negative affect and self-concept (pp. 212–13).

QUESTIONING THE 'TAKEN-FOR-GRANTED'

Given the inextricable link between memory and intellectual functioning it is perhaps salutary to finish by quoting at some length from an article by Schaie and Willis (1986). Although it will certainly be far from the last word on this contentious subject, more than any other recent paper it makes us question taken-for-granted assumptions about intellectual and by inference memory decline in old age.

This experimental study is the most recent phase of a descriptive, longitudinal program of research that has examined intellectual change in adulthood over the past 28 years. In this study we focused on the modifiability of change occurring from late midlife into old age. A major finding of the Seattle Longitudinal Study has been the observation of wide individual differences in the onset and magnitude of intellectual decline. The initial phase of this study, which involved the classification of individuals with regard to decline status on two primary abilities, provides further support for the variability of cognitive functioning in later adulthood. Almost one half (46%) of the subjects exhibited no statistically reliable decline on either of the primary abilities studied over the previous 14-year period. The finding that less than one quarter of the subjects showed decline on both Space and Reasoning argues further that the onset of decline varies significantly across various abilities. For most individuals the pattern of decline appears to be selective, perhaps even ability specific, rather than global and catastrophic. The considerable stability in intellectual functioning is noteworthy given that both of the abilities studied (Inductive Reasoning, Spatial Orientation) involve abstract reasoning on speeded measures and would thus be expected to exhibit normative patterns of decline if one were to extrapolate from the widely accepted classical pattern of cognitive aging (Botwinick, 1977) . . . .

. . . Whereas subjects showing no decline were on average 2 years younger than those having declined, there is a wide age range (64–85 years) for those classified as stable, suggesting that for some individuals cognitive decline may be a condition of old-old age, rather than occurring in middle or young-old age. We do not construe these data to imply that there is no cognitive decline in old age, although some have in the past accused us of this position (Donaldson, 1981; Horn and Donaldson, 1976). Rather, we believe these data to argue for large individual differences in the onset and pattern of intellectual aging (pp. 228–9).

That older people can learn and remember information, and reproduce it successfully enough under examination conditions to obtain degrees, is evidenced in those persons studying with the Open University, of whom in 1986 there were 2875 finally registered undergraduate students aged 60 and over: some 4.3% of all undergraduate students. Academically, over-60s students at the OU have a slightly lower drop-out rate than the under-60s, do slightly better in continuous assessment, but slightly worse in examinations. The overall pass rate is similar for all ages and in terms of pass rate, those aged 60 to 64 are among the most successful of OU students (Clennell *et al.*, 1984). Most

of the 'older' students experienced less difficulty than they expected.

The very existence of the 'University of the 3rd Age' (Midwinter, 1984)—run for and by retired people—suggests we take care not to overgeneralize incorrectly from the many excellent experimental laboratory-based studies of facets of memory which do demonstrate age-decrement effects in memory for certain stimuli, especially when other tasks have to be attended to at the same time (Kausler, 1982). If gradually such changes reveal themselves to the older person, it is likely that he or she will adopt strategies that ameliorate any 'problems' they cause. It is when it is thought that nothing can be done to ameliorate the problem 'because it's old age' that the practical everyday real-life problems increase.

REFERENCES

Baddeley, A. (1983). *Your Memory: A User's Guide*, Penguin Books, Harmondsworth.

Baddeley, A. (1986). *Working Memory*, Clarendon Press, Oxford.

Botwinick, J. (1977). 'Intellectual abilities'. In J.E. Birren and K.W. Schaie (eds.), *Handbook of the Psychology of Aging*, Van Nostrand Reinhold, New York, pp. 580–605.

Cavanaugh, J.C., and Perlmutter, M. (1979). 'A diary study of adult's memory'. Paper presented at the Annual Meeting of the Gerontological Society, Washington, D.C. (November).

Charness, N. (1985). 'Aging and problem-solving performance'. In N. Charness (ed.), *Aging and Human Performance*, John Wiley, London, Chap. 6, pp. 225–59.

Clennell, S., *et al.*, (1984). *Older Students in the Open University*, Open University, Regional Academic Services, Milton Keynes.

Cohen, G. and Faulkner, D. (1986). 'Does "Elderspeak" work? The effect of intonation and stress on comprehension and recall of spoken discourse in old age', *Language and Communication*, **6**, 112, 91–98.

Donaldson, G. (1981). 'Letter to the Editor', *Journal of Gerontology,* **36**, 634–6.

Horn, J.L., and Donaldson, G. (1976). 'On the myth of intellectual decline in adulthood', *American Psychologist*, **31**, 701–19.

Kahn, R.L., and Miller, N.E. (1978). 'Adaptational factors in memory function in the aged', *Experimental Aging Research*, **4**, 273–90.

Kahn, R.L., Zarit, S.H., Hilbert, N.M., and Niedereke, G. (1975). 'Memory complaint and impairment in the aged', *Archives of General Psychiatry*, **32**, 1569–73.

Kausler, D.H. (1982). *Experimental Psychology and Human Ageing*, John Wiley, Chichester.

Kausler, D.H. (1985). 'Episodic memory: memorizing performance.' Chapter 3 in Charness, N. (ed.) *Aging and Human Performance*, London, Wiley, pp. 101–140.

Kermis, M.D. (1984). *The Psychology of Human Ageing: Theory, Research and Practice*, Allyn and Bacon, London.

LaRue, A. (1978). 'An overview of measures of cognitive functioning: comparative performance of depressed, organic and normal aged patients'. Paper presented at the Annual Meeting of the Gerontological Society, Dallas, Texas (November).

Lowenthal, M.F., Berkman, P.L., Beuhler, J.A., Pierce, R.C., Robinson, B.C., and Trier, M.L. (1967). *Aging and Mental Disorder in San Francisco*, Jossey-Bass, San Francisco.

Midwinter, E. (1984). *Mutual Aid Universities*, Croom Helm, London.

Reber, A.S. (1985). *The Penguin Dictionary of Psychology*, Penguin Books, Harmondsworth.

Schaie, K.W., and Willis, S.L. (1986). 'Can decline in adult intellectual functioning be reversed?', *Developmental Psychology*, **22**, 223–32.

Sunderland, A., Harris, J.E., and Baddeley, A.D. (1983). 'Do laboratory tests predict everyday memory? A neuropsychological study', *Journal of Verbal Learning and Verbal Behavior*, **22**, 341–57.

Tulving, E. (1972). 'Episodic and semantic memory', in E. Tulving and W. Donaldson (eds.), *Organization of Memory*, Academic Press, New York.

Welford, A.T. (1985). 'Changes of performance with age: an overview'. In N. Charness (ed.), *Aging and Human Performance*, John Wiley, London, Chap. 9, pp. 333–69.

Wilson, B.A. (1987). *Rehabilitation of Memory*, The Guilford Press, London.

Wilson, B.A., and Moffat, N. (1984). 'Rehabilitation of memory for everyday life'. In J.E. Harris and P.E. Morris (eds.), *Everyday Memory Actions and Absent-mindedness*, Academic Press, London, Chap. 12, pp. 207–33.

Zarit, S.H., Cole, K.D., and Guilder, R.L. (1981). 'Memory training strategies and subjective complaints of memory in the aged', *The Gerontologist*, **21**, 158–64.

Zelinski, E.M., Gilewski, M.J., and Thompson, L.W. (1980). 'Do laboratory memory tests relate to everyday remembering and forgetting?'. In L.W. Poon, J.L. Fozard, L.S. Cermak, D. Aronberg and L.W. Thompson (eds.), *New Directions in Memory and Aging: Proceedings of the George A. Tallard Memorial Conference*, Lawrence Erlbaum, Hillsdale.

Cognitive loss in old age—myth or fact?

ROBERT WOODS* and PETER BRITTON†

*Lecturer in Clinical Psychology at Institute of Psychiatry, University of London and Honorary Principal Psychologist at Bethlem Royal and Maudsley Hospitals;
†Senior Lecturer in Applied Psychology at University of Newcastle-upon-Tyne and Honorary Clinical Psychologist with Newcastle Health Authority

METHODOLOGICAL ISSUES*

The main problem in considering cognitive change is to distinguish between changes which reflect the ageing process, as a *maturational process*, and those which can be attributed to underlying changes in the culture and environment of the individual, or *cohort influences*. In the studies of Savage, Britton, Bolton and Hall (1973), for example, the population of elderly people assessed had been subjected to a wide variety of influences in early childhood. Some had their education cut significantly by war or economic depression. Indeed, length of education often bore little relationship to the official school-leaving age. Individuals born as little as ten years apart or in urban as against rural environments could have very different early experiences relevant to intellectual development.

As well as education, there might be differences in nutrition, early medical care, occupational opportunities and so on. Thus, someone reaching the age of 70 in 1960 might have had quite a different set of influences than someone in the cohort of people reaching the age of 70 in 1980 (the 1910 cohort). Furthermore, *at the time of assessment* different cultural influences may be operating. For example, conceivably our 70-year-old assessed in 1960 may have had more negative expectations regarding his performance than his counterpart 20 years later, who will have been exposed to numerous TV programmes extolling what can be achieved in later life!

Cross-sectional studies

In this method groups of individuals aged say 20, 40 and 60 are compared on the basis of data obtained at a single point in time. As far as possible the groups involved are matched on the obvious socio-economic, demographic or other non-experimental variables involved. Conclusions are then drawn from comparison of each age-group's results. [. . .] This procedure can, however, only show age *differences* not age *changes*.

Cultural effects are very strong and evident between cohorts in this type of study. However well-matched the samples there is no way that the 20-year-old group will have comparable early life experiences to the 60-year-old group. So many changes have occurred between 1920 and 1960! How then can one separate the effects of age and cohort differences? In cross-sectional studies it is almost impossible.

Longitudinal studies

These studies follow a group of individuals over a series of assessments. Thus age-related changes in an individual or group can be followed in that individual or group. [. . .] Longitudinal studies reduce the cohort effects which confuse the interpretation of cross-sectional studies but they do not eliminate them. It is quite possible that changes can occur in a lifetime or in the span of the study due to environmental effects which obscure and confound actual age changes. This problem is particularly acute at times of considerable change in cultural or environmental factors. [. . .]

From Chapters 2 and 3 of R. Woods and P. Britton (eds) *Clinical Psychology with the Elderly*, Croom Helm, London, 1985. Reproduced by permission of Croom Helm Limited.
© R. T. Woods and P. G. Britton.
For a fuller account of these complex issues the reader is referred to the extensive account in Chapters 19 and 20 of Botwinick (1978) or Chapter 11 in Bromley (1974).

Practice effects, arising from familiarity both with the specific test items and with the testing situation, could potentially mask an age-related decline. The severity of these effects will relate to the number of reassessments required, and the interval between them. Certain types of test items may be particularly susceptible to practice, further confusing the findings.

The most serious fault of longitudinal studies is that inevitably some subjects are not available to be reassessed. Some have moved away, others are too busy, some are too ill or have died, others feel once was enough! Whatever the reasons, especially in an elderly population it seems to be impossible to follow a complete group over an extended period. This would not be so damaging if drop-out was a random process, if any subject were as likely as any other to be unavailable. Siegler and Botwinick (1979) point out that it is 'mainly the intellectually, and perhaps physically superior' who persevere and are available to be tested on each occasion. The more demanding the study, in terms of number of re-tests and their frequency, the more marked is this selective attrition. [. . .] At each reassessment those still available have on average a higher *initial* test score than those available at the previous assessment point.

It is clear that longitudinal studies do *not* lead directly to indications of age-related changes.

Sequential designs

The problems outlined above led in the late 1960s and early 1970s to serious thinking about appropriate new methodologies. The most notable work was by Schaie (1967) and Baltes (1968) which produced designs said to be capable of clarifying the distinction between age effects, cohort effects and time of measurement effects. In essence they carried out a series of cross-sectional studies at different points in time. For example, Schaie, Labouvie-Vief and Buech (1973) and Schaie and Labouvie-Vief (1974) report data from their extensive study of cognitive ability. A cross-sectional study was initially carried out in 1956, with subjects aged from 21 to 70 years. In 1963, a further cross-sectional study was undertaken, using fresh subjects drawn from the same pool (members of a medical insurance plan) over the whole age-range. Similarly in 1970, a third cross-sectional study with a new batch of subjects aged from 21 to 84 took place. In addition, in 1963 as many as possible of the subjects first tested in 1956 were re-tested, and similarly in 1970 subjects first tested in 1956 or 1963 were re-tested where possible. [. . .]

The cross-sequential studies reported by Schaie and his colleagues have demonstrated the extent of cohort effects. [. . .] Cohort effects, it is argued, can be as large as age differences for most of the life span.

Unfortunately, not even this most complex methodology can provide all the solutions and satisfy all the critics! [. . .]

The statistical treatment of the results has been the subject of some controversy (see, for example, Horn and Donaldson, 1976, 1977; and replies by Baltes and Schaie, 1976; Schaie and Baltes, 1977). Botwinick (1978, p.372) provides a useful discussion of the limitations of this methodology.

There is then no easy answer in the study of age-related changes; it is important to be aware of the limitations of each and the potential confounding that may occur. The cross-sequential method is attractive, with its combination of the other methods allowing comparisons to be made in several ways, but it can be difficult to implement in practical situations. Certainly increased knowledge of cohort and time-of-measurement effects may prevent us from being drawn into the mythology of inevitable age-related decline, and help us face a real world where a number of complex, dynamic, interweaving factors interact to produce age differences.

INTELLECTUAL CHANGE

Earlier in this chapter we drew attention to the traditional model of age-related decline in intellectual abilities. The previous discussion on methodology will have suggested that reinterpretation of such findings is required. However, it is fair to say that some aspects of intellectual performance do show decline on average in older age-groups. The point where this decline becomes evident has been grossly underestimated. It is likely to be at the age of 60 or 70 rather than at 25! The problem is to find out just what is happening; to define the nature of the changes precisely, within groups and individuals, and to identify factors related to the decline.

Psychologists have approached this problem in two ways. The global intelligence test has been a favourite psychometric measure in the past. It has the advantage of sampling a range of intellectual functions using well-defined subtests, in a standardised manner. This should reduce experimenter, subject and environment bias, and to an extent this is so. However, there are many difficulties with these tests and we will mention a few below. The second approach has been to use tasks from experimental psychology.

Much controversy has surrounded the relative merits and demerits of these approaches. A review of the contrasting approaches of psychometrician and experimental psychologist is given in the papers by Kendrick (1982a, 1982b) and Rabbitt (1982).

There can be little doubt that current psychometric tests of cognitive function lead to a blunderbuss approach with little finesse. Tests developed primarily for the assessment of children and young people, to predict educational attainment and work performance, may produce effective discrimination and reliability with a younger adult population but be very poor measures of the extent and subtlety of cognitive change in the elderly. Subtests may contain few items which effectively discriminate at appropriate ability levels. The quest for test reliability may have excluded just those very items or subtests which may have proved to be sensitive indicators of cognitive change in the elderly. Any changes found in the elderly may merely reflect cultural or educational biases in the application of the tests across age-groups.

With these cautions in mind we can examine some of the findings from studies using global intellectual measures. [. . .] If one looks beyond full-scale IQ to the verbal and performance components of the Wechsler Adult Intelligence Scale (WAIS) it becomes evident that different patterns of age differences are found for different aspects of intellectual ability. Performance IQ is found to decline faster than verbal ability in middle age although in the elderly the declines are roughly parallel.

Explanations for these effects have varied from a consideration of the psychological function involved to methodology. Speed of processing information, involving input systems, central processor time and motor output, has been thought to affect performance tests more acutely, especially the timed tests. However,

studies summarised by Botwinick (1977) suggest that the elderly cannot improve to the level of younger subjects even if given unlimited time. The cross-sectional methodology used brings in all of the cohort, environmental and other problems seen earlier, which could in theory differentially influence verbal and performance abilities.

In one of the few studies covering a large part of the life span, Owens (1966) reported longitudinal findings (on the Army Alpha Test, a general cognitive measure) on a group of subjects followed up from the age of 19 to the age of 61, with an intermediate assessment at about the age of 49. Subjects showed a general *improvement* in the first 30 years, with hardly any loss evident as the subjects entered their sixties.

Longitudinal studies following intellectual change in elderly people have reported some inconsistent findings. Eisdorfer and Wilkie (1973) assessed subjects initially aged 60–69 on four occasions over ten years, finding a decrement in performance ability (on the WAIS) but no substantial overall decline. Jarvik, Kallman and Falek (1962), following a group with an initial average age of 67.5 years over an eight-year period, similarly reported a decline on the performance tasks. Blum, Fosshage and Jarvik (1972) carried out a 20-year follow-up on these same subjects, when an overall decline was evident. In contrast Savage *et al.* (1973) found an *increase* in performance ability in their sample (mean initial age 71), who were assessed four times in seven years. A slight decline in verbal level also emerged.

The effects of selective subject attrition (only one-sixth of Savage *et al.*'s sample were re-tested at seven years), different frequencies of reassessment (and so different practice effects) and different ages at the commencement of the studies probably account for these differences between studies. The overall trend seems to be of stability to the age of 60 or so, then a decline in performance level to about the age of 70, when verbal abilities show some decline.

Cross-sequential data (Schaie *et al.*, 1973; Schaie and Labouvie-Vief, 1974) on the Primary Mental Abilities Test suggest that age-related decline is minimal until at least the age of 60 or so. Verbal abilities show decline later than performance, speeded measures. Longitudinal analyses show least decline, cross-sectional most, with the independent measures analysis showing an intermediate level of decline. Age-related decline, if it occurs, is a feature of old age (not middle age as was once thought) and varies greatly for different aspects of intellectual function. For most of the life span, cohort differences are probably of greater significance. The extent of age-related decline in old age does not in general appear to be dramatic enough seriously to affect the adaptive ability of the majority of the elderly.

INDIVIDUAL DIFFERENCES AND PATTERNS OF INTELLECTUAL CHANGE

The use of global composite intelligence tests in studies such as those quoted above has led to many attempts to examine the *pattern* of intellectual change in ageing. We have already referred to broad differences in age-related decline seen in verbal and performance components of tests such as the WAIS. More specific cognitive functions reflected in individual subtests have also been related to the ageing process.

This led to a great deal of interest in the construction of Deterioration and Ageing Indices related to tests such as the WAIS. These were based on an approach by Wechsler who developed a Deterioration Index for the Wechsler–Bellevue Scale. This attempted to assess abnormality of deterioration based on differential combinations of subtests described as 'hold' and 'don't hold' respectively according to whether they were thought to remain stable in ageing or to show a marked decline.

Similar indices were developed by many others, perhaps reaching their climax in the work of Hewson (1949) who produced a multi-component index of bewildering complexity. These endeavours continued well into the WAIS era and even to the present day, e.g. Savage (1981). In 1966, Bolton, Britton and Savage concluded that many of the indices developed at that time were dubious in origin, and suspect in practice, with respect to practical validity and reliability. Miller (1977) compared the search for the right Wechsler subtest combinations to the medieval alchemist's quest for the philosopher's stone!

One of the problems with the indices has been confusion as to whether they are intended to reflect a pattern of deterioration related to ageing or to dementia. [. . .]

Whilst this pursuit of patterns of decline has proved to be rather futile to date, it is based on the clear awareness that individual changes do exist. All types of study, cross-sectional, longitudinal or cross-sequential, reveal that within the patterns of general stability or gradual change in overall ability there may be significant changes in specific facets of cognition in individuals. This is an area where it is likely that large sample studies may tend to obscure important individual variability. The results observed could be explained in part by the combination of data from individuals who retain to a great extent their capacities together with data from those more severely declining. Siegler and Botwinick (1979), summarising longitudinal data over a 20-year period from the Duke University ageing projects, concluded that 'there is a sizeable proportion of old people who decline very little as old age advances, or decline not at all, except perhaps in extreme old age'. Average findings tell us about the average elderly person, but obscure important individual differences that may be of great practical importance.

The concept of 'plasticity' has been introduced by Baltes and Willis (1979) who suggest that cognitive functioning in individuals is not a fixed feature but a growing and developing function. To those involved in the area of child development, this is not a novel concept. Children are known to differ considerably in the pace and nature of their intellectual development, in response to genetic and environmental stimuli. Baltes and Willis argue that it is reasonable to expect an equivalent range of rate and type of change in the elderly, subject as they are to a number of powerful environmental and intrinsic influences. This long-term plasticity may well be a reason why generalisations about the intellectual changes in ageing (such as Deterioration Indices) may be very poor predictors in the individual case.

Most middle-aged psychologists have been brought up accepting some model of stability of IQ, and this is reflected in a reluctance to accept easily the concept of long-term plasticity. Even more problems arise when the concept is extended to short-term changes in intellectual ability. The man in the street will tell you that some mornings, some days he is not 'with it'. Arithmetical ability is impaired, memory 'goes', car driving, musical instrument playing and similar over-learned activities are performed very badly. Psychologists have been slow to look for correlates of these everyday feelings. However, the intellectual performance of old people can be improved by various interventions (Baltes and Barton, 1977; Patterson and Jackson, 1980) and a number of factors have been identified that have a specific, adverse effect on elderly people's performance. These include tiredness (Furry and Baltes, 1973), cautiousness (Birkhill and Schaie, 1975) and the effects of elderly people evaluating their own performance negatively. For a variety of reasons elderly people may not be performing at their optimal level when tested cognitively. Intellectual ability, as assessed, is not then a fixed attribute of the elderly person. It may fluctuate in the short term, and show idiosyncratic changes in the long term.

Some apparent under-functioning has been attributed to the nature of the tests and tasks used. The concept of ecological validity of tests has been discussed by Kendrick (1982). He suggests that tests which do not relate to the day-to-day life of the subject are perceived as (at best) irrelevant. He refers to the phenomenon familiar to most psychologists who have used the WAIS with the elderly of the individual faced with the Block Design subtest who says 'I've never done this since I was a child'. Such tests are held to be prone to exacerbate motivational and attitudinal problems and so reduce their validity as an accurate guide to cognitive performance. Volans and Woods (1983) refer to the need for a fuller consideration of exactly what factors are involved in 'ecological validity' and point out that in some circumstances task difficulty may be just as important in influencing the subject's attitude and motivation.

A more extreme position is taken by Labouvie-Vief, Hoyer, Baltes and Baltes (1974) who state that deficits seen in the intellectual abilities of the elderly reflect *only* a lack of practice and familiarity with the tasks used. The intervention studies mentioned above, showing elderly people to improve with practice on intellectual tests, are often taken as support for this position. Few have included a younger control group; one study that did (Hoyer, Hoyer, Treat and Baltes, 1978) showed that younger subjects actually improved *more* with the same amount of practice.

Current intellectual tests are far from ideal and probably do lack relevance for older people. Often quoted is a study by Demming and Pressey (1957) who developed a test of practical information that seemed more relevant to the culture and life-style of the elderly. Scores *increased* with age on this test!

Not all the apparent age-related changes can be blamed on IQ tests. They almost certainly do produce underestimates of functioning in some older people, which hampers the accurate identification of individual differences in patterns of change as the person ages. It has been shown that a number of factors influence cognitive performance; physical and mental health and sensory loss are of particular importance. [. . .]

PERSONALITY CHANGE

The literature on personality change with advancing age follows a similar pattern to that on cognitive change. The great majority of studies use cross-sectional methodology. Most use the personality assessment equivalent of the intelligence test, the major personality questionnaires. Most date from before the advent of cross-sequential methodologies. Most studies cover well the adult age-range from 20 to 60, have fewer subjects in the 60–70 group and are very weak in extreme old age (Neugarten, 1977).

How relevant are these major personality inventories to the aged? This topic is discussed in detail by Savage, Gaber, Britton, Bolton and Cooper (1977) and by Lawton, Whelihan and Belsky (1980). They are generally based on item pools derived from work on normal adults. Most inventories seem to be derived from the same source pool of questions, whether from the Minnesota, Cattell or Eysenck schools. A close examination of the questions used raises many queries about their relevance in extreme old age.

Items are often inappropriate in language or content to the social and environmental context of the aged. The same question could relate to different aspects of personality in different age cohorts. Some of the many factors influencing personality questionnaire responding, such as social desirability biases, may not operate in the same fashion in different age cohorts. Indeed, the general attacks on trait-based measures (Mischel, 1968) may be even more appropriate to assessment in the aged.

The continued use of these questionnaires has been defended, for example by Hogan, De Soto and Solano (1977) and Lawton et al. (1980). They emphasise that care is required in interpretation of results, as normative data and validity are either non-existent or less reliable in the elderly.

The results from these studies may be summarised as showing a general stability in personality (Neugarten, 1977). In the few cross-sequential studies age changes have been relatively small (Schaie and Parham, 1976). The changes which do occur tend to be towards social withdrawal and introversion. Once again individual variability in scores is great and tends to increase with age.

On the Minnesota Multiphasic Personality Inventory (MMPI), Calden and Hokanson (1959) found higher scores in the elderly on hypochondriasis, depression and the social-introversion scale. Swenson (1961) and Britton (1967) present data on non-hospitalised or community elderly which suggest relatively similar findings of an increased bias towards anxiety-related scales and more social introversion.

Savage (1981) reports very little work with the elderly on the Eysenck scales. He suggests that the few studies which have been published tend *not* to support any general swing towards increased introversion in old age, contrary to the initial finding of Gutman (1966) on the Maudsley Personality Inventory.

The Cattell scales, notably the Sixteen Personality Factor Questionnaire (16PF) in its various forms, have been extensively used in studies on the elderly. One of these is worth specific comment since it presents rare longitudinal personality data. Costa and McCrae (1978) administered the 16PF to adult males in a study where initial assessments were carried out between 1965 and 1967. Several other scales were also used in this extensive study which employed the combined A and B forms of the 16PF—a formidable array of questions! The 16PF was again included in a ten-year follow-up of the sample. Analysis of their results suggests an overall stability of personality. They suggest that 'When longer, and thus more reliable, scales are used, measuring the broader dimensions of general anxiety and extraversion, stability coefficients reach the 0.80 mark'. Savage *et al.* (1977) also report on 16PF findings for an elderly group. Their subjects over 70 differed from the Cattell norms by a general tendency towards introversion and social withdrawal. Again, this relatively well-preserved

community sample showed very little change in personality across an age span from 70 to death.

Attempts have been made to use other types of personality measure with the elderly. An extensive review of the use of projective measures is given by Kahana (1978). Whilst drawing attention to the difficulties of applying standard administration and scoring protocols, it is suggested that these tests may be satisfactorily completed by the elderly. Various tests are reviewed and some studies report age-related trends. As with questionnaire measures, changes in personality do not appear to be major as age advances. However, we share the doubts expressed by Savage (1973) concerning the validity of such techniques.

CONCLUSIONS

What may we conclude from these investigations? It would appear that there is a general stability in personality in the ageing individual with no gross changes. The personality measures which have been employed suggest an increase in introversion and a degree of social withdrawal. These may be artifacts of the application of tests designed for younger persons; the questions may be inappropriate. The clinical implications of these results are clear. Excessive change in personality variables is *not* a reasonable expectation in the normal elderly. If such change is observed it is likely to reflect significant abnormality, or perhaps, the total irrelevance of the test to the individual.

REFERENCES

Baltes, M.M., and Barton, C.M. (1977). 'New approaches to ageing: a case for the operant model', *Educational Gerontology*, **2**, 383–405.

Baltes, P.B. (1968). 'Longitudinal and cross-sectional sequences in the study of age and generational effects'. *Human Development*, **11**, 145–71.

Baltes, P.B., and Schaie, K.W. (1976). 'On the plasticity of intelligence in adulthood and old age: where Horn and Donaldson fail', *American Psychologist*, **31**, 720–5,

Baltes, P.B., and Willis, S.L. (1979). 'The critical importance of appropriate methodology in the study of ageing: the sample case of psychometric intelligence'. In F. Hoffmeister and C. Muller (eds.), *Brain Function in Old Age*, Springer-Verlag, Berlin, pp. 164–87.

Birkhill, W.R., and Schaie, K.W., (1975). 'The effect of differential reinforcement of cautiousness in intellectual performance among the elderly'. *Journal of Gerontology*, **30**, 578–83.

Blum, J.E., Fosshage, J.L., and Jarvik, L.F. (1972). 'Intellectual changes and sex differences in octogenarians: a twenty-year longitudinal study of ageing'. *Developmental Psychology*, **7**, 178–87.

Bolton, N., Britton, P.G., and Savage, R.D. (1966). 'Some normative data on the WAIS and its indices in an aged population', *Journal of Clinical Psychology*, **22**, 184–8.

Botwinick, J. (1977). 'Intellectual abilities'. In J.E. Birren and K.W. Schaie (eds.). *Handbook of the Psychology of Ageing*. Van Nostrand Reinhold, Cincinnati.

Botwinick, J. (1978). *Ageing and Behaviour*, Springer, New York.

Britton, P.G. (1967). 'An investigation of cognitive and personality functions in a sample of the aged in the community', Unpublished PhD dissertation, University of Newcastle upon Tyne.

Bromley, D.B. (1974). *The Psychology of Human Ageing*, 2nd ed., Penguin, London.

Calden, G., and Hokanson, J.E. (1959). 'The influence of age on MMPI responses', *Journal of Clinical Psychology*, **15**, 194–5.

Costa, P.T., and MacCrae, R.R., (1978). 'Age differences in personality structure revisited'. *Ageing and Human Development*, **8**, 131–42.

Demming, J.A., and Pressey, S.L. (1957). 'Tests "indigenous" to the adult and older years', *Journal of Counselling Psychology*, **4**, 144–8.

Eisdorfer, C., and Wilkie, F. (1973). 'Intellectual changes with advancing age'. In L.F. Jarvik, C. Eisdorfer and J.E. Blum (eds.), *Intellectual Functioning in Adults*, Springer, New York.

Furry, C.A., and Baltes, P.B. (1973). 'The effect of age differences in ability extraneous performance variables on the assessment of intelligence in children, adults and the elderly'. *Journal of Gerontology*, **28**, 73–80.

Gutman, G.M. (1966). 'A note on the MPI: age and sex differences in extraversion and neuroticism in a Canadian sample'. *British Journal of Social and Clinical Psychology*, **5**, 128–9.

Hewson, L. (1949). 'The Wechsler–Bellevue scale and the substitution test as aids in psychiatric diagnosis'. *Journal of Nervous and Mental Disease*, **109**, 158–83, 246–65.

Hogan, R., De Soto, C.B., and Solano, C. (1977). 'Traits, tests and personality research', *American Psychologist*, **32**, 255–64.

Horn, J.L., and Donaldson, G. (1976). 'On the myth of intellectual decline in adulthood', *American Psychologist*, **31**, 701–9.

Horn, J.L., and Donaldson, G. (1977). 'Faith is not enough:

a response to the Baltes–Schaie claim that intelligence does not wane', *American Psychologist*, **32**, 369–73.

Hoyer, F.W., Hoyer, W.J., Treat, N.J., and Baltes, P.B. (1978). 'Training response speed in young and elderly women'. *International Journal of Ageing and Human Development*, **9**, 247–54.

Jarvik, L.F., Kallman, F.J., and Falek, A. (1962). 'Intellectual changes in aged twins'. *Journal of Gerontology*, **17**, 289–94.

Kahana, B. (1978). 'The use of projective techniques in personality assessment of the aged'. In M. Storandt, I.C. Siegler and M.F. Elias (eds.), *The Clinical Psychology of Ageing*, Plenum, New York, pp.145–80.

Kendrick, D.C. (1982a). 'Why assess the aged? A clinical psychologist's view'. *British Journal of Clinical Psychology*, **21**, 47–54.

Kendrick, D.C. (1982b). 'Psychometrics and neurological models. A reply to Dr. Rabbitt'. *British Journal of Clinical Psychology*, **21**, 61–2.

Labouvie-Vief, G., Hoyer, W.J., Baltes, M.M., and Baltes, P.B. (1974). 'Operant analysis of intellectual behaviour in old age' *Human Development*, **17**, 259–72.

Lawton, M.P., Whelihan, W.M., and Belsky, J.K. (1980). 'Personality tests and their uses with older adults'. In J. Birren and R.B. Sloane (eds.), *Handbook of Mental Health and Ageing*, Prentice-Hall, Englewood Cliffs, New Jersey.

Miller, E. (1977). *Abnormal Ageing: The Psychology of Senile and Presenile Dementia*, Wiley, Chichester.

Mischel, W. (1968). *Personality and Assessment*, Wiley, New York.

Neugarten, B.L. (1977). 'Personality and ageing', In J.E. Birren and K.W. Schaie (eds.), *Handbook of the Psychology of Ageing*, Van Nostrand Reinhold.

Owens, W.A. (1966). 'Age and mental abilities: a second adult follow-up', *Journal of Educational Psychology*, **51**, 311–25.

Patterson, R.L. and Jackson G.M. (1980). 'Behaviour modification with the elderly', *Progress in Behaviour Modification*, **9**, 205–39.

Rabbitt, P. (1982), 'How to assess the aged? An experimental psychologist's view. Some comments on Dr. Kendrick's paper', *British Journal of Clinical Psychology*, **21**, 55–9.

Savage, R.D. (1973). 'Old age'. In H.J. Eysenck (ed.), *Handbook of Abnormal Psychology*, 2nd ed., Pitman's Medical, London.

Savage, R.D. (1981). 'Intellect, personality and adjustment in the aged'. In R. Lynn (ed.), *Dimensions of Personality: Papers in Honour of H.J. Eysenck*, Pergamon, Oxford.

Savage, R.D., Britton, P.G., Bolton, N., and Hall, E.H. (1973). *Intellectual Functioning in the Aged*, Methuen, London.

Savage, R.D., Gaber, L.B., Britton, P.G., Bolton, N., and Cooper, A. (1977). *Personality and Adjustment in the Aged*, Academic Press, London.

Schaie, K.W. (1967). 'Age changes and age differences', *Gerontologist*, **7**, 128–32.

Schaie, K.W. and Baltes, P.B. (1977). 'Some faith helps to see the forest; a final comment on the Horn and Donaldson myth of the Baltes–Schaie position on adult intelligence', *American Psychologist*, **32**, 1118–20.

Schaie, K.W. and Labouvie-Vief, G. (1974). 'Generational versus ontogenetic components of change in adult cognitive behaviour: a fourteen year cross-sequential study', *Developmental Psychology*, **10**, 305–20.

Schaie, K.W., Labouvie-Vief, G. and Buech, B.U. (1973). 'Generational and cohort specific differences in adult cognitive functioning: a fourteen-year study of independent samples', *Developmental Psychology*, **9**, 151–66.

Schaie, K.W., and Parham, I.M. (1976). 'Stability of adult personality traits: fact or fable', *Journal of Personality and Social Psychology*, **34**, 146–58.

Siegler, I.C., and Botwinick, J. (1979). 'A long term longitudinal study of the intellectual ability of older adults—the matter of selective subject attrition', *Journal of Gerontology*, **34**, 242–8.

Swenson, W.M. (1961). 'Structured personality testing in the aged: an MMPI study of the geriatric population', *Journal of Clinical Psychology*, **17**, 302–4.

Volans, P.J., and Woods, R.T. (1983). 'Why do we assess the aged?', *British Journal of Clinical Psychology*, **22**, 213–14.

Biological factors in the etiology of mental disorders of old age

ANDREW PROCTER

Lecturer in Psychogeriatrics, United Medical and Dental Schools, Guy's Hospital, London

1. THE MENTAL DISORDERS OF OLD AGE

The elderly are at risk of developing a similar range of psychiatric conditions as their younger counterparts. However, some conditions are markedly more prevalent in old age. Prominent among these is the group of diseases causing impairment of cognitive function (Hemsi, 1982) either irreversibly (i.e. the dementias) or reversibly (variously called delirium, confusional states or transient organic psychoses).

The relationship between age and psychiatric illness in the absence of gross brain or systemic disease is less clear, in part because the nosology of such conditions is more controversial. Such psychiatric illness can be broadly divided into the affective psychoses (which include severe depression), non-affective psychoses (which include the paranoid psychoses) and the neuroses. When comparable criteria are used the prevalence of both severe depression and the neuroses appear to be similar in the young and old (see Comfort, 1982; Philpot, 1986). The non-affective psychoses are particularly heterogeneous and include various clinical types of schizophrenia and other psychoses with prominent paranoid delusions. Some authorities define schizophrenia as only occurring for the first time before the age of 45 years, and so defined it is primarily a disease of young adults. Paranoid illnesses in the elderly are almost certainly a heterogeneous group, some related to young-onset schizophrenia and others being transient organic psychoses with prominent organic etiology (Pitt, 1982).

Thus some of the functional illnesses of the elderly superficially resemble those of younger patients. However, there are important differences. These include differences in symptomatology—for example depression appears to be characterized by predominantly somatic complaints. Importantly, the response to treatment is generally worse in the elderly and for this and other reasons, the prognosis is usually poorer (see Philpot, 1986).

The aim of this review will be to consider those biological factors which may play a part in the etiology of psychiatric conditions at all ages, but especially those specific to the elderly which may modify the presentation and course of the illness.

2. THE BIOLOGICAL CHANGES OF AGING

Almost all the organ systems of the body show structural and functional changes with increasing age. However it is those which affect the function of the nervous system which most influence the development and manifestation of psychiatric disease.

2.1 Structural and functional changes in the brain

2.1.1 Atrophy Numerous studies have confirmed that a reduction in brain size occurs with increasing age in psychiatrically normal individuals (reviewed by Perry and Perry, 1982). The simplest measure of this determined post-mortem is total brain weight which shows a 5% to 10% decline from maturity to the ninth decade, most marked in the male. Brain weight is subject to variability due to irregular trapping of cerebrospinal fluid, and it fails to give any information about the previous size of the brain or those areas most affected.

More detailed pathological studies comparing brain size and cranial cavity volume indicate that the reduction of brain size occurs after the sixth decade and affects predominantly the cerebral cortex in the parasagittal frontal and parietal areas. Brain imaging techniques such as X-ray computed tomography and magnetic resonance imaging have generally confirmed the findings in life without the introduction of peri-mortem artefacts.

Detailed histological examination indicates that certain brain regions are relatively unaffected by ageing while others show marked loss of cells. Because lost neurones are not replaced to any detectable extent in the mature mammalian brain, neuronal loss has been most extensively investigated. In many brain-stem structures neuronal numbers are stable with increasing age, while in others, nerve cell loss occurs. Importantly, cell loss occurs in the locus coeruleus and substantia nigra which give rise to ascending noradrenergic and dopaminergic fibres respectively.

The cerebral cortex shows the most marked age-dependent changes which have received much attention in view of the role of the cortex in higher cognitive function. Loss of neurones has been observed in all areas of cortex differing only in degree from region to region. There is, however, much controversy regarding the identity of the cells lost and the regions most affected.

The cerebral cortex is a highly organized structure with complex intrinsic neuronal circuitry and interconnections with other regions of the nervous system. The neuronal elements broadly consist of the terminals of ascending nerve fibres of subcortical neurones, and intrinsic cortical neurones which can be classified as either pyramidal cells or non-pyramidal cells (Braak and Braak, 1986). The pyramidal cells give rise to the major output from an area of the cortex with fibres up to one metre long, while the non-pyramidal cells form the local circuitry with shorter fibres which terminate near the cell body. The exact extent to which these cells are affected by ageing is unclear, but many studies have shown a loss of large neurones which are probably pyramidal cells. However, experimentally induced 'loss' of large cells in other areas of the brain appears to be due to shrinkage so that the cells remain but are smaller (Pearson, Gatter and Powell, 1983). When the morphology as well as size is taken into consideration, there appears to be proportionally greater loss of non-pyramidal cells (Braak and Braak, 1986).

Studies of this type depend upon the examination of a relatively small area of the cortex and fail to take account of shrinkage of the total area of the cortex. The neurones of the cerebral cortex are interconnected functionally in columns arranged perpendicularly to the pial surface. In pathological conditions where cortical atrophy is prominent and possibly also ageing, a loss of entire columns may occur and mask the true extent of cell loss unless the entire cortex is considered (Hauw, Duychaerts and Partridge, 1986).

More evidence for the greater loss of local neurones is provided by neurochemical investigations. The assignment of neurotransmitters to cortical cell types is far from complete, but it seems likely that the amino acids, glutamic and aspartic acids or closely related substances are the transmitters of pyramidal cells. The majority of non-pyramidal cells appear to use gamma-aminobutyric acid (GABA) as transmitter, while others contain neuropeptides including somatostatin. Other important cortical neurotransmitters, such as acetylcholine and the monoamines, dopamine, noradrenaline and serotonin, are present in the nerve terminals of cells in subcortical structures (Jones, 1986). The exact interconnections of these neuronal elements is unknown at present but GABA and somatostatin-containing neurones and pyramidal cells appear to bear receptors to serotonin. An age-dependent loss of such receptors has been observed in a number of brain regions (Procter, Middlemiss and Bowen, 1987).

2.1.2 Other histological changes
In addition to loss of neurones, abnormal structures may be seen in an aged brain, the significance of which remain unclear (reviewed by Perry and Perry, 1982).

Various organic pigments and minerals accumulate in the brain throughout life. The most characteristic of these is lipofuscin which is probably composed of lipid and proteinaceous material. This may occupy up to 75% of the cytoplasm of a neuronal cell body, but no deleterious effects on the cell metabolism have been demonstrated. Similarly amyloid, an apparently insoluble extracellular fibrillary material, accumulates in many organs including the brain, yet a direct effect on physiology has not been demonstrated. In the brain it is located primarily in two sites, one in the walls of blood vessels and the other at the core of senile plaques. These plaques are recognized microscopically as minute areas of abnormal tissue in the grey matter of the cerebral cortex and elsewhere. Electron microscopy has shown them to be composed of glial and neuronal elements including nerve terminals, axons and dendrites. Plaques have been observed in the brain from the fourth decade onwards, and in cognitively normal individuals they are most abundant in the medial temporal lobe structures (amygdala and hippocampus) but may be present in all cortical areas. The pathophysiological significance of plaques in a cognitively normal individual remains unclear, although in demented patients with Alzheimer's disease (see 3.2.2) there is a well-established relationship between the cognitive impairment and the number of plaques. This too is the case for another abnormal structure, the neurofibrillary tangle. This intracellular structure comprises aggregated bundles of filaments within the cell bodies of pyramidal cells. Electron microscopy shows that the main structural features are twisted fibrils or tubules, each composed of a pair of filaments wound round each other. In cognitively normal individuals neurofibrillary tangles of the hippocampus are present in 5% by the fifth decade, and are almost universal by the tenth. The presence of tangles in other areas of the cerebral cortex is rare in the cognitively normal.

2.2 Structural and functional changes of other organs influencing brain function

In many organ systems it is difficult to separate the effect of normal ageing from that of pathological conditions which have increased prevalence amongst the elderly.

2.2.1 Sense organs
The relationship between psychiatric illness and impairment of vision and hearing has been examined, as of all the senses these show the most clear deterioration with age.

The frequency of eye disease rises sharply in people over 65 years of age. Cataracts and glaucoma are approximately eight times more common than in the general population and retinal disorders six times more common (MRC, 1983). Estimates from the United Kingdom and the United States suggest that 5% of those over 65 have visual impairment sufficient to prevent them reading newsprint even with spectacles.

Deafness is also common in the elderly; one study found a prevalence of 60% for hearing impairment in those over 70 years of age (Herbst and Humphrey, 1980).

2.2.2 Cardiovascular system
The blood supply to the brain may be impaired by arteriosclerosis of the blood vessels supplying it. Arteriosclerosis, while not an invariable concomitant of ageing, is more common amongst the elderly, and together with other disorders of the heart and great vessels appears to directly cause brain damage as a result of reduction or complete cessation or cerebral blood flow. The consequences and possible mechanism of this are discussed below (3.2.1).

The regulatory mechanism of the blood pressure is frequently impaired in old age and hypertension with its associated risk of cardiovascular disease tends to be more common. Also, however, disorder of the autonomic nervous system can occur and the reflexes involved in maintaining blood pressure may be impaired resulting in postural hypotension. This occurs as a result of loss of reflex vasoconstriction and increased heart rate on standing. It is of importance when drug treatment is considered (see Trotter, 1982).

2.2.3 Endrocrine system
Age-related changes are seen in a number of hormonal systems without any obvious functional deterioration. In particular many elderly patients have decreased concentrations of circulating thyroid hormones (both free and total thyroxine and tri-iodothyronine; Seth and Beckett, 1984).

Corticosteroid metabolism in the human is subject to many influences and the investigation of any relationship with normal ageing is difficult. However, in experimental animals confounding influences can be controlled and it appears that aged animals have impaired ability to terminate secretion of corticosteroid when a potent stimulus, stress, abates. This may have a role in the etiology of nerve cell loss in normal ageing as well as depression and dementia, because corticosteroids appear to enhance the effect of a number of neurotoxins (Sapolsky, 1987).

2.2.4 Other metabolic changes Several physiological changes occur with ageing. These are particularly important when drug treatment is initiated as the elderly person's response to drugs may be different from that of a younger person. In particular, the distribution and elimination of drugs may be so altered that an oral dose produces higher blood concentrations in the elderly than woud be expected. The factors underlying this are summarized in Table 1.

3. BIOLOGICAL FACTORS IN THE ETIOLOGY OF SPECIFIC PSYCHIATRIC DISORDERS

3.1 Transient organic psychoses

These generally short-lasting disorders arise in conjunction with recognizable disorder of cerebral function of the types summarized in Table 2. While persons of all ages may develop such a confusional state during major illness, the elderly appear to be particularly at risk. In part this is because the elderly are more likely to suffer physical illnesses, but preexisting impairment of cognitive ability or vision and hearing predispose to the development of confusion. Furthermore, as discussed above, elderly people are particularly susceptible to the effects of certain drugs or to drug interactions, all of which may directly cause confusion.

3.2 Dementia

This syndrome of global deterioration of orientation, memory, comprehension, calculation, learning capacity and judgment is of a chronic, often progressive nature

Table 1   Factors affecting the response to drugs in the elderly

Factor		Effect	Example
Pharmacokinetics			
Absorption	Altered gut motility	Apparently no effect on drug absorption	
	Reduced small intestine surface area		
	Reduced small intestine blood flow	Impaired absorbsion of enteric-coated preparations	Enteric-coated preparations
	Reduced gastric acidity		
Distribution	Increased body fat	Accumulation of lipid soluble drugs	Benzodiazepines, tricyclics
	Reduced muscle bulk		
	Reduced total body water	Higher plasma levels of water soluble drugs	Diazepam, phenytoin
	Reduced plasma proteins	Enhanced effect of protein-bound drugs	
Metabolism	Reduced activity of liver enzymes	Increased circulating drug levels	Chlormethiazole, beta-blockers
Excretion	Asymptomatic reduced renal function	Slow excretion of drugs	Digoxin, lithium
Pharmacodynamics	Increased receptor sensitivity	Proportionally greater effect of drugs	Digoxin, benzodiazepines
Drug Interactions	Greater risk of multiple pathology and therefore multiple prescriptions	Increased risk of drug interactions	
Compliance	Complex drug regimes	Reduced compliance, therefore lack of effective treatment	
	Poor labelling, inadequate instructions		
	Poor eyesight, poor hearing		
	Cognitive impairment		

Table 2 Important causes of transient organic psychoses in the elderly

Infections	At most sites (but especially cerebral, pulmonary and urinary)	
Hypoxia	Of pulmonary cause	e.g. bronchopneumonia
	Of cardiac cause	cardiac failure
		dysrhythmia
		myocardial infarction
		hypotension
Metabolic/endocrine	Renal failure	
	Liver failure	
	Hypoglycaemia/diabetic pre-coma	
	Hypo- and hyperthyroidism	
	Hypo- and hyperparathyroidism	
	Vitamin deficiency	(thiamine, nicotinic acid, B_{12} and folate)
	Dehydration and electrolyte imbalance	
	Acid–base disturbance	
Cerebral	Epilepsy and post-ictal states	
	Space-occupying lesions	
Cerebrovascular	Cerebral thrombosis or embolism	
	Subarachnoid haemorrhage	
	Hypertensive encephalopathy	
Traumatic	Cerebral trauma	
	Major fractures (resulting in hypotension)	
Toxic drugs	Psychotropic drugs	
	Withdrawal of drugs	barbiturates
		benzodiazepines
		alcohol
	Drug interactions	

and if untreated is usually irreversible and terminal. There are many causes of the syndrome which may occur at any age from childhood to old age. However, at different ages there are certain diseases which are more likely to be the cause.

In old age two conditions appear to predominate, cerebrovascular disease and Alzheimer's disease (in the over 65 year age group often called senile dementia of the Alzheimer type). Dementia in the elderly may be caused by many other conditions, some of which are potentially treatable and others which are not. These are summarized in Table 3. The precise prevalence in the elderly of these various causes of dementia is not known. This is generally because the diagnosis can only be established at post-mortem examination, and the differentiation on clinical grounds alone is usually impossible. When interpreting the results of post-mortem studies it must always be remembered that these are almost without exception made of hospitalized patients, who are only a small proportion of the demented elderly and may therefore have atypical features (Procter and Bowen, 1987).

3.2.1 Cerebrovascular disease Cerebral infarction or ischaemia may occur either as a result of disease of the cerebral vessels themselves or as a result of emboli from diseased extracranial vessels or the heart itself. Cerebral infarcts are easily recognized post-mortem as local areas of softening of the brain. The development of cognitive impairment following brain infarction appears to depend more on the size of the lesion than its site (see Perry and Perry, 1982).

Of all the organs in the body the brain seems to be

Table 3 Important causes of dementia in the elderly

Infective	Sequelae of meningitis and encephalitis	
	Creutzfeld-Jakob disease	
	Syphilis	meningovascular
		general paralysis
Hypoxia	Sequelae of cerebral hypoxia	
Metabolic/endocrine	Sequelae of hypoglycaemia	
	Hypothyroidism	
	Vitamin deficiency	B_{12}
		nicotinic acid
	Hypopituitarism	
	Hypocalcaemia	
	Wilson's disease	
Cerebral	Demyelinating diseases	
	Subdural haematoma	
	Subarachnoid haemorrhage	
	Cerebrovascular disease	
	Cerebral tumour	
	Communicating hydrocephalus	
	Neurodegenerative disorders:	
		Alzheimer's disease
		Pick's disease
		Huntingdon's disease
		spinocerebellar degeneration
		Parkinson's disease
		etc.
Traumatic	Head injury/post-traumatic encephalopathy	
Toxic	Heavy metal poisoning	

particularly susceptible to ischaemic damage. Recent experimental work suggests that glutamic acid, the likely transmitter of cortical pyramidal cells, plays a key role in ischaemic brain damage responsible for cerebral palsy in children and stroke and dementia in adults. Glutamic acid and its analogues have been shown to be neurotoxic in a number of experimental systems, and one effect of hypoxia is to increase the release of glutamic acid from nerve terminals and to inhibit its uptake by terminals and glial cells. The neurotoxic effect of ischaemia can be dramatically reduced by the administration of an antagonist of glutamic acid which is active at a class of synaptic receptors for glutamic acid, the N-methyl-D-aspartate receptor. The future use of such compounds may provide exciting therapeutic prospects (Schwarcz and Meldrum, 1985; Rothman and Olney, 1986).

Some patients with dementia and vascular disease have lesions in the white matter which can be demonstrated with X-ray computed tomography, in the apparent absence of grey matter infarction as described above. The term 'leukoariosis' has been applied to this condition but its etiology and precise relationship to cerebrovascular disease and Alzheimer's disease are not yet established (Hachinski, Potter and Merskey, 1987).

3.2.2 Alzheimer's disease The term Alzheimer's disease has previously been applied only to those patients who develop dementia before the age of 65 characterized by senile plaque and neurofibrillary tangle formation in most of the areas of the cerebral cortex. Patients over 65 years old with a similar condition have been considered to have 'senile dementia of the Alzheimer type'. This distinction is made less frequently now except for research purposes and Alzheimer's disease is the term applied to all patients regardless of age. Differences have been described between young and old patients; young patients appear to have a more rapidly progressive disease, more severe pathological changes and derangement of more neurotransmitter systems (Rossor et al., 1984). While this has been taken as evidence of distinct subgroups of the disease, an alternative explanation is that the younger patients, being physically in better health, survive to a more advanced stage of the disease.

Controversy also surrounds the relationship between Alzheimer's disease and normal ageing. No type of change has been found in the brain of a demented patient with Alzheimer's disease that is not also present to some extent in the brain of an undemented subject, although neurofibrillary tangle formation is usually confined to the hippocampus in the normal elderly and present throughout the cortex in the demented. The severity of 'pathological' changes in an undemented subject consistently appears to fall below a definable limit. If these changes exceed that limit dementia was usually present in life. These observations have led to an ongoing controversy—some workers are of the opinion that Alzheimer's disease is an extreme variant of normal ageing while others suggest that it results from specific insults to the brain, the effects of which are influenced by the age of the subject (see Lauter, 1985).

In addition to the histological changes, deficits of numerous neurotransmitters have been reported. In studies of brains obtained at post-mortem examination, loss of the cortical innervation by ascending fibres using acetylcholine, serotonin, noradrenaline and dopamine have been reported. Also loss of the markers of neurotransmitters associated with intrinsic cortical cells has been found, including loss of GABA, glutamic acid and somatostatin. However, post-mortem studies may be complicated by the debilitated state of the patients before death, and biochemical changes after death. Importantly, the brains are only examined after many years of illness, which is not the case for tissue obtained surgically at diagnostic operations performed soon after the onset of symptoms. In such tissue only a deficit of cholinergic innervation has been found, although histological examination indicates a greater loss of synapses than can be accounted for by this loss alone (Procter and Bowen, 1987).

The cortical cholinergic deficit occurs early in the disease and appears to be related to the clinical and pathological severity. Yet the results of therapy aimed at restoring cholinergic transmission has been disappointing (Bartus et al., 1982).

The cholinergic deficit is due to a loss of ascending fibres of cell bodies in a subcortical structure, the nucleus basalis of Meynert (nbM). The relative importance of cortical and subcortical structures in the pathogenesis of Alzheimer's disease is not clear. Senile plaques appear to contain cholinergic terminals, among other structures, and it has been suggested that a primary lesion of the nbM gives rise to the cortical pathology. However, experimental lesions of the cortex can cause secondary atrophy of the cells in the nbM, which suggests that the primary lesion in Alzheimer's disease could be in the cortex (Pearson, Gatter and Powell, 1983).

It is becoming apparent that the distribution of senile plaques and neurofibrillary tangles is not random, but appears to reflect the known functional anatomy of the cerebral cortex, which supports the idea that certain cells are selectively vulnerable. The exact nature of the lesion is unknown. Genetic factors are undoubtedly important in some patients. The well-known association of Down's syndrome (Trisomy 21) and Alzheimer neuropathology (Wisniewski et al., 1985), and the recent demonstration that the gene for familial Alzheimer's disease is located on chromosome 21 (St George-Hyslop et al., 1987), indicate a major role for the genes of this chromosome.

Several mechanisms whereby this genetic factor may exert its influence have been proposed (reviewed by Lauter, 1985). These include the loss of trophic factors responsible for nerve cell integrity, or the production of endogenous neurotoxins possibly active at glutamic acid receptors (see 3.2.1; Maragos et al., 1987). Exogenous agents which may act through these mechanisms or interact with genetic factors include viruses which have been shown to cause some neurodegenerative conditions; ionizing radiation which causes the production of oxygen free radicals to which the brain is particularly sensitive; and environmental toxins. Of the last, aluminium has received the most attention because of the demonstration that it can cause Alzheimer-like pathology in animals, and aluminium silicates seem to be present in senile plaques

(Candy *et al.*, 1986). Whether this deposition of aluminium silicates is a primary event in the formation of plaques or whether plaques once formed accumulate aluminium salts is yet to be established.

Further clues to the etiology of Alzheimer's disease are likely to be obtained from investigation of the selective vulnerability of certain nerve cells. Cholinergic and glutamatergic cells are considered by some to be particularly vulnerable and in view of recent demonstrations of deranged energy metabolism in Alzheimer's disease (Sims *et al.*, 1987), it may be of note that the precursors of both these neurotransmitters also have a role in the cells' energy production.

3.3 Depression

That form of depression in which biological factors seem to be most important, depressive psychosis, appears to have a similar prevalence in the elderly as in younger subjects. Certain forms of depression are undoubtedly more common in the elderly and the best example is that following a stroke. About one-third of patients become depressed after a stroke, and although this may be explained by the associated loss of physical and social abilities, other biological factors seem to be important. In particular the depression is said to be associated with lesions of the left frontal lobe and to respond to antidepressant treatments (see Wade, Legh-Smith and Hewer, 1987).

Although genetic factors have been implicated in the etiology of depression in the elderly (Mendlewicz, 1976), biological factors may not play a unique role in etiology, but determine the response to treatment. Most antidepressant drugs appear to act on monoaminergic neurotransmission, in particular they influence the reuptake of serotonin and thereby the numbers of postsynaptic serotonin receptors (Philpot, 1986). As has already been described, normal ageing is associated with a reduction in the numbers of serotonin receptors and this may be expected to influence the efficacy of antidepressants. At a cortical serotonergic synapse, the postsynaptic cell is a cell intrinsic to the cortex including those which use GABA as transmitter. Some of these are probably lost as a result of normal ageing. Recent reports suggest that antidepressants and electroconvulsive treatment may also influence GABA receptors, and some drugs known to affect GABA metabolism may also be efficacious in affective disorders. GABA cells may therefore be important in determining the response to a variety of treatments for depression (Meldrum, 1987).

Ageing is associated with other changes which may alter the response to antidepressants. Thyroid hormone supplementation of antidepressants may be effective for the treatment of younger patients with depression resistant to standard treatment, even in the absence of hypothyroidism (Loosen and Prange, 1982). As discussed above, elderly people have low levels of thyroid hormones which may hinder their response to usual treatment.

Some patients with depression have cerebral atrophy demonstrable by brain imaging and, at post-mortem, in the absence of dementia (Standish-Barry *et al.*, 1986). Hypersecretion of corticosteroids appears to occur commonly in depression (Philpot, 1986), and as discussed above (2.2.3) this may have a role in nerve cell death.

Finally, it must not be forgotten that for pharmacokinetic and other reasons (Table 1 and 3.1) the elderly are at particular risk of developing serious side effects from the three major physical treatments of depression: drugs, electroconvulsive therapy and psychosurgery. This may make effective treatment difficult or impossible.

3.4 Paranoid disorders

The nosology of paranoid disorders of the elderly is confused, as paranoid symptoms are common features of transient organic psychoses and early dementia. Many series of patients with paranoid disorders probably include patients with such varied conditions.

A major etiological factor in the development of paranoid illnesses appears to be impairment of hearing or sight. The present state of the classification of paranoid disorders makes further comment difficult, but it is probably significant that many are alleviated by neuroleptic drugs which act as dopamine antagonists (Pitt, 1982).

3.5 Neuroses

Of the neurotic condition, biological factors have only been implicated to any great extent in anxiety. An important condition in the differential diagnosis of anxiety is caffeine intoxication which has identical symptoms to free floating anxiety. Anxiety symptoms due to caffeine are more frequent at increased age (Greden, 1980) which probably reflects the elderly person's greater sensitivity to drugs in general.

Common pharmacological treatment of anxiety includes the benzodiazepine class of drugs which appear to act at a neuronal receptor closely associated with the GABA receptor (Meldrum, 1987). The increased sensitivity of the elderly to benzodiazepines (Comfort, 1982) probably reflects the alteration in the activity of GABA neurones at increasing age.

4. CONCLUSION

Future understanding of psychiatric illness in the elderly will depend on research into the normal function of the nervous system and a better understanding of all the neurotransmitters and neuropeptides rather than the limited numbers studied hitherto. This will hopefully increase the numbers of drugs available and help us to differentiate between normal ageing and pathological degenerative conditions which, because they are common, are often regarded as normal.

REFERENCES

Bartus, R.T., Dean, R.C., Beer, B., and Lippa, A.S. (1982). 'Cholinergic hypothesis of geriatric memory dysfunction', *Science*, **217**, 408–17.

Braak, H., and Braak, E. (1986). 'Ratio of pyramidal cells versus non-pyramidal cells in the human frontal isocortex and changes in ratio with aging and Alzheimer's disease'. In D.F. Swaab, E. Fliers, M. Mirmiran, W.A. Van Gool and F. Van Haaren (eds.), *Progress in Brain Research*, Vol.70, Elsevier Science Publishers BV.

Candy, J.M., Klinowski, J., Perry, R.H., Perry, E.K., Fairbairn, A., Oakley, A.E., Carpenter, T.A., Atack, J.R., Blessed, G., and Edwardson, J.A. (1986). 'Aluminosilicates and senile plaque formation in Alzheimer's disease', *Lancet*, i, 354–7.

Comfort, A. (1982). 'Anxiety in old age'. In D. Wheatley (ed.), *Psychopharmacology of Old Age*, Oxford University Press.

Greden, J.F. (1980). 'Caffeine and tobacco dependence'. In H.I. Kaplan, A.M. Freedman and B.J. Sadock (eds.), *Comprehensive Textbook of Psychiatry*, 3rd ed., Williams and Wilkins, Baltimore.

Hachinski, V.C., Potter, P., and Merskey, H. (1987), 'Leukoariosis', *Archives of Neurology*, **44**, 21–3.

Hauw, J.J., Duychaerts, C., and Partridge, M. (1986). 'Neuropathological aspects of brain aging and SDAT'. In Y. Courtols, B. Faucheux, B. Forette, D.L. Knook and J.A. Treton (eds.), *Modern Trends in Aging*, Vol. 147, John Liby Eurotext, London, Paris.

Hemsi, L. (1982). 'Psychogeriatric care in the community'. In R. Levy and F. Post (eds.), *The Psychiatry of Late Life*, Blackwell, Oxford.

Herbst, K.G., and Humphrey, C. (1980). 'Hearing impairment and mental state in the elderly living at home', *Br. Med. J.*, **281**, 903–5.

Jones, E.G. (1986). 'Neurotransmitters in the cerebral cortex', *J. Neurosurg.*, **65**, 135–53.

Lauter, H. (1985). 'What do we know about Alzheimer's disease today?', *Danish Med. Bull.*, **32** (Suppl. 1), 1–21.

Loosen, P.T., and Prange, A.J., Jr (1982). 'Serum thyrotropin response to thyrotropin releasing hormone in psychiatric patients: a review', *Am. J. Psychiatr.*, **139**, 405–16.

Maragos W.F., Greenamyre J.T., Penney J.B., and Young A.B. (1987). Glutamate dysfunction in Alzheimer's Disease: an hypothesis, *Trends in Neurological Sciences* **10**: 65–68.

Meldrum, B. (1987). 'Classification of GABA and benzodiazepine receptors', *J. Psychopharmacol.*, **1**, 1–5.

Mendlewicz, J. (1976). 'The age factor in depressive illness: some genetic considerations', *J. Gerontol.*, **3**, 300.

MRC (1983). 'Diseases of the eye', working party report submitted to Neurobiology and Mental Health Board, Appendix 10, MRC 1983, p.7.

Pearson, R.C.A., Gatter, K.C., and Powell, T.P.S. (1983). 'Retrograde degeneration in the basal nucleus in monkey and man', *Brain Res.*, **261**, 321–6.

Perry, R., and Perry, E. (1982). 'The aging brain and its pathology'. In R. Levy and F. Post (eds.), *The Psychiatry of Late Life*, Blackwell, Oxford.

Philpot, M.P. (1986). 'Biological factors in depression in the elderly'. In E. Murphy (ed.), *Affective Disorders in the Elderly*, Churchill Livingstone, Edinburgh.

Pitt, B. (1982). 'Paranoid psychosis in the elderly'. In D. Wheatley (ed.), *Psychopharmacology of Old Age*, Oxford University Press.

Procter, A.W. and Bowen, D.M. (1987). 'Aging, the cerebral neocortex and psychiatric disorder'. In P. Davies and C.E. Finch (eds.), *Neurochemistry of Aging: Banbury Report*, Cold Spring Harbor Laboratory.

Procter, A.W., Middlemiss, D.N., Bowen, D.M. (1987). 'Selective loss of serotonin recognition sites in the parietal cortex in Alzheimer's disease', *Int. J. Ger. Psychiat.* (submitted).

Rossor, M.N., Iversen, L.L., Reynolds, G.P., Mountjoy, C.Q., and Roth, M. (1984). 'Neurochemical changes in early and late onset types of Alzheimer's disease', *Br. Med. J.*, **288**, 961–4.

Rothman, S.M., and Olney, J.W. (1986). 'Glutamate and the pathophysiology of hypoxic-ischaemic brain damage', *Ann. Neurol.* **19**, 109–11.

Sapolsky, R.M. (1987). 'Protecting the injured hippocampus by attenuating glucocorticoid secretion'. In P. Davies and C.E. Finch (eds.), *The Neurobiology of Aging: Banbury Report*, Cold Spring Harbor Laboratory.

Schwarcz, R., and Meldrum, B. (1985). 'Exitatory amino acid antagonists provide a therapeutic approach to neurological disorders', *Lancet*, **ii**, 140–3.

Seth, J., and Beckett, G.J. (1984). 'Thyroid function tests', *Medicine International*, 2nd series, **11**, 463–7.

Sims, N.R., Finegan, J.M., Blass, J.P., Bowen, D.M., and Neary, D. (1987). Altered mitochondrial function in primary degenerative dementia', *Brain Res.* (in press).

Standish-Barry, H.M.A.S., Bouras, N., Hale, A.S., Bridges, P.K., and Bartlett, J.R. (1986). 'Ventricular size and CSF transmitter metabolite concentrations in severe endogenous depression', *Br. J. Psychiat.*, **148**, 386–92.

St George-Hyslop, P., Tanzi, R.E., Polinski, R.J., *et al.* (22 authors) (1987). 'The genetic defect causing familial Alzheimer's disease maps on chromosome 21', *Science*, **235**, 885–90.

Trotter, C. (1982). 'Drugs in psychogeriatrics'. In P.J. Tyrer (ed.), *Drugs in Psychiatric Practice*, Butterworths, London.

Wade, D.T., Legh-Smith, J., and Hewer, R.A. (1987). 'Depressed mood after stroke: a community study of its frequency', *Br. J. Psychiat.*, **151**, 200–5.

Wisniewski, K.E., Dalton, A.J., McLachlan, C., Wen, G.Y., and Wisniewski, H.M. (1985). 'Alzheimer's disease in Down's syndrome: clinicopathological studies', *Neurology*, **35**, 957–61.

Characteristics of depression in the elderly

BRICE PITT

Professor of Psychiatry of Old Age, St Charles Hospital, London

Major depressive illness in the elderly is often much the same as in younger patients, but there may be features which mask, complicate or give an unusual quality to the underlying mood disorder. For example, cognitive impairment of a degree to suggest dementia (pseudodementia—Kiloh, 1961 has been estimated by Post (1975) to occur in as many as 10% of elderly patients admitted to hospital with depressive illness. Depressed old people frequently do not actually complain of depression, belonging to a generation which had not learnt to do so, but are inclined to present physical symptoms, notably insomnia, constipation and pain, or simply to 'fail to thrive', in a state of anorexia and anergy.

Physical illness is one of the commonest precipitants of depression, and the attribution of symptoms to one disorder rather than the other can be as difficult as it is important. Possibly because depression greatly increases the dependency upon others which is the lot of many elderly people, frank regression and quite florid behaviour disorder—incontinence, screaming, food refusal, aggression—may compound and over-shadow the lowered mood. Exotic psychotic features may be rather more common in old people, including paranoia which goes well beyond what is readily comprehensible as secondary to severe despondency, and markedly impaired self-esteem. Not only may elderly depressives be thought demented because they appear (or indeed are) confused, but also because the condition persists far longer than expected by those used to treating younger patients.

Minor depression is probably five times as common as major depression in the elderly (Gurland et al., 1983) but is very likely to be overlooked (e.g. Williamson et al., 1964) or regarded as a normal reaction to the vicissitudes of old age. Attempts have been made to distinguish between the dysphoria of the disaffected elderly (Blazer and Williams, 1980; Gillis and Zabow, 1982) and true depression, albeit writ small.

This paper deals with those special features that make depression in old age such a stimulating challenge to a diagnostician, reviewing evidence, such as there is, of their prevalence and speculating on their nature and any clues they may give to the causation of depression in old age and the contribution made by ageing.

First, however, a brief general account of the signs and symptoms of depression will be given.

THE MAIN FEATURES OF DEPRESSION

A good description of the features of a major depressive episode is given in the 'American Diagnostic and Statistical Manual (DSMIII) (American Psychiatric Association, 1980). The first diagnostic criterion is a dysphoric mood or loss of interest or pleasure in all or almost all usual activities and pastimes. The mood is characterised by such symptoms as: depressed, sad, 'blue', hopeless, low, 'down in the dumps', irritable. This mood disturbance must be prominent and persistent, but not necessarily the dominant symptom. In the more severe form of depression which the manual terms 'melancholia', the depressed mood is perceived as having a distinctly different quality from the kind of feeling experienced after, say, the death of a loved one, and a lack of reactivity to

From *Affective Disorders in the Elderly*, E. Murphy (ed.), Churchill Livingstone, London, 1986. Reproduced with permission.

pleasurable stimuli is noted—the patient does not feel much better, even temporarily, when something good happens.

The manual lists eight other symptoms, at least four of which should have been present nearly every day for a period of two weeks or more:

1. Poor appetite or significant weight loss, increased appetite or significant weight gain. (The latter, usually ascribed to 'comfort' eating, is uncommon in the elderly.)
2. Insomnia or, again much less common in the elderly, hypersomnia. The insomnia typically takes the form of waking at least two hours before the usual time. However, there may be difficulty in getting to sleep, or a tendency to wake in the middle of the night, when sleep may be regained with some difficulty.
3. Psychomotor agitation or retardation. Agitation takes the form of restless pacing, inability to sit still, wringing of the hands, moaning, groaning, pressure of speech and flamboyant displays of anguish or importunate pleading for help and reassurance. Retardation includes feeling slowed up and showing delay in initiating speech, replying and in actions.
4. Loss of interest or pleasure in usual activities (already, in fact, mentioned under mood) or decrease in sexual drive.
5. Loss of energy; fatigue. A combination of fatigue, loss of interest and despondency makes many depressed people withdrawn, avoiding the company they normally enjoy.
6. Feelings of worthlessness, self-reproach, or excessive or inappropriate guilt—exaggeratedly low self-esteem.

   Such ideas may, in psychotic depression, be delusional. Delusions are usually mood-congruent: guilt, impoverishment, punishment, nihilism and sometimes bizarre hypochondria predominate. 'I'm not ill, I'm wicked; I should be punished, not treated. I'm making other people ill!' 'I'm ruined, I'll be evicted, I'll go to prison for debt!' 'I can't eat, everything's blocked up, I've no insides, I'm dead!' Occasionally fleeting hallucinatory voices echo these thoughts and berate the patient.

   Less often the voices are mood-incongruent, and the patient believes that (s)he is persecuted,

frequently feeling unable to explain why this should be so (see later).

7. Complaints or evidence of diminished ability to think or concentrate, such as slowed thinking, or indecisiveness.
8. Recurrent thoughts of death, suicidal ideas, wishes to be dead, suicide attempts: 'I wish I could die in my sleep', 'Life isn't worth living', 'If only I had the courage I'd take my life'. The physically ill may reject treatment for these reasons.

Delusions of unworthiness and guilt and suicidal attempts are unlikely to be overlooked, nor are agitation and weight loss, though they may be misinterpreted, but it is clear from the above that major depressive illness can be present without any of these manifestations, in which case it may be easily missed. Withdrawn depressed old people do not visit their doctors all that readily and even if they do, the malaise may well be ascribed to physical disorder, a normal reaction to the vicissitudes of old age or even to normal ageing rather than to depression. The Edinburgh study by Williamson *et al.* (1964) showed that general practitioners were unaware of most of the depression suffered by their elderly patients.

Still more often missed or dismissed is the milder neurotic depression (Pollitt and Young, 1971), less pervasive than the major type, varying from day to day, though the predominant mood is one of unhappy apprehension. Diurnal variation often takes the form of worsening towards the end of the day, while initial is more common that late insomnia. Any weight loss is less than 3–4 kg, and weight gain from 'comfort' eating is much more common than in the major illness. Noise intolerance, irritability, querulous hypochondriasis and uneasy apathy are characteristic. Tears flow more freely than in the major disorder. Guilt is not marked and suicidal tendencies are small. There is far more reactivity than in major depression—the patient can be 'bucked up' or 'taken out of (him)herself', but sooner rather than later the dysthymic tendency will reassert itself.

Major and minor depressive illness are endogenous illnesses, and though up to a point understandable as reactions to distressing life-events (Murphy, 1982) differ qualitatively from purely reactive depression. Reactive depression is the normal reaction to a grievous circumstance, and only comes to medical attention when the loss is very profound or the loser's tolerance is especially low. It is deemed to be wholly comprehensible in terms of the misfortune which occasioned it, being closely related in time (within hours or days), perceived by the sufferer as due to that loss and varying in intensity according to how keenly that the deprivation is felt; distraction can relieve the distress, and time is a great healer. Pharmacological measures in management are less appropriate than psychological help to 'work through' the distressing feelings about the lost object, whereas medication is a mainstay of the treatment of major and even minor depressive illness.

ENDOGENOUS DEPRESSION IN THE ELDERLY

Clinically it may be helpful to classify endogenous depression in the elderly not only as mild, moderate or severe, but also as agitated or retarded.

Severe agitated depression in old age has an importunate quality which may arouse concern or irritation in the beholder. If there are delusions the diagnosis of a serious mental illness is unlikely to be missed, but if hypochondria, exaggerated helplessness and 'attention seeking' are to the fore, there may be the misleading suspicion that the condition is largely simulated for some obscure purpose, probably as retaliation at someone or to manipulate more intensive care. Such a diagnostic error may prove embarrassing to the doctor and fatal to the patient!

The classical late life depressive illness was thought to be involutional melancholia (Stenstedt, 1959). The features of a severe agitated depression, with an extravagant, even histrionic quality and extreme nihilistic hypochondriacal delusions (Cotard's syndrome), in which the intestines are thought to be completely blocked or the insides are rotted away, are indeed encountered more commonly in older than younger patients, but not exclusively. The almost boisterous quality of such a presentation is sometimes explicable by a mixture of mania with melancholia. Mixed affective states—'miserable mania' or manic misery, in which actual flights of ideas have a generally melancholy theme—are not exceptional in the elderly.

In severe retarded depression, speech may be delayed so that to answer a simple question can take more than a minute, or reduced to the point of total silence. Movements may be slowed to the point of immobility and stupor (akinetic mutism) with refusal of food or fluids. This retarded state may not be recognised as a serious illness demanding urgent treatment. The picture is consistent with the old-time physician's concept of turning the face to the wall, and may be managed as if the patient's evident wish to die should be respected. The patient may indeed look and become so ill that the administration of electroconvulsion therapy (ECT) may seem like kicking a corpse, yet this is often the means whereby not only may the life be saved but mental health restored.

Mild to moderate retarded depression, in which the patient is withdrawn, inert, apathetic and peevish, is so like the stereotype of 'crabbed age' that it may readily be regarded as part of the spectrum of normal ageing. Mild to moderate agitated depression is the same as the neurotic or atypical depression described above.

HYPOCHONDRIASIS

One feature which older depressives show so much more than younger patients that it may, perhaps, be regarded as characteristic, is hypochondria. When this is as florid as in involutional melancholia there can at least be no doubt that there is a mental illness, if some uncertainty about which one. Hypochondria in the setting of mild to moderate agitated depression, however, readily misleads and perplexes the unwary diagnostician. The expectation that older patients may have diverse physical ills means that these are considered first as the cause of the somatic complaints with which most elderly patients present, and pains are taken to exclude them. This is not necessarily bad practice, but the high morbidity of the elderly for depression needs also to be recognised; undue delay in starting treatment worsens the prognosis.

De Alarcon (1964) found hypochondria in just under two-thirds of depressed elderly patients admitted to the Bethlem Hospital. The main complaints concerned the bowels. Hypochondria was the first manifestation in 30% of the patients, preceding overt depression by two to three months. In only 20% of those with hypochondria was it a previous personality trait. There was an association between hypochondria and attempted suicide: one-quarter of those who were hypochondriacal tried to kill themselves, compared with 7% of those who were not. Gurland (1976) compared older and younger depressives using the Present Mental State examination. The only significant difference was the more frequent somatic (hypochondriacal) colouring to the older patients' mental state.

Zemore and Eames (1979) used the Beck scale to compare depressive symptoms in old people resident in homes or waiting to go in to those in young adults, drawn from first year psychology students. While the elderly had no more affective or cognitive symptoms than the young, they did show more somatic symptoms. Murrell *et al.* (1983) found a strong relationship between depression (scores above a cut-off point on a Depression Scale) in a Kentucky community sample over the age of 55 and self-reported physical ill health.

The question then arises whether these somatic symptoms are those of depression or of the various physical disorders to which older subjects are evidently more liable. Such fundamental signs and symptoms as anorexia and weight loss, anergy, malaise, aches, pains, constipation and insomnia have several possible causes other than depression, and their evaluation in the patient who is known to be physically ill but may be depressed too is very difficult. Sometimes they have to be largely discounted, while evidence is sought from the previous personality and history, the mood, thought content and behaviour.

Steuer *et al.* (1980) studied the relationship between depression (measured by the Zung scale), somatic symptoms based on self-reports and health based on medical evaluation in 60 older (median age of 64.5 years) persons in relatively good health. There was a significant relationship between physicians' rating of health, depression scores and a somatic symptom subscale. Items on this included 'My heart beats faster than usual'; 'I get tired for no reason'; 'Mornings are when I feel best'; 'I have trouble sleeping at night'; 'I eat as much as I used to'; 'I still enjoy sex'; 'I notice that I am losing weight'; and 'I have trouble with constipation'. Fatiguability, diurnal variation and enjoyment of sex (i.e. loss thereof) significantly related to both depression and physical health. Otherwise, however, for this relatively healthy group of elderly people who had considered themselves depressed and sought help for that depression (i.e. unlike most depressives in a psychogeriatric practice) somatic symptoms seemed to contribute less to depression than lack of hope, decreased activity, difficulty in doing things, feelings of uselessness, and problems in decision making.

DISTINGUISHING DEPRESSION FROM DEMENTIA

Blazer *et al.* (1985), in a community study, found a prevalence of 4% of major depression and dysthymia in the population aged 35–50 and only 2.8% in those aged over 60. The older patients were more likely to somatise their depression, complaining especially of abdominal and back pain, but headache was as common in each age group. Although the elderly cried less, they felt more helpless. Twice as many older as middle-aged patients complained of sleep difficulty, and four times as many of feeling tired. In neither group was there cognitive impairment, and the elderly did not complain more of difficulty in concentration, but they had more difficulty with short-term memory. Popkin *et al.* (1982) found that while depressed elderly patients in the community complained more of memory problems, their actual performance on tests of immediate and delayed recall did not differ significantly from that of older adults who were not distressed.

This lack of cognitive impairment is in line with clinical experience that most depressed old people referred to a psychiatric service show no deficiencies of intellect or memory which suggest that they may be demented. True, those bogged down in an extremity of guilt or misery may not readily apply themselves to matters of less than obvious urgency such as serial sevens (taking 7 away from 100, 7 from the remainder and so on), the years of the Second World War or learning the address of an unknown gentleman residing somewhere on the South East coast. Agitation is inimical to concentration, and retardation delays responses so that the hasty assessor may assume that the patient does not know the answer when, given time, (s)he might have come up with the right one.

The greatest contribution to the misdiagnosis of depression in old age as dementia, indeed, appears to be the doctors. Psychiatrists, physicians and family practitioners who know little about the manifestations of depression in late life (their number is presumably dwindling) but are aware of how common dementia becomes with ageing may ascribe the abnormal mental state of the depressed to the latter. Likewise, those unaware of the unfortunately often refractory nature of old age depression (Murphy, 1983) may attribute their therapeutic reverses to an underlying dementia. Duckworth and Ross (1975) reported that psychiatrists in the Queens, New York, overdiagnosed organic mental disorder in affectively ill old people, and did so far more than their counterparts in Toronto, and London, England.

PSEUDODEMENTIA

An important minority of elderly depressives do, however, show perplexing cognitive impairment which is very hard to distinguish from that arising from mild to moderate organic dementia. Wells (1979) has devised a checklist to distinguish pseudo from organic dementia by a short rapid course, clear onset, past psychiatric history, the patient's complaints of a poor memory along with other malfunctions and woes, equal impairment of remote and recent memory, a lack of effort on psychological testing, 'don't know' answers and variable performance. Post (1975) remarks that confabulation is a feature of organic, not pseudodementia, and any patient who makes gross errors (such as claiming still to live with parents who are known to be dead) is probably organically demented. Rabins et al. (1984) compared the outcome of depressed, depressed/demented and demented elderly patients. A past history of depression, self-reports of depressed mood, self-blaming, hopeless and somatic delusions, appetite disturbance, acute and subacute onset, differentiated the depressed/demented from the demented group, as did the course over the next two years. Nearly all the depressed/demented group but none of the demented only group were cognitively normal.

The unwary should be warned against being unduly swayed by results of clinical psychological testing much at odds with the patient's performance elsewhere, unless the tester is very experienced in the field; also the finding of 'cortical atrophy' on the computerised axial tomography (CAT) scan by no means alone clinches the diagnosis, and can be another pitfall.

Depression sometimes heralds and quite often accompanies dementia, when it is known as organic depression. Roth (1983) states that this is particularly the case in multi-infarct dementia, one-quarter of patients being so affected. The Hachinski scale (Hachinski et al., 1975) uses depression as one of the features distinguishing multi-infarct from Alzheimer's dementia. However, Knesevich et al. (1983) found depression to be uncommon in patients in whom they diagnosed Alzheimer's disease and Bucht et al. (1984) did not confirm that affective symptoms were more common in multi-infarct patients.

As patients with multi-infarct dementia tend to show more insight and better preservation of personality than those with Alzheimer's disease they might be expected to feel affliction and to demonstrate that feeling more keenly. They are liable to emotionalism, which is sometimes facile but probably more often indicates deep suffering than the term 'mock-turtle syndrome' would suggest, and therefore should not be underestimated. Depressed demented patients can be in a state of continuous agitation, incoherent grief, eat little, lose weight, show diurnal variation of mood and early waking which cause their carers great concern. Sometimes a form of antidepressant therapy can help.

DEPRESSION PRESENTING AS A DISORDER OF BEHAVIOUR

The literature on behaviour disorder in the elderly, whether or not related to depressive illness, is relatively meagre, though it looms large in psychogeriatric practice. The present author therefore will draw mainly on his own clinical experience to describe it. In behaviour disorder associated with depression, one particular manifestation of the depression, sometimes typical, is so exaggerated as to dominate the clinical picture and become the therapist's prime target.

A typical depressive feature which may predominate is anorexia, or, more exactly, food refusal and even regurgitation of what little has been eaten, with consequent alarming weight loss. Similarities to anorexia nervosa (Crisp, 1966) in the young are superficial, although Kellett et al. (1976) have described a post-menopausal anorectic syndrome. The behaviour of the young anorectic resembles that of the older patient and denial (of the extent to which food is being refused) is common to both, though is usually more blatant in the elderly. There is no body image distortion in the elderly, no obvious desire to be thin, and the anorexia is initially secondary to depressive illness. At first it may be linked to the depth of misery, suicidal intent or to hypochondria, but in due course these traditional manifestations of a severe depressive illness—profound melancholy, guilt, sleep disturbance and diurnal variation of mood—fade into the background and the eating disorder predominates. A battle of wills between the patient on the one hand and the family and the therapeutic team on the other is then frequently joined, and seems sometimes relevant to the dynamics of the phenomenon, analogous to the child who will not eat. It cannot be claimed, though, that such a concept often proves more helpful in treatment than antidepressives, tranquillisers, hypoglycaemic agents or ECT. A behavioural approach is generally best rewarded, but even so, many of these patients make little progress, and die of what is euphemistically termed 'inanition' or 'intercurrent infection'.

Incontinence of urine or faeces is not an uncommon association with depression in the elderly. Sometimes it may be a factor in inducing mild or reactive depression in those who feel humiliated by their loss of sphincter control. Depressive apathy and retardation may contribute to 'accidents', and antidepressants, by inducing heavy sleep, constipation or urinary retention (and thereby overflow), may cause a little, sporadic incontinence. Constipation and faecal impaction may be features of depression itself. Sometimes, however, in depressed inpatients, there is a seemingly perverse refusal to eliminate in the right place and a contrary incontinence in what is obviously the wrong place occasionally compounded by faecal smearing, which seems voluntary and purposeful—a form of angry regression—and analogies with enuresis and encopresis in childhood suggest themselves.

A little less common, but still familiar to most psychogeriatricians, are the screaming depressives. These patients alarm their neighbours by their shrieks in the small hours, the time, of course, when major depression is at its worst, which they either disown or acknowledge but seem dissociated from. Such screams, which might be interpreted as a cry for help in someone alone and in anguish, may even persist for a while if the patient is admitted to hospital. Any explanation offered by the patient is, as is usual when such behaviour disorders are discussed, facile, perfunctory and inadequate.

Screaming at least arises comprehensibly from the disinhibited lonely despair of the depressive. Harder to understand in a depressive context are those who scratch, kick or bite the hand which feeds them (usually a nurse). The dynamic view that aggression contributes to depression, that some symptoms may be perceived as anger turned inwards, and that suicide, the ultimate act of aggression towards the self, also hurts those who are left behind gains some support here (Kendell, 1973).

All these behaviour disorders, indeed, seem to attack others where the patient is in a state of perhaps resentful dependency. It may be that certain attitudes of the carers reinforce the disordered behaviour, in which the patient may persist, for example, for the reward of attention, even if this is exasperated! It is noteworthy that staff attention is one of the most effective reinforcers in behaviour therapy programmes for the elderly. There may also be an element of more or less covert spite which thus finds an outlet. It does seem that the institutional setting is productive of behaviour disorder which is a function of the dependency so readily begotten by being in care.

DEPRESSION PRESENTING AS PAIN

Another depressive manifestation which may so dominate the clinical scene as to mask the underlying depression is pain. This may arise from a potentially depressing physical illness such as shingles or a stroke, or be central to deep-seated hypochondria. Typically, the only respite is that afforded by sleep, though the pain may vary diurnally in line with the depressed mood. The history may indicate that the pain initiated in a depressive setting, and then took it over, or that it was present long before but the depression has made it worse, probably by lowering tolerance.

Typically the description of the pain is elaborate but imprecise. Its location is vague, and where the main theme is its persistence aggravating or relieving factors are difficult to determine. Analgesics, tranquillisers and hypnotics are requested even though the patient will not admit that they are beneficial. The pain is complained of almost as a grievance, and is inflicted with some relish on those who must hear about it! Though usually extensively investigated it lacks a convincing 'organic' quality, and the disability it causes is both more and less than its intensity would appear to warrant: the pain-preoccupied patient leads a passive, indolent existence, requiring the assistance of others (especially an attentive spouse) in most daily activities, and yet when it comes to the point there are few, if any, such activities of which (s)he is incapable.

Tinnitus and insomnia are other insistent and persistent complaints which may comparably have a depressive basis. Tinnitus is, of course, symptomatic of an organic disorder, but is both depressing and becomes much less tolerable at times of depression. The subject of insomnia in old age is too vast to be considered here, but again, depression is a not infrequent cause, makes sleeplessness still less tolerable and may become focused on that particular symptom with an urgency which makes the doctor grudgingly prescribe ever stronger hypnotics in ever larger doses. Any chronic physical disorder may be exacerbated and rendered less endurable by the presence of depression (Williamson, 1978). It is then important to recognise that the patient's complaints may require more attention to the mood than to the underlying bodily disease.

It appears that whenever pain, insomnia, tinnitus or behaviour disorder colour the depressive picture the prognosis worsens. However, that is not to say that antidepressive treatment cannot be rewarded in depressive insomnia, and Feinmann et al. (1984) have shown the value of dothiepin in the treatment of psychogenic facial pain.

DEPRESSION PRESENTING AS LONELINESS

Depression in old age may also present as acute loneliness. When an old person who has long been alone and content to be so urgently seeks a place in a home, depression should always be suspected. There may have been an alarming intimation of failing health, like a fall, or failing memory, or a traumatic experience such as a burglary or a mugging, generating a state of anxiety which is quite understandable; but when the complaint is less rational the patient

may be better served by the uncovering and treatment of the underlying depression than a change to communal accommodation which (s)he may soon detest.

DEPRESSION WITH PARANOID IDEAS

Yet another facet of depression in old age is the paranoid. Paraphrenia, the circumscribed paranoid psychosis of the elderly (Kay and Roth, 1961; Post, 1966) generally runs a course true to itself, and is more likely to end in dementia than normal old age. The reaction of most paraphrenics to their imagined persecution is one of robust opposition; some, however, get very nervous and a few very depressed, even to the point of no longer wishing to live. From the history it is clear that the depression is secondary to the paranoia.

Paranoia is sometimes a feature of severe psychotic depression. The usual explanation is that the profoundly guilty patient feels that others must know of his or her misdeeds and go so far as to talk about them, reproach and plan dire punishments. Not infrequently a very depressed and deluded patient suspects that those treating him or her are merely biding their time before bringing in the police, arranging a transfer to a place of torture, or expiation in prison. Here the paranoia can be seen to be in line with and secondary to the deep distribution of mood.

There are two sorts of patients, however, who blur the generally useful and valid distinction between paraphrenia and depressive illness. One is the patient who has bouts of illness, some of which are paraphrenic, others frankly depressive with little or no paranoid content. For example, the present author recalls a lady who was always abrasive, but when paraphrenic blamed her landlord for all her woes, and when depressed was hypochondriacally concerned about her bowels and would irritably dismiss reference to her erstwhile paranoia. Logsdail (1984) has described three cases in which previous affective illnesses were replaced in later life by paranoia.

More common, perhaps, are those whose paranoia evidently develops in the wake of depression but intensifies and persists so that it no longer seems justified by the severity of the mood disorder, but on the contrary is felt to be a merciless over-reaction to misdemeanours, or frankly undeserved persecution. Here it seems as if the depression has precipitated a state of paraphrenia, and treatment is needed for both.

THE BOUNDARY BETWEEN DEPRESSION AND DYSPHORIA

Finally, the question may be asked whether all persistent states of depression in the elderly are to be regarded as cases of depressive illness, or whether an alternative concept such as dysphoria (Gillis and Zabow, 1982) should be invoked, reserving the concept of depressive illness to those for whom psychiatric treatment is indicated, while the dysphoric elderly are likely to be amenable only to fundamental changes in society's attitudes and modes of care. The question is pertinent when considering the findings of Mann *et al.* (1984) who surveyed residents in old people's homes in the London Borough of Camden using the Brief Assessment Schedule, derived from the Geriatric Mental State examination (Copeland *et al.*, 1976) and the CARE (Comprehensive Assessment and Referral Evaluation) (Gurland *et al.*, 1977). They found that no less than one-third of these residents were severely demented, and of the rest 38% were depressed. What is one to make of such a finding? Are depressed old people selectively admitted to old people's homes by social workers who respond thus to their complaints of loneliness and helplessness? Or did the survey turn up a number of disaffected, apathetic, querulous, self-absorbed old people feeling stranded and somewhat stigmatised, with too much time to brood and too little else to do? One is aware of homes where a large proportion of the residents sit with their backs to the wall, saying or doing nothing, jealously guarding their personal space, where inertia appears to reign supreme!

The likelihood is that there are limits to what psychiatry can achieve for the depressed elderly by the means directly at its disposal, rather than advocacy of more choices for old people, more help at home and better institutional care, and that the term dysphoria refers to those whom medication can help least. Care must, however, be taken not to consign gloomy exasperated and perhaps sometimes exasperating old people too readily to a category of 'understandably' depressed and in need of environmental change. Knowing when and when not to prescribe is the art as much as the science of psychogeriatrics, adding to extensive clinical experience and a keen evaluation of the evidence an intuitive insight into how this old person has changed and how much present malfunction may be ascribed to present and continuing environmental stress.

REFERENCES

American Psychiatric Association (1980). *Diagnostic and Statistical Manual of Mental Disorders*, 3rd ed., American Psychiatric Association, Washington, D.C.

Blazer, D.G., and Williams, C.D. (1980).'Epidemiology of dysphoria and depression in an elderly population', *American Journal of Psychiatry*, 439–44.

Blazer, D.G., George, L., Landerman, R., Pennybacker, M., Melville, M.L., Woodbury, M., *et al.* (1985). 'Psychiatric disorders: a rural/urban comparison', *Archives of General Psychiatry*, **42**, 651–6.

Bucht, G., Adolfsson, R., and Winbald, B. (1984).'Dementia of the Alzheimer type and multi-infarct dementia—a clinical description and diagnostic problems', *Journal of American Geriatric Society*, **32**, 491–8.

Copeland, J., Kelleher, M., Duckworth, G., and Smith, A. (1976). 'Rehabilitation of psychiatric assessment in older patients', *International Journal of Aging and Human Development*, **7**(4), 313–22.

Crisp, A. (1966). 'A psychosomatic study of anorexia nervosa: a controlled study of some aspects of the constitution and premorbid feeling of patients', MD Thesis, University of London.

De Alarcon, R.D. (1964). 'Hypochondriasis and depression in the aged', *Gerontology Clinic*, **6**, 266–77.

Duckworth, G.S., Ross, H. (1975). 'Diagnostic differences in psychogeriatric patients in Toronto, New York and London, England', *Canadian Medical Association Journal*, **112**, 847–85.

Feinmann, C., Harris, M., and Cawley, R. (1984). 'Psychogenic facial pain: presentation and treatment', *British Medical Journal*, **288**, 436–8.

Gillis, L.S., and Zabow, A. (1982). 'Dysphoria in the elderly', *South African Medical Journal*, **62**, 410–13.

Gurland, B. (1976). 'The comparative frequency of depression in various adult age groups', *Journal of Gerontology*, **31**, 283–92.

Gurland, B., Copeland, J., Sharpe, L., Kelleher, M., Kuriansky, J., and Simon, R. (1977). 'Assessment of the older person in the community', *International Journal of Aging and Human Development*, **8**, 1–8.

Gurland, B., Copeland, J., Kuriansky, J., Kelleher, M., Sharpe, L., and Dean, L. (1983). *The Mind and Mood of Aging*, Croom Helm, London.

Hachinski, V.C., Iliff, L, Zilhka, E. Du Boulay, R., McAllister, V., Marshall J. *et al.*(1975). 'Cerebral blood flow in dementia', *Archives of Neurology* **32**: 632–637.

Kay, D.W.K., Roth, M. (1961) 'Environmental and hereditary factors in the schizophrenia of old age ('late paraphrenia') and their bearing on the problem of causation in schizophrenia', *Journal of Mental Science* **107**: 649–686.

Kendell, R.E. (1973) 'The relationship between aggression and depression', In Lader M., Garcia R (eds) *Aspects of depression*. WPA.

Kellett, J.M., Trimble, M., Thorley, A.P., 1976 'Anorexia nervosa after menopause', *British Journal of Psychiatry* **128**: 555–558.

Kiloh, L.G. (1961) 'Pseudo-dementia', *Acta Psychiatrica Scandinavica* **37**: 336–351.

Knesevich, J.W., Martin, R.L., Berg, L., Danziger, W. (1983) 'Preliminary report on affective symptoms in the early stages of senile dementia of the Alzheimer type', *American Journal of Psychiatry* **140**: 233–235.

Logsdail, S., (1984) 'Affective illness changing to paranoid state: report on three elderly patients', *British Journal of Psychiatry* **144**: 209–210.

Mann, A.H., Graham, N., Ashby, D. (1984) 'Psychiatric illness in residential homes for the elderly: a survey in one London Borough', *Age and Aging* **13**: 257–265.

Murrell, S.A., Himmelfarb, S., Wright, K. (1983) 'Prevalence of depression and its correlates in older adults', *American Journal of Epidemiology* **11**: 173–185.

Murphy, E. (1982) Social origins of depression in old age, *British Journal of Psychiatry* **141**: 135–142.

Murphy, E. (1983) 'The prognosis of depression in old age', *British Journal of Psychiatry* **142**: 111–119.

Pollitt, J., Young, J. (1971) Anxiety state or masked depression? A study based on the actions of monoamine oxidase inhibitors' *British Journal of Psychiatry* **119**: 143–149.

Popkin, S.J., Gallagher, D., Thompson, L.W., Moore, M. (1982) Memory complaint and performance in normal and depressed older adults, *Experimental Aging and Research* **8**(3–4): 141–145.

Post, F. (1966) *Persistent Persecutory States in the Elderly*, Pergamon Press, London.

Post, F. (1975) Dementia, depression and pseudo-dementia, In Benson, D., Blumer, D.F., (eds) *Depression*. Spectrum Publications Inc., New York.

Rabins, P., Merchant, A., Nestadt, G. (1984) Criteria for diagnosing reversible dementia caused by depression: validation by 2 year follow up, *British Journal of Psychiatry* 488–492.

Roth, M. (1983) 'Depression and affective disorders in later life'. In Anget (ed) *The Origins of Depression: current concepts and approaches*', Springer-Verlag, New York.

Stenstedt, A. (1959) 'Involutional melancholia: an aetiological, clinical and social study of endogenous depression in later life with special reference to genetic factors', *Acta Psychiatrica et Neurologica Scandinavica* **32**: suppl. 127.

Steuer, J., Bank, L., Olsen, E., Jarvik, L. (1980) 'Depression, physical health and somatic complaints in the elderly: a study of the Zung self-rating depression scale', *Journal of Gerontology* **35**: 683–688.

Thielman, S., Blazer, D. (1986) 'Depression and dementia', In Pitt, B. (ed) *Dementia in Old Age*, Churchill Livingstone, Edinburgh.

Wells, C.E. (1979) Pseudo-dementia *American Journal of Psychiatry* **136**: 895–900.

Williamson, J. (1978) 'Depression in the elderly', *Age and Aging*, **7** (suppl.) 35–40.

Williamson, J., Stokoe, I.H., Gray, S., Fish, M., Smith, M., McGhee, *et al.* (1964). 'Old people at home: the unreported needs', *Lancet*, **1**: 1117–1120.

Zemore, R., Eames, N. (1979) 'Psychic and somatic symptoms of depression among young adults, institutionalised aged and non-institutionalised aged', *Journal of Gerontology* **34**: 716–722.

The contribution of psychology to the understanding of senile dementia

TOM KITWOOD

Lecturer, Interdisciplinary Human Studies, University of Bradford

I would like to begin this article with two vignettes from my own recent experience. Both relate to a symposium organized by the Alzheimer's Disease Society in Britain, of which I am member. After a presentation on the aetiology of dementia a discussion developed about one of the most puzzling, yet well-established findings of recent research: that there is a higher prevalence of dementia, in all degrees of severity and throughout the whole age range, in New York than in London (Gurland *et al.*, 1983). Various hypotheses were aired: there might be differences in the metallic content of the water, in atmospheric pollution, in diet, in ethnic (and hence genetic) mix, and so on. No one suggested the possibility that New York might be a more stressful environment than London for those in later life. Had our discussion been about cardiac disorder or diabetes mellitus, this surely would have been raised at least as a possibility. I was reminded of the memorial service for a member of my family, who had practised for many years as a doctor and psychoanalyst in New York, but who had returned to an English village for the last months of her life. Her best friend, herself a New Yorker, had said in her short speech of remembrance: 'New York is a wonderful place in which to live: but it is a terrible place in which to die'.

The other vignette concerns disclosures made to me by a woman to whom I was a total stranger. Her husband had developed a dementing illness. He had been employed for over thirty years in industry; then, when his company began to contract its operations, his job became threatened, and eventually he took early retirement. Apparently he showed no emotional reaction to this, either at the time or later. He then had a year at university, attempting to gain a teaching

qualification. Here he found the work very difficult, although he would not admit it, and eventually he failed. After this he took on some part-time teaching in further education, but in due course he was told he was no longer required. Around this time the older daughter qualified as a doctor, and was preparing for marriage. One day, so my acquaintance told me, she arrived home to find her husband in a totally confused state, which lasted about 24 hours. Soon afterwards he was diagnosed as a case of Alzheimer's disease. It seems that none of the medical professionals gave even the faintest hint that the affliction might be related in some way to his life-experiences; Alzheimer's disease was simply a mysterious and tragic 'bolt from the blue'. My acquaintance, however, had wondered whether there were connections. As she told me the story, I felt that I had heard something like this a number of times before (Kitwood, 1987a).

In certain respects our understanding of dementia is in a state resembling that of cancer some twenty or thirty years ago. At that time the main emphases in research were upon identifying environmental carcinogens, examining the details of cellular change, and so on. Since then the emphasis has changed to some degree, as it has become clear that cancer-formation is linked to a weakening or breakdown of the immune system; the key problem is not so much why cancer cells are produced, as why they are not rejected. Moreover some cancers, at least, appear to be linked both to personality type and to psychosocial stress (Cooper, ed., 1984). In other words, the way is gradually being opened up for viewing cancer as an illness of the person.

We may make distinction, then, between two possible ways of framing human ill-being, whether of body or of mind: the *technical* and the *personal*. Those who adopt a technical approach see illness very much in the way that a mechanic might look at the breakdown of an automobile, or an electronics engineer the malfunction of a computer. Medical science in the West is strongly committed to this approach, which has indeed yielded some remarkable victories. In the case of dementia in old age it holds sway virtually to the exclusion of all other possibilities. The brain is failing: discover, then, precisely what is going wrong, using such natural-scientific disciplines as neurology, biochemistry, virology, pathology and genetics, with the hope of eventually uncovering and controlling the causal process. The point about my two vignettes, of course, is this. It is not that the framing of dementia in personal terms has been 'weighed in the balance and found wanting'; on the contrary, it is not on the official agenda at all. And yet, as we shall see, the findings of neuropathological research themselves point to the need for a complementary psychological understanding. Moreover, the literature shows that promising beginnings were made some years ago; but as research from a technical standpoint gained in momentum, these were either forgotten or ignored.

THE TECHNICAL FRAME

According to geriatric medical science there are several fairly well defined organic diseases which cause dementia in old age, of which two are especially significant. The first (AD) is a condition in which the cerebral grey matter shows clear degenerative changes, including the plaques first identified by Simchowicz and the neurofibrillary tangles identified by Alzheimer early in this century. The second (MID) is associated with the destruction of tissue that follows some form of circulatory failure in the brain (multiple infarction). The two conditions are sometimes, but not always, distinguishable at a clinical level. Authorities vary considerably in their accounts of the relative prevalence. According to a typical report (Albert, 1982), over 50% of senile dementias are of the first type; 10–15% are of the second; another 10–15% are a mixture of both; and the remainder belong to a number of minor categories, relating to metabolic dysfunction, alcoholism, hydrocephalus, tumours, etc. There are also several 'pseudodementias', in which the symptoms are reversible; these are associated with such factors as depression, metabolic imbalance, or the side effects of drugs. In sound clinical practice, of course, the possiblity of pseudodementia must be eliminated before the final diagnosis of an organic dementia can be sustained. MID can often be diagnosed positively. AD tends to be diagnosed by default; it is something of a residual category.

So far as aetiology is concerned, the core of the technical research consists of 50 or so papers, dating from the late 1960s, which deal with the relationship between the state of the brain and the degree of dementia as assessed by clinical judgement and/or psychological testing. These papers are not read by many doctors, let alone those involved in the day-to-day business of geriatric care; indeed, it is likely that they have been scrutinized closely by only a very few persons. Somehow it has come to be assumed widely that they have established beyond all reasonable doubt the case for exclusive neuropathological causation in the 'true' dementias. This, however, is some way from the truth, although of course this work has made an absolutely fundamental contribution to our understanding of the organic basis to these disorders.

Research on the neuropathological correlates of dementia may be divided into several main categories. The 'classical' work consists of observations made on the brains of old people after death, using either macroscopic or histopathological techniques. Another corpus of research is based on computed tomography. This is a sophisticated development from photography using X-rays, where data from successive sections of the brain are reconstructed by a computer. In recent developments the technique has been extended beyond its original use, to include nuclear magnetic resonance and positron emission. The latter looks as if it may prove to be a very powerful tool in due course, since it can give many indications of brain metabolism (Hawkins and Phelps, 1986).

Among the other categories of technical research particular mention must be made of biochemical studies, particularly of neurotransmitter levels; of regional blood flow; and of nerve conduction velocity outside the brain. Only the first two categories will be discussed here. They are complementary, in that they provide evidence about the state of the dead and of the living brain. In their fine detail the findings reported here may not, in the end, prove to be definitive, and some may have been superseded already. The most important point for our purposes, however, is the type of research, and the general approach to the problem of dementia, that they exemplify. For a more detailed discussion, see Kitwood (1987b).

1. Evidence from post-mortem studies

The first major quantitative study of a neuropathological correlate of dementia was that of Blessed, Tomlinson and Roth (1968). Using the very reliable, although not very sensitive, technique of plaque counting, they examined the brains of 60 subjects, 26 of whom had been diagnosed clinically as demented. Very strikingly, they found 'no one kind of pathological change peculiar to the severely demented individuals . . . the differences between the 'senile dements' and other subjects reflect a quantitative gradation of a pathological process common in old age, rather than qualitative differences' (p.805). For the whole group there was a highly significant correlation between the plaque count and degree of dementia as assessed by two tests. This, however, was much reduced for the 'senile dements' alone; only about 16% of the variance could be accounted for. Moreover, if the data are examined in detail, it is apparent that those with a high dementia score are randomly distributed according to plaque count. A parallel set of data for MID are presented by Roth (1980), with correlations and scatter rather similar to those found with dementia of the Alzheimer type. Thus although, in general, dementia is associated with neuropathic change, a very considerable part of the variance remains unexplained.

In two further papers (Tomlinson, Blessed and Roth, 1968, 1970), the same authors report a more detailed examination of the brains of 50 old people who had become demented and of 28 who had remained mentally intact. One of the most remarkable features here, too, was the degree of overlap between the state of the brains of the dements and of the controls. For example, 40% of the dements showed no cerebral atrophy (controls 46%); 28% showed no neurofibrillary change (controls 39%). The most severe neuropathology, however, both Alzheimer type and multi-infarct, was shown only in the brains of the demented persons. Among the dements, two brains were highly anomalous, in that they showed no significant damage of either type.

These are among the foundational studies that have set the tone for many other more detailed investi-

gations. To give but one example, Ball et al. (1985) report their observations on the hippocampal region of the brain and claim that neuropathology here, and here alone, is specific to AD. This hypothesis, however, runs into difficulties. There is considerable variation in the amount of neuropathic change that is associated with dementia; dementia has been shown in some cases without hippocampal damage as detectable by current methods; and most crucially, as Collerton and Fairbairn (1985) have pointed out, the total non-function of the hippocampus results not in dementia but amnesia. In work such as this the loose fit between dementia and neuropathology still remains.

Findings from post-mortem studies certainly suggest that when the degeneration of grey matter has passed beyond certain limits, dementia is the inevitable outcome. To assert this, however, is a very different matter from assigning causation uniquely to neuropathology. The data have shown consistently that the state of the brains of some dements are well within the range of those of the mentally well preserved, and that a psychological condition of dementia can accompany varying degrees and kinds of neuropathic change. This point was emphasized repeatedly in the earlier work of Rothschild. In one paper (Rothschild and Sharpe, 1941), for example, detailed case studies were presented of three persons who were severely demented, but whose brains appeared to be virtually 'normal', and of two who had remained mentally intact despite severe brain damage.

2. Evidence from computerized tomography

Here we will look at a small body of research, based on the scanning of the brains of 50 well-preserved old people, 40 who were assessed clinically as probably demented and 41 who were suffering from an affective disorder, principally depression (Jacoby, Levy and Dawson, 1980; Jacoby and Levy, 1980a, 1980b). The data indicated a slow, age-related process of atrophy in the grey matter of the cortex among all three groups. Although this was significantly greater for the dements, there was considerable overlap with the other two groups. No clear point could be established where the CT measures would unequivocally indicate dementia; depending on the measure, the authors estimated that up to 40% of the subjects might be misclassified. Thus although CT is very useful in screening out other conditions (for example tumours), it is of limited value in the positive diagnosis of dementia. A similar point was made by Wells and Duncan (1977), who report on the way CT has been implicated in the misdiagnosis of this condition.

A reexamination of 27 survivors was carried out after an interval of about 4 years (Bird, Levy and Jacoby, 1986). Taking the group as a whole, no significant changes were found either in the CT measures or in cognitive function. When CT was used to identify a putative dementing subgroup, no significant cognitive differences emerged between these persons and the rest. The authors conclude:

It is important not to place undue significance on cut-off points of dementia; it is now clear that those determined in our earlier studies cannot be used to define a dementing group. . . .Atrophy does not necessarily indicate dementia; the diagnosis must still be made by means of a global clinical assessment (p.83).

Thus if these studies are typical, CT certainly indicates an association between dementia and a degenerative process in the brain, but not the conclusion that dementia is caused exclusively by neuropathic change. The research group whose work we have examined estimates that about 20% of normal old people have enlarged ventricles, and that about 25% of demented persons have ventricles within the normal range. In giving these figures, they point out candidly that workers such as Earnest et al. (1979) find an even greater degree of overlap. In general, then, these findings corroborate those obtained from post-mortem studies, although of course they are far less precise.

Looking at the whole body of work carried out within the technical frame, the key facts relevant to our discussion are as follows:

1. In clinical terms the dementias fall into a small number of overlapping syndromes, only loosely correlated to recognizable neuropathology as identified *post mortem.*
2. The neuropathology can roughly be classified into two main types, Alzheimerian and multi-infarct, although many brains show a mixture of both.
3. the neuropathic changes found in the demented are present, to some degree, in many well-preserved old people.
4. 'Alzheimer's disease' is a very loose category, almost certainly covering several different conditions.
5. A form of neuropathology clearly specific to AD, or to one of its types, has not yet been discovered.
6. Some people become demented with very little accompanying neuropathology. The correlation between degree of dementia and severity of neuropathology for both AD and MID falls far short of a basis for sufficient explanation.
7. There is probably a neuropathological threshold beyond which a demented state is inevitable, although this may vary from person to person.

A certain determinism does seem to be built into the technical frame. For example, the assertion 'the true dementias of old age are irreversible (and hence incurable)' is now immune to falsification. If any condition is found to be reversible it is simply not held to be one of the genuine conditions, organic in the old-fashioned sense. The 'saving of the appearances' is aided by another device, quite commonly used in clinical work. Suppose an old person suffers an accident, or undergoes an operation, or has an extended period away from home, and that thenceforward a process of senile impairment clearly ensues. This is often explained by saying that he or she already 'had' a dementing illness, but that it was 'unmasked' by the critical life events. In ways such as this the possible contribution of psychology to the genesis of dementia tends to be excluded from consideration; as also the existence of a hinterland where dementia might be reversible, that lies en route to the terminal condition.

BRAIN AND MIND IN DEMENTIA

At this point we must face a question that has never been prominent in the work of those who have framed dementia in a technical way: it is the relationship between states of the brain and states of the mind—a relationship that is as important in 'mental sickness' as in 'mental health' (cf. Rose, 1984). If we reject dualism and assume that mental and neurophysiological descriptions refer to the same reality, to talk in psychological terms is never to be dealing with a domain that is mysteriously independent of brain function. To propose that some part might be played by psychological factors in the aetiology of dementia is thus to talk about exceedingly subtle events and states in a way that is readily accessible to experience and investigation, although with less precision than that to which natural science aspires. Moreover, and most crucially, the human being who is the subject of the inquiry can still be regarded a person, even for the purpose of research.

Let us suppose, for a moment, that the correlation between the most powerful neuropathological indices and the most robust measures of dementia approached 1.0; in other words, that all the variance was accounted for. If so, the proximal causation of dementia might be entirely attributable to neuropathology; this, however, would still have to be clearly demonstrated, because correlation does not in itself prove causation. Even then, psychology might be involved in more distal aspects of causation, by analogy with diseases such as cancer (see p. 123). In the case of the senile dementias, however, matters are more complex. The present state of research indicates that some 50% of the variance might be accounted for; although as we have seen, if cases of low dementia and small neuropathic change are excluded, the amount is much smaller. It seems highly improbable that this falling short of 100% is solely due to error variance. Thus psychology seems to be implicated proximally in the causation of dementia, even if it contributes to the distal causation as well. Putting matters in a way that does not do justice to the subtlety of the mind–brain problem, but which accords with a technical mentality, dementia in old age is not only caused by malfunction of the hardware but by faulty software as well.

Perhaps the most crucial question posed by neuropathological research, and which at present it seems unable to answer, is what brings about the change from normal to demented functioning in an individual, granted a certain degree of degeneration of grey matter. It may, of course, be the case that there are obscure pathogens yet to be discovered, or biochemical disturbances too subtle to be monitored by today's techniques, and so on. There seems to be a strong case, however, for the inquiry to include factors of a personal kind. It is irrational to rule them out *a priori*.

THE TECHNICAL FRAME AND THE TAKEN-FOR-GRANTED WORLD

Why, then, has one particular type of approach to dementia achieved such prominence during the last 20 or so years, virtually to the exclusion of all others? Very speculatively, it may be suggested that there has been a convergence of interests in adopting a purely technical frame, and that as research within it has gathered momentum, clearly achieving results, other approaches have come to appear irrelevant or absurd.

Most significantly, perhaps, medicine in the West has increasingly tended to view human illness by analogy with problems in engineering. Moreover, as high technology has become available to medical science, those carrying out research have often been lured by what is 'technically sweet'. Their good faith is not in question here. The point is that their milieu, the world with which they are familiar by training and experience, is one deeply impregnated by technology and natural science, and the objectifying mode that accompanies them. The skills of interpersonal understanding, on the other hand, belong to another milieu, which only a minority of health professionals have entered. The technical framing of dementia, it need hardly be added, has had powerful support from some drug companies, which could then produce specific sedatives and palliatives; and even, in certain instances, complete schedules for the assessment and management of the dementing illnesses. Within the medical profession there are, however, some indications of dissent; for example recently a group of doctors openly rejected the 'medicalization of dementia' at a symposium of the American Gerontological Society (Klass, 1985).

The technical frame is generally adopted, too, by nurses and others who are employed in geriatric care—even if there are times when it conflicts with their more direct intuitions. The majority of carers will have absorbed the standard view without subjecting it to critical appraisal. Also, since their professional life-position is one of subservience and deference to medical authority (Salvage, 1983), there is a very strong pressure on them to continue with taken-for-granted views. But there is a further point. Under the current provision for medical and social services for old people it is virtually impossible for them to engage in a fully personal way with their confused, fearful and sometimes despairing patients. It is often merely a matter of 'managing' their behaviour. The professional carers are not sufficiently resourced themselves, either at an organizational or an individual level, to do more. Thus the technical frame provides a kind of distancing; it helps to make their working life more bearable, and rationalizes the woes that they encounter day by day.

But we must consider also the predicament of relatives and, in some cases, friends. For them, too, the technical frame is helpful, for it enables them to cope with the feelings of grief, anger, fear, guilt and inadequacy in which they are often enveloped. Also, it can give grounds for an apologia, since it is far easier to describe the afflicted person as 'having' Alzheimer's disease or some other condition than to express matters in everyday terms. Moreover, by adopting the technical frame the caretakers are relieved of having to face the immensely threatening possibility that there might have been, and might still be, psychologically malignant processes going on within the family, including even their own relationship to the dementing person. Perhaps this is why the associations of carers contain people for whom the technical frame virtually provides a mythology, and why some of their own written contributions express a touching yet tragic combination of sentiment and subservience to the technical view.

If we move even further onto speculative ground, we come upon another possible reason why the technical frame has come to be accepted so widely. Does it aid a widespread and collusive denial of what is involved in ageing and dying in the modern world, and even perhaps the denial of death itself? The disintegration of the embodied person that we witness as a slow process during a dementing illness is something that will happen to us all. It is liable to activate our deepest forms of *angst*, attached to the ultimate facts of isolation and mortality. In a society such as ours the age of retirement involves, for many people, a disastrous disempowerment through lack of income, work role and mobility; great personal insecurity; a progressive loss of social connections; and possibly an entry into a world where there is little genuine love and understanding. Some of the burdens and losses bear especially heavily on women, who may have spent much of their lives attending to the needs of others, while their own needs were unrecognized or

unfulfilled. Many of these problems arise from the structural position of old people; they are not the necessary accompaniment of the ageing process (Phillipson, 1984).

These are hard truths to face existentially, when the culture makes so great a fetish of youth and beauty, and when social structures are so firmly embedded. To view dementia as a problem in neurological or biochemical engineering provides a small consolation, insulating people from certain deeply disturbing truths which, at some level, they do not wish to know. The technical framing of dementia is a paradigm of the technical framing of the universal facts of ageing and death. There are only very few settings, perhaps most notably some of the hospices for the dying, where the technical frame is genuinely transcended.

TOWARDS A PSYCHOLOGICAL UNDERSTANDING OF DEMENTIA

To consider dementia as an illness of the whole person, rather than merely a disease of the brain is, of course, not a new idea. Some of the relevant literature is reviewed by Gilhooly (1984), who comes to the very proper conclusion that while there may be something of significance here, it is clearly an instance of 'case not proven'. Her discussion, however, is somewhat unsympathetic. In some of this earlier work there is a richness that is lacking in the more precise research carried out within the purely technical frame. It has, however, remained as little more than a collection of fragments, and never been coordinated into a coherent research programme. One reason for this, undoubtedly, is the power, prestige and success of work in medical science such as we have examined. But it is also arguable that the more psychologically oriented research never had a theoretical basis adequate to the task. It required, but lacked, a well-founded concept of the person as an embodied being in a social setting. Thus systematic psychological work in this field has yet to be carried out.

Of course, all that is said from a psychological standpoint must, ultimately, be compatible with the established findings of neurophysiology and neuro-pathology. But the key to a psychological approach that is genuinely personal is that it does not 'stand outside', taking the position of a detached, unaffected observer. Its aim is to work interpretively and empathically, going far beyond the measurement of indices or the codification of behaviour. This involves personal risk for the researcher, for his or her own self-hood becomes involved, engaged, and thereby subjected to all manner of psychodynamic processes such as identification, projection and counter-transference. These are not to be guarded against, but to be used as data. It is on the ground of our own experience in relationship that we can gain some inkling of what is happening to another. Yet when we encounter deep distress we often defend ourselves against it, lest we too should be engulfed.

From a psychological standpoint the more obvious symptoms of dementia, such as impairment of short-term memory, emotional disinhibition, paranoid reactions, and the failure to complete schemata of action, might be understood as aspects of a slow and progressive 'loss of self'. The continuing thread of 'I am' experience, which was first spun together from tiny strands during infancy, becomes disturbed, fades from view, or is fragmented. This is often compounded by fear and bewilderment, because the person lacks sufficient insight to recognize what is happening. If he or she did, this meta-level understanding might itself be a sufficient basis for continuing identity, as in Luria's famous case of the 'man with a shattered world', whose brain had suffered massive damage from a bullet wound (Luria, 1972). Our task, then, is to give a psychological account of this loss of self, and this requires a theory or model of the self that is lost.

Here we need a distinction, conceptualized in various ways in the theories that have arisen from psychoanalysis and psychotherapy. It is between the experiencing, sentient centre (sometimes, but ineptly, called the 'true self') and the self that is formed in everyday interaction, as a person adapts, often without awareness, to existing social reality. Modern social psychology, with its strongly cognitive emphasis, tells us mainly about the latter, showing how a self-concept arises out of processes such as social feedback and social comparison. The experiential self is what many forms of psychotherapy seek to recover, by enabling the person to be more in touch with his or her own organismic life, less subject to the distortions of

experience that are imposed by others. The experiencing self, so depth psychology suggests, develops mainly in contexts where a person is valued, where he or she is attended to with respect, where discourse is available in which sentient experience is accepted, named and shared. To be in touch with this self is to be psychologically healthy, and this would be highly conducive also to physical well-being. The experiencing self is often impaired, obscured, malnourished; how could it be otherwise, when that which would enrich and validate it is largely absent? In some people this self is hidden away, put into cold storage and then forgotten, in the secret hope that one day it will be allowed to grow and flourish. Meanwhile, living in the taken-for-granted world, they exist on the ground of their adapted selves, mistaking this for the true psychic reality. They have a certain kind of stability, but only so long as that world remains intact.

If we view self-hood in this kind of way, a problem area comes into focus. Dementia might be understood, psychologically, as the consequence of the removal of the main cognitive supports that had preserved a person's sense of ontological continuity, even if in an alienated state, through loss of roles, impoverishment of social life, and so on. But not only this; these losses are likely to be far more damaging in those whose experiential self is poorly developed; who cannot genuinely assimilate them, and ward them off by such defences as denial. In short, we might hypothesize that the psychological precondition for dementia is an underdeveloped experiencing self, while the adapted self is seriously undermined. The secret hope of being really understood and validated by another is finally abandoned. All this, of course, has its neurophysiological correlates, and it is not inconceivable that it might have neuropathological consequences as well. These ideas could certainly be related to the two vignettes with which this paper began. The social environment of modern urban America might be regarded as highly 'dementogenic' for those in later life. The case of the man who developed dementia soon after being made redundant seems to be a paradigmatic example of what we have been discussing.

Thus, from what has been found in the more technical research, and from directly psychological considerations, there is a strong case for viewing dementia in personal terms. The technical frame is not likely to deliver anything like the full aetiological picture, despite the power of its research methods and the precision of some, at least, of its results. There are other kinds of inquiry to be made into dementia, grounded in that intersubjective sensitivity that lies at the heart of psychotherapeutic work. Dementia is an existential plight of persons—not simply a problem to be investigated and managed through technical skill.

AUTHOR'S NOTE

I wish to thank the editors of *Free Associations* for their permission to draw on papers of mine which they have already published. These are listed in the references.

REFERENCES

Albert, M.S. (1982). 'Geriatric neuropsychology', *Journal of Consulting and Clinical Psychology*, **49**, 835–50.

Ball, M.J., Blume, W., Fisman, M., Fox, A., Fox, H., Hachinski, V., Kral, V.A., Kirsher, A.J., and Merskey, H. (1985). 'A new definition of Alzheimer's disease: A hippocampal dementia', *Lancet*, 5 January, 14–16.

Bird, J.M., Levy, R., and Jacoby, R.J. (1986). 'Computed tomography in the elderly: changes over time in a normal population', *British Journal of Psychiatry*, **148**, 80–5.

Blessed, G., Tomlinson, B.E., and Roth, M. (1968). 'The association between quantitative measures of dementia and of senile change in the cerebral grey matter of elderly subjects', *British Journal of Psychiatry*, **114**, 797–811.

Collerton, D., and Fairbairn, A. (1985). 'Alzheimer's disease and the hippocampus', *Lancet*, 2 February, 278–9.

Cooper, C.L. (ed.) (1984). *Psychosocial Stress and Cancer*, Wiley, Chichester.

Earnest, M.P., Heaton, R.K., Wilkinson, W.E., and Manke, W.F. (1979). 'Cortical atrophy, ventricular enlargement and intellectual impairment in the aged', *Neurology*, **29**, 1138–43.

Gilhooly, M. (1984). 'The social dimensions of senile dementia'. In I. Hanley and J. Hodge (eds.), *Psychological Approaches to the Care of the Elderly*, Croom Helm, London.

Gurland, B., Copeland, J., Kuriansky, J., Kellever, M., Sharpe, L., and Dean, L.L. (1983). *The Mind and Mood of Ageing*, Croom Helm, Beckenham.

Hawkins, R.A., and Phelps, M.E. (1986). 'Positron emission tomography for evaluation of cerebral function', *Current Concepts in Diagnostic Nuclear Medicine*, **3**, 1–13.

Jacoby, R.J., and Levy, R. (1980a). 'Computed tomography in the elderly: 2. Senile dementia: diagnosis and functional impairment', *British Journal of Psychiatry*, **136**, 270–5.

Jacoby, R.J., and Levy, R. (1980b). 'Computed tomography in the elderly: 3. Affective disorder', *British Journal of Psychiatry*, **136**, 270–5.

Jacoby, R.J., Levy, R., and Dawson, J.M. (1980). 'Computed tomography in the elderly: 1. The normal population', *British Journal of Psychiatry*, **136**, 249–55.

Kitwood, T.M. (1987a). 'Dementia and its pathology: in brain, mind or society?', *Free Associations*, **8**, 81–93.

Kitwood, T.M. (1987b). 'Explaining senile dementia: the limits of neuropathological research', *Free Associations*, **10**, 117–40.

Klass, D. (1985). 'Medicalization of dementia: gain or loss?', Gerontological Society of America (unpublished).

Luria, A.R. (1972). *The Man with Shattered World*, Basic Books, New York.

Phillipson, C.(1984). *Capitalism and the Construction of Old Age*, Pluto Press, London.

Rose, S.P.R.(1984). 'Disordered molecules and diseased minds', *Journal of Psychiatric Research*, **18**, 351–60.

Roth, M.(1980). 'Senile dementia and its borderlands'. In J.O. Cole and J.E. Barrett (eds.), *Psychopathology in the Aged*, Raven Press, New York.

Rothschild, D., and Sharpe, M.L. (1941). 'The origin of senile psychoses: neuropathologic factors and factors of a more personal nature', *Diseases of the Nervous System*, **2**, 49–54.

Salvage, J. (1983). *The Politics of Nursing*, Heinemann, London.

Tomlinson, B.E., Blessed, G., and Roth, M. (1968). 'Observations on the brains of non-demented old people', *Journal of Neurological Science*, **7**, 331–6.

Tomlinson, B.E., Blessed, G., and Roth, M. (1970). 'Observations on the brains of demented old people', *Journal of Neurological Science*, **11**, 205–42.

Wells, C.E., and Duncan, G.W. (1977). 'Danger of over-reliance on computerised cranial tomography', *American Journal of Psychiatry*, **134**, 811–13.

Self-awareness in early dementia

ALISON FROGGATT

Lecturer in Sociology, University of Bradford

SOUNDINGS: EXPLORING THE EXPERIENCE OF EARLY DEMENTIA

In this paper I wish to share some explorations of the self-awareness of people experiencing the earliest stages of dementia. In view of the increased prevalence and recognition of these forms of brain failure it is worth considering approaches which may ameliorate the process, or act as a preventive measure. The disease model alone offers insufficient explanation of such disorders. Psychological understanding of the experience may be able to contribute to a fuller knowledge of ways of retaining and reconstructing a sense of self in this context. The self-perceptions of the old people concerned are immensely valuable, so despite research problems this paper suggests ways of increasing our awareness of the early stages from inside dementia.

It is easy to talk somewhat glibly about the loss of the self in people with dementia. 'He's not himself somehow', 'She never used to be like that' are the cries of saddened frustrated relatives. As a social worker these cries of pain hit home, and there is an urge to explore further, to speculate, conceptualize and try to find out more of how people with early dementia perceive themselves, and how they can be helped to retain a sense of themselves. Personal experiences have encouraged me in the search.

Dementia is more than a disease; social and psychological experiences leave their mark upon a sufferer, just as much as any organic changes in the brain. Alzheimer's work has led to his name being associated with static dementia, leaving multi-infarct or arteriosclerotic dementia as the name for fluctuating dementia, affected by changes in the blood supply. The characteristics of the _disease entity_ are memory loss, and impairment of orientation, judgement and abstract reasoning. (Filinson, 1985, p.329). The subjective experience of both kinds of dementia will be considered as particularly in the early stages the differences between the two are less clear cut.

The incidence of dementia was thought to be around 22 per cent of those 85 and over (Health Education Council, 1985). A lower figure was indicated by Ineichen (1987): 'A rule of thumb is suggested: 1% of 65–74, 10% of 75 and over', giving a large increase, 17.2 per cent, in the number of sufferers between 1983 and 2001, with more if the local health district contains a very large elderly population.

Attention is usually drawn to dementia through the distress experienced by carers of those with brain failure. The pain is often about the loss of the person who is stripped down, losing first the higher order functioning and then gradually the lower capacities leading to incontinence, inability to eat when hungry or go to bed when tired. Significantly much research around the experience of dementia focuses on the carers who have an urgent need for support in their care work (Gilhooley, 1984; Levin _et al._, 1984; Gilleard, 1984). At times it seems as though the sufferers are of less importance, for they have caused the alienating exhausting experience the carers are going through. It is part of the incipient ageism in our society that is is easier to identify with the carers than the sufferers. It is rather less painful and frightening too.

The rationale for a fresh empirical enquiry into the experience of early dementia is firstly that there is evidently a dissonance between post-mortem findings in the brain and observed behaviour prior to death. More is going on than can be explained organically. In other circumstances we recognize the holistic interplay of social, psychological and biological factors. Let us explore early dementia in the same light.

Secondly, close observation and discussion with people identified as dementia sufferers show that at least in the early stages they have some insight and awareness of what is happening to them. The person is reachable at that point. Can one continue to reach out and explore the experience? Can the sufferer then bear the pain for longer and retain some hold on the reality of his/her world, and keep his/her mind working, on details of daily life or in reviewing past experience and memories with a sympathetic audience? I want to share what I have gleaned of the subjective experience, before reviewing existing studies and proposing a way to do more research.

THE SUBJECTIVE EXPERIENCE

While it is not easy to give credence to fragmented thought, it is only by listening attentively to the fragments that we can begin to grasp what this experience feels to be about. Is it like being imprisoned in your own mind? Is it like having a TV set in your head with the electricity switched off? To sense that one is 'losing grip mentally', as one woman put it, must be one of the most isolating experiences in life, because as this grip slips, so also does the confidence and capacity to understand and explain to other people what seems to be happening. Memory failure ties in quickly with social isolation. Once neighbours realize the sufferer is forgetting to keep to arrangements, invitations tend to diminish. Precisely because it is so hard to communicate the experience it becomes an invisible one.

From the outside it is very easy to define confusion. To the person concerned it is not confusion but an episodic mixture of forgetfulness over recent events, absentmindedness and internal preoccupations with thoughts and day dreams. There is difficulty in making decisions, even about what to eat or wear, and in relating to people in terms of remembering about their lives and recent events. Unless some effort is made to piece together these kinds of clues about inner realities of people with dementia, all decisions about 'their' future care and treatment will be made by others on their behalf, thus marginalizing and objectifying sufferers even more.

OBSERVING EARLY DEMENTIA

It is important to give careful observation to the dementing processes, for these are happening to people in families who may go through months of puzzlement, trying to piece together and explain what is happening to the affected person (Gubrium and Lynott, 1985). At this early stage it is observable that the activities which are given priority tend to go back to early childhood. For one person it will be the importance of looking after one's clothes or the obsession to keep the place clean and tidy, and for another to save and economize, wrapping 'treasures' up very carefully. Absentmindedness leads to accidents—pans boiling dry, gas left on, unlit. This creates more anxiety in the sufferer, and those around. The combination of a limited insight with engulfing feelings of anxiety, needing constant reassurance is an underlying feature of the person who feels the cognitive self slipping away. A heavy burden is placed on the spouse or carer to provide as much routine and reassurance as possible. People in the earlier stages of brain failure are often embarrassed and caught out by their incapacity, fearful of being scolded, rejected or mocked (Lee, 1981). One achieves more with such a person by warmth and affection, staying with him/her while he/she tries to make sense of the task in hand. But the realities of being a carer do not always allow for that.

People with dementia seem to have difficulty in executing a plan, even in writing a letter or making a shopping list. It requires concentration of effort over time, and it is hard to complete these tasks. Similarly incontinence, a particular trouble, is often less about bladder capacity than about the ability to interpret the signal and translate it into immediate action with foresight and hindsight about the effect of failing to do so.

The social repertoire, one of the skills retained longest, includes politeness, being agreeable to strangers and putting on a good presentation of self. Even where the repertoire is limited to just a few sentences before repetition sets in, this remains true. Thus one needs to know people over time to get beyond the social self. Memory failure can be masked by confabulation or ploys of activity. The wide variation in behaviour with sufferers must surely relate to previous life events, as well as present location. Thus the energetic restless wandering behaviour characteristic of severe dementia is also a characteristic in unresolved grief (Gray and Isaacs, 1979).

Creating and maintaining trust is one of the chief ways of holding on to someone going through this very frightening process. The fluctuating pattern with good days and bad ones shows that steady irreversible decline is somewhat rare and that some behaviour is a response to recent events or anxieties.

EXISTING STUDIES

A misfit between the disease as evidenced in post-mortem findings and the behaviour exhibited by the sufferer has been recognized (Gilleard, 1984, p.17). Kitwood (1987) examined the neuropathological evidence for the disease of dementia and found that more explanation in social and psychological terms was required. He made it clear that this journey of exploration was likely to be painful. But then so is the experience for sufferer, family and friends. A 'disease' explanation is reassuring in that it is socially accept-able: the causes are seen to lie outside the person and the family network. However, the present state of medical knowledge does not hold out any hope of a cure. If by grasping the nettle that personal experience and disposition play a part in the aetiology, we can lessen the rate of decline or maintain more sense of self, then the effort to cope with the pain would be worth while.

Gilleard (1984) showed an understanding of the realities of the dementing process for the sufferer. He differentiated the experience of a mentally handi-capped person with limited cognitive ability who knew who he was, and to which family he belonged, from that of people either with a brain trauma or a head injury, who while affected retain their sense of self, all seen in relation to the person with dementia, for whom the struggle to retain a sense of personal reality produced difficulties. 'This personal reality seems to depend upon the intactness of memory, the ability to continue to interpret the present within the structure of personal experience in the past, and the ability to extend this continuity to one's future intentions' (Gille-ard, 1984, p.20). His view is that the combination of different types of brain impairment, the 'onslaught from all sides', is what makes it impossible for the demented

person to retain a hold on 'orientation and personal integrity'. He drew attention to the 'yet unattended problem of mildly or questionably demented elderly' (Gilleard, 1984, p.41), the focus of this paper.

There is a distinction between the cognitive self which may be affected by memory loss and the experiencing feeling self which may be much less impaired, but hampered by an incapacity to verbalize. Our understanding of this distinction is helped by Epstein (1985) who gives a worked-out exploration of the distinction between the cognitive rational processes and the preconscious processes of experientially based information associated with the experience of emotions, particularly from earlier life. He sees four main motivating forces in which it is necessary to maintain a balance: the pleasure/pain equation, a stable coherent conceptual system, a level of self-esteem and relationships with significant others. Behaviour consists in a balancing act between the three conceptual systems of the unconscious, the preconscious and the conscious, with the latter trying to integrate all three. In practice, our behaviour is as much determined by what *feels* good, and right or bad, as by what we *know* is good or bad. Epstein believes that most balancing-up takes place between the need to maintain a stable conceptual system and one's need to maintain a sense of self-esteem, and this seems to shed some light on the processes of early dementia.

A sense of self, maintained by keeping these motivating forces in balance, seems essential to maintain a hold on the incremental losses of ageing. Circumstances may bring excessive and unmanageable losses which combine with memory failure, leading to low self-esteem, a lost sense of self and thus dementia. Bereavement, change of residence, hospitalization, surgery, day care, institutionalization, further bereave-ments, all combine for more people in later life than we like to admit.

Thus Kitwood (1986) has developed a paradigm for explaining dementia as a triple combination of aspects of a person being involved: the underlying dispositions of character arising from the adaptations the person has made, the significant life events and losses, and the more recent social and psychological events which interact. A person who adopts a pattern of tending to pass around rather than through the middle of feelings may be caught up in life events, death of a spouse, divorce of a daughter, with which the experiencing self is unable to deal. If the adaptive capacity is overstrained and further psychosocial pressures intervene, the person may give up the effort to retain a hold on the sense of self. Memory and information overload are compounded by extreme anxiety leading to withdrawal or confusion.

Anxiety is a feature which occurs in accounts of dementia. Newroth and Newroth (1980) identified fear as a major component of Alzheimer's disease, recurrent and intermittent fear with support needed through these periods. For a sufferer 'the only appropriate response to this increase of fear and anxiety is for others to develop a sensitivity to the reality of his emotional experiences, and his inability to understand the changes that are happening to him' (Newroth and Newroth, 1980, p.6). These feelings were borne out in the interviews which I undertook. Nervous anxious laughter about 'forgetting a lot' masked a good deal of panic.

PROBLEMS OF RESEARCH

There are formidable obstacles to doing qualitative research with people known to be suffering from early dementia, which include ethical methodological and psychological considerations:

1. The underlying morality of asking those who are already mentally precarious about aspects of themselves which it may be painful to contemplate.
2. Gaining access to sufferers can only be through a general practitioner, psychogeriatrician, community psychiatric nurse or social worker.
3. Research probably needs to be conducted by a variety of methods: semi-structured conversations with the sufferer, additional interviews with the key relatives and principal carer, and consulting records (with consents), to build up a psychobiography.
4. Researchers/interviewers need to be experienced and/or trained, as interviews are likely to be emotionally costly. It is painful to see someone confronting their grief at fading faculties, particularly those of mind and memory.
5. Funding may be difficult to obtain, in the light of prevailing ageism and sexism in society. Due to the greater longevity of women, dementia sufferers were thought to be predominantly female, but doubt has been cast on this (Ineichen, 1987). The cost

of institutional care in relation to care in the community (Audit Commission, 1985) should encourage research in ways to keep sufferers active, alert and in touch with themselves as much as possible.
6. Getting consent from the sufferer to talk about his/her life as lived now. If a person witholds consent because of anxiety this must be respected. Building trust, warmth and empathy into the encounter can balance the anxiety for those who do consent.
7. There is reticence about research in this area for fear of increasing anxiety (Gilhooly, 1984). To legitimate that anxiety as being reasonable in the circumstances could be a way of strengthening the person's hold on reality.
8. Interviews with sufferers may need to be relatively short and spaced close together to benefit memory. One social worker realized her client liked a bright/red colour and always wore a red scarf to visit her. That kind of attention to detail is of the essence to the time-consuming qualitative research required.
9. Interviews with relatives may need to be lengthy as they puzzle over the minutiae of observed behaviour, trying instinctively to make sense of it.

INITIAL RESEARCH

An exploratory study was undertaken to test out the feasibility of research in these circumstances and interviews were held with three women already receiving help from a community support programme because they were thought to have symptoms of Alzheimer's disease. Asking each of them how they found life produced different answers.

Mrs D., living with an alert and vigorous husband, a second marriage, said, 'I can't think. My mother would be so upset if she could see me now, part wrong in the head.' Her husband made repeated reassuring comments; 'We don't think so do we, love.' She persisted: 'It's Ken I worry about. Its bad sometimes; I forget. He looks after me. He keeps me in line.'

Exploring with this couple their daily routine, it seemed Mrs D. was often restless; she could no longer even watch television with satisfaction. Of the daily management he said, 'We do things together, I help her with washing, cooking and all.' He found she had peeled a second pan of potatoes one day and exploded, 'You daft creature.' She was so upset and restless following this that he had to lock the doors to keep her in the house that night. He was even more unnerved that the next day she had forgotten the incident. Thus for the supporter there is not only the strain of the continual 24 hour alertness, but the stress of trying not to get annoyed, in order to reduce anxiety and keep the situation manageable.

A lady aged 82, living alone, presented a different picture, living passively. Asked how she was she said, 'I'm not doing so well, I can't get off the sofa,' Her thoughts went round in a small cycle which then repeated. She was concerned about paying the lady upstairs £1 every time she gave a bit of help; another concern was that her son did not visit enough. She seemed to lack insight into the limitations of her life, reliant on a home help giving lunch each day. When she said again 'I'm stalled (bored) lying here on this sofa' I asked 'What would you be doing if you could?' 'Why, seeing to my people of course; I was a home help until I was 72.' Hidden underneath the struggle of daily living was the strong identity of herself as a coping person; given more stimulation through day care earlier in her life she might have been able to build on that identity with reminiscences about the people she used to help.

The third woman aged 78 lived with an alert but physically disabled husband. A recent hospital admission had accelerated her decline, so that she failed to recognize a son who visited from a distance. In the interview she recognized her lack of memory and diverted my attention by offering to make tea, and describing their domestic arrangements in detail. While it was clear her husband played an increasing part domestically, in her own home with his support she was holding her own.

UNDERSTANDING DEMENTIA

These extracts from interviews show the kind of fragments from which our understanding of dementia from the inside must be built; it is of the essence of the problem that no logical coherent subjective account is possible. However, it may be possible to distinguish the response of those who are more severely demented from those who have a fluctuating degree of brain failure, and again from those who have some mental illness. Thus the explanation 'I must lie on this sofa' as above is presented as a mandatory command from higher authority; someone with fluctuating dementia might recognize (on a good day) that 'I feel safer on the sofa', rather than stumbling restlessly around the flat. The anxious Mrs D. seemed to demonstrate that her habitual pattern of life-long worry was now focused on her forgetfulness; part of her self recognized that there was a problem in not being able to remember.

In a different example of insight from a mentally ill old lady for whom a diagnosis of dementia was not yet confirmed in hospital, she said to the social worker, 'I'm so terrified I cannot think clearly or get my words right. Are you another one they have sent to stop me going home, and because I'm so confused I can't get my words out to defend myself?' This comment showed much more self-awareness of the pressures the person was under in grappling with confusion amongst other difficulties.

A person with severe dementia is much less likely to be anxious about the impact of her behaviour and may well be euphoric, responding to strangers and close family in incongruent ways. Research could usefully explore the differential impact of institutionalization on a person with early dementia. In addition one needs to understand the significance of the general experience, as with bereavement, in order to particularize the different response and experience of a person with dementia. Admission to hospital or residential home is initially disorientating and deskilling; for a sufferer who has an insecure memory this effect is magnified.

The importance of the experiencing feeling self must also be borne in mind. The very act of listening to the anxieties expressed enlarges our vision of the pain experienced, and simultaneously gives validity and value to the person experiencing the self vanishing. That person is not always anxious; moments of joy, apppreciation and contentment can be shared with a friend or confidante. Dementia is not fast killing, nor as demonstrated all encompassing, in the early stages, although the complete loss of a loved person, bit by bit is seen as the present likely outcome. Could that outcome be postponed by working to retain a person's sense of self, by maintaining physical mental and emotional health around the cognitive impairment? A totally protective environment may not be the answer. It can be positive to ask the sufferer to go on taking risks, facing up to new experiences and to cope with anxiety, given support. Groups for sufferers could be supportive, too, given the tendency noted earlier for groups to focus on carers.

In this paper I have tried to exemplify ways of understanding dementing people within a cognitive and psychosocial framework, using sensitive observation, speculation and conceptualization. As dementia comes to be more widely recognized as a partial response to adverse circumstances and experience and not solely as an incurable disease, further research of this kind will be necessary. It would also be interesting to see further exploration of the effect of strongly held religious or ideological beliefs, and of the presence of close affectionate relatives, or a confidante, on maintaining the self. Disentangling these different aspects would require careful assessment with imaginative lateral thinking and feeling from the researcher, such as is also required in work with people with severe deafness, or severe mental handicap, or other communication difficulties. Meanwhile, carers, supporters and professionals can reach out to strengthen with affection and respect the often frightened and struggling person with early dementia.

ACKNOWLEDGEMENTS

I wish to thank David Froggatt, Tom Kitwood, Barbara McCabe and Margaret Mathieson, and the people with whom conversations were held, for help in many different ways with this paper.

REFERENCES

Audit Commission (1985). *Managing Social Services for the Elderly More Effectively*, HMSO, London.

Epstein, S. (1985). 'The implications of cognitive-experiential self-theory for research in social psychology and personality', *Journal for Theory of Social Behaviour*, **15**, 3.

Filinson, R. (1985). 'Chronic illness and care provision—a study of Alzheimer's disease'. In W.A. Peterson and J. Quadagno (eds.), *Social Bonds in Later Life*, Sage Publications, California.

Gilhooly, M. (1984). 'The social dimensions of senile dementia'. In I. Hanley and J. Hodge, *Psychological Approaches to the Care of the Elderly*, Croom Helm, London.

Gilleard, C. (1984). *Living with Dementia*, Croom Helm, London.

Gray, B., and Isaacs, B. (1979). *Care of the Elderly Mentally Infirm*, Tavistock Publications, London.

Gubrium, J.F. and Lynott, R.J. (1985) 'Alzheimer's disease as biographical work'. In W.J. Peterson and J. Quadagno (eds.), *Social Bonds in Later Life*, Sage Publications, California.

Health Education Council (1985). *Who Cares*, HEC, London.

Ineichen, B. (1987). 'Measuring the rising tide', *British Journal of Psychiatry*, **150**, 193–200.

Kitwood, T. (1986). Review article of *Another Name for Madness*, M. Roach, in *Free Associations*, **8**.

Kitwood, T. (1987). 'Explaining senile dementia: the limits of neuropathological research', *Free Associations*, **10** (in press).

Lee, J.A. (1981). 'Human relatedness and the mentally impaired older person', *Journal of Gerontological Social Work*, **4**, 2.

Levin, E., *et al.* (1984). *The Supporters of Confused Elderly Persons at Home*, National Institute of Social Work, London.

Newroth, A., and Newroth S. (1980). *Coping with Alzheimer's Disease*, National Institute for Mental Retardation, Downsview, Ontario.

Norman, A. (1982). *Mental Illness in Old Age*, Policy Studies in Ageing No. 1, Centre for Policy on Ageing, London.

Section IV

Assessment of mental health in older people

Biographical influences on mental health in old age

MALCOLM JOHNSON

Professor of Health and Social Welfare, The Open University

It ought to be lovely to be old to be full of the peace that comes of experiences and wrinkled ripe fulfillment. . . .
And a young man should think: By Jove, my father has faced all weathers, but its been a life!

D. H. Lawrence

INTRODUCTION

It was fashionable for a time to repeat the adage 'we are what we eat' as an injunction to 'healthy eating' resulting in greater physical health. Like many such claims it contains more than a morsel of truth. But whatever we eat we are what we have experienced. Whether it be a high fibre and low cholesterol diet or one oozing with fats and sweets, bodily fuel forms only one element in the totality of life. Individuals can be classified by their occupation, gender, class, intelligence, beauty or height, but none of these characteristics encapsulates the whole person. The essence of our being is rooted in the way we have lived our lives and conducted ourselves in the world.

Recognition of the importance of life history is easy to come by, but it is found more readily in the world of the arts than in the realm of scientific study. In everyday life there is an endless fascination with other people's lives. Much of what is reported in the popular press concerns the private lives and personal backgrounds of public figures. Television and radio thrive on factual and fictional accounts of how people, groups and communities cope with the exigencies of life, focusing on 'the human interest' of personal struggle, success and failure. Biography is one of the most popular genre of literature. The desire to look into other people's lives and to contrast them with our own is an eternal feature of human social life. Indeed, it is a powerful mechanism for social cohesion and cultural transmission. The way in which societies establish norms of behaviour and notions of what is healthy derives from a perpetual process of mutual observation, judgement and response.

Just as societies are constantly analysing current events in terms of their history, so individuals are in a state of lifelong self-reflection and reassessment of who they are and where they are going.[1] The universality of these two related processes led Ralph Waldo Emerson to observe 'There is properly no history; only biography'. Just as Marx argues that all capital is merely an artefact of labour, so too it can be seen that the tide of human affairs is no more than the sum of its biographical parts.[2]

Despite the pervasiveness of interest in life experience and the passage from birth to the grave, the social and biological sciences have not seen fit to give serious attention to the matter. For understandable reasons scientific study has had to be cut into manageable portions, but it is interesting that these divisions tend to militate against any appreciation of the subjective lifetime experience of individuals. The biological sciences which feed medicine attend to bodily subsystems, their functioning and pathology. Similarly, the medical specialities which determine the shape of both knowledge and practice are either functional (e.g. urogenitary, cardiology) or related to particular characteristics like age (paediatrics) or gender (obstetrics). As a result our knowledge of the social, psychological and physical processes which interact throughout normal life expectancy has been segregated into 'developmental stages'—early childhood, childhood and adolescence, early adulthood, middle age, old age.[3,4]

If we are to fully understand the needs, preoccupations, aspirations and maladies which occur in later life it is essential that the biographical context is part of the analysis. This is no more self-evident than in the diagnosis, treatment and amelioration of mental illness, influenced as it is by the peculiar shape of knowledge about ageing and psychological well-being.

THE KNOWLEDGE MAP OF AGEING

The last fifteen years has seen a noticeable shift, particularly within the study of ageing, towards a lifespan approach in psychology and to the broad acceptance of biographical approaches in sociology. Psychologists had for many decades built an elaborate body of research data which depicted later life as one of unrelieved decline. Memory, cognition, learning and creativity all showed a downward path. Intellectual functioning was described as progressively decremental throughout life after a peak in the early twenties.[5]

The work of Shaie, Baltes and Nesselroade[6-8] from the early 1970s undermined this view by demonstrating that prior studies used inappropriate research designs and failed to take account of significant intervening variables related to education levels, cohort and cultural differences. In short, the attempts by earlier researchers to decontextualize assessments of intellectual ability were seriously flawed.[9] Scientifically proper comparisons would only be made taking into account biographical factors and making judgements within groups of individuals whose life experiences were similar in most significant respects.

As a consequence of this reorientation, psychologists of ageing consistently report remarkable stability in intellectual performance within identified groupings over time, where age is an unimportant variable. But significant and sustained differences are found at all ages between groups like scientists, lawyers, teachers and artisans who have different *levels* of education and different *patterns* of problem solving. Similarly older people perform less well, across the board, than young people in dealing with intellectual tasks which are recent in origin and have no part in their established repertoire of skills. It is inevitable that older people unfamiliar with modern technology and the language associated with it will display poor command of its content; but this must not be seen as a decrement of capacity.

Lifespan psychology has provided a less degenerative picture of later life, but not one which denies the observable deficits which come mostly in the late stages of old age. On the present evidence it seems prudent to accept Labouvie-Vief's view[9] that there is stability then gradual decline within the elderly population, but precipitous individual decline in the short period before death. This dramatic loss of ability is usually associated with severe physical disability or the acute phase of life-threatening diseases. This is a view also propounded by Fries and Crapo,[10] whose notion of the 'rectangular curve' presents a graph of extended survival, where major incapacity and heavy claim on helping services is largely confined to the final three years of life.

Psychology has a century-old tradition of psychoanalysis which is rooted in the prompted telling of life stories. Indeed, a range of investigative methods and treatments have grown up which acknowledge and build upon the therapeutic value of biographical accounting. Out of the psychoanalytic schools created by Freud and Jung have developed well-established practitioner and lay 'talking therapies': Included amongst these would be counselling in its many forms and the co-counselling methods. A great deal of standard psychiatric assessment is grounded in life review.[11] For all of these styles of helping, there are two fundamental ingredients. One is the unfolding of a person's personal past to an interested stranger. The other is the role of sympathetic and intelligent listener. Simply talking about oneself even in the absence of response can be gratifying, but awareness of a concerned and interested (but uninvolved) audience is vital. In some of these situations the 'audience' is consciously no more than an alert and active listener. In others the 'audience' may engage in detailed exploratory questioning, interpretation and advice giving.[12-14] The act of autobiography can therefore be one of self-recreation or a tool to be used by helpers. Psychology and psychiatry have places and procedures for both.

In common with other disciplines, sociology in this century has balkanized the study of personal and corporate life experience. Specialisms have flourished in the analysis of social class differences, gender, urban and rural dwelling, education, work, health, the family, etc. More recently we have seen a focus on particular sets of activities: the sociology of . . . science, law, deviance, leisure, religion and many others. This construction of the sociology of knowledge has served to illuminate areas and territories of social existence whilst putting the total lifetime experience into shadow. Despite this tendency there is a robust if somewhat neglected sociological tradition which is not only in the listening mode, but takes the lifespan as the unit of analysis.

It was through the monumental work, *The Polish Peasant in Europe and America*, published 1918–20, by W. I. Thomas and Florian Znaniecki[15] that 'human documentary accounts' research made its appearance. Based not only on oral statements, but also on letters, diaries, essays, photographs and memorabilia, this form of study was concerned with the reconstruction of the life lived. These stories did not seek to deny that there were such structural entities as class or community, but to indicate that these structures are human artefacts which rely upon social recognition and interaction with individuals to have continuing existence.

In the early 1970s a number of social scientists and historians in the United States and northern Europe, influenced by the interpretive studies of Erving Goffman, Howard Becker, Anselm Strauss and others, rediscovered biographical research. They were largely motivated by an unease with the hard positivism of the survey tradition of social enquiry and the abstraction of the grand theory of Parsons, Merton and their successors. As a contributor to that emergent literature, in an essay about the assessment of need in old age I wrote:

So far we have talked of studies which set universal standards on such dimensions as health, income, housing etc and result in bad decisions about need. These decisions are bad in the sense that they are meant to result in an increased life satisfaction for the receiving party and often fail to do so. They are also bad at another level. They take little or no account of the individual's personal assessment and concentrate on decision making, based upon immediately *observable* and *present* features of his or her life. Such an approach denies the historical roots of personal 'needs' and implies an unrealistic homogeneity in the face of knowledge that as they get older they become more idiosyncratic.[16]

These observations remain largely true more than a dozen years after they were written. Yet there are signs of change both in the intellectual landscape which provides a backdrop to personal and cultural conceptions of old age and in the field of practice. In the intervening period the work of Daniel Bertaux[17] in studying the social experiences of French bakers, Glen Elder[18] on Americans in the Great Depression, Martin Kohli[19] on the compulsorily early retired in Western Germany and Xavier Gaullier[20] on their counterparts in France have contributed to a new articulation of what can be considered as *normal ageing*. Through this interpretation of reminiscence as a *normal* feature of everyday life Peter Coleman[21] has taken this biographical understanding into the realm of clinical practice. Mary Marshall[22] has carried out a similar task in demonstrating the need for biographical listening and action planning by social workers with elderly clients.

What can be distilled from recent life history research may be briefly categorized as follows: (1) those who listen to the life stories of older people whom they wish to help gain markedly different pictures of the needful person, from those who administer traditional assessment techniques; (2) self-esteem can be greatly enhanced by skilful encouragement of reminiscence; (3) the way people cope with the multiple losses associated with later life is directly dependent on earlier preparatory experiences and on the remaining core of valued relationships, statuses and activities; (4) that joint or corporate life story telling for the purposes of generating oral history can be both intrinsically satisfying and of importance in reestablishing self-confidence. Hence it is widely incorporated into reality orientation programmes in hospitals and residential homes.

Here we can see the relevance of biographical work in relation to mental health and illness.

LIFE HISTORY AND MENTAL WELL-BEING

Like fingerprints, life histories are individual and unique. They are influenced by the common experiences of their cohort contemporaries (the present group of over 75s shares the trauma and excitement of two world wars) and the prevailing pressures of culture, fashion, politics and social order. Yet within this framework of external structures, each life is significantly different from all others. When 'helpers' enter the lives of elderly people to 'deal with' behavioural changes which might be represented as disorders, it is this uniqueness which must provide the backcloth to assessment and assistance.

Very often, the prescribed course of action involves additional support from kin or neighbours. Where there is a history of fractured relationships this will not prove to be either workable or therapeutic. More positively biographical accounts can identify important strands of activity which can be used in a positive fashion. For one older lady in Leeds, the preparation of food for others had been central to all her significant relationships. Harnessing this talent and need was the route back to self-esteem. Another 85 year old woman with delusions about her house being likely to fall or burn down, was overtired and undernourished. She had been regularly subsidizing her married daughter's family from her only income source, the old age pension. Another suffering from endogenous depression, low self-esteem and an acute sense of relative deprivation, had been an only daughter with nine brothers. From early childhood she had been expected to serve the needs of her brothers and father and was denied opportunities for education and employment. The burden of caring for her father until he was 90 built up a resentment which was nurtured by the greater prosperity of her brothers.

Mental well-being is most likely to occur when the pattern of values, relationships, activities, home living arrangements and self-image, built up prior to and during mid-life, can be sustained into retirement and later life. However idiosyncratic this configuration might be it represents what is normal for that individual. It is the tried and tested product of more than six decades of trying at life. Within it there will be elements of failure and guilt as well as achievement and success. What characterizes successful ageing is the ability to create continuity and the avoidance or management of assaults on personal stability. Alas such challenges are plentiful in the third age.

Physical ill health has a profound impact on mental health, for it represents a constant threat to continuity. Chronic illnesses of a disabling sort, like arthritis or heart disease, are often the cause of abandonment of long-established patterns. Such 'losses' are just as likely as events like bereavement and retirement to cause acute depression and behavioural deterioration. As depression is the epidemic condition of old age, it is the most common cause of deterioration. Treatment only of the symptoms in isolation from concern with the significance of the loss and the understandable nature of the response will provide no more than medicated suffering. Replacement or acceptable substitution of lost relationships or opportunities for personal development may not be possible, but attempts to replenish the stock of biographically valued activities will be of more value than biochemical interventions which at best can only provide changes of mood. As Brown and Harris[23] demonstrated so convincingly in their study of middle-aged women, pharmaceutical preparations alone rarely provide solutions to depression. In the later stages of life multiple strategies are equally important.

Confusional states are a common consequence of life events, episodes of illness, poor nutrition, excessive cold, death of a pet and falls alike. Psychological equilibrium can be disturbed by a wide range of happenings, some of which may appear trivial. Further examination usually uncovers a lowering of morale and loss of self-confidence based upon subjective estimates of decline. The 'It's because of my age' response is the culturally transmitted formulation of a widespread misunderstanding of intellectual decline with age, which professionals all too often reinforce. Thus personal uncertainty is amplified and reinforced. Moreover, the associated confusion is seen not as a reasonable reaction, but as confirmation of incipient dementia. Yet so often the precipitating events, when seen in a biographical context, can be appreciated as challenges to self-identity and ego strength. The professional response should then be one of empathetic remediation of a treatable circumstance. The context of diagnosis must begin with the subjective interpretation.

Even when organic brain disease is the cause of behavioural disorder, there is a place for biographically based therapy. Coleman[21] points out that not all older people find reminiscence profitable and some find it only leads to distress; but for most it has therapeutic properties. Woods and Britton[24] report the value of personality and identity reconstruction through rehearsal of central lifetime activity. At a simpler level of skill relearning through reality orientation, the projected model of past performance provides both a goal and a measure of progress.

A further cause of confusion is the challenge of entirely new situations for which life experience has provided no usable equipment. Low levels of education (common in the present group of over 75s most of whom left school at 14) make changes of currency, measurement systems and high technology beyond comprehension. As was signalled earlier, these are biographically associated problems, not signs of intellectual deterioration. The inability to cope is real and problematic, but it is societally caused rather than individually pathological. In this context modern technology is increasingly the provider of solutions to its own challenge. Agencies like Age Concern and Help the Aged have gathered information on a growing range of domestic devices, mobility aids and electronic alarms which can overcome the competence gap.

Others in this volume have written about the spectrum of other mental illnesses which afflict people of all ages and have their cumulative presence in the elderly population. Here it must suffice to draw attention to the impact that long-established mental illnesses such as schizophrenia will have had on earlier life. It will have become part of the past and like any significant element of personal history will have fashioned the current shape of self-expectation, family and other relationships, even income and housing. Such chronic conditions are the most intractable problems in older people, not only because no solutions have been found earlier but because the will and the incentive to respond to new initiatives has atrophied in the light of earlier failure.

This enlargement of existing problems which are carried into old age applies also to people who are problematic to others but not diagnosable as being mentally ill. The experience of ageing may have a benign effect as individuals mature and establish themselves in mid life. But there is little evidence of a similar process in passing into the third age. We carry our portfolio of strengths and weaknesses with us. In short, nice younger people will tend to become nice older people. Those who were cantankerous, intolerant, spiteful, mean, narrow minded, selfish or indolent will continue to be. Without an awareness of these transported traits, the helper may be deceived into treating the manifestations of uncharitable behaviour as signs of mental disorder.

Low income, lack of support services, exclusion from decision-making bodies and the low social valuation of retired people also serve to undermine the competence of elderly people. This reduction in their citizenship which Peter Townsend[25] has called 'struc-tured dependency' has an impact on the mental well-being of the whole population of older people, particularly those in the later age groups beyond 75. Eric Midwinter,[26] in arguing against this ageism, asserts: 'Society must therefore acknowledge both the sameness and the difference of the various human groups. It must accept, for instance, that there might be goodness in frailty and other qualities negatively associated with old age.' Thus there is a broader community mental health message which needs to be set alongside the over-individuated approach we have to mental well-being and disorder.

CONCLUSIONS

It has been argued that a better understanding of the last third of life is emerging from the biological and social sciences. The more realistic and less pathological view which is now being assembled does not take away the illness and disability which is associated with great age, but it does provide a more differentiated and positive picture. A linkage of this body of knowledge with an appreciation of the biographical influences on physical and mental health, it is suggested, would generate better understanding and more effective helping practice.

It is important not to overstate the case. Biographical analysis is not and should not become the only tool of research or practitioner diagnosis. Nonetheless, it has an important role to play in illuminating the whole person who is at the centre of the holistic medical and social care many professionals now strive for.

REFERENCES

1. William Earle, *The Autobiographical Consciousness: A Philosophical Enquiry into Existence*, Quadrangle Books, Chicago, 1972.
2. Leopold Rosenmayr, 'On the social constitution of the life course and of ageing: a multi-disciplinary gerontological perspective', in Manfred Bergener (ed.), *Geropsychiatric Diagnostics and Treatment*, Springer Publishing Co., New York, 1985.
3. Tamara Hareven, 'Life course and ageing in historical perspective', in Tamara Hareven and Kathleen Adams (eds.), *Ageing and Life Course Transitions: An Interdisciplinary Perspective,* Tavistock, London and New York, 1982.

4. Martin, Kohli, *Retirement and the Moral Economy: An Historical Interpretation of the German Case*, Institut fur Soziologie der Freien Universitat Berlin, 1986.

5. J.L. Horn, 'Organisation of data on lifespan development of human abilities, in L.R. Goulet and P. B. Baltes (eds.), *Lifespan Developmental Psychology*, Academic Press, New York, 1970.

6. K.W. Shaie, 'Towards a stage theory of adult development', *International Journal of Ageing and Human Development*, **8**, 129–38 (1977).

7. J.R. Nesselroade, K. Shaie and P.B. Baltes, 'Ontogenic and generational components of structural and qualitative change in adult cognitive behaviour', *Journal of Gerontology*, **27**, 222–8 (1972).

8. P.B. Baltes and K. Shaie, 'On the plasticity of adult and gerontological intelligence: where Horn and Donaldson fail', *American Psychologist*, **31**, 720–5 (1976).

9. Gisela Labouvie-Vief, 'Individual time, social time and intellectual ageing', in T. Hareven and K. Adams (eds.), *Ageing and Life Course Transitions: An Interdisciplinary Perspective*, Tavistock, London and New York, 1982.

10. J.F. Fries and L.M. Crapo, *Vitality and Ageing: Implications of the Rectangular Curve*, W. H. Freeman, San Francisco, 1981.

11. Robert N. Butler, *Why Survive? Being Old in America*, Harper and Row, New York, 1975.

12. Paul Thompson, *The Voice of the Past: Oral History*, Oxford University Press, Oxford, 1978, Chap. 6.

13. Malcolm L. Johnson, *An Ageing Population: Relations and Relationships*, The Open University, Milton Keynes, 1979.

14. Ken Plummer, *Documents of Life*, Allen and Unwin, London, 1983, especially Chap. 5.

15. W.I. Thomas and F. Znaniecki, *The Polish Peasant in Europe and America*, 2 vols, Dover Publications, New York, 1958 (original editions 1918–20).

16. Malcom L. Johnson, 'That was your life: a biographical approach to later life', in J.M.A. Munnichs and W.J.A. van den Heuval (eds.), *Dependency and Interdependency in Old Age*, Martinus Nijhoff, The Hague, 1976. Reprinted in V. Carver and P. Liddiard (eds.), *An Ageing Population*, Hodder and Stoughton, London, 1979.

17. Daniel Bertaux (ed.), *Biography and Society: The Life History Approach in the Social Sciences*, Sage, Beverly Hills, 1981.

18. Glen Elder, *Children of the Great Depression: Social Change in Life Experience*, University of Chicago Press, Chicago, 1974.

19. Martin Kohli, 'Expectations towards a sociology of the life course', in M. Kohli (ed.), *Sociologie des Lebenslaufs*, Luchterhand, Darmstadt, 1978.

20. Xavier Gaullier, 'Economic crisis and old age—old age policies in France', *Ageing and Society*, **2**(2), (July 1982).

21. Peter Coleman, *Ageing and Reminiscence Processes: Social and Clinical Implications*, Wiley, Chichester, 1986.

22. Mary Marshall, *Social Work and Elderly People*, Allen and Unwin, London, 1984.

23. G.W. Brown and T. Harris, *The Social Origins of Depression: A study of psychiatric disorder in women*, Tavistock, London, 1978.

24. R.T. Woods and P. G. Britton, *Clinical Psychology with the Elderly*, Croom Helm, London, 1985.

25. Peter Townsend, 'The structured dependency of the elderly: creation of social policy in the twentieth century', *Ageing and Society*, **1**(1), March 1981.

26. Eric Midwinter, *Redefining Old Age*, Centre for Policy on Ageing, London, 1987.

Clinical and neuropsychological assessment of dementia

Felicia Huppert* and Elizabeth Tym†

*Department of Psychiatry, University of Cambridge; † Hinchingbrooke Hospital, Huntingdon, Cambridgeshire

While biological methods for investigating dementia have in recent years become increasingly precise and stringent, methods for assessing behavioural change have lagged far behind. This is a serious problem, since the diagnosis of dementia in life relies on evidence of behavioural change, including impairment of cognitive functions, personality and the ability to cope with everyday activities. Crude forms of behavioural assessment may suffice when behavioural changes are gross, but more refined methods are essential for the early detection of dementia, and the measurement of behavioural change over time. [. . .]

PART 1. CLINICAL ASSESSMENT OF DEMENTIA

Dementia is the most serious psychiatric disorder of old age. It is also very common, occurring in about 5% of those over 65 and in 15% of those over 80 years of age. Its clinical manifestations may be widespread and diverse, so that dementia can seldom be omitted from consideration in diagnosing mental illness in old age. [. . .]

Clinical features of Alzheimer's disease

In the first stage, impairment of memory for recent events is usually the prominent feature. Spatial perception and topographical memory decline, and disorientation, especially in time and place, frequently occurs. Impaired concentration and fatigue may be noticed, alongside restlessness and anxiety. Depression, when it occurs, is fleeting and variable, and does not occur without other features of dementia. It is at this stage that an exaggeration or alteration of lifelong personality traits may appear, though it is rarely unaccompanied by obvious manifestations of memory or intellectual deficit.

Gustafson and Nillson[1] and Lauter[2] found some focal neurological deficits occurring early in AD, but these are more prominent in presenile cases where they occur in a setting of relative intellectual cohesion. In the second stage of AD, all aspects of memory fail progressively and expressive dysphasia appears in association with parietal lobe deficits such as dyspraxia and agnosia. Epileptic fits occur in 5–10% of cases. Blunting of emotions and apathy begin to take over the mood state. Judgement and the capacity for abstract thought and calculation have also disappeared by this stage. [. . .]

In the third and final stage, there is gross disturbance of all intellectual functions. There are marked focal neurological deficits, and an increase in muscle tone appears with accompanying slow, wide-based and unsteady gait. There is gross emotional disinhibition, and the former personality becomes submerged. Patients cannot recognize relatives or even their own face in the mirror. They are bedfast and increasingly incapacitated through spasticity and myoclonus. Double incontinence is almost invariable at this stage. There is progressive wasting despite a voracious appetite, but life may continue for one or more years in an almost entirely vegetative state.

Differential diagnosis

Because deterioration of intellect, personality and conation are not unique to dementia, it is necessary to exclude other possible causes of the observed

From British Medical Bulletin, 42(1), 1986 (edited). Reproduced with permission.

changes. Among the elderly, the presence of severe sensory deficits resulting in impaired perception or comprehension often makes diagnosis very difficult. There are a number of other conditions from which dementia needs to be differentiated. [. . .]

Depressive illness. The common occurrence of depressive symptomatology in the elderly may be hard to differentiate from the apathy, loss of initiative and general decline in performance which may be manifest in the early stages of dementia. Conversely, cognitive impairment may be manifest in a depressive illness, leading to the diagnosis of 'pseudodementia'.[3,4] However, in most cases, dementia can be differentiated from depression on the basis of historical information including duration, mode of onset, character of the early symptoms, the variable and uneven nature of the cognitive impairment and a past history of depression.

Acute confusional states Occurring in the elderly, especially when precipitated by chest or urinary tract infection or chronic cardiac disease, these may give rise to difficulty in diagnosis. [. . .]

A history of recent onset (weeks or months), fluctuation in the degree of confusion and clouding of consciousness usually permits a clear diagnosis of acute or subacute confusional state. There may be evidence of preservation of intellect during lucid intervals, and delusions and hallucinations, when present, are more detailed, coherent and well defined than in dementia.[5] However, a hitherto undetected underlying early dementia may be associated with such states.

Once the diagnosis of dementia has been made, it is important to differentiate between different forms of the disorder both for clinical practice and for research where groups need to be as homogeneous as possible. Differentiation is required between the most common forms of dementia, namely AD and multi-infarct dementia (MID).[6] A number of the rarer forms of dementia need also to be differentiated from AD and MID, as do the secondary dementias. In general, cognitive impairment is more patchy and personality better preserved in the secondary dementias than in AD.

Multi-infarct dementia The main features of MID are its abrupt onset, fluctuating course, history of stroke, focal symptoms or signs, and stepwise deterioration. [. . .]

At post mortem, a proportion of the brains of patients dying with dementia show pathological changes that characterize both MID and AD.[7] Thus, an additional category of dementia of dual aetiology has been suggested by a number of workers (e.g. Emerson et al.[8]) [. . .]

Early detection of dementia

As indicated above, it is not an easy task to establish a diagnosis of dementia even when the behavioural changes are well established. The task is even more difficult in the early stage. Impairment of memory, name-finding difficulty and slowing of responses are relatively common and frequently complained of among the healthy elderly. Further, the range of competence within the elderly population is extremely large, thus making the determination of a threshold level of morbidity very difficult. One consequence of this variability has been the overdiagnosis of dementia in persons of limited intelligence or poor education.[9,10] For these reasons, there are as yet no agreed criteria for the diagnosis of mild dementia, and estimates of its prevalence range widely from 2.6% in Britain to 52.7% in Japan in community residents aged 65 and over. [. . .]

Progress towards early detection is needed to understand the natural history of the disorder, to ensure early intervention to avert crises, sustain viability within the community, and to introduce potential pharmacological treatments at a stage when they are most likely to prove effective. [. . .]

Establishing a diagnosis

The diagnosis of dementia and a judgement regarding the type of dementia must be based largely on clinical findings supported by appropriate radiological and laboratory investigations. Assessments of many of the clinical features and information pertaining to the development of the disorder and the record of previous illness require evidence from an informant, usually a close relative.

The following steps have to be taken to establish a diagnosis of dementia:

1. A history as full as possible needs to be obtained from the patient. In addition, an informant should give an account of the patient's premorbid intellectual attainments, personality and social functioning as well as current behaviour patterns and competence. [. . .]
2. Systematic examination of mental state, which should comprise both an objective examination of cognitive functions and draw upon a wide range of observations including appearance, demeanour, mood, speech, thought content and perceptual disturbance.
3. A physical examination to include blood pressure, CNS examination, examination of sight and hearing, and assessment of gait.
4. Laboratory investigations. These will include a full blood count, urea and electrolyte profile, and tests of thyroid and liver function.
5. Radiological investigation. Chest and skull X-rays are routinely undertaken. As far as computerized tomography (CT) scans are concerned, the overlap that exists between measures of cortical atrophy in demented and normal elderly individuals means that the findings must be integrated with the results of clinical observation before a final diagnosis of dementia is made. [. . .]

Standardized diagnostic interviews

Several structured or semi-structured diagnostic interview schedules are currently in wide use.

The Geriatric Mental State (GMS) of Copeland *et al.*[11] [. . .] has been used in the USA/UK diagnostic project for comparing mental disorders in the elderly in New York and London[12] and in other surveys. [. . .]

The GMS has been shown to be effective in the discrimination of organic brain syndromes from functional psychiatric disorders but it does not provide a differential diagnosis between MID, senile dementias of Alzheimer type (SDAT) and confusional states.

The Comprehensive Assessment and Referral Evaluation (CARE) of Gurland *et al.*[13] is a long semi-structured interview covering psychiatric symptoms, physical disability and performance in the activities of daily living along with information about nutritional status and economic and social aspects of illness. It incorporates most of the GMS and has been widely used in community surveys. The CARE is reported to be a valuable aid in determining whether an elderly person requires referral to health or social services. An abbreviated form, the SHORT-CARE, is also available.[14] [. . .]

Although these instruments provide a valuable body of systematic information about many features relevant to the diagnosis of dementia, they cannot themselves generate a definitive diagnosis for two fundamental reasons: (i) information concerning past history is either omitted or inadequate; and (ii) there is no provision for the seeking of evidence from an informant. [. . .]

Behaviour rating scales

Once a diagnosis of dementia has been established, there is frequently a need to obtain a more detailed picture of the patient's competence in the activities of daily living including self-care, instrumental tasks and social functioning. A variety of brief behaviour rating scales have been developed specifically for this purpose.

The Crichton Geriatric Behavioural Rating Scale[15] is easy to use and has been employed in clinical trials. The Clifton Assessment Procedure for the Elderly (CAPE)[16] is widely used, particularly in connection with allocation to various types of health and social services facilities. These and many other ward rating scales have been comprehensively reviewed by Hall.[17]

Some scales have been devised for use by relatives and others in the community. One of the most popular is the Instrumental Activities of Daily Living (IADL)[18] and its derivatives which rate performance on using the telephone, shopping, food preparation, housekeeping, laundry, transportation and taking medication.

Grading the severity of dementia

Clinical assessment of dementia should include an estimate of the severity of the disorder, and it is standard practice for clinicians to make a global rating in terms of mild, moderate or severe dementia. A global clinical rating is usually adequate for purposes of prognosis and the counselling of relatives, and correlates well with objective measures of cognitive performance.[19]

However, to improve reliability of severity ratings, and hence comparability between investigators, it is desirable to employ a standardized instrument. The Blessed et al. dementia scale[20] is an early and still widely used instrument for quantitative measurement of deterioration. It examines competence in the practical tasks of everday life and changes in personality, interests and drive based on evidence from an informant. The scale's popularity derives largely from its correlation with plaque counts in the cerebral cortex of elderly demented patients and normal, well-preserved old people.

More recently developed scales have attempted to take account of a wider range of the features of dementia. The Clinical Dementia Rating (CDR) of Hughes et al.[21] rates dementia along a five-point scale (none, questionable, mild, moderate, severe) on the basis of the person's performance in six areas of daily living: memory, orientation, judgment/problem solving, community affairs, home/hobbies, and personal care. Since it is recognized that the different areas of functioning may not be equally impaired, a complicated algorithm has been produced for converting the profile of performance into a single severity rating. A shortcoming is the omission of language or praxis. [. . .]

Although there are many purposes for which it is useful to assign a value to the overall severity of dementia, it is clear that this procedure sacrifices information about the relative impairments which patients manifest in different areas of functioning. In the clinical study of dementia, as outlined above, it is essential to take account of a wide range of information and to rate patients along a number of dimensions. It is hoped that the new generation of assessment instruments will meet this need.

PART 2. ASSESSMENT OF COGNITIVE FUNCTION

Deterioration of cognitive function is a central feature in well-established dementia and forms part of every published set of operational criteria for its diagnosis. [. . .]

Choice of cognitive tests

As cognitive impairment predominates among the features of dementia, some form of cognitive assessment is mandatory when making a diagnosis. The choice of suitable measures depends on two major considerations. First, the purpose of the assessment being made; whether for diagnosis, for devising a management regime, or for measuring change prospectively. Measures appropriate for one purpose may be inappropriate for another. For example, evidence of impaired remote memory may be of great value in arriving at a diagnosis, but have few implications for the patient's management and be insensitive to ongoing change. When recommendation for management is the primary goal of assessment, the measures used must be clearly relevant to the activities of daily living (ADL). When the aim is to measure prospective change in cognitive functions, the most appropriate measures are quantitative ones which yield a wide range of scores and are sensitive to change.

The second consideration is what source of information is most appropriate: patient's self-report, informants' evaluations, clinical observations, rating scales or objective tests. In fairly severe cases of dementia, the clinician will have to rely on evidence from informants to provide background information and on rating scales to assess behavioural change. But often there is a choice. Assessment of ADL for the purpose of management is frequently based on clinical observations or behaviour ratings, but a number of good objective tests have been recently developed, including the Performance of Activities of Daily Living (PADL) test,[22] the Rivermead Behavioural Memory Test[23] and the Cognitive Competency Test.[24] Any source of information can be used as a basis for measuring change, but objective tests are also likely to be the most sensitive, particularly where the time to perform the task is measured as well as its accuracy. It is in this area of measuring change that computerized mental testing is likely to have its greatest impact. Computerized tests are acceptable to the elderly and, when the procedure is simple enough, can be used to good effect even with moderately demented patients.[24]

One type of information which has to be interpreted with particular caution is the patient's self-report of deteriorating mental function. An obvious difficulty is that many patients lack insight or deny their failing abilities. There is also the frequently replicated finding of Kahn et al. [25] that complaints about poor memory are more closely related to depressive symptoms than to poor performance on memory tests. This finding has recently been extended to other areas of cognitive function. Subjects' self-reports of orientation, language, concentration and thinking as well as memory function do not correlate significantly with objective measures of cognitive performance but there is a very high correlation ($p<0.001$) between informants' reports and patients' performance.[19] Therefore, while cognitive complaints may provide useful information about the patient's mood, they are not a trustworthy measure of the individual's competence.

Although cognitive function can, as indicated, be assessed in a variety of ways, there is little doubt that objective measures of performance are likely to be the most valid, reliable and sensitive. The psychometric approach to testing, in which individuals are assigned a number based on their test performance, has given way to an increased interest in analysing the separate functions which together contribute to the test score. In the case of IQ tests such as the Wechsler Adult Intelligence Scale (WAIS), these functions include attention, memory, language, praxis, perception, calculation and abstract thinking. An approach that takes such functions as its principal focus is neurospychological assessment.

Neuropsychological assessment

[. . .] A number of shorter instruments sometimes known as 'dementia scales' have been developed specifically for use with the elderly. They can be usefully employed in population screening for dementia, provided one accepts that they assess cognitive impairment of whatever cause. These brief mental status examinations are usually concerned only with memory and orientation and, having been designed for use with a very impaired population, are insensitive to mild degrees of impairment. Yet evidence is accumulating (see below) that there are subtle impairments across a broad range of cognitive functions even in the early stage of dementia. Assessment should therefore cover a broader range of functions.

A test of wider scope is the Clifton Assessment Scale[16] which, in addition to memory and orientation, samples concentration, reading, writing and psychomotor performance. Even more broadly based is the new Alzheimer's Disease Assessment Scale.[34] It provides good objective measures of most psychological functions, but unaccountably bases assessment of language on the subjective evaluation of the interviewer. An attractive alternative is the Extended Dementia Scale of Hersch[35] which provides a very good coverage of cognitive functions and is well suited for use with moderate to severely demented patients.

One of the more popular instruments for assessing a range of cognitive functions in elderly and demented patients is the Mini Mental State Examination (MMSE) of Folstein et al.[26] Its popularity derives partly from its brevity; it takes only 5–10 minutes to administer. Its value as a screening test for cognitive impairment has recently been established in a number of large community studies. [. . .]

Clearly a test is needed which, while remaining brief, provides an adequate coverage of individual cognitive functions and a sufficient range of scores to ensure that ceiling effects are avoided. An attempt to achieve these objectives has been made in the Cambridge Cognitive Examination, a newly developed mini-neuropsychological investigation which forms part of the CAMDEX[19] and is currently being used in community and patient samples.

The nature of the cognitive deficit

The assessment of cognitive impairments in dementia should take account of two important points: (i) that cognitive functions such as memory and language are not unitary; and (ii) that the deficits which result from diffuse brain damage may not be the same as those resulting from focal brain damage. The implications of these points will be discussed in relation to three selected areas of cognition: memory, language and spatial function.

Memory Memory denotes two broadly different processes: remembering previously acquired information and learning new information. In the early stage of dementia, it is chiefly the learning of new information that is deficient. As the disease progresses, learning becomes increasingly impaired and the retrieval of even very familiar information from the remote past may be affected. [. . .]

Subjects do better when the words are organized in a meaningful way rather than presented at random. Weingartner et al.[36] report that AD patients fail to benefit from such organization in contrast to elderly normal and depressed patients. To the extent that this reflects a general failure to process the semantic or meaningful features of information, poor retention would be expected. Good retention is largely a function of the depth and elaboration of initial encoding.[27] [. . .]

There is abundant evidence[23] that some aspects of the memory performance of healthy elderly people are impaired in comparison with that of young or middle-aged people. Although the term 'benign senescent forgetfulness',[28] has been with us for over 20 years, we still lack data to differentiate between senescent forgetfulness and senile forms of memory loss. Nor have there been follow-up studies using sufficiently sensitive memory tests to confirm that this form of senescent forgetfulness is indeed benign. Since increasing forgetfulness is common in the normal elderly, but not inevitable, there is reason to question whether its presence indicates a benign prognosis.

Language Language is a communication skill involving both the ability to express oneself and to comprehend others in speech as well as in writing. Language can be described in terms of its structure (phonology, syntax) or its meaning (semantics). Advanced dementia is usually associated with a severe impairment of all aspects of language functioning. Most clinical descriptions of moderate dementia regard language impairment as an optional extra. More recently, with the advent of detailed psycholinguistic studies of the language of demented patients, Bayles and other investigators have concluded that some form of language impairment is invariably present in dementia.[30]

Whereas structural features of language may be preserved even in moderately severe cases of dementia, patients lose their knowledge of meaning and reference. Demented patients can recognize and correct morphological and syntactic errors (e.g. 'she lost John book') but even mildly demented patients have difficulty with semantic errors (e.g. 'she lost John's temper'). Detailed prospective studies of language in AD patients[31] show that, in the early stages, the form

of conversational speech is relatively normal with articulation, phrase length and grammar showing little impairment. Neologisms and phonemic substitutions are rare. However, the content of speech is abnormal, with patients showing naming problems and relying on stock phrases. At all stages of the disease, generative naming is more impaired than confrontation naming, and errors tend to be perseverative or semantically related to the target. Aural comprehension is poor. Although reading ability is well preserved, reading comprehension is very poor and disorders of written language are common. All aspects of language become more impaired as the disease progresses, though the rate of deterioration varies for different components, with structural features, repetition of words and simple phrases and reading aloud showing the slowest deterioration. [. . .]

Spatial function It has been known for some time that obvious impairments of drawing, copying, constructional ability, left–right and topographic orientation and perceptual discrimination are a useful prognostic indicator in dementia. [. . .] The use of spatial function tests which are graded in difficulty reveals subtle impairments even among mildly demented patients.[32] [. . .]

Moore and Wyke[33] recently made a detailed analysis of drawing and copying ability in 15 elderly AD patients and compared their performance to that of patients with unilateral focal lesions. [. . .] The characteristic features of the drawings of demented patients were gross impoverishment with essential features omitted, the addition of verbal labels and the small, cramped appearance of the drawings. [. . .]

Implications of neuropsychological findings

In summary, recent evidence from studies of spatial function, language and memory has established that it can no longer be assumed that the cognitive deficits seen in dementia are the same as those in patients with circumscribed focal lesions. Thus, the view that the global deterioration of dementia represents the sum of cognitive deficits associated with focal brain damage, i.e. a 'mosaic' of individual deficits, cannot be retained. [. . .]

It can be seen that neuropsychological assessment,

which provides a functional approach to cognition, has proved fruitful in the study of dementia. By partitioning cognitive functions and examining their subcomponents, a clearer picture has emerged of the intact as well as the impaired aspects of cognitive function.

REFERENCES

1. L. Gustafson and L. Nillson, 'Differential diagnosis of presenile dementia on clinical grounds', *Acta Psychiatr. Scand.*, **65**, 194–209 (1982).

2. H. Lauter, and J.E. Meyer, 'Clinical and nosological concepts of senile dementia'. In C.H. Muller and L. Ciompi (eds), *Senile dementia. Clinical and Therapeutic Aspects*, Huber. Berne, 1968.

3. L.G. Kiloh, 'Pseudodementia', *Acta Psychiatr. Scand.*, **37**, 336–51 (1961).

4. C.E. Wells, 'Pseudodementia', *Am. J. Psychiatry*, **136**, 895–900 (1979).

5. M. Roth, and D. H. Myers, 'The diagnosis of dementia', *Br. J. Hosp. Med.*, **1969** 705–17 (1969).

6. E.H. Liston and A. La Rue, 'Clinical differentiation of primary degenerative and multi-infarct dementia. A critical review of the evidence. Part II: Pathological studies', *Biol. Psychiatry*, **18**, 1467–85 (1983).

7. B.E. Tomlinson, G. Blessed and M. Roth, 'Observations on the brains of demented old people', *J. Neurol. Sci.*, **11**, 205–42 (1970).

8. T.R. Emerson, J.R. Milne, and A.J. Gardner, 'Cardiogenic dementia—a myth', *Lancet*, **2**, 743–44 (1981).

9. B.J. Gurland, 'The borderlands of dementia: the influence of sociocultural characteristics on rates of dementia occurring in the senium'. In N.E. Miller and G.D. Cohen (eds.), 'Clinical aspects of Alzheimer's disease and senile dementia', *Ageing*, **15**, 61–84 (1981).

10. M. Kramer, P.S. German, J.C. Anthony, M. von Korff and E.A. Skinner, 'Patterns of mental disorders among the elderly residents of eastern Baltimore', *J. Am. Geriatr. Soc.*, **33**, 236–45 (1985).

11. J.R.M. Copeland, M. J. Kelleher, J.M. Kellett, *et al.*, 'A semistructured clinical interview for the assessment of diagnosis and mental state in the elderly. The Geriatric Mental State Schedule I. Development and reliability', *Psychol. Med.*, **6**, 439–49 (1976).

12. B.J. Gurland, J.R.M. Copeland, J. Kuriansky, M.J. Kelleher, L. Sharpe and L.L. Dean, 'The mind and mood of ageing: mental health problems of the community elderly in New York and London', Haworth Press, New York, 1983.

13. B. Gurland, J. Kuriansky, L. Sharpe, R. Simon, P. Stiller and P. Birkett, 'The comprehensive assessment and referral evaluation (CARE). Rationale, development and reliability', *Int. J. Aging Hum. Dev.*, **8**(1), 9–42 (1977).

14. B. Gurland, R.R. Golden, J.A. Teresi and J. Challop, 'The SHORT-CARE: an efficient instrument for the assessment of depression, dementia and disability', *J. Gerontol.*, **39**, 166–9 (1984).

15. R.A. Robinson, 'Some problems of clinical trials in elderly people', *Gerontol. Clinica*, **3**, 247–57 (1961).

16. A.H. Pattie and C.J. Gilleard, 'A brief psychogeriatric assessment schedule. Validation against psychiatric diagnosis and discharge from hospital', *Br. J. Psychiatry*, **127**, 489–93 (1975).

17. J.N. Hall, 'Ward rating scales for long-stay patients: a review', *Psychol. Med.*, **10**, 277–88 (1980).

18. M.P. Lawton, and E.M. Brody, 'Assessment of older people: self-maintaining and instrumental activities of daily living', *Gerontologist*, **9**, 179–86 (1969).

19. M. Roth, E. Tym, C.Q. Mountjoy, F.A. Huppert, H. Hendrie, S. Verma and R. Goddard, 'CAMDEX: a standardized instrument for the diagnosis of mental disorder in the elderly with special reference to the early detection of dementia', *Br. J. Psychiatry* 1986, **149**, 698–709.

20. G. Blessed, B.E. Tomlinson and M. Roth, 'The association between quantitative measures of dementia and of senile change in the cerebral grey matter of elderly subjects', *Br. J. Psychiatry*, **114**, 797–811 (1968).

21. C.P. Hughes, L. Berg, W.L. Danziger, L.A. Coben and R. L. Martin, 'A new clinical scale for the staging of dementia', *Br. J. Psychiatry*, **140**, 566–72 (1982).

22. J.B. Kuriansky, B.J. Gurland, J.L. Fleiss and D. Cowan, 'The assessment of self-care capacity in geriatric psychiatric patients by objective and subjective methods', *J. Clin. Psychol.*, **32**, 95–102.

23. B. Wilson, J. Cockburn and A.D. Baddeley, *The Rivermead Behavioural Memory Test*, Thames Valley Test Company, Reading, Berkshire, 1985.

24. P.L. Wang and K.E. Ennis, 'Competency assessment in clinical populations. An introduction to the cognitive competency test'. In Uzzell, B.P., Gross, Y. (eds.), *Clinical Neuropsychology of Intervention*, Kluwer–Nijhoff, Boston, 1986.

25. R.L. Kahn, S.H. Zarit, N.M. Hilbert and G.M. Niederehe, 'Memory complaint and impairment in the aged', *Arch. Gen. Psychiatry*, **32**, 1569–73 (1975).

26. M.F. Folstein, S.E. Folstein and P.R. McHugh, '"Mini-Mental State". A practical method for grading the cognitive state of patients for the clinician', *J. Psychiatr. Res.* **12**, 189–98 (1975).

27. F.I.M. Craik, 'Age differences in remembering'. In N. Butters and L.R. Squire (eds.), *Neuropsychology of Memory*, vol. 3, Guilford Press, New York, 1984, p. 12.

28. L.W. Poon, J.L. Fozard, L.S. Cermak, D. Arenberg and L. W. Thompson (eds.), *New Directions in Memory and Aging. Proceedings of the George A. Talland Memorial*

Conference, Lawrence Erlbaum, New Jersey, 1980.

29. V.A. Kral, 'Senescent forgetfulness: benign and malignant', *J. Can. Med. Assoc.* **86**, 257–60 (1962).

30. K.A. Bayles, 'Language function in senile dementia', *Brian Lang,* **16**, 265–80 (1982).

31. A.W. Kaszniak, and R.S. Wilson, 'Longitudinal deterioration of language and cognition in dementia of the Alzheimer's type'. Paper presented at the 13th Annual Meeting of the International Neuropsychological Society, San Diego, California, 1985.

32. J.W. Largen and D. Loring, 'Spatial dysfunction in early putative Alzheimer's disease'. Paper presented at meeting of International Neuropsychological Society, 1983.

33. V. Moore, and M.A. Wyke, 'Drawing disability in patients with senile dementia', *Psychol. Med.,* **14**, 97–105 (1984).

34. W.G. Rosen, R.C. Mohs, and K.L. Davis, 'A new rating scale for Alzheimer's disease', *Am. J. Psychiatry*, **141**, 1356–64 (1984).

35. E.L. Hersh, 'Development and application of the extended scale for dementia', *J. Am. Geriatr. Soc.*, **27**, 348–54 (1979).

36. H. Weingartner, W. Kaye, S.A. Smallberg, M.H. Ebert, J.C. Gillin, and N. Sitaram, 'Memory failures in progressive idiopathic dementia', *Journal of Abnormal Psychology,* **90**, 187–96 (1981).

Psychiatric and physical assessment

JOHN WATTIS* and MIKE CHURCH†

* Consultant in the Psychiatry of Old Age, St James's University Hospital, Leeds; † Top grade Clinical Psychologist, Towers Hospital, Leicester

The skills needed to assess and formulate the management of elderly patients are best developed in clinical practice and by review of outcome in individual patients. If we are to learn from this experience, we must be meticulous in recording our findings and opinions in individual cases and in comparing our initial impressions with outcome. The self-discipline of careful assessment, problem formulation and review of outcome is the foundation for professional growth. The scheme outlined here is intended as the framework for such learning.

HISTORY

Most elderly patients referred for psychiatric assessment should be seen initially in their own homes. The advantages of this practice hold true for all health workers and include:

1. The patient is seen in the situation with which he or she is familiar. The confusion and disorientation which may be engendered by a trip to hospital, general practice surgery or consulting rooms are avoided.
2. The environment can be assessed as well as the patient.
3. The patient's function in his or her own environment and the level of social support can easily be assessed.
4. Neighbours and relatives are often readily available to give a history of the illness and its impact on them.

From *Practical Psychiatry of Old Age*, J. Wattis and M. Church, Croom Helm, 1986 (edited). Reproduced by permission of Croom Helm Limited.

Elderly patients who have to be seen for the first time in hospital should be interviewed in a quiet, distraction-free environment, and every effort must be made to put them at their ease. It is quite impossible to conduct a satisfactory psychiatric assessment of an elderly person who may have poor sight or hearing or both in a ward environment where there is a lot of noise and distraction. Unless care is taken to make an assessment in a suitable environment, any confusion will be compounded and a falsely pessimistic opinion of the patient's mental function may be formed. The patient's family and neighbours often have an important role to play in assessment and continuing management. A good relationship with them as well as with the patient is essential. At the initial interview, the patient and family will have many different anxieties, some of which may be founded upon their own ideas about the purpose of the assessment. It is vital that the doctor spends time listening to the problems as they are seen by the patient and relatives. A popular misconception is that the doctor has come to 'put away' the patient in the local institution. Social workers may suffer from a similar problem in that elderly clients may think that the social worker has come to arrange for them to be taken into 'a home'. The elderly patient's idea of what institutional care involves may also be quite different from that of the person conducting the assessment. Old people still refer to what we think of as modern hospitals by their workhouse names and find it difficult to conceive that an admission to hospital or a residential home could be anything other than permanent. The doctor needs to take time to listen to these fears and to explain why he is visiting and the scope and limitations of any help he can offer. Anxiety may inhibit the patient's and relative's ability to grasp and remember what is being said. It may be necessary to repeat the same information several times and to ask the patient or relative questions to clarify whether they have really understood what has been said. Those of us who work in the health field should never forget that although an assessment may be commonplace to us, for the patient and relative it is taking place at a crisis point in life. An empathetic manner, reflecting back the patient's and relative's concerns, will help them to realise that their worries have been acknowledged and will help to form a useful relationship.

The psychiatric history starts with the presenting complaint. Quite often, the patient lacks insight and believes that nothing is wrong. In these circumstances, careful probing is appropriate. Even early in the interview it may sometimes be necessary to ask direct questions about memory loss, mood or persecutory ideas, though a more oblique approach starting with personal history is usually better. As well as delineating the presenting complaint, it is important to obtain a history of how long it has been present and how it developed. Sometimes, when it is difficult to obtain a clear history of the time course of an illness, it is useful to resort to 'time landmarks'. These are things like the previous Christmas or some important personal anniversary which can often help to clarify the picture. Often a proper history of the presenting complaint can only be obtained by talking to an informant. Sometimes one can arrange to talk to a relative before seeing the patient and this is often helpful. In other cases, there may be no relatives available and information may have to be pieced together from a variety of sources such as the home help, the social worker and friends and neighbours. After delineating the presenting complaint and often even before this, it is helpful to get the patient to give an account of his previous life. Old people generally enjoy talking about the past and it is quite easy to introduce the subject. A useful opening line is 'tell me a bit about yourself; were you born in these parts?' One can then lead the person through their life history, often unobtrusively testing their memory (for example, their date of birth and the dates of important events) at the same time. The family history and the history of past physical and nervous complaints can be woven into this brief account of the patient's life-time and an assessment can be made of the patient's personality and characteristic ways of dealing with stress. Old people, like young people, respond well to those who have a genuine interest in them. Courtesy is also vital. Talking 'across' patients

to other professionals or to relatives generates anxiety and resentment, as does lack of punctuality.

MENTAL STATE EXAMINATION
Level of awareness

At an early stage in the interview, the patient's level of awareness should be assessed. The patient may be drowsy as a result of lack of sleep or medication or because of physical illness. Rapidly fluctuating level of awareness is seen in acute confusional states and a level of awareness that fluctuates from day to day is one of the clues to the diagnosis of chronic subdural haematoma. Impaired awareness can lead to poor function on tests of cognition and memory and, if it is not recognised, can lead to an under-estimation of the patient's true abilities. The patient's ability to *concentrate* and pay *attention* are closely related to level of awareness. Sometimes, however, they may be distracted by more mundane things. If the patient is, for example, in pain, it may be very hard for him to understand the relevance of giving an account of his mental state. Disturbance of mood and abnormal perceptual experiences can also impair attention and concentration.

Behaviour

On a home visit the patient's behaviour can not only be observed directly but can also be deduced from the state of the house. The patient's general appearance, his dress, personal hygiene and the attitude to the interviewer can all be assessed. Incontinence can often be smelled and the patient's mobility checked by asking him to walk a few steps. Especially if the patient lives alone, inconsistencies between the patient's state and the state of cleanliness and organisation of the household indicate either that there is a good active social support network or that the patient has deteriorated over a relatively short period of time. There are available various behavioural schedules which enable the systematic assessment of the patient's abilities.[1] A shortened form of the Crighton Royal Behavioural Assessment Form is shown in Table 1. It enables a numerical value to be attached to a person's performance in various important areas of behaviour. [. . .]

Table 1 Modified Crighton Royal Behavioural Scale

Dimension		Score
Mobility	Fully ambulant including stairs	0
	Usually independent	1
	Walks with minimal supervision	2
	Walks only with physical assistance	3
	Bed-fast or chair-fast	4
Orientation	Complete	0
	Orientated in ward, identifies persons correctly	1
	Misidentifies persons but can find way about	2
	Cannot find way to bed or toilet without assistance	3
	Completely lost	4
Communication	Always clear, retains information	0
	Can indicate needs, understands simple verbal directions, can deal with simple information	1
	Understands simple information, cannot indicate needs	2
	Cannot understand information, retains some expressive ability	3
	No effective contact	4
Co-operation	Actively co-operative, i.e. initiates helpful activity	0
	Passively co-operative	1
	Requires frequent encouragement or persuasion	2
	Rejects assistance, shows independent but ill-directed activity	3
	Completely resistive or withdrawn	4
Restlessness	None	0
	Intermittent	1
	Persistent by day	2
	Persistent by day, with frequent nocturnal restlessness	3
	Constant	4
Dressing	Correct	0
	Imperfect but adequate	1
	Adequate with minimum of supervision	2
	Inadequate unless continually supervised	3
	Unable to dress or retain clothing	4
Feeding	Correct, unaided at appropriate times	0
	Adequate, with minimum supervision	1
	Inadequate unless continually supervised	2
	Needs to be fed	3
Continence	Full control	0
	Occasional accidents	1
	Continent by day only if regularly toileted	2
	Urinary incontinence in spite of regular toileting	3
	Regular or frequent double incontinence	4

Another form which could be recommended is the behavioural assessment form of the Clifton Assessment Procedure for the Elderly.[2]

Mood or affect

[. . .]Mood affects not only how we feel but also how we think and even the functioning of our motor and gastro-intestinal systems. Old people are not always used to talking about their feelings and it can sometimes be quite difficult to find the right words. 'How do you feel in your spirits?' can evoke the appropriate response but will sometimes produce an account of the patient's alcohol drinking behaviour! Especially where there are communication difficulties, one may have to resort to direct questioning, for example 'do you feel happy or sad?' Although the patient's account of her mood should always be sought, it cannot always be relied upon. Some elderly patients who are quite depressed, even to the point of being in tears throughout the interview, do not confess to a depressed mood, perhaps because they are afraid this may result in hospitalisation. Psychomotor retardation (the slowing of thought and action) can be so profound that patients are unable to report their mood or may even say 'I feel nothing'. The person conducting the assessment will, of course, observe the patient's facial expression, any tears and other signs of depressed mood. In addition, specific questions should be asked about whether the patient feels guilty about anything, whether they have any worries about money or health and, if there is depressed mood, enquiry should also be made in all cases about suicidal feelings. [. . .]

Often, if psychomotor retardation is present, the answer will take some time to come and it is very easy to rush on to the next question before the patient has had time to respond to the previous one. One group of symptoms is often associated with severe 'biological' depression. This includes early morning wakening, mood worse in the morning and profound appetite loss and weight loss. The opposite of depressed mood is elated mood which is seen in hypomania. [. . .] In older patients, irritability and querulousness are often more prominent than happiness although the patient may still experience a feeling of elation and special powers. [. . .]

Anxiety is felt by many elderly patients, often in response to the stresses of ageing. Sometimes the patient may be so worried about falling that, in order to avoid anxiety, she restricts her life severely. Thus, a patient who has had one or two falls may, instead of seeking medical help, restrict herself to a downstairs room in the house and never go out. As long as the patient continues to restrict her life, she experiences little anxiety. Whereas in a young person such behaviour would almost certainly lead immediately to the patient being defined as 'sick' and a call for medical attention, in the elderly patient, this restriction is all too easily accepted as 'normal'. When assessing anxiety, attention should therefore be paid not only to how the patient is feeling during the interview (which may, in itself, provoke anxiety!) but also to whether he or she can engage in the tasks of daily living without experiencing undue anxiety. Anxiety is an effect which has physiological accompaniments; a racing pulse, 'palpitations', 'butterflies in the stomach', sweating and diarrhoea are all found. Patients not infrequently use the term 'dizziness' to describe not true vertigo, but a feeling of unreality associated with severe anxiety.

Perplexity is the feeling which commonly accompanies acute confusional states and may also be found in some mildly demented patients. The patient in an acute confusional state may be experiencing visual or auditory hallucinations and may also be subjected to a whole series of changes in the environment which she cannot properly grasp. [. . .]

Thought

The form, speed and content of thought are all assessed. Formal thought disorder occurs in schizophrenia and includes thought-blocking when the patient's thoughts come to an abrupt end, thought withdrawal when thoughts are felt to be withdrawn from the patient's head, and thought insertion. Slowing of the stream of thought (thought retardation) is found in many depressive disorders. Slow thinking is also characteristic of some of the organic brain syndromes caused by metabolic deficiencies. Thought is speeded up in hypomania, often leading to 'flight of ideas' where one thought is built upon another in a way that is founded upon tenuous associations. The patient with flight of ideas can be seen to have a logical thread running through their thoughts even if the subject develops and changes rather rapidly. In dementia, spontaneous thought is often diminished, so-called 'poverty of thought'. The patient with an acute confusional state also finds difficulty in maintaining a train of thought due to fluctuating awareness. In dementias of metabolic origin and in some cases of multi-infarct dementia, slowing of thought processes may be accompanied by great difficulty in assembling the necessary knowledge to solve particular problems. The observer gets the impression that the patient grasps what the problem is but is frustrated by her own inability to cope with it. Content of thought is profoundly influenced by the patient's mood. The depressed patient will often have very gloomy thoughts and ideas of poverty, or physical illness may be pervasive. The anxious patient's thoughts may be taken up with how to avoid various anxiety-provoking situations and there may be unnecessary worries about all aspects of everyday living. This kind of anxiety is also found in depressed patients, particularly if their normal personalities incline towards anxiety. The patient who feels persecuted may think of little else. Every noise or happening will be fitted into the persecutory framework. Except when patients are deeply suspicious, their *talk* generally reflects their thought. In addition, however, to the form, speed and content of thought, talk is also influenced by various motor functions. Slurred speech may be found in the patient who is drowsy or under the influence of drugs or alcohol. Sometimes it also results from specific neurological problems such as a stroke. Patients with Parkinson's disease may produce so-called 'scanning' speech where words are produced without inflexion and with hesitation between words. [. . .] A degree of difficulty in finding words and putting speech together appropriately is found in many patients with dementia, particularly those with Alzheimer's disease. This is one form of dysphasia. A stream of apparent nonsense, so-called fluent dysphasia, may occur in dementia but is also sometimes associated with a small stroke.

[. . .] Occasionally, fluent dysphasia, especially when it includes new words 'invented' by the patient (neologisms) may be mistaken for the so-called 'word salad' produced by some schizophrenic patients. [. . .]

Hallucinations

These can be defined as perceptions without external objects. Visual hallucinations are usually seen in patients with acute confusional states or dementia although occasionally they occur in patients with very poor eyesight without measurable organic brain damage, especially if the patient is living alone in a relatively under-stimulating environment. Auditory hallucinations (hearing voices) occur in a variety of mental illnesses. They are predominantly found in schizophrenia when they may consist of a voice repeating the patient's thoughts or of voices talking about the patient in the third person. They also occur in severe depressive illness when they are often derogatory in nature. In hypomania, too, auditory hallucinations in keeping with the patient's mood are sometimes found. Hallucinations of touch and smell also occur. Hallucinations of being touched, especially those with sexual connotations, occur in the late-onset form of schizophrenia ('late paraphrenia') and hallucinations of smell, especially of the patient believing herself to smell 'rotten', in severe depression.

Delusions

A delusion can be defined as a false unshakeable belief out of keeping with the patient's cultural background. Delusions occur in fragmentary forms in organic mental states but well-developed delusions are usually found only in severe affective disorders and schizophrenia. The ideas of poverty, guilt or illness found in the less severely depressed patient may develop into absolute convictions in the more severely depressed. The patient may, for example, firmly believe that she has cancer in the face of all available medical evidence. Occasionally, of course, she will be right but in many cases the belief will be founded upon the depressed mood and will disappear when that is treated. Ideas of persecution are also sometimes found in patients with depression of moderate severity and these, too, can develop into full-blown delusions. This can make the differential diagnosis of atypical affective states and paraphrenia particularly difficult in old age. Delusions of grandeur, for example that the patient has extraordinary powers of perception or is fabulously rich, are also found in hypomanic states. In paranoid schizophrenia, the delusional content is often very complicated and may involve persecutory activities by whole groups of people. These delusions may be supported by hallucinatory experiences.

Obsessions and compulsions

Obsessions occur when the patient feels compelled to repeat the same thought over and over again. They can be distinguished from schizophrenic phenomena such as thought insertion by the fact that obsessional patients feel that these thoughts come from within themselves and try to resist them. Sometimes such thoughts may result in compulsive actions, for example, returning many times to check that the door has been locked. Although characteristically a part of obsessional neuroses, obsessional symptoms also occur in depressed patients and apparently compulsive behaviour can also be a result of memory loss. Some patients, for example, with early dementia may not be able to remember that they have locked the door so may return many times to check it, but not as a result of any inner feelings of compulsion.

Illusions

Illusions occur when a patient misinterprets a real perception. Some hypochondriacal worries can be based on this. For example, many old people have various aches and pains but sometimes patients may become over-concerned by these and may begin to worry that they indicate some physical illness. Such misinterpretations of internal perceptions are not usually described as illusions although the term would be quite appropriate. Acute confusional states also produce illusions when the patient seeing the doctor approaching, misinterprets this as someone coming to do him harm and strikes out. [. . .]

Orientation/memory

Orientation for time, place and person should be recorded in a systematic way. The degree of detail would depend upon the time available and the purpose of the examination. Orientation for time can easily be split into gross orientation, for example the year or approximate time of day (morning, afternoon, evening, night), and finer orientation, for example the month, the day of the week and the hour of the day. Orientation for person depends upon the familiarity of the person chosen as a point of reference. Orientation for place also depends upon familiarity. A useful brief scale which includes some items of orientation as well as some items of memory-testing is the scale developed by Hodkinson.[3] [. . .]

Orientation is, to a large extent, dependent upon memory although it should never be forgotten that the patient may not know the name of the hospital she is in, simply because she has never been told. Memory for remote events can be assessed when taking the patient's history. The ability to encode new material can be assessed by the capacity to remember a short address or to remember the interviewer's name. Many patients with dementia will have great difficulty in encoding and storing new memories. Sometimes, especially in the metabolic dementias, one can form the impression that the patient is encoding and storing new material but that she is having great difficulty in retrieving the memory when asked to. This has been described as 'forgetfulness'.

Other areas of organic brain dysfunction

When a patient has impaired memory, it is important to ascertain whether this is an isolated deficit or whether it is associated with other signs of more generalised brain damage. In everyday clinical practice, some areas are relatively easy to test. *Right/left orientation* can be ascertained by asking the patient to lift her right or left hand. More complicated tasks such as 'touch your left ear with your right hand' are more discriminating but also more difficult to interpret. *Visuospatial function* can easily be tested by asking the patient to copy designs of increasing complexity. For example, asking the patient to copy in turn a square, a triangle and a simple house. This should be done on paper without lines. *Nominal aphasia* can be tested using everyday objects. An object such as a pen or wrist-watch and its smaller parts can be used. *Frontal signs* may be picked up when patients perseverate on some of the tasks given to them. They may get stuck, for example, on their date of birth, repeating their year of birth when asked the current year or their age. Apraxia and perseveration may also be seen in tasks of everyday living such as dressing. [. . .]

Insight and judgement

In severe psychiatric illness insight is often lost. Depressed patients may be unable to accept that they will get better despite remembering many previous episodes of depression which have improved with treatment. Hypomanic and paraphrenic patients may act on their delusions with disastrous consequences. Patients with severe dementia often do not realise their plight, which is perhaps fortunate. Patients with milder dementia may have some insight, especially in the metabolic and multi-infarct types of dementia where mood is, not surprisingly, also often depressed. Closely related to insight is judgement. This can be a particularly difficult question with a moderately demented patient living alone or living with relatives but left alone for a substantial part of the day. Patients may be leaving gas taps on and frankly be dangerous to themselves and others but at the same time maintain that they are looking after themselves perfectly well and do not need any help, much less residential or nursing home care. [. . .]

Other cognitive functions

Mental arithmetic is used to test cognitive ability. The patient's educational level should be taken into account and tasks should be related to everyday tasks (e.g. shopping) whenever possible. Many British old people still find it easier to reckon up in pre-decimal coinage. Tasks like serially subtracting seven from one hundred assess concentration as well as arithmetic and may be seen as irrelevant by many old people. They should generally be avoided. Asking the meaning of *proverbs* is also said to test abstract reasoning ability. Such tests rarely reveal clinically useful material in old people. [. . .]

The psychiatric history and examination of the elderly patient takes time. It must be tailored to the patient's tolerance of questions and must be approached in a sympathetic way. The doctor who initiates his interview by firing a series of seemingly random questions designed to test memory and orientation is unlikely to get the best out of his patient. Time taken in proper assessment is not wasted. A poor assessment can result in treatable illness going untreated or a potentially independent old person being forced into dependency in an institution. [. . .]

In addition, medical treatment for psychiatric disorder can cause physical illness and vice versa. No psychiatric examination, particularly in the elderly, is complete without a thorough physical examination. [. . .] Psychiatric illness in the elderly is often complicated or precipitated by acute or chronic physical illness.

Diminished sensory input, one of the techniques used in 'brain washing', is often inflicted on the elderly due to medical slowness in recognising and correcting defects of sight and hearing. Sensory deprivation may be instrumental in producing paranoid states and in precipitating or worsening confusion. At least a crude estimate of visual and auditory acuity is part of the examination of every old person. Wax in the ears is an easily remedied cause of poor hearing. Other forms of deafness may require a hearing aid. A good deal of patience may be needed to train the elderly person to use an aid properly, especially if poor hearing has been present for some time. The doctor should be on the look-out for flat batteries or dirty battery contacts in hearing aids. For assessment purposes, more powerful amplifiers may be needed and there are several useful portable types. [. . .]

One of these aids is an important part of the equipment of any psychiatrist working with the elderly. In extremity, a stethoscope used in reverse may help. Visual defects, like hearing defects, vary from those that are easily corrected by spectacles and other aids to those like cataract and glaucoma that require more complicated surgical or medical intervention.

Medication for physical and psychiatric disorders is particularly likely to produce side effects in the elderly and, unless a careful *drug history* is taken, these side effects may be mistaken for a new illness. Many drug interactions occur in old people who are more often subject to polypharmacy than the young. When an elderly patient presents with a new symptom, present medication, which may well be causing the symptom, should be reviewed before anything else is added.

Investigations may be planned in the light of findings from the history and examination. There is need for research into the cost-effectiveness of 'screening tests' for potentially reversible dementia. Many doctors would confine themselves to haemoglobin, full blood count and film, urea and electrolytes and thyroid function tests; some would routinely add serum B_{12} and folate and a serological test for syphilis. Other tests such as chest X-ray, skull X-ray, radio-isotope brain scan and computerised axial tomography (CAT) are at present only justified by specific indications. Hopes that CAT might provide an easy and definitive diagnosis of senile dementia by demonstrating brain atrophy have not been realised due to wide overlaps in the picture between normal, functionally ill and demented patients. Nevertheless, research series have shown a small proportion of clinically undetected space-occupying lesions.[4-6]

The collection of information is only the first part of the assessment process. Nevertheless, it is vitally important and demands attention to detail and, especially with the elderly, considerable patience.

REFERENCES

1. L. Israel, B. Kozarevic and N. Sartorius, *Source Book of Geriatric Assessment*, S. Karger AG, Basle, 1984.

2. A. Pattie and C. Gilleard, *Manual of the Clifton Assessment Procedures for the Elderly (CAPE)*, Hodder and Stoughton Educational, Sevenoaks, 1979.

3. H. M. Hodkinson, 'Evaluation of a mental test score for assessment of mental impairment in the elderly', *Age and Ageing*, **1**, 223–8 (1972).

4. R.J. Jacoby, R. Levy and J.M. Dawson, 'Computed tomography in the elderly: 1. The normal population', *British Journal of Psychiatry*, **136**, 249–55 (1980).

5. R.J. Jacoby, R. Levy and J.M. Dawson, 'Computed tomography in the elderly: 2. Senile dementia, diagnosis and functional impairment', *British Journal of Psychiatry*, **136**, 256–69 (1980).

6. R.J. Jacoby, R. Levy and J.M. Birch, 'Computed tomography and the outcome of affective disorder: a follow-up study of elderly patients', *British Journal of Psychiatry*, **139**, 288–92 (1981).

Section V

Approaches to treatment and care

New approaches in services for mentally ill older people

CHRIS CLOKE

Former Health and Social Services Information and Policy Officer, Age Concern, England

Services for mentally ill elderly people remain largely underdeveloped and hospital based. The extent of unmet need was emphasized in the Health Advisory Service report *The Rising Tide*[1] which followed a three and a half year study involving visits to 130 health districts. The HAS, perhaps oversensationally, argued that the need to provide services for elderly mentally infirm people is quite unprecedented since never before have so many people survived into great old age. Ten per cent of people over the age of 65 and 20 per cent over the age of 80 show signs of dementia. Failure to provide specialist services 'is likely to result in most other kinds of health and social service being overwhelmed by the sheer weight of numbers'. As a result of the report the Department of Health and Social Security allocated the small sum of £6 million, to be spent over the three year period 1983–4 to 1986–7, to fund 28 demonstration projects for the elderly mentally ill. An analysis of the applications for these funds clearly shows the lack of provision that existed in the early 1980s. One successful applicant wrote that 'The special problems faced by (this authority) in starting off with an extremely low base of provision present an opportunity for developing services for the elderly mentally ill in a planned, co-ordinated way whilst hoping to avoid the extensive provision of long stay beds for these patients'. Another authority reported that 'There is no psycho-geriatric hospital provision within the district. Similarly there are no local authority elderly mentally infirm residential or day care facilities.'

The projects that were funded include day centres, night sitting and nursing, community support services and the appointment of additional community psychiatric nurses and other staff to build up services. Similar initiatives have been undertaken by a variety of statutory and voluntary agencies both within and outside these demonstration districts. The experience of family carers shows, however, that there are still insufficient services to support mentally ill old people living in the community. A shortage of funding in the current economic climate has been used as one reason for failure to develop services. In fact many of the services which have proved effective are relatively inexpensive to run. Moreover, community services can be no more costly than the institutional care that might otherwise be required and they are the preferred option.

A RANGE OF MENTAL ILLNESSES

In planning to meet the mental health needs of older people it is important to remember that they are tremendously varied. They may be suffering from conditions such as dementia, clinical depression and paraphrenia which require specialist services, but they may also be coping with bereavement, feeling lonely or experiencing difficulties following retirement. In some areas there has been a tendency to concentrate on providing a dementia service to the detriment of the other conditions. In addition, how a particular condition presents will vary from individual to individual and it will also progress at different rates. This indicates a need to provide accurate diagnosis, careful monitoring and regular reassessment. Furthermore, these elderly people are also likely to suffer with other illnesses and physical disabilities, which can often be overlooked by care providers, and so a multidisciplinary approach is essential.

SUPPORTING FAMILIES, NEIGHBOURS AND FRIENDS

At least 80 per cent of elderly people with dementia and a higher proportion of those with other mental illnesses are cared for in the community.[2] The bulk of the care provided to them comes not from the statutory services but from families, friends and neighbours. All the research suggests that the strain of caring for someone with dementia can be intolerable, affecting health, family life, finances and work. Statutory services still tend to be allocated overwhelmingly to those elderly people living on their own. The National Institute for Social Work survey of carers of elderly people with dementia found 'evidence that a considerable proportion of the supporters and their elderly relatives were not receiving services relevant to their problems, had not been offered them and would accept them if offered. For example, 45 per cent of the elderly persons who were heavily incontinent were not visited by community nurses: 83 per cent of the supporters whose elderly relative had not been admitted to relief care had not been offered such a break.'[2] This highlights the need to ensure that in providing for the elderly mentally infirm the needs of their family carers are also met.

Gilleard's[3] survey of referrals to psychogeriatric day care found that only 34 per cent were visited by a district nurse or, less commonly, by a health visitor, 32 per cent had home helps and 10 per cent had meals on wheels. While mentally frail elderly people are more likely to receive community health and social services than the average older person there still remains a substantial number who receive no help at all. Moreover, the appropriateness of the traditional range of these services for mentally impaired older people has been questioned. Usually these services—home helps, meals on wheels, day care, community nursing, for example—are only available on weekdays during usual working hours. The needs of very confused elderly people do not conform to these requirements and twenty-four hour care or surveillance, seven days a week, may be necessary. Many of the projects and special initiatives which have been undertaken with this group of patients are either extensions of current provision or have sought to fill in 'the gaps' between services.

A number of day and, less frequently, night sitting services and attendant schemes—such as those run by Age Concern Plymouth and Crossroads Care Attendant Schemes—have been set up to provide care to confused elderly people and relief to their carers. These initiatives may be seen as 'gap filling' and have often proved inexpensive to run, sometimes because volunteers are recruited to provide the service or because the attendants are paid a modest fee. They are successful because the attendants 'stand in' for the carers and provide care in the familiar surroundings of the dependant's own home. The attendants can often build up a close relationship with both the dependants and their families.

HOME CARE SERVICES

Recognizing that the traditional home help service undertaking basic household chores, cooking and shopping, is of limited value to frail and confused elderly people, a number of local authorities have abandoned it in favour of domiciliary aide or attendant services or have set up special projects alongside the usual provision. Oldham Metropolitan Borough Council's home care service, for example, has as its philosophy the aim of making the service meet the needs of the client rather than make clients fit the service.

This has been achieved by recruiting all new home helps to work any time between 8 a.m. and 10 p.m. over a seven day period. Home helps arrive early to get the clients out of bed, help with toileting and dressing, provide breakfast and get them ready for day care and at the end of the day receive them home, make tea and, if necessary, put the client to bed. To cover hours when the area office is closed there is a team of home helps who work a rota system to cover emergencies.

The home care or domiciliary aides in this and similar schemes are a cross between the home help and a good neighbour. In some cases quasi nursing duties may also be performed. It has been suggested that the efficacy of such initiatives for elderly mentally infirm people living on their own is largely dependent on the availability of day care support which can be complemented.

Several projects have sought to provide an even more flexible system of support which is based on the Kent

Community Care Project[4] which was started in 1977 and subsequently replicated in Anglesey and Gateshead. The project has been closely monitored and documented by the Personal Social Services Research Unit at the University of Kent.

'PACKAGES OF CARE' FOR CONFUSED ELDERLY PEOPLE

The Kent experience was in part the inspiration behind Age Concern England's action research project in the London Borough of Newham and in Ipswich. Like the Kent project it sought to provide packages of care to elderly people, in this case suffering from senile dementia, so that they could avoid or postpone admission to residential care and enjoy an enhanced quality of life. For the purposes of the research only people who have already been assessed by a psychogeriatrician can be referred to the scheme and the care provided to each client should not exceed the cost of institutional care—£200 a week in 1985. A local development worker coordinates a package of domiciliary care which might be provided around the clock and could include home help, district nursing, community psychiatric nursing, day centre attendance, day hospital care, social work support and help from voluntary agencies. Each element is costed. In addition, the development officers can recruit community carers who are paid at the standard care attendant rate to complement or enhance existing services provided by other agencies. The development officers, who manage the scheme, assess the clients' needs, liaise with other agencies and recruit, train and support the community carers.

The development officers have described the complex nature of their work. The tasks performed by the community carers are varied, reflecting the needs of the clients, and fall into two main categories: physical help and basic psychological support. Tasks in the first group include: helping people to the lavatory, emptying commodes and dealing with incontinence; washing people; being in charge of the supply of gas and going into the home several times a day to switch it on and off; making meals for people who had refused meals on wheels because they believed they were still cooking for themselves; and giving regular medication. Basic psychological support largely involves helping the client to orientate to time and place: reminding people to wash and dress; reminding clients to take their medication; helping clients to recognize their meals on wheels; reminding them to get ready for the day hospital or day centre; going out with clients to friends, the post office, the hairdresser, the chiropodist, dental and hospital appointments. The development officers comment 'We see going out with clients as an important service to people who would either get lost and perplexed if they went out alone or would become increasingly housebound. Most domiciliary services are designed to help people in their homes, but we tried to make sure that we did not imprison them there'.[5] While this system of care is *not* suitable for all clients referred to it, a substantial number of confused elderly people can benefit. The community carers live quite close to the clients and can get to know them very well and gain their trust. They can also respond very quickly, including during antisocial hours. The development worker also has a keyworker role and liaises closely with a wide range of professionals. Above all, the 'packages of care' are flexible and meet the needs of the elderly person. The staffing requirements are few and the ceiling on the amount of money that could be spent a week on a client ensure that the costs did not exceed that of residential care. As the vast majority of elderly people, including those who are confused, wish to stay in the community, this scheme enabled the clients to enjoy an enhanced quality of life.

NIGHT CARE

Night care causes problems in the Ipswich/Newham project as it proves prohibitively expensive to provide care throughout the night. Many projects have faced similar problems all stemming from the fact that confused elderly people have the ability to turn night into day and go wandering when most people are fast asleep. Loss of sleep is a principal cause in the breakdown of family care. Night sitting and night nursing can make an important contribution to supporting confused elderly people and their carers. Such services, however, are still very few and far between and, in any case, are not always appropriate.

The German Hospital Night Shelter operated by City and Hackney District Health Authority was opened in 1983 as a response to the problems faced by a woman in her fifties who was caring for her husband in his eighties and an elderly mother. One of the dependants was confused and very active at night. A night nurse was found to offer very little relief because the council flat was very small and the carer would still be disturbed in her own room. The aim of the night shelter is to relieve relatives caring for mentally infirm people to enable them to have occasional evenings and nights without their dependant.

The day hospital, located in the grounds of the psychiatric hospital, is converted to a night shelter. The accommodation includes kitchen, bathroom and personal laundry facilities. It is located away from the hospital but skilled help is close by if required. The shelter started offering care to five people at night, both men and women, but this number can now be increased. High quality 'Z' beds have been purchased and privacy is secured through the use of movable screens—the equipment can be easily stacked away during the day. It was also necessary to buy some additional bed linen.

The day hospital has a driver who, once he has delivered the day patients home, then collects the night patients who arrive at about 7 p.m. They then have supper and between 9 and 10 p.m. the patients are bathed and dressed in hospital night clothes. Some patients may be bathed in the morning. The patients are allowed to go to bed when they like and some do not retire until the early hours of the morning. Videos are shown to entertain the patients and *Gone with the Wind* is a regular favourite! After breakfast the elderly people are collected at 8 a.m. and this allows time to prepare for the arrival of the day patients.

Referrals come from the psychogeriatrician, general practitioners, community psychiatric nurses, geriatric liaison nurses, community physicians, social workers, and relatives themselves. They are made to the Head of Nursing at the hospital who, with the registrar and the social worker, assesses each case and offers night shelter relief according to need. Some people may be offered other forms of help. It is recognized that the night shelter may confuse some elderly people even further and so the first night is always considered a trial period. Sometimes relatives, quite understandably, will worry about how their dependants will settle, but they can phone in to find out.

The staffing comprises two psychiatric nurses, one on duty each night, Monday to Friday, equipped with a telephone and an alarm. Relief for meal breaks is provided by nurses from wards in the Hospital. The duty senior house officer provides medical cover as necessary. The scheme is funded from the psychiatric nursing budget and 'soft' money was used for equipment. No great organization is needed.

While the night shelter is not appropriate for every confused person, it has managed to enhance the quality of life for many people and their carers. If the users attend the day hospital they are already familiar with the building and are thus unlikely to become further disorientated. The project capitalizes on existing resources, including transport which so often can be a vexed problem. In providing carers with an occasional and planned break they are better able to cope.

DAY CARE

The availability of day hospital and day centre provision only on weekdays and often between 9 and 5 limits its usefulness. If carers are working they may have to leave home before their dependant is collected and not be able to get home until after their relative has returned home. This indicates a need for small, localized day centres which are within walking distance of the home, and which can operate flexible hours. While not all day centres match this ideal, day care is increasingly being used to meet the needs of mentally frail elderly people and their carers. It is a service in which both statutory and voluntary agencies have become involved. There are many examples of innovative day centres for confused elderly people.

The Halewood Day Centre, opened in 1974 and run by Age Concern Bracknell, is rather unusual in that it is situated on a large housing estate in a two-bedroom ground floor council flat which the attenders recognize as a 'home from home'. It is also staffed entirely by volunteers who the paid organizer has recruited and trained and there are always at least three of them on duty. The Centre is run five days a week and about nine to twelve patients attend each day. It aims to enable elderly mentally infirm people to remain in their own homes or those of their carers for as long as possible and provide relief to their families. The Centre works closely with the statutory agencies which also make referrals, especially the community psychiatric nurse, the geriatric liaison officer and the home helps. The CPN has been a source of support for the scheme as a whole and is a frequent caller at the Centre, making checks on patients who attend and offering guidance to the volunteers. A range of activities and services are provided at the Centre: games, music, basket weaving, bathing, hairdressing, shaving, clothes washing and administration of medicine. Health and social service professionals will visit their clients/ patients at the Centre and the volunteers liaise well with them. Much of the success of the project derives from the importance which the organizer and volunteers attach to creating a secure and friendly atmosphere in which each individual is given personal attention.

A TRAVELLING DAY HOSPITAL

Transport to day centres is a recurring problem and is partly overcome if the centres are very local, either enabling the driver to return to the home of attenders who might have forgotten to get ready or staff to go and collect them. In rural settings such an approach is not always possible but one solution is to take the therapy to the users. This is what the Travelling Day Hospital for elderly mentally ill patients run by the South East Hampshire Health Authority since 1982 sets out to do.[6] Its title is rather a misnomer since it is the staff and not the hospital which do the travelling to four centres in areas of high psychiatric morbidity and sizable elderly populations. The multidisciplinary team comprises a sister or charge nurse, one SEN, a senior occupational therapist, part-time social worker and a clerical officer. The consultant psychogeriatrician does one session a month for a full case conference and also keeps in regular contact with each centre. Two or three volunteers help at each centre. The team goes to a different centre four days a week and sets up the day hospital in non-medical premises. Fifteen patients attend each day and they comprise elderly people who have suffered a functional illness and are returning to a normal life, the lonely, the isolated and the bereaved. The team provide remedial and preventive mental health care and meet a very great

need, at a relatively low cost, in a scattered rural area. Part of the project's success lies in the fact that local people see the travelling day hospital as far less stigmatizing than going to the mental hospital itself. Moreover, the day hospital can be changed, moved or discontinued in the light of changing local needs.

The day centre can form the focus of a number of activities which can be run for the attenders and their carers. The groups running some day centres have set up sitting and attendant services in recognition of the fact that families may need relief care when their dependants are not attending the centre. Relative support groups have also developed out of day centres.

HOLIDAYS FOR CONFUSED ELDERLY PEOPLE

The MIND and Age Concern groups in Greenwich broke new ground when they took a group of the confused elderly people attending their jointly run day centre on a week's holiday to Hastings in 1984. Ten pensioners supported by volunteers and paid staff stayed in caravans and enjoyed a series of day outings. Fears that the elderly people would become too disorientated to enjoy themselves were misplaced with the exception of one lady whose son came and took her home. Because the group were living in compact accommodation, knew each other and the helpers from the day centre and were given a lot of support they settled down very well. The holiday also enabled their regular carers to have a break. The pensioners thoroughly enjoyed their holiday and with the total expenditure coming to just over £1000, which the local authority paid, it was certainly cheaper than the possible alternative option of providing residential care for a week, which might have taken more time to get used to.

A week's holiday for a group of carers and their elderly relative at a small seaside hotel run by a person who formerly worked in residential care arose out of a relatives support group organized by Merton MIND. Both carers and dependants had a break from their routine lives and because the carers went on the holiday they may have worried less than had they been separated from their dependants.

CARERS SUPPORT GROUPS

The family carers of the elderly mentally infirm often feel under an intolerable physical and emotional strain, they feel unrecognized and are often ignorant of what services and benefits are available. In supporting the carers their dependants are enabled to stay in the community. Although more services are being established there are still far too few available.

Many carers benefit and gain support from an opportunity of meeting together to share their experiences and frustrations and to learn, sometimes from professionals, about the nature of their dependants' illness and how to cope with it. A number of carers support groups have been established by both statutory and voluntary agencies and with professional and non-professional workers taking a lead. The DHSS-funded Informal Caring Programme based at the Kings Fund Centre is to publish in 1988 a manual on setting up such groups.

Following suggestions from a local consultant psychogeriatrician on how a voluntary group could help local confused elderly people, Merton MIND decided to assist relatives by forming support groups. The first was set up in 1981 and several have been established since. The project employs a part-time social worker/counsellor whose telephone number is given by the consultant, GP, social worker or existing carers to carers who may need help. It is then for the carer to take the first initiative and make contact. This is felt to be less intrusive than when the counsellor makes the first contact. The counsellor then visits the carer and listens to the problems, offers advice and introduces the idea of joining a group. This may take as many as three hour-long visits. If the carer does not like the idea of joining a group continuing support in the form of visits and telephone contact is offered.

The groups meet monthly in social services establishments and one of the staff there works with the counsellor during the sessions and in monitoring the group's development. The groups comprise eight to ten members as it is felt that many carers, because they lead isolated lives, would find larger numbers rather offputting and everyone might not otherwise get a chance to speak. The groups are very supportive to new members who are quickly offered companionship. While it was originally thought that the counsellor would withdraw once the group got underway this has not happened as it was found that the carers welcomed the continuity of her involvement as they tend to have little spare time to help each other. One group came to a natural end after three members whose parents had died had shared their bereavement. The two remaining members joined another group. The project aims to facilitate leaving a group when a carer feels ready. Funding is from the local social services department and the district health authority.

Some carers groups have found that as their members grow in confidence they wish to become involved in organizing services and also campaigning for changes in public attitudes to mental infirmity and for improvements in statutory provision. SEMI (Support for Elderly Mentally Infirm) in Bristol which, in 1978, was one of the earliest carers groups to be formed attaches priority to both these activities. It is now a registered charity with paid workers and runs day centres and a sitting service. These services can also be used by carers who choose not to belong to SEMI. Members of SEMI, throughout its short history, have always welcomed the opportunity to speak at meetings about the needs of mentally infirm elderly people and their carers since they, after all, are the people who have most knowledge and experience.

CHANGING ATTITUDES

Public and professional ignorance about mental infirmity needs to be tackled if attitudes and services are to improve. For this reason a number of agencies have organized surveys, campaigns and weeks of action around this broad theme. In some cases there was very little or no health or social provision before these activities highlighted the need. When, in 1981, Age Concern Bexley widely circulated a questionnaire to people looking after a forgetful elderly person to assess the problems they were experiencing, they found that statutory services were under pressure, with no specialist day care facilities, no short term or respite care available in the one residential home, only two community psychiatric nurses in post and most of the support being given by social work assistants. As a result Age Concern Bexley, in collaboration with health and social services, developed a relief and support scheme for the carers of elderly confused dependants using regular weekly placement of volunteers in their homes. This project is now joint financed.

In 1982 Age Concern Metropolitan Salford held a citywide Mental Health Week comprising activities, conferences and exhibitions, not only for professionals but also for elderly people themselves, their supporting relatives and friends, and the general public. For professionals there was a major conference on *Who Cares for the Carers?*, a film day on the nature, diagnosis and management of confusion, and a series of talks on such subjects as working with mentally frail elderly people, the role of the voluntary sector and reality orientation. Entertainment and excursions were arranged for elderly people, an Over 60s Club held a conference on *A Positive Approach to Retirement* and a carers' evening was held. Mental Health Weeks, such as this one, have sought to emphasize the importance of statutory authorities providing a comprehensive, multidisciplinary assessment and treatment service which actively seeks out those in need and undertakes preventive work.

This paper has sought to demonstrate that mentally ill elderly people do not form a homogenous group but instead may be suffering a variety of mental and physical conditions. This requires a wide range of flexible responses. Many statutory services are too rigid in their approach with only limited provision being offered. It is therefore necessary to adapt and extend existing services and develop approaches for meeting the needs of the elderly mentally infirm. Such initiatives are being successfully undertaken at comparatively low cost as the projects described here have sought to demonstrate. It should be emphasized, however, that too few such schemes exist and that, often by intention and quite appropriately, they cater for only a small number of people. Moreover, they should be seen not as substituting for but as complementing an effective base of statutory care.

REFERENCES

1. *The Rising Tide: Developing Services for Mental Illness in Old Age*. Health Advisory Service, 1982.
2. Enid Levin *et al., The Supporters of Confused Elderly People in the Community*, National Institute of Social Work, 1982.
3. Chris Gilleard, *Living with Dementia: Community Care of the Elderly Mentally Infirm*, Croom Helm, 1984.
4. See David Challis and Bleddyn Davies, *Case Management — Community Care*, Gower, 1986.
5. Denise Murphy and Crys Rapley, 'Still living at home', *Community Care*, 31 July 1986.
6. Neil Evans *et al., An Evaluation of a Travelling Day Hospital for Elderly Mentally Ill People*, Social Services Research and Intelligence Unit, Portsmouth Polytechnic, 1986.

FURTHER READING

Mental Illness in Old Age: A Collection of Projects, compiled by Christopher Cloke, Age Concern England, 1983.
Mental Illness in Old Age: Meeting the Challenge, Alison Norman, Centre for Policy on Ageing, 1982.

The organization Good Practices in Mental Health (380 Harrow Road, London W10) publishes information on a range of services and projects for mentally ill elderly people.

Meeting the challenge of coordinated service delivery

Dᴀᴠɪᴅ Hᴜɴᴛᴇʀ

King's Fund Institute, London

INTRODUCTION

A major consequence of government policy to develop community care alternatives to hospital care for the priority care groups—mentally ill, mentally handicapped, physically disabled and elderly people—has been the need to encourage service providers across various departments and agencies to work more closely together. Repeated pleas from central government and elsewhere to foster joint planning and collaboration between health and local authorities in order to make a reality of community care have become commonplace.

The report of the working group on joint planning, published in 1985, is the latest in a long line of official statements stressing the virtues of collaboration (Working Group on Joint Planning, 1985). That it exists at all is testimony to the growing concern over the pace of and the uneven way in which joint planning has been conducted (Hunter and Wistow, 1987). When launched as a policy initiative in the mid 1970s, joint planning was seen uncritically to be 'a good thing'. A touching faith in organizational altruism prevailed and the complexities and politics of organizational life were conveniently, but misguidedly, overlooked. Attempts to get the *structures* for joint planning right are now seen to be insufficient—attention also has to be directed to the *processes* of joint planning. In particular, there have to be incentives to encourage collaboration.

In its critique of community care policy, the Audit Commission pointed to the fragmented organizational and professional arrangements which remained a major obstacle to progress (Audit Commission, 1986). The government's response to the mounting criticism of the policy of community care, to which all governments have subscribed over the past 20 years or so, has been to ask its health adviser, Sir Roy Griffiths, to review community care policies. The review was announced in December 1986 and Sir Roy is expected to report to ministers by the end of 1987.

If coordination between agencies, services and professionals remains ever popular at the level of rhetoric, at the level of practice it is fraught with difficulties. The social policy arena is littered with the debris of unsuccessful attempts to improve coordination. There are, however, important successes and these generally receive less attention than the failures.

Following a brief review of the various pleas for coordination, their origins and validity, the second half of this article describes two successful examples of mechanisms whose purpose was to promote collaborative activity among groups of professionals in different agencies. The analysis is aimed at identifying some of the conditions under which health and social service professionals may be able to work together on the frontline as distinct from higher levels of collaboration between, for instance, health and local authorities. The reason for this emphasis on joint working as distinct from joint planning is to demonstrate that there is much which individual professionals themselves can do to coordinate their activities and interventions more effectively.

WHY COORDINATE?

Pleas for improved coordination between agencies, services and professionals have their origins in at least four sets of concerns. First, there is the frontier or boundary problem—boundaries and territorial demarcations between professionals, services and agencies militate against coordinated action in respect of care groups, like the elderly mentally infirm, whose needs cross sectoral divisions. Second, and partly arising from the frontier problem, is a perceived overlap and duplication of coverage by services. Third, there is a sense that services which ought to be working together in practice pull in different directions and operate at cross purposes. Finally, an all too evident outcome of a compartmentalized approach to service delivery is the appearance of gaps or discontinuities in services.

Improved coordination is seen as one, if not *the*, remedy for any, or all, of these ills, even if their root causes go deeper and lie elsewhere. Calls for coordinated service provision have generally been based on a number of untested and unproven assumptions about the nature of service operation and professional decision-making (Norton and Rogers, 1981; Glennerster *et al.*, 1983; Gray and Hunter, 1983). These are predicated on a rational model of planning which makes no allowance for the multiple, and sometimes conflicting, objectives of agencies, services and professionals who do not share a unitary perspective on service issues or the needs of clients. Misleadingly, therefore, it is believed that frontier problems are organizational in design and can be resolved through structural means; that the necessary skills to ensure coordinated approaches are already present but merely require the appropriate structural forum in order to prosper; and that every service already operates as effectively as possible within its own boundaries with no allowance made for possible *intra*-service malfunctions which could constrain *inter*-service collaboration.

These assumptions have been challenged on a number of grounds. Most important is the fact that improved coordination, whether between agencies, services or professionals, is no substitute for a certain clarity and agreement over aims. As Rein (1983, p. 67) argues, the search for improved collaboration can camouflage 'the multiple, conflicting hopes that parents, politicians, administrators and professional service providers and interest groups impose'. Moreover, many problems in service delivery are not problems of coordination alone, or even at all, although they may be presented as such. Rather they have to do with the needs of clients which may not fit available

services: a shortage of resources (human or financial); a refusal by an individual to take a service; and professional differences over how a case should be managed.

While it would be quite wrong to undervalue the benefits of cooperation in remedying some of the problems noted above, it would be equally wrong to regard coordination as the solution to every organizational and professional problem. Ambiguous legislation, organizational inertia, confused aims and professional resistance can all conspire to influence the outcome of attempts to improve coordination. Successful coordination among agencies, services and professionals is therefore no simple matter. It may, for instance, prove possible at an agency level but be unworkable at a provider level, or vice versa.

LEVELS OF COORDINATION

There are three interconnected levels of joint planning and coordination embracing health and related services such as personal social services, housing and education:

1. National level: interdepartmental
2. Local level: interagency
3. Street level: interprofessional

Most attention is devoted to the first and especially the second levels and the third is generally neglected (e.g. Central Policy Review Staff, 1975; JASP Team, 1984; Working Group on Joint Planning, 1985). Yet, as the Audit Commission acknowledged in its discussion of locally integrated community care schemes, joint *working* in the actual care setting at street level—as distinct from joint *planning* at the other levels—is important for the success of collaborative activity at all levels. Poor or non-existent cooperation between practitioners in the field is likely to undermine the effectiveness of plans or policies mutually agreed by local agencies. Similarly, good interprofessional coordination but poor joint planning is likely to result in effective joint activity being confined to isolated and precarious small-scale initiatives rather than becoming widespread within mainstream services.

Most innovations occur in a small-scale context involving a handful of practitioners. Innovation is not generally the product of high-level joint planning machinery although such machinery may be necessary to sustain a particular innovation or to extend its coverage. At the end of the day, however, it is vital for the success of joint activity that those charged with implementing policy are committed to it. While joint working at street level perhaps ought to infuse joint planning at higher levels, in practice joint planning proceeds independently of activities at street level which are often neglected.

The remainder of this article focuses upon joint working at street level in the belief that this level can be the starting point for effective coordination among services and ultimately agencies. It is also the level at which individual service providers can make an immediate contribution to the shape of services and their direction. If joint working fails at this level, where services and clients meet, then efforts at higher levels can hardly be expected to succeed. As Booth (1981, p. 224) has said: 'lack of cooperation between practitioners in the field undermines the effectiveness of mutually agreed plans or policies as much as lack of resources'. As important as resources or even structures are the roles and skills which can facilitate joint approaches.

STREET LEVEL JOINT WORKING: TWO ILLUSTRATIONS

While descriptions of successful innovative examples of joint activity abound (several are described in the Audit Commission's report on community care), the roles and skills required to make a reality of joint working have been little explored. A useful notion in attempting to understand them is 'reticulist activity' (Friend, Power and Yewlett, 1974). A reticulist is a networker or broker, someone who endeavours to blur organizational and professional boundaries by creating and nurturing links between organizations and professionals, and by linking together the 'right' people on the 'right' problems (Schon, 1971).

A reticulist must appreciate when to bargain, when to seek to persuade, and when to seek to confront in situations ranging from those where there is a high degree of consensus to those where there is inherent conflict between the interested parties. Typically, reticulists operate on the margins, or in the interstices, of organizations and occupy liaison roles. They have

been referred to as 'responsible schemers' in the successful maintenance of joint working networks (Friend, 1983). Although fulfilling an important function, reticulists receive scant attention, possibly because the work is less obviously valued than orthodox skills due to its outcomes being less immediately evident or tangible. The work has no recognized status. Reticulist activity underpins the two examples of joint working described below. In each, the liaison role performed by a particular group of professionals was central to its success.

(a) Community Services for the Elderly Team

The Community Services for the Elderly Team operated in one of the four major Scottish cities and was funded by the local health board (equivalent to an English district health authority). The Team comprised four clinical medical officers. The account which follows draws heavily upon McKeganey and Hunter (1986) where a fuller description of the Team may be found.

The origins of the Team lay in the recurring disputes which took place between geriatric medicine and residential care over the appropriate placement of particular elderly people. While the Team was originally conceived as a mechanism for bridging the gap between these services, its role broadened so that members advised on patients transfers; on exchanges between acute and geriatric beds, and between geriatric, psychiatric and residential care; on discharges from hospital into the community; and on the allocation of sheltered housing.

A founder member of the Team described its reticulist or networking role in the following terms:

My remit is to advise the social work department, housing department and anyone else involved in the care of the elderly and to try and pull all the services together, acting as a referee if necessary. We see all the old people who go into residential care from hospital—geriatric units, psychogeriatric units and acute wards. We act as a sort of buffer between the consultants and the social workers. Our part of the service works quite well in keeping everybody speaking to each other. I see this as being a major part of my job.

As this description implies, joint working between the services was seen as something which had to be worked at rather than, as is so often the case, assumed at the outset. Among the reasons were those factors considered earlier in the article, that is the different backgrounds and training of the various professional groups, their different power bases, their differential status and their respective territorial concerns. While each professional group is concerned with individual patients or clients each is also concerned with issues of resource allocation and use. It was very often in terms of conflicting views as to what was perceived to be the correct use, or disposal, of resources such as beds that disagreements surfaced between professionals which the Team sought to resolve.

While Team members were in part chosen for their clinical skills, the Team leader also noted the importance of sensitivity, tact and the ability to appear non-threatening in accomplishing their work. Members needed 'a fair degree of sympathy, compassion and commonsense and an ability to try and understand what the problems were without pushing their own ideas'.

Team members did not function as completely neutral arbiters between different professional groups. Though on occasion they performed in such a fashion, much of their work was more practical and directive in nature. A key aspect of the Team's functioning consisted of being on hand to be called in by social workers as an ally in their negotiations with hospital staff. Indeed, it was partly because of the close alliance that the Team had been able to foster with social workers that it was able to help influence outcomes. Had the Team remained wholly independent it would have been seen as an external imposition on the work of the various professionals and would probably have been ignored or been less effective. In short, the Team's leaning towards social work gave it a power base, or leverage, from which to operate and persuade those who were dependent upon the social work department.

Team members were well aware of the complexities of their work and often described themselves as 'walking a tightrope' between competing and often conflicting claims. Speaking for, or on behalf of, social workers in their negotiations with other services (particularly hospital services) at points of apparent disagreement was one aspect of the Team's reticulist role. It was at least in part as a result of their clinical training and the experience acquired over the years of their operation that Team members were able to perform such a role. Being clinically trained, Team members were able to negotiate with staff in hospitals from a shared knowledge base and were able to translate items of relevant medical knowledge to the social workers and other ancillary staff involved in a case, thereby maximizing the flow of information between different professionals. The clinical training of Team members together with their expertise in the care of the elderly acquired over many years were therefore important sources of legitimacy. In addition, while there was an acknowledged social work leaning in much of the Team's work, members had no axe to grind or territory to defend. They could move relatively freely within and between professional groups in their endeavours to find common ground upon which mutually agreed outcomes to difficulties could be sought. In this work it would be hard to overestimate the importance of such interactional skills as charm, patience, tolerance and good humour.

Although the situations into which the Team would be called were invariably highly specific, pertaining to a particular client at a particular time, nevertheless, such occasions often provided the Team with an opportunity to sensitize a diverse range of professionals to the nature and the difficulties, of each other's work. Thus much of the Team's work involved a combination of both reactive and proactive elements: reactive in the sense that the team was often called into an existing dispute or disagreement, the lines of which had already been fairly clearly drawn, and proactive in the sense that the Team would often attempt to utilize such occasions for positive educational purposes.

In assessing the Team's significance and value, it fulfilled an integrative, connective role as social broker in its attempts to mobilize services around individuals. This is in contrast to the operation of separate services each of which may try to fit an individual to the available resource.

(b) The liaison physicians

The liaison physicians operating in a major city in the North-East of England performed a similar function to the Community Services for the Elderly Team described above. The work of the liaison physicians has been documented by Hutchinson, Evans and Greveson (1984), the source for the following account.

The creation of two posts of liaison physician arose from a recognition that (1) social workers experienced difficulty in obtaining appropriate medical assessments for their clients and (2) apportioning responsibility for care of individual elderly people between the health and social services could present problems. As Hutchinson and his colleagues point out:

This has to be primarily a matter of local agreement on policy since if government guidelines, both prescriptive and permissive, were to be followed literally, their ambiguities and absurdities would lead to some elderly people not receiving necessary care at all. It is by no means unknown for elderly patients in hospital to be found not fit enough for residential care but fit enough to be discharged home (pp. 50–1).

It is against the background of such anomalies that the post of liaison physician was created. In this respect, its origins parallel those of the Team described above.

The functions of the liaison physicians included the following:

1. Assessing applicants for residential care
2. Assessing hospital patients applying for entry or transfer to residential care
3. Choosing residential homes most appropriate to individual clients
4. Advising general practitioners and social workers on management of elderly patients or clients
5. Advising residential home staff

One of the most important functions of the liaison physicians was organizing the medical assessment of applicants for residential care. They arranged attendance and supervised assessment on behalf of the consultant to whose responsibility the patient was allocated. They were responsible for seeing patients in hospital who were initiating applications for residential care, or who were seeking transfer back to a residential home after admission to hospital. In such cases the liaison physician did not act simply as an unhelpful doorkeeper to residential care but tried to respond with practical alternative suggestions for care.

The liaison physicians also received referrals from general practitioners which generally fell into the category of non-specific cries for help. Cases referred in this way often lay in the no-man's land between medicine, psychiatry and social services where the experience and position of the liaison physicians could be of special relevance.

In addition, the liaison physicians were on hand to give advice about elderly residents to residential staff. In this way they contributed to the formal and informal in-service training and experience of residential home staff. One of the key topics dealt with concerned the appropriate use of health services for elderly people. Like the work of the Team operating in a Scottish city, much of the educational function was carried out 'on the job' rather than in formal seminars or lectures. This approach was possible because the liaison physicians visited all the residential homes in the city on a regular basis.

The liaison physicians performed two roles which were not evident in the Scottish Team's remit: educating medical students by contributing to undergraduate courses and contributing to the running of the day hospital service.

As in the case of the Team members, the effectiveness of the liaison physicians depended crucially on their being seen as having a broad and independent view of services for elderly people as a whole. In the words of Hutchinson and his colleagues:

The work is a combination of clinical medicine and practical administration, involving a great deal of personal contact and cooperation with patients, their families and with staff at all levels in the health and social services. An interesting combination of diplomacy and decisiveness is called for, not least in the relationship with consultants in the geriatric service (p. 54).

ASSESSMENT AND CONCLUSION

This article has reported on two attempts at interprofessional, or street level, joint working in order to examine not only the context within which joint working may be attempted and the sorts of problems for which it may be seen as a partial solution but also the sorts of skills that are likely to be required by those charged with the responsibility for bringing it about. In assessing the value of the initiatives described above for other localities a number of observations may be made.

First, common solutions to common problems probably do not exist. Both the creation of the Team and the post of liaison physician were products of their respective environments – they were 'bottom up' rather than 'top down' responses to perceived problems in each locality. What may work in one locale may be less successful or even fail if transferred and imposed elsewhere without adaptation to fit local circumstances. While it is possible to learn from successful initiatives, any mechanism for joint working must be custom-built for the particular environment in which it is to be introduced.

Second, there needs to be an identified purpose for which some kind of coordinated response is seen to be appropriate. Often joint working is not directed at a particular objective but is invoked at a general catchall level. There needs to be agreement on both the nature of the problem and the response to it before joint working can hope to succeed. Both initiatives described above offered legitimate responses to perceived problems.

Third, in joint activity of the kind described the work is sensitive and political and requires particular skills for its successful execution. The skills are not principally technical or clinical (although they may serve as an important source of legitimacy) but social and interpersonal. Although only a single profession has been involved in each of the initiatives, whether only clinicians are able to play such a reticulist, brokerage role between health and social services personnel is an open question. On the evidence available, the clinical background appeared crucial for the effective operation of the two initiatives, particularly in those situations where negotiations with hospital clinicians were necessary.

Fourth, the organizational standing of the Team and of the liaison physicians and the absence of 'axes to grind' enabled members to appear reasonably detached and unbiased. At the same time, complete neutrality and detachment would certainly have lessened the effectiveness of the Team and probably that of the liaison physicians. Some leverage or stake in the system was therefore essential. Success flowed from a tricky combination of coalition building and the formation of a loose alliance with social workers while simultaneously maintaining a degree of independence from all interested parties – hence the aptness of the tightrope metaphor.

Fifth, joint working cannot be expected to compensate for basic resource shortages or for services under severe pressure. Solutions to these problems lie elsewhere.

Sixth, successful joint working arrangements are those for which service providers perceive a need. The Team and the liaison physicians survived because service providers, or at any rate a sufficient number of them, were of the opinion that their respective activities merited support. They felt helped and supported by the existence of the initiatives, certainly in overall terms if not on every occasion. Without such support, it is unlikely that mechanisms to facilitate joint working could survive for long.

In conclusion, while the two examples described in this article of mechanisms designed to make a reality of joint working offer possible models for similar initiatives elsewhere, whatever arrangements are established must be of the bespoke variety, tailored to fit the particular political and organizational context prevailing in a locality.

REFERENCES

Audit Commission (1986). *Making a Reality of Community Care*, HMSO, London.

Booth, T. (1981). 'Collaboration between the health and social services: Part II. A case study of joint finance'. *Policy and Politics*, **9** (2), 205–26.

Central Policy Review Staff (1975). *A Joint Framework for Social Policies*, HMSO, London.

Friend, J.K. (1983). 'Planning—the art of responsible scheming'. *Linkage*, **7**, 8–15.

Friend, J.K., Power, J.M., and Yewlett, C.J.L. (1974). *Public Planning: The Intercorporate Dimension*, Tavistock, London.

Glennerster, H., with Korman N., and Marsden-Wilson, F. (1983). *Planning for Priority Groups*, Martin Robertson, London.

Gray, A.M., and Hunter, D.J. (1983). 'Priorities and resource allocation in the Scottish health service: some problems in planning and implemention', *Policy and Politics*, **11**(4), 417–37.

Hunter, D.J., and Wistow, G. (1987). *Community Care in Britain: Variations on a Theme*, King Edward's Hospital Fund for London, London.

Hutchinson, P., Grimley Evans, J. and Greveson, G. (1984). 'Linking health and social services: the liaison physician'. In J. Grimley Evans and F.I. Caird (eds.), *Advanced Geriatric Medicine*, Vol. 4, Pitman, London.

JASP Team (1984). 'Joint approach to social policy'. Report

of Research Funded by Social Science Research Council (now Economic and Social Research Council), University of Bath, Loughborough University of Technology and Royal Institute of Public Administration.

McKeganey, N., and Hunter, D. (1986). '"Only connect . . . ": tightrope walking and joint working in the care of the elderly', *Policy and Politics*, **14**(3), 335–60.

Norton, A., and Rogers, S. (1981). 'The health service and local government services'. In G. McLachlan (ed.), *Matters of Moment*, Oxford University Press for the Nuffield Provincial Hospitals Trust, London.

Rein, M. (1983). *From Policy to Practice*, Macmillan, London.

Schon, D. (1971). *Beyond the Stable State*, Penguin, Harmondsworth.

Working Group on Joint Planning (1985). *Progress in Partnership*, DHSS, London.

Issues in the therapeutic use of reminiscence with elderly people

Peter Coleman

Senior Lecturer in Social Gerontology, University of Southampton

CHANGING ATTITUDES TO REMINISCENCE

The study of ageing, gerontology, has witnessed many changes in the last 20 years. One of the most remarkable has been the change in attitude by gerontologists themselves towards reminiscence as a healthy rather than an unhealthy activity of elderly people. An almost totally negative view to talking or thinking about the past has been replaced by a much more positive one. [. . .]

Even now reminiscence therapy cannot be said to stand on a very solid base, and recent commentators, notably Merriam (1980), have been led to criticise simplistic thinking about reminiscing and its value. Talking or thinking about the past may serve various functions, and one must try to be more discerning in one's observations. Also, reminiscence may mean different things to individuals in different situations. For example, a frail, disabled, elderly person may learn to appreciate thinking back on past memories in a way yet inconceivable to a younger, active person. In a study of 300 adults aged from 18 to 90 years, Merriam and Cross (1982) showed that older adults more frequently experienced feelings of satisfaction and well-being with reminiscence than did other age groups. Moreover recent work on 'differential gerontology' (for example Thomae, 1976) has taught that one must no longer expect to find common laws of social or psychological ageing. Whether a person stands to gain from reminiscence will depend on his past history as well as his present needs. Therefore, more detailed analysis of individual cases seems to be called for, using diverse samples of elderly people.

From Chapter 3 of *Psychological Therapies for Elderly People*, I. Hanley and M. Gilhooley (eds.), Croom Helm, 1986 (edited). Reproduced by permission of Croom Helm Limited. © I. Hanley and M. Gilhooley.

FUNCTIONS OF REMINISCENCE

It is important to note that even in the first writings on reminiscence, quite a divergence of views was expressed on the function reminiscence might play in old age. Butler (1963) stressed that the life review was a normative process in later life, prompted by the realisation of approaching death. It was 'characterised by the progressive return to consciousness of past experience, and, particularly, the resurgence of unresolved conflicts'. He stressed, as have later writers (for instance, Kaminsky, 1984), that the life review is not necessarily easy to recognise. It can appear fragmentary with key themes occurring in dream material as well as in conscious daydreaming and more purposeful thinking. Typically, ordinary daily occurrences may trigger thinking on associated events in the past. [. . .] The outcome of the life review is not necessarily positive. The individual may remain obsessed with events and actions he regrets, finds no solution and no peace, and develop chronic feelings of guilt and depression. It is also possible that the individual may 'block' the life review process altogether, succeed in avoiding certain thoughts and reject the past. This might be a successful way of avoiding a negative outcome, particularly if the individual has plenty of present interests, but it denies the potentiality of growth inherent in the life review process. [. . .]

McMahon's and Rhudick's (1964) observations on how much time the veterans of the Spanish–American war they interviewed devoted to talking about the past led them to speculate on a number of other uses of reminiscence: 'the maintenance of self-esteem in the face of declining physical and intellectual abilities; coping with grief and depression resulting from personal losses, finding means to contribute significantly to a society of which older persons are members; and retaining some sense of identity in an increasingly estranged environment'. [. . .]

The close link between reminiscence and preservation of identity is made by a number of other writers (Castelnuovo-Tedesco, 1978; Zinberg and Kaufman, 1963). 'Reaching out to share recollections with others may be motivated by the need to convince oneself of a continuity between the past and present' (Carlson, 1984). A similar point is made by Blythe: 'One of the reasons why old people make so many journeys into the past is to satisfy themselves that it is still there' (Blythe, 1979). The past represents a platform of security which may give strength and effort to continue.

However, maintaining a sense of identity is quite a distinct idea from the life review. Indeed, McMahon and Rhudick (1964) dispute the implication of Butler's view that all individuals feel a need for self-justification at the end of their lives, and rather go to the other extreme by denigrating this function as characteristic of 'obsessive-compulsive subjects who, we may suspect, have been reviewing their past behaviour in the same judgemental and evaluative way all their lives', that is, it is evidence of a lifelong and ongoing pathological process.

For McMahon and Rhudick, if there is an ideal use of reminiscence it is the one traditionally ascribed to older men in primitive societies, as bearers and transmitters of their culture's stories and traditions. They describe their 'best-adjusted' group, quite simply, as storytellers, 'recounting past exploits and experiences with obvious pleasure in a manner which is both entertaining and informative'. Moreover, these storytellers seemed to have little need to depreciate the present or glorify the past, as did other members of their sample. Rather their reminiscing is a happy instance of behaviour serving both personal ends and social goals: 'The older person's knowledge of a bygone era provides him with an opportunity to enhance his self-esteem by contributing in a meaningful way to his society' (McMahon and Rhudick, 1964).

It has to be admitted that the storytelling function of the old has become devalued in modern societies, both because of the fast-changing nature of society which has appeared to make the past seem less relevant, and because of the development of many other means of preserving and communicating information. Nevertheless, the recent growth of interest in oral history has done something to reverse this trend. It has led to a revaluing of the memories ordinary individuals possess of the times they have lived through. The memories of the oldest generations have come to appear especially valuable, with the realisation that the possibility of collecting records of experiences of a whole era, such as the Edwardian period before the First World War, dies with them.

When I first began to research the functions of reminiscence in the late 1960s, I took care to try to distinguish between the two types of reminiscence, 'life review' reminiscence, as described by Butler, and 'informative' or 'teaching' reminiscence, as described by McMahon and Rhudick. I also included basic assessments of the amount of conversation individuals devoted to past events and of the extent to which they said they thought about the past. There was no evidence that 'simple' reminiscence per se was related to adjustment in general or at some particular level of social loss or physical disability, and this has also been the finding of a number of other studies.

But the more particular measures of the individual's conversations about the past did produce interesting results. 'Life reviewing', defined in terms of questions or statements about the kind of person the individual had been in his life and why he had done the things he had, did seem to be adaptive for those individuals who were also dissatisfied with their past lives. Likewise, 'informative' reminiscing, defined in terms of communication of historical facts or attitudes to the world based on past experience, also seemed adaptive, at least for the men in the author's sample (Coleman, 1974). These findings convinced the author of the value of trying to be more specific in describing the meaning or function of reminiscence.

ATTITUDES OF ELDERLY PEOPLE TO REMINISCENCE

If one wants to know what elderly people are doing when they reminisce, one can do worse than ask them directly. Of course, it is likely that their attitudes will reflect to some degree the attitudes of society as a whole, but it is also interesting to observe what variations there might be in attitude and what implications, if any, these have for other aspects of the individual's life.

Through the 1970s I have carried out three studies in which either as a main or subsidiary part of the research, elderly people were asked about the past and their reminiscences. The smallest study (in numbers), but the most intense, has been a longitudinal study of elderly people living in sheltered housing schemes in London, which was started in 1969 (Coleman, 1986). [. . .] The second study was a survey of elderly people living in the Dutch city of Nijmegen in the Netherlands. A large number of people were interviewed (455) and some questions on reminiscence were included in the questionnaire. The third study was another large-scale community survey of elderly people living in Southampton (*n* = 366) in 1977 to 1978, in which questions on reminiscence were also included.

The answers given to questions in the studies reveal a varying attitude to reminiscence according to the phrasing of the questions. Thus, whereas only a quarter to a third of the elderly people interviewed say they 'live in the past more and more', two-thirds to three-quarters say they 'like to think about the past'. The former statement has a negative connotation in society, and it was therefore not surprising that those who assented to it were more likely to be depressed and to have low morale. The latter statement, on the other hand, was found to have a much more positive connotation, and indeed assent to this statement was correlated with high morale. When asked to choose between thinking abut the future and the past, the split was almost 50–50 in all three studies. [. . .]

A consideration of all the data seemed to bear out Lewis's point (1971) that it makes sense to speak of 'reminiscers' and 'non-reminiscers'. A substantial number said they enjoyed thinking about the past and thought it a good and helpful thing to do, whereas an equally substantial number did not enjoy it and thought it a pointless and useless thing to do. [. . .]

In order to gain insight into people's attitudes, however, it is important not only to describe their content but also the reasons underlying them, and it was clear that not all those who reminisce did so for the same reasons, and the same applied to those who did not reminisce. Whether people reminisced or not was not in itself associated with whether they also expressed a sense of well-being. But there was an association between well-being and the reasons for reminiscing and not reminiscing. Thus, reminiscing could have a positive or negative association, depending on the individual's attitude to what he was doing. 'Living in the past' for most people tended to reflect a negative activity, whereas 'liking to think about the past' reflected a positive one.

Looking carefully at all the data from the London study, including most importantly what people actually said about their own reminiscing, it made sense to divide the group into four regarding their orientations towards reminiscence.

The first is a large group of 21 individuals who indicated that reminiscence played an important and positive part in their lives. The characteristic the past had for all of them was that of a treasured possession, even with and sometimes because of its difficulties. [. . .]

The second group of eight people is particularly interesting because they could be called 'compulsive' reminiscers. The reminisced a lot although it made them feel bad about their past lives to a significant extent. They were dissatisfied with their lives as a whole or had significant and troubling areas of regret. They could not repress their memories. [. . .]

The third group of fifteen is the most heterogeneous. They saw no general value in reminiscence. The majority had found other ways of coping with life. Certainly, and this is important, they seemed no less well-adjusted than those in the first group. Some had striking life histories to tell. But they did not feel any need to dwell on them further. [. . .]

The fourth group indicates another important distinction. These were six people who, like the previous group, did not reminisce and did not want to reminisce, but, like the second group, their relationship with the past was an uneasy one. They had to avoid reminiscing because it made them feel depressed. This was not because there was anything to regret in the past; on the contrary, the past had been fuller and happier, and the contrast with the emptiness of the present made them more sad than they need be. [. . .]

Thus those who had a positive attitude to reminiscing and actually reminisced were by and large well-adjusted. Those who saw no point in reminiscing and so did not reminisce were likewise well-adjusted. On the other hand those who could not bear to reminisce, although their memories were happy, tended to be depressed. And those who could not avoid reminiscing—although their memories were painful—were troubled people.

The same people have been followed up over a period of more than ten years, so it is possible to analyse what happened to the members of each of the above groups. [. . .]

Briefly expressed, the large group of those who reminisced, valued their memories highly and found them helpful in coping with life in old age, and appeared to adapt well to the vicissitudes that faced them. They maintained positive attitudes to reminiscence. [. . .]

The second group is particularly interesting since it seems to exemplify the life review process. Five of the eight died within two years. From the evidence collected, it was clear that two at least showed increasing psychological disturbance. According to the reports of wardens and neighbours, they had become alcoholics and did not look after themselves. [. . .]

Of the people who discounted the importance of reminiscence, the interesting question is whether they were able to adapt to the vicissitudes of old age as well as the reminiscers. The answer seems to be that they were. One of the sixteen was 'lost' when he moved out of his housing complex, but of the remaining fifteen, twelve remained well-adjusted until their deaths. Three became depressed and, of these, two did so in the face of considerable disability. The rest maintained much the same attitudes. They had found successful ways of coping with old age which did not involve reminiscence. Nearly all had plenty of outside interests and they did not feel any need to look back.

From the evidence available on the six people in the final category, who in 1971 did not like to reminisce because of the contrast with their present situation, five were at that time clearly depressed. [. . .] These five retained the same negative attitudes to their present life and an avoiding attitude towards reminiscence. [. . .]

IMPLICATIONS FOR THERAPY OF A DIFFERENTIAL VIEW OF REMINISCENCE

[. . .] Any helping individual, professional or otherwise who is considering using reminiscence as a means of therapy, should try, before making any specific intervention, to understand from the elderly person's perspective his/her life history and circumstances. The same applies to any offer of practical help: one should consider beforehand what the likely benefit is going to be. The distinctions drawn between types of attitudes to reminiscence offer a framework around which to consider various approaches to therapy.

In those who already reminisce readily and have a positive attitude to memories of their past lives, these memories constitute strengths which can be tapped in the face of difficulties. But the links between past and present can be broken. The stresses and strains of old age may be so great that they disrupt the person's sense of continuity between past and present. Reminiscence then can come to seem irrelevant to the present situation. Thus, although reminiscence occurs naturally and spontaneously in many elderly people, there can be times when an outsider does need to promote it. For example, it may be the task for a social worker to remind an elderly client that he or she has met crises before, and has struggled and persevered. Such an interpretation of one's life history can serve as a powerful motivation to try and cope with the new demands of the present.

Of course, a social worker may initially know little about the individual's past, but the very activity of exploring it with the individual concerned will likely help them both to understand better the situation they are now in. At the least the client should feel that the social worker has a better appreciation of him/her as an individual. The social worker may be able to spot ways in which the individual has coped in the past which can be used again. Information collected also from others about the client's previous life may be useful to the social worker in challenging an elderly person's depressed view of himself and the world, and to help him reach a more positive view of his current efforts.

Moreover, it is not only that people may 'forget' about their own individual histories; they may also have adopted from society at large a general attitude to what has happened in the past as irrelevant, uninteresting or of no further value. Individuals in a group setting such as a long-stay hospital or residential home may have done worthwhile and interesting things in their lives and may have contributed to society in various ways, but may need encouragement to reevalute these things—perhaps by the act of having to tell others about them. It is in such circumstances that the various forms of group reminiscence therapy, around particular themes and/or using visual and other aids (objects, pictures, slides and so on) are most helpful in stimulating memories and the sharing of experiences. A skilled leader is needed who can search beneath self-effacing attitudes and elicit important memories, and not allow the more talkative and assertive individuals to dominate conversations. [. . .]

Creative reminiscing needs to be distinguished from a brooding on the past, such as was shown by people in the second group in the study described. Their thoughts were often dominated by regretful memories about things they wish they had or had not done in their lives, or about sad things that had happened to them and their families. Short-term counselling offers a number of possibilities for helping such individuals. Again, it is important to be clear about what one is dealing with. One needs, for example, to try and develop a sense of how justified or rational the person's accusations are. Many individuals may have a tendency to blame themselves and feel guilty for past events for which they really had little or no personal responsibility, especially if they are depressed. Also, they may feel profoundly unlucky in a way which makes luck appear as something directed against them personally rather than a random occurrence.

Beck (1976) writes of the 'depressogenic error of generalization' whereby selective negative thinking is projected into the past. Various techniques have been suggested for countering such thinking by cognitive therapists; for example, 'disattribution' which involves teaching the client to stop attributing all blame to himself by recognising the role played by fate and others in events (Rathjen, Rathjen and Hiniker, 1978); or rational disputation of thoughts (Ellis, 1974) which encourages people to appreciate and then modify the way irrational beliefs about events often determine their feelings about things that happen to them; or by simply changing the forms of attention and seeing that there were positive things in the past as well as negative, and attending to them for a change. Some therapists specialising with the elderly, as Sherman (1981), regard such types of 'cognitive therapy' as being especially relevant to the elderly. Circumstances in old age may not easily be changed, but it is possible

to be more hopeful about changing an elderly person's perception of them.

However, it would be very naive to think that all problems with a difficult 'life review' can be solved in these ways. A person's sense of guilt may be well-founded. As Sherman himself points out, where actual wrong has been done to someone and that person is dead, the wrong has to be accepted, not disputed. To do this would tend to make matters worse by making the client attest to his or her guilt all the more, as well as reducing confidence in the counsellor. One should listen to the client carefully, hear him out fully and completely, provide the necessary catharsis and then help to move him from a sense of guilt to a sense of forgiveness.

The importance of the help that can be provided by religious practices, as the Christian confession, cannot be denied, and it would be foolish to omit religion from a discussion of forgiveness, and also of the healing of tragic and hurtful memories (Linn and Linn, 1974). [. . .]

The life review, as described by Butler (1963) and later writers (for example, Kaminsky, 1984) should be seen as a natural activity, perhaps especially but not exclusively related to old age (Molinari and Reichlin, 1985), and one that needs respect. [. . .] For some it may be an entirely private matter. But for those with deep feelings of regret and dissatisfaction, it may be vital that they are not left alone with their thoughts. Creative use can also be made of negative reminiscences, and writing an autobiography for a small group of interested others or for a therapist is better than sitting around and brooding about past events. [. . .]

Many negative phenomena in old age, such as hypochondriasis and prejudiced views, may reflect fears about loss of identity and inferiority. Bringing a person to a less egocentric view of life and to develop interest in the happiness of others may be the best way of combatting such feelings. Therefore, rather than staying with the individual in his morbid thoughts about the past, it may be much more profitable to try to encourage an orientation to the world around him, to develop social interests and contacts. Again, it must be stressed, judgement is required as to whether reminiscence is a productive or counterproductive activity, and whether some other intervention might be called for.

In those who deny the importance of reminiscence to them—the third group in my study—one should not lightly dismiss their view as (over) defensive. Most of the people interviewed who came into this category had very understandable reasons for not reminiscing. They were too busy with other things they preferred to do. It surely makes more sense to help them to continue with their chosen way of life and special interests—for example, find ways of transporting them to their old clubs or provide special aids to compensate for disabilities—rather than to say they should sit quietly and contemplate their past. [. . .]

The final group in the same study were those who tried not to reminisce although they said that their past lives had been very happy. The reason for their avoidance was because, they said, it was too painful to reminisce. It made them more sad than they need be. All these people were depressed when first spoken to, or subsequently became so. All had been bereaved or had suffered another important loss (for example, severe disability or separation from a previously close family) and had not come to terms with these changes. In retrospect, it seemed evident that the inability to reminisce had reflected their inability to overcome these losses, and perhaps resulted from their failure to grieve satisfactorily. The same link between reminiscence and grieving has also been made recently by Pollack (1981) and Castelnuovo-Tedesco (1980). Reminiscence, they observe, may be functionally analogous to the grieving process. Like the work of mourning, reminiscence involves a reorganisation of one's relationship to the lost other. Reminiscence, too, can involve obsessive recounting. It can appear to reflect self-absorption. In some it can also result in a failure to give up what has been lost. Indeed, in those who never give up wishing for the return of the past, reminiscence may not be pleasurable because they are unable to detach themselves from and freely enjoy their memories of the past, as memories.

This outcome may occur most where people have become very dependent on past relationships and roles for their idea of themselves. Worden views highly dependent relationships as especially difficult to grieve (Worden, 1982). He cites the research of Horowitz and colleagues who suggest that a person who has a highly dependent relationship and then loses the source of that dependency experiences a change in self-image from that of a strong person, well-sustained by the relationship with a strong other, to the pre-existent structure of a weak, helpless waif supplicating in vain for rescue by a lost or abandoning person (Horowitz et al., 1980) [. .]

Therefore, proper consideration of reminiscence raises many other issues of importance in old age, and it seems right that increasing attention is being given to it. The main point here, however, has been to emphasise that one cannot make simple generalisations about the value of reminiscence. Each person needs to be considered in a special way. Whether reminiscence is a positive or negative factor in their lives, whether they can be helped with reminiscence which disturbs them or causes them pain, whether reminiscence should be avoided or stimulated, are all questions which call for a careful appraisal. Certainly, memories can be a source of great creativity, and this is an important point to stress, but elderly people should be offered many other possibilities as well to express themselves. Research on the value of formally stimulated reminiscence—for example, in institutional settings—should take a differential view, paying due attention to each individual's life history and circumstances.

REMINISCENCE AND MENTAL DETERIORATION

The previous view that reminiscence was related to or even caused mental deterioration has been turned on its head. Now, reminiscence is seen as the 'new' means of preserving mental functioning in old age. A number of recent papers have pointed to the benefits of organised reminiscence in psychogeriatric institutions both to patients and staff (Kiernat, 1979; Lesser, Lazarus, Frankel, et al., 1981; Norris and Abu El Eileh, 1982; Cook, 1984). Although most of the evidence is of an anecdotal nature rather than quantitative, it is consistently positive. The writers point to improvements such as increased participation in discussion and more spontaneity on the part of elderly people, greater socialisation before and after the sessions and even higher self-esteem and behavioural improvements.

The nurses and other staff involved have been said to benefit from knowing the elderly people better and, as a result, being able to form closer relationships with them. Other valuable spin-offs are referred to (for example, the formation of activity programmes based on the interests expressed in the groups). Evidence has also been collected that structured reminiscence exercise leads to improvement in cognitive functioning as measured by the Raven Standard Progressive Matrices (Hughston, 1976). At the least, activities involving reminiscence seem to be an eminently suitable means of attracting and maintaining the engagement of many elderly people.

Comparison with the enthusiasm expressed for reality orientation comes readily to mind. As Woods and Britton point out in their recent text (Woods and Britton, 1985), research on the benefits of reminiscence in institutions for the elderly will now probably mushroom and researchers should take notice of the lessons emerging from the previous research on reality orientation.

However, there is some danger that this association will lead, at least as far as mentally deteriorated elderly people are concerned, to an exclusive concern with the 'cognitive' and 'activity' benefits of reminiscence therapy, and a neglect of the broader issues of the relationship between reminiscence and psychological adjustment that have been the focus of this paper. Yet these same issues, such as maintenance of identity, present themselves as much with people suffering from dementia as with mentally intact elderly people, perhaps even more so. For example, one often needs to look beyond the immediate content of the reminiscence towards its meaning for the individual. Reminiscence may be a means of communicating feelings which, if expressed directly, would be difficult to handle both for the elderly person and the people who care for them. One illustration of this is talk about parents. Elderly people, and elderly women in particular, seem to reminisce a lot about childhood (Coleman, 1986). But why do confused elderly people speak so often about their parents as if they were alive? Does this tell us something about their sense of security and need for roots (Miesen, 1985)? In recognising reminiscence as a valuable activity for mentally deteriorating elderly people, one should not thereby become insensitive to what is said. Nor should one assume that reminiscence activities will suit everyone equally.

REFERENCES

Beck, A.T. (1976). *Cognitive Therapy and the Emotional Disorders*, International Universities Press, New York.

Blythe, R. (1979). *The View in Winter: Reflections on Old Age*, Allen Lane, Harmondsworth, London.

Butler, R.N. (1963). 'The life review: an interpretation of reminiscence in the aged', *Psychiatry*, **26**, 65–76.

Carlson, C.M. (1984). 'Reminiscing: towards achieving ego integrity in old age', *Social Casework: The Journal of Contemporary Social Work*, February 1984, 81–9.

Castelnuovo-Tedesco, P. (1978). 'The mind as a stage: some comments on reminiscence and internal objects', *International Journal of Psychoanalysis*, **59**, 19–25.

Castelnuovo-Tedesco, P. (1980). 'Reminiscence and nostalgia: the pleasure and pain of remembering'. In S.I. Greenspan and G.H. Pollack (eds.), *The Course of Life: Psychoanalytic Contributions toward Understanding Personality Development, Adulthood and the Aging Process*, US Department of Health and Human Services, Washington D.C., pp. 115–27.

Coleman, P.G. (1974). 'Measuring reminiscence characteristics from conversation as adaptive features of old age', *International Journal of Ageing and Human Development* **5**, 281–94.

Coleman, P.G. (1986). *Ageing and Reminiscence Processes: Social and Clinical Implications*, John Wiley, Chichester.

Cook, J.B. (1984). 'Reminiscing: how it can help confused nursing home residents', *Social Casework: The Journal of Contemporary Social Work*, February **1984**, 90–3.

Ellis, A. (1974). *Humanistic Psychotherapy: The Rational-Emotive Approach*, McGraw-Hill, New York.

Horowitz, M.J., *et al.* (1980). 'Pathological grief and the activation of latent self-images', *American Journal of Psychiatry*, **137**, 1157–62.

Hughston, G.A. (1976). 'The effects of two educational interventions on the cognitive functioning of older people', doctoral dissertation, Pennsylvania State University, University Park, Pa37 (5).

Kaminsky, M. (1984). 'Transfiguring life: images of continuity hidden among the fragments'. In M. Kaminsky (ed.), *The Uses of Reminiscence. New Ways of Working with Older Adults*, The Haworth Press, New York.

Kiernat, J.M. (1979). 'The use of life review activity with confused nursing home residents', *American Journal of Occupational Therapy*, **33**, 306–10.

Lesser, J., Lazarus, L.W., Frankel, J., *et al.* (1981). 'Reminiscence group therapy with psychotic geriatric inpatients', *The Gerontologist*, **21**, 291–6.

Lewis, C.N. (1971). 'Reminiscing and self-concept in old age', *Journal of Gerontology*, **26**, 240–3.

Linn, D., and Linn, M. (1974). *Healing of Memories*, Paulist Press, New York.

McMahon, A.W., and Rhudick, P.J. (1964). 'Reminiscing: adaptional significance in the aged', *Archives of General Psychiatry,* **10**, 292–8.

Merriam, S. (1980). 'The concept and function of reminiscence: a review of the research', *The Gerontologist,* **20**, 604–9.

Merriam, S. and Cross, L. (1982). 'Adulthood and reminiscence: a descriptive study', *Educational Gerontology,* **8**, 275–90.

Miesen, B. (1985). 'Meaning and function of the remembered parents in normal and abnormal old age'. Paper presented at the XIIIth International Congress of Gerontology, New York.

Molinari, V., and Reichlin, R.E. (1985). 'Life review reminiscence in the elderly: a review of the literature', *International Journal of Aging and Human Development,* **20**(2), 81–92.

Norris, A.D., and Abu El Eileh, M.T. (1982). 'Reminiscence groups', *Nursing Times,* **78**, 1368–9.

Pollack, G.H. (1981). 'Reminiscences and insight', *Psychoanalytic Study of the Child,* **36**, 279–87.

Rathjen, D.P., Rathjen, E.D., and Hiniker, A. (1978). 'A cognitive analysis of social performance'. In J.P. Foreyt and D.P. Rathjen (eds.), *Cognitive Behaviour Therapy: Research and Application*, Plenum Press, New York.

Sherman, E. (1981). *Counseling the Aging. An Integrative Approach*, The Free Press, New York.

Thomae, H. (ed.) (1976). *Patterns of Aging*, Karger, Basel.

Woods, R.T., and Britton, P.G. (1985). *Clinical Psychology with the Elderly*, Croom Helm, London/Aspen, Rockville, Maryland.

Worden, J.W. (1982). *Grief Counseling and Grief Therapy*, Springer, New York.

Zinberg, N. and Kaufman, I. (1963). 'Cultural and personality factors associated with aging: an introduction'. In N. Zinberg and I. Kaufman (eds.), *Normal Psychology of the Aging Process*, International Universities Press, New York.

Elder abuse: issues, treatment and support

MARK KINNEY*, ROBERT WENDT† and JOSEPH HURST‡

*Associate Professor of Theory and Social Foundations, University of Toledo, Ohio; †Professor of Counselor Education, University of Toledo, Ohio; ‡Professor of Social Foundations, University of Toledo, Ohio

INTRODUCTION

This paper is about taking a stand—a stand to declare an end to abuse on the planet by the year 2020. Let's together look forward to that day when we can have '20–20 hindsight' about what steps were taken worldwide to cope with, reduce, prevent and finally end abuse of children, spouses, parents and the elderly. This paper is about creating the commitment to the belief that abusing another human being physically, psychologically, emotionally and materially is an unacceptable way of relating to others under any circumstance. Estimates of the number of 'abused, neglected or exploited' elderly persons in the United States alone range from 600 000 to over a million (Eastman, 1981).

ISSUES IN RESPONDING TO ELDER ABUSE

Extensive discussions of elder abuse have taken place in the last few years. The work on definitions has been fruitful. Today professionals generally agree that abuse includes physical, psychological and material abuses (Hickey, Douglass and Noel, 1983; Galbraith and Zdorskowski, 1984). Underlying the issue of abuse are several assumptions to which many of us still adhere. It is *outside* of these assumptions that effective action will occur.

1. Some of us assume that abuse is just too big a problem to solve. The difficulty in identification, the lack of adequate staff and staff training in social service agencies and churches, the blindness of the populace and other societal factors confirm this view. Elder abuse will never end.
2. Some of us assume that family abuse leads to elder abuse, and that the history of abuse in families is deeply rooted, too deep to make it possible to change.
3. Some of us assume that the abused persons and the abusers should handle the problem themselves. They may even have brought it upon themselves! They are the ones most affected. They should do something about it themselves.
4. Some assume that abuse grows from the dependent relationship inherent in growing old, a relationship which will always be present in our society.

Taking a position on elder abuse results in others taking the opposite view. When someone says that it is caused by the history of abuse within the family, then others say 'No!', it is caused, for instance, by the unfairness of the economic system and financial problems. The solution to this problem comes by listening to all sides of the issue and producing action consistent with our stand to end abuse. The solution lies in widespread action, not in argumentative dialogue.

This paper, then, is about possibilities. There are several underlying principles of group process which impact this issue. The first principle is that circumstances can be shifted through the involvement of people. Second is the principle that all relevant persons need to be involved in finding solutions to problems they have created or of which they are a part. Third is the principle that the affected persons can create a

From *Elder Abuse: Perspectives on an Emerging Crisis*, Michael W. Galbraith (ed.), Convergence on Ageing, Mid-America Congress on Ageing, Vol. 3, 1986, Kansas. Reproduced with permission.

solution if given the support and occasions to do so.

What can the individual do? First, create a personal commitment to resolving the issues. Look at each new situation in terms of bringing to bear whatever it takes to remove or alleviate the abuse.

Second, pursue the solutions which you see in your own spheres of influence. We do not need to re-do the whole world to impact on this issue.

Third, we professionals can work toward systematic approaches to ending abuse through ensuring that steps are taken in each of the following spheres: (1) the definitions of abuse; (2) the identification and reporting of abuse; (3) the treatment of the abused and abuser; and (4) the prevention of abuse.

To move in that direction we will (1) focus on treatment in families and (2) discuss the development of support groups as a way for the abuser and abused and the professionals interacting with them to reach out to the community for assistance.

TREATMENT MODALITIES

The psychotherapeutic treatment of violence and neglect in families involving elder abuse is undergoing rapid development. In terms of direct intervention, it appears that family level approaches hold the most promise for success involving crisis interventions and longer term treatment.

Traditionally, treatment approaches have focused on changing the individual who is the abuser while offering support to the victims. More recently, there have been attempts to broaden this perspective by focusing less upon intrapsychic factors of behavior and placing greater emphasis upon interpersonal and systemic causation of behavior and upon familial and intergenerational factors. While certain personality and organic variables are linked with abusive behavior, understanding the family relationships from a systems perspective is a necessary step to providing effective interventions. An interactional model of pathological behavior has evolved from family theory (Bowen, 1978) which in turn emanated from family therapy. The viewpoint that abuse may have adaptive consequences in maintaining the stability of a family is a radical departure from previous theory.

Increasingly, theorists and therapists have come to view abuse in terms of such complex variables as marital strife, alcohol intake and intergenerational transmission of violent behavior. Elder abuse as well as any form of family violence operates in terms of circular causation of behaviors (L'Abate, 1976) rather than the traditional linear model of cause and effect. More clearly stated, behaviors within violent families involve circular patterns of behavior which are rigid and repetitive involving the whole family, not just the abuser and the victim. Therefore, it is important to view elder abuse as one component of interaction between all family members.

Several factors substantiate the need for family intervention:

1. Multiple generations are often involved directly or indirectly in the abuse of the elder.
2. The stress level within the family is usually extremely high with a significant 'pile-up' of stressors over time which has eroded the family's ability to cope.
3. There is a lack of psychological, social and interpersonal resources to cope with the stress of caring for the personal needs of the elderly and the needs of the rest of the family.

Therefore, such families have built and maintained inadequate and dysfunctional patterns of communication marked by low self-esteem of their members. This also contributes to members being unable to be supportive and to problem-solve, which results in conflict. Underlying these patterns is a pervasive sense of family members being unable to control themselves or events.

These family factors need to be empirically validated and should not ignore biological and organic contributions to violence and subsequent abuse (Elliott, 1982). Herr and Weakland (1978) point out that while families are an important component of clinical intervention, important questions exist regarding: (1) empirical knowledge to decide when to apply individual, group or family oriented interventions; (2) how to combine clinical counseling into agencies not designated or trained in family counseling; and (3) on what basis to select a framework for intervention.

Consistent with a growing trend (McCuan et al., 1983) we recommend that family crisis intervention be introduced as soon as possible after abuse has been identified. This would be followed, when appropriate, by longer term family therapy. Support groups and individual counseling could be adjunctive treatment modalities occurring after the abuse and victimization of the elder has ceased to exist.

FAMILY CRISIS INTERVENTION

Tomita (1982) has suggested that direct interventions are more feasible when the patient admits the need for help and when there are repeated contacts with the patient. He identifies three types of intervention: the therapeutic plan, the educational plan and the resource linkage.

Tomita feels a family oriented assessment is a necessary prerequisite for the formulation of each plan. Psychological, economic, health and social factors must be considered from the perspective of the victim, abuser and other family members. This requires the participation of the whole family, preferably in the home setting. Techniques for involving family members are employed by family therapists and will not be elaborated in this chapter. Gurman (1981) and Gurman and Kniskern (1981) have dealt with these issues extensively.

In cases in which a family is at a crisis point and the abuse is affecting the physical well-being of the elder, then immediate interventions may be necessary. This may include separation of the abuser and victim and possible institutionalization of the abuser in the event of uncontrolled physical violence, alcoholism, drug addiction and/or an acute psychotic episode. When the abuse involves violent behavior, then immediate action has to be taken to stop the violence. In order to accomplish this, the therapist must deal with the issues openly and establish a rule that forbids physical abuse. This can be set in the initial session or as part of the treatment plan. Generally, the abuser and elderly are very unhappy with the situation and do not wish to continue the situation, or have enforced separation or legal involvement in the problem.

It is, however, usually apparent to the family that they cannot change the situation by themselves. The abuser in certain situations cannot control the violent action and the victim and other family members are unable to exert the power necessary. If the victim or family attempts to stop the abuse, the abuser perceives this

as a threat which triggers an abusive response. The therapist who is a neutral expert with implied legal and professional power, has the leverage to impose rules and make them work. The therapist needs to have a backup facility for separating the elder or abuser should further violence occur.

In families exhibiting problems other than physical abuse, crisis intervention is still a necessary first step. Overmedication or overuse of alcohol, as well as undermedication need to be given priority. Issues of alcohol consumption and medication need also to be confronted immediately with the requirement that appropriate medication be resumed. Consultation with medical experts is often the first step. Alcoholism, on the other hand, is unlikely to be curtailed as a directive and the alcoholic will most likely need a comprehensive treatment program in an inpatient setting which should also involve the entire family.

Although material abuse and neglect need to be addressed, there is not the urgency of the other situations. Principles and techniques of family crisis intervention have been developed by Langsley *et al.* (1968) and Rueveni (1985).

EXTENDED FAMILY TREATMENT ISSUES

Family theory has developed into a number of approaches based upon systems theory. Structural family therapy (Minuchin, 1974; Minuchin and Fishman, 1980) offers the most direct and concrete approach. Strategic therapy (Haley, 1976; Madanes, 1981, 1984) offers techniques that are specific to persistent family problems.

It is important for the therapist in working with these families to assume a strong stance. The therapist needs to control the sessions and prevent outbreaks of hostility and verbal assaults. Blaming and uncontrolled anger can escalate into more abuse outside the sessions, sometimes with other members of the family when the abuse with the elder subsides.

The control problem in working with these families is both a lack of education regarding the therapeutic process and the covert resistance to change on the part of the whole family. This results in a variety of defensive positions taken by various family members involving the abused elder.

Essentially those families may seek help or are open to assistance because of stress created by the referral of the family by an outside authority which presents itself as a crisis situation. However, once the crisis is passed and the tension level subsides, the motivation to continue in treatment subsides. The fear of uncontrolled anger and/or lack of love seems to create a deep fear of the family dissolving—leaving people, including the elder, isolated without support or emotional connection. Therefore, interventions based upon honest thoughts and feelings are seen as threatening a perception, which is in direct conflict with the therapy process.

In order to deal with this dynamic, the therapist needs to form alliances with the more flexible members of the family. It is especially important that the elder feels that the therapist is caring, responsive and competent. Using the elder as a consultant to the rest of the family whenever possible neutralizes the victim role and enhances self-esteem. Establishing a working relationship with other family members of the abuser is equally important.

At times the spouse of the abuser may be resistant because of the positive nature of their rigid role. The children may be resistive, especially adolescents, because of the image factor with peers and the community.

Therapists need to control, yet give empathy and support, which enables the deflection away from power struggles at heightened moments of resistance. The use of paradoxical techniques (Palazzoli et al., 1978), ordeals (Haley, 1985) or pretending interventions (Madanes, 1981) are better suited for healing than for direct confrontation.

The abuser also needs to be brought back into a more functional role in the family which is very difficult, especially when the problems have persisted for many years. This can only be done when the family system has become more flexible, which happens after the more flexible members of the family begin to interact at a more functional level.

A particular problem for therapists are the emotional reactions associated with elder abuse which are similar in nature to child abuse situations. It is very easy to regard the victim with sympathy and to fall into recurring options which more often than not fail and create counteractive anger from the entire family. At the same time it is very difficult initially to be objective in dealing with the abuser. The more immediate reaction is one of fear and anger relative to the abuser. The therapist must engage the abuser in the therapy, despite the strong negative feelings. However, as the therapist gains understanding of the pervasive anger within the family and the personal dynamics of the abuser, these feelings tend to subside. History-taking relative to the family of origin of the abuser, while not necessarily therapeutic for the family, does aid immensely the understanding of the therapist. It lessens the aversiveness and creates a more objective stance with the family.

As the therapy progresses, support groups and other community resources for the elder can be effectively utilized. As therapy ends, individuals within the family may have separate issues, including the marital dyad, for which other forms of treatment, such as individual and marriage counseling, would also be timely and effective.

PERSONAL SUPPORT

The word support is commonly used in everyday personal and professional language. Most often it refers to 'assistance that seeks to bolster deficient persons by the provision of such material and non-material resources as comfort, encouragement, advice and environmental manipulation' (Pearson, 1983, p. 362). However, personal support has many dimensions.

Gibb (1961) distinguishes supportive from defensive communication. Supportive messages result in reduced threat, increased accuracy and listening, and emotional backing for people (i.e., support for people's self concepts, needs, goals, ideas and actions). According to Gibb, supportiveness results from messages that are *descriptive* rather than evaluative, *problem oriented* rather than controlling, *spontaneous* rather than manipulative, *empathic* rather than neutral, *equal* rather than superior and *flexible* rather than certain.

Richard Pearson (1982) describes thirteen emotional, cognitive or idealized dimensions of personal support.

These dimensions are outlined and defined in Table 1.

Although it can be and has been narrowly viewed as an extraordinary, focused intervention to end a crisis or to remove some deficiency, support is a continual reserve of personal resources and relationships upon which people can draw to develop, maintain, renew and expand their personal effectiveness and a sense of well-being. Like a reservoir of water, personal support is there to be tapped when needed. In the case of elder abuse, there is a low reserve for the abused, the abusers and other family members.

PROVIDING SUPPORT

In efforts to cope with and to prevent elder abuse, there are two avenues for providing personal support to elderly citizens and those who do, or may, abuse them: (1) expanding and strengthening their natural support systems, and (2) fostering their membership in other supportive groups. Natural support systems include family, friends, neighbors, co-workers and other people (e.g., church-goers and leaders, club members, senior center participants). According to Pearson (1982), personal support can be extended and strengthened by working with individuals and people in their natural support systems and by providing or making referrals to additional groups. When individuals have a sufficient network of support and there are barriers to effective relating, then counseling, therapy and educational programs can focus on helping elderly people and others around them to communicate, give and receive support, cope with problems and expand their resources.

When people's natural support systems are insufficient or incapable of improvement, then additional personal support is required. As professionals and lay persons, we need to refer people in this situation to appropriate sources of support (e.g., individual and group counseling, family therapy, self-help groups, educational programs, recreational activities, service organizations, peer counseling and support groups).

Table 1 Dimensions of support

Emotionally-oriented support

1. Love: caring, emotional sharing, affection and warmth
2. Intimacy: physical contact, pleasure and sexual satisfaction
3. Companionship: sharing activities, belonging and togetherness
4. Acceptance: respect, empathy, understanding and trust
5. Help: material assistance and doing things for someone
6. Example: modeling how life can be

Cognitively-oriented support

7. Encouragement: confidence, affirmation and reinforcement
8. Comfort: reassurance, forgiveness and reliance
9. Guidance: direction, spiritual assistance and suggestions
10. Knowledge: intellectual stimulation, expertise, information and instruction
11. Honesty: feedback, other perspectives and listening

Idealized support

12. Admiration: attention, interest and praise
13. Satisfaction: serving and contributing to others' lives

SUPPORT GROUPS

Professionals can act to establish support groups for the abused and for abusers which offer several dimensions of support to replace eroded natural forms of support. For instance, support groups run by trained counselors or therapists might focus on material support, honest feedback, acceptance, help, guidance, empathy and encouragement lost because of rejection by formerly supportive people (Rueveni, 1985). Similarly, support groups for the abused could focus on their needs for companionship, affection, comfort, encouragement, guidance and help. Such support groups can serve as an adjunct to any other form of treatment.

In addition, when elderly people are identified who may potentially be involved in some form of abuse, they need to be invited to participate in a variety of activities that broaden their network of support, meet their needs for particular dimensions of support and develop strengths in seeking and obtaining it. [. . .]

According to Hulse (1985), homogeneous groups made up of subcultural or cultural minorites and people with a common problem may be, at this point in time, the primary means to provide support and validation. Such groups also provide a wide range of opportunities for developing social support networks for individuals who need enduring nurturance and help in coping with day to day life (Rueveni, 1985). Retirees, having a wealth of experiences, motivations and needs for participation, can be trained in group methods and techniques so they can work as co-leaders in such groups (Rueveni, 1985). [. . .]

Support group leaders need to screen their potential membership, use co-leaders whenever possible and have leader support (e.g., supervision, groups, consultants) as a network of support. Specific guidelines and goals regarding the length of sessions (two hours works very well), number of sessions, confidentiality, giving support versus advice and judgments, the 'non-therapy' nature of the group and miscellaneous details are necessary. These may be printed in a pamphlet, brochure or handout and need to be discussed and agreed upon during the first two sessions. [. . .]

CONCLUSION

In our work to end elder abuse, we now see the need to go beyond our assumptions as to how and why the abuse occurs. As professionals, we must work with families, develop support groups and other community supports. By utilizing the modalities which are well developed for use with families, and applying them to the needs of elder abuse families, productive growth can occur. By utilizing the techniques which are available in setting up support groups, many instances of abuse can be avoided. By supporting each other, professional to professional, we can increase our overall effectiveness in dealing with these issues.

Now is the time for ending elder abuse as part of our stand *for* human beings and humanity and *against* inhumanity and violence. Let's join together now in support of any and all action consistent with this end.

REFERENCES

Bowen, M. (1978). *Family Therapy in Clinical Practice*, Aronson, New York.

Eastman, P. (1981). 'Elders under siege', *Psychology Today*, **15**(1), 30.

Elliott, F. (1982). 'Clinical approaches to family violence: biological contributions to family violence', *Family Therapy Collection*, **3**, 35–8.

Galbraith, M., and Zdorskowski, R.T. (1984). 'Heuristic models of elder abuse: implications for the practitioner',

Lifelong Learning, **7**(8), 16–21, 24.

Gibb, J. (1961). 'Defensive communication', *Journal of Communication*, **11**(3), 141–8.

Gurman, A.S. (ed.) (1981). *Questions and Answers in the Practice of Family Therapy*, Brunner/Mazel, New York.

Gurman, A.S. and Kniskern, G. (1981). *Handbook of Family Therapy*, Brunner/Mazel, New York.

Haley, J. (1976). *Problem Solving Therapy: New Strategies for Effective Change*, Jossey Bass, San Francisco.

Haley, J. (1985). *Ordeal Therapy*, Jossey Bass, San Francisco.

Herr, J.H., and Weakland, J.H. (1978). 'The family as a group'. In: I. Burnside (ed.), *Working with Elderly Groups: Processes and Techniques*, Duxbury, North Scituate, Mass.

Hickey, T., Douglass, R., and Noel, C. (1983). *A Study of Maltreatment of the Elderly and Other Vulnerable Adults*, Institute of Gerontology, University of Michigan, Ann Arbor.

Hulse, D. (1985). 'Overcoming the socio-ecological barriers to group effectiveness: present and future', *Journal for Specialists in Group Work*, **10**(2), 92–7.

L'Abate, L. (1976). *Understanding and Help the Individual in the Family*, Grune and Stratton, New York.

Langsley, D.G., Kaplan, D., Pittman, F., Manchota, P., Flomenha, K., and Dekoving, C. (1968). *The Treatment of Families in Crisis*, Grune and Stratton, New York.

McCuan, E., Travis, A., and Voyles, B. (1983). 'Family intervention: applying the task centered approach'. In J. Kosberg (ed.), *Abuse and Maltreatment of the Elderly: Causes and Interventions*, John Wright PSG, Boston, pp. 355–75.

Madanes, C. (1981). *Strategic Family Therapy*, Jossey Bass, San Francisco.

Madanes, C. (1984). *Behind the One-Way Mirror: Advances in the Practice of Family Therapy*, Jossey Bass, San Francisco.

Minuchin, S. (1974). *Family and Family Therapy*, Harvard University Press, Cambridge, Mass.

Minuchin, S., and Fishman, H.C. (1980). *Family Therapy Techniques*, Harvard University Press, Cambridge, Mass.

Palazzoli, M., Cecchin, G., Prata, G., and Boscolo, L. (1978). *Paradox and Counterparadox*, Aronson, New York.

Pearson, R.E. (1982). 'Support: exploration of a basic concept in counseling and informal help', *Personnel and Guidance Journal*, **61**(2), 83–7.

Pearson, R.E. (1983). 'Support groups: a conceptualization', *Personnel and Guidance Journal*, **61**(6), 361–5.

Rueveni, U. (1985). 'The family as a social support group now and in 2001', *Journal for Specialists in Group Work*, **10**(2), 88–91.

Tomita, S. (1982). 'Detection and treatment of elderly abuse and neglect: a protocol for health professionals', *Physical and Occupational Therapy in Geriatrics*, **2**(2), 37–51.

How to help the bereaved

LILY PINCUS

Formerly at Tavistock Clinic Institute of Marital Studies, now deceased

Shakespeare has Hamlet's mother say, 'Thou know'st 'tis common; all that live must die.' It is equally common, therefore, that bereavement through death has to be faced as a fact of life. Yet however honestly it is faced, bereavement brings about a crisis of loss, probably the most severe crisis in human existence. In this situation of inevitability and crisis, what help does the bereaved need and what help can be offered?

We have seen from the accounts of bereaved children how vitally important the attitude of those around them, their teachers, their relations, is for their recovery from the crisis of loss. Although the adult mourner is not so totally dependent on his 'outer world' and is more able to understand the reality of his bereavement, many of the people to whom I spoke told me how lost and bewildered they felt, how frightened about the 'grave departures from their usual attitude toward life', and that they did not know where to turn for help. Some were afraid of going mad or of getting themselves into irrevocable situations, such as hastily giving up their homes. Many developed symptoms of physical illness, but even if they did not go to a doctor or some other helper the symptoms were a disguised request for help of some sort.

In physical as well as mental health, it has become at least theoretically accepted that prevention is better than cure. We cannot prevent bereavement, in fact, one of the most important preventive measures would be to acknowledge the inevitability of death and bereavement, not as a horrible threat looming over us, but as an important part of our lives, for which we can prepare ourselves. In our culture there are now attempts at preparation for most situations we all have to meet: for marriage, for parenthood, ever earlier nursery education in preparation for school, all sorts of preparation for jobs and professions, preparation to cope with retirement and with hospital stays—and probably many more. But there appears to be nothing to prepare people for the most fundamental and universal task, which might have to be met at any age: death and bereavement.

Thinking and talking about death need not be morbid; they may be quite the opposite. Ignorance and fear of death overshadow life, while knowing about and accepting death erases this shadow and makes life freer of fears and anxieties. The fuller and richer people's experience of life, the less death seems to matter to them—as if love of life casts out fear of death. A child therapist once said to me, 'Children of parents who are not afraid of death are not afraid of life'. In that sense, education for death is education for life, and should be an underlying feature in all education in schools, universities, and through the media.

Yet while one part of me firmly believes that education for death is a major task in our time and culture, I also know that our attitude toward death and bereavement is not easily affected by rational learning; it has its roots in the unconscious and often is expressed with a degree of irrationality which appears to be out of keeping with the personality of the mourner. A friend of mine lost her mother, who was nearly ninety. This once intelligent and gracious woman had badly deteriorated in the previous two years, and it became impossible to look after her in her own home. Just when her daughters were struggling with the painful decision to find institutional care for her, she became ill, went into the hospital, and died peacefully within a couple of weeks. My friend, a very competent, sensible woman, freely admitted her relief that her mother had been spared suffering and upheaval, and acknowledged that a great burden had been taken off her. Nevertheless, she showed all the symptoms of distress, confusion, and disturbance with which we are familiar in bereavement situations. And in *A Very Easy Death* Simone de Beauvoir describes the sudden

Reprinted by permission of Faber and Faber Ltd from *Death and the Family* by Lily Pincus, Faber and Faber, 1974 (edited).

outburst of tears that almost degenerated into hysteria when she heard of the terminal illness of her seventy-eight-year-old mother. 'I had understood all my sorrows up until that night: even when they flowed over my head I recognized myself in them. This time my despair escaped from my control: someone other than myself was weeping in me.'[1]

I have attempted to understand such 'irrational' responses in terms of early childhood reactions to loss and abandonment which are revived whenever loss is experienced in later life. The insights of depth psychology have helped us to make the link between emotional processes in infancy and later life situations in which we feel helpless and dependent, such as illness, old age, and dying. In spite of the apparent dichotomy of birth and death, both they and sex are closely connected in our fantasies and in the reality of nature.

There has been a remarkable shift in taboos in the last two centuries. In the nineteenth century, when every family expected to lose some of its children, when many mothers died in childbirth, and people died at an earlier age, death in all its aspects was often exhibited in a spectacular way, while sex and birth were unmentionable. While the literature of the nineteenth century was a literature of death, the literature of our time is about sex. Sex is now hectically displayed and limelighted and death has become unmentionable. A newspaper editor recently commented to one of his contributors, "Don't mention death, it loses readers."

Birth, and copulation, and death.
That's all the facts when you come to brass tacks:
Birth, and copulation, and death.

—T.S. Eliot[2]

If we can truly (not only intellectually) accept the connections between these fundamentals of life, our attitude toward them all may become more realistic, better balanced, and we may then be able to retrieve death and bereavement from the dark corners in which we try to keep them hidden.

Since the majority of patients now die in the hospital, death is kept away from the home. Children are protected from knowing about it, and relatives are prevented from being in close touch with a dying patient, who is generally too sedated to die consciously.

Sedation may, of course, be necessary to ease pain and discomfort but we should realize the vital importance of using it with utmost discretion, in order not to deprive the dying patient and his relatives of the most fundamental experience of 'awakenings' on the threshold of death and the message they convey.

Again and again bereaved people have complained with sorrow and bitterness that they were not allowed to be present at the moment of death, that they were ushered out at the last minute 'for their own good'. They felt cheated, wondering whether there might not have been a last contact, a word, a glance—but even without that, they felt that the finality of their loss might have become more real if they had been allowed to stay. One of the major tasks of mourning, accepting the reality of loss, might have been made easier.

When talking to the relatives, it often became clear, however, that they had willingly colluded with the hospital staff because of their own fears of what the encounter with death would mean to them, especially without the privacy so essential for this encounter. There are situations, of course, such as death through an accident and certain illnesses, where the deceased is so changed and distorted that it may be better for those who loved the living person not to see him. But these are exceptions, and almost all the relatives to whom I spoke who were present at the moment of death or able to see their dead mentioned the relief, the feeling of peace this gave them. One young man of eighteen who was with his grandmother when she died said, 'I ought to have had this experience long ago, then I would not have been so frightened of death.' One widow said that seeing her dead husband was an unforgettable experience. 'He looked so young, so beautiful, so relaxed—I felt with deep gratitude: this is the body of my lover.' This widow became a counsellor for the bereaved, partly because she wanted to share her experience with others.

In our culture, the attempts not to know about death, not to be reminded of it, are predominant. The house of a deceased person no longer is marked in any way, no drawn blinds, no indication of recent death. The bereaved rarely wear mourning clothes or any other outward sign. No respect is paid, no notice is taken of funeral processions. Funerals and cremations are 'got over' as hurriedly as possible. I recently attended one that lasted altogether seven minutes.

There seems to be a general conspiracy that death has not occurred. This glossing over allows for no psychological transition, no 'rites de passage' to help the bereaved to adjust from relating to the living to relating to the dead person or to the change in his own status from a wife (husband) to a widow (widower). It does not create a climate in which grief and mourning are accepted, supported, and valued. Yet human beings need to mourn in response to loss, and if they are denied this, they will suffer, psychologically, physically, or both. The first therapeutic task in our society, therefore, is to give sanction to mourning.

Loss through death is not only an individual concern, it also affects the community in which the loss occurred, and the bereaved needs the understanding and support of this community. In the past, community support found expression in rituals. These 'rites de passage' gave sanction to mourning, helping the bereaved to make adjustments to the world in which he had to live without the lost person. The world around him, be it his family, neighborhood, parish, work group, also had to make adjustments to life without the deceased and with the bereaved in a new status. If there is some interaction in this groping toward reorientation between the community and the mourner, the mourner feels less isolated. This has been one of the functions of rituals.

Some religious communities in our society still observe mourning rituals: Quaker meetings, the Irish wake, the Jewish shared mourning, come to my mind. In the latter, relatives, friends, and members of the Jewish congregation gather in the mourner's house for a full week and take care of everything that has to be done, setting him free to grieve. Such care and sympathy provide comfort for the mourner at the moment of greatest distress. How much this helps him to find a way back to life I do not know.

Many societies offer social solutions as substitutes for rituals, which seem to be designed primarily to define a place for the widow. In a Portuguese fishing village in which many husbands die young at sea, there is a particularly large group of widows whose work and identity before their bereavement is based on their function as wives of fishermen. When the man dies the widow immediately joins what looks like a widows' club. They all wear the same clothes, and on Sundays they go together to visit their husbands' graves, each with a bunch of flowers in her arms and a bucket of sand on her head. They find some security in their joint fate and in the obligations and privileges appropriate to their status.

The Beguines in Belgium, though more sophisticated, perform a similar task for themselves by doing good deeds collectively.

In China today the government provides individual workshops for widows. They make, among other things, the blue clothing which is the standard feature of Chinese dress. In this way the widow feels useful and caring, earns her living, and establishes a new type of contact with the community at large and with her individual customers.

The East African ritual of the second burial seems to be designed to care for both the living and the dead. This funeral takes place one year after the death. During the year the dead person is kept alive in the minds of the family with grief and mourning and endless talks about him, and any child born during this time is named after him. Meanwhile the whole family is also preparing for the second funeral, to which relatives, friends, and clan members come from all over the country. If the dead person is a man, his son prepares an effigy of him. On the day of the anniversary of death the grave is slightly reopened and with much lamenting and grieving, the effigy is put on top of the body but facing in the opposite direction. This means that the dead man has now left the living world and joined his ancestors, and the surviving are free to live ther own lives. His widows (there may be as many as four), who throughout the year have worn mourning cords around their waists, remarry, and their new husbands cut the cord at the grave. The atmosphere changes from mourning to rejoicing. Through this ritual, the step from death to life and sex and birth is sanctioned, and the bereaved can take it without guilt. Since the wife has no ancestors in her own right, being connected to the past through her husband, it is vitally important that she remarry before she dies. If the dead person is a woman, she receives a second burial but no effigy and her husband does not have to remarry.

Rituals express the collective unconscious of the culture, for which they perform a religious, social, or therapeutic function. For our Western society, with its emphasis on the importance of close personal relationships, different—more personal—forms of 'rites *de passage'*—are necessary. In their absence, an increasing number of counseling services, set up by both voluntary and statutory organizations, are offering help to the individual bereaved or to small groups of mourners.

I am not concerned here with discussing the work of these services but rather with exploring more generally the needs of the bereaved and the ways in which they might be met, bearing in mind that the majority of mourners may not actually make use of therapeutic services. Nevertheless, it may help them to know that they can do so, just as physical symptoms sometimes disappear as soon as the patient knows that he can go to see a doctor.

The experience of counselors for the bereaved confirms that help is most needed and most effective in the period immediately after the funeral. It is when the first numbness and the distractions preceding the funeral are over that the pain of loss is most severe. At that time, too, adjustments to a changed life have to be made, and the bereaved needs somebody to hold his hand, just as the baby who experiences loss needs to be firmly and lovingly held.

As I myself have never done counseling work with newly bereaved people, I owe some of the following observations to discussions with social workers who have.

The immediate task may consist mainly of letting the bereaved talk, letting him tell all the details of the last weeks and days again and again, and just listening in the knowledge of how important this is. The need to talk, to complain, 'to mope', to 'get it off my chest', and to be listened to is great.

In a climate of trust the bereaved may be able to express his feelings of guilt about having failed or harmed the deceased, or not having loved him enough. He may be frightened by his occasional feelings of hatred, perhaps a wish for the patient to die quickly, to 'get it over with', so that he would no longer have to watch and participate in the suffering. There may also be guilt about the fury against the dead person who has left him with all the pain of loss. To have these feelings accepted and understood as a normal part of bereavement is true therapeutic help which a counselor or good friend can give.

The need for a person who is simply around and quietly gets on with the various tasks which otherwise the bereaved would have do do—thus setting him free to grieve—may be equally great. In his grief, he may be as self-centered as an infant, and totally unaware of the needs of the other person, who after some time may be desperately in need of a cup of coffee or completely exhausted. It is not easy to be a helper in bereavement. Our usual way of behaving may not be relevant for the bereaved. True help consists in recognizing the fact that the bereaved has a difficult task to perform, one that should not be avoided and cannot be rushed. He not only has to accept the ultimate loss of the loved person, he also has to assimilate the experience of having been in touch with death. John Donne's words will always be true: 'Any man's death diminishes me because I am involved in mankind.'

Colin Murray Parkes has said, 'There is an optimal "level of grieving" which varies from one person to another. Some will cry and sob, others will betray their feelings in other ways. The important thing is for feelings to emerge into consciousness. How they appear on the surface may be of secondary importance.' While the mourner is in great need of sympathy, pity is the last thing he wants. Pity puts him at a distance from and into an inferior position to the would-be comforter. 'Pity makes one into an object; somehow being pitied the bereaved person becomes pitiful.'[3]

Any sensitive friend can provide comfort for a mourner by regular contact at times of special vulnerability. A telephone call at the moment of waking may take the sting out of the early morning depression that another day of loneliness and misery has to be faced. If this call can be counted on every day at the same time it may be of great therapeutic value.

Saturday afternoons, which may have been a married couple's regular time for a joint outing, may be another vulnerable time. A friend of mine who had adjusted exceptionally well to her widowed life told me that even years after her husband's death she avoided being alone at home on a Saturday afternoon, in order not to watch compulsively and with envy her married neighbors going out together. And Mary Stott writes, 'My own best help came from a friend who turned up almost every Saturday evening to play two piano duets, bringing the pudding for our supper in the boot of his car.'[4]

The regularity of such arrangements is what is most helpful, because it is the routine of married life, often little things taken for granted, which has been lost and is so sadly missed.

All such help derived from affectionate understanding of the needs of the bereaved, whether given by counselors, neighbors, or friends, can be termed therapy in bereavement situations in which there is no evidence of complications. If there are signs that all is not going well, if the bereaved is suffering from lasting physical symptoms, excessive guilt or anger, persistent depression, or uncontrollable grief, then more direct therapy may be indicated.

Absence of grief in bereavement is one such sign. Yet those who cannot mourn are also likely to deny any need for help. 'Therapy is only for mad people,' said one such widower. [. . .]

It may not be the bereaved himself but rather the people around him who first sense that all is not well. An example of this was a recently widowed woman of seventy-two who since her husband's death had caused much trouble in her local clinic by turning up at all hours and shouting abuse at the doctors who, she claimed, had killed her husband and were now killing her. The puzzled doctors felt that this women needed frequent home visits and asked a social worker to call on her. On his first visit, after knocking at the door, the social worker heard energetic movements in the apartment, but when the woman opened the door and recognized the caller, she collapsed into his arms. She seemed to have to impress on him her need for support. Her first verbal communications were complaints about being let down by everyone since the death of her 'angel-husband'. She produced photos of him and also of her only daughter, who had married a Swiss and lived abroad. She, too, was described as an angel. Everyone else was nasty: her friends exploited her, her neighbors annoyed her, nobody cared about her or was prepared to help her. What help she needed she could not say but it was clear that she expected the social worker to provide it. On each of his subsequent visits she collapsed into his arms when he arrived, but as soon as he had guided her to a chair, she got up, went into the kitchen to make tea for him, and showed that she was perfectly capable of looking after herself. On the one and only occasion when, early in their contact, the social worker brought one of his students with him, the widow showed her disapproval of this interference in their relationship by dropping the tea-tray and then collapsing on the floor. She needed one person to herself.

Soon the stories about the angel-husband began to change. It emerged that for many years and up to his death he had been having an affair with another woman and had on several occasions deserted his wife. When he died suddenly she must have felt that her hatred and resentment about his desertions had killed him, and transferred this self-accusation onto the doctors and all the others who had 'killed' him and would now 'kill' her. It also emerged that the 'angel-daughter' showed no interest in her mother. She had gone abroad when she was still very young, there was little contact, and she had not even come home for her father's funeral. Obviously no one could stand this woman's demands and confused communications—her anger had driven everyone away.

The social worker was well aware that he must not repeat this pattern. He had to watch his own reactions in order to stick by her in spite of all her frenzies and provocations. Only then could he hope to help her to show her pain and anger more directly and not to act it out so madly. He understood that this woman had probably always felt unacceptable and insecure, and since her husband's death, which she saw as his greatest, most punishing act of desertion, her anxieties about her own badness had become overwhelming. Her only chance for recovery was to feel understood and accepted as she was. After she had been able to tell the truth about her husband and to face her hatred of him and her resulting self-hate, she no longer collapsed when the social worker came to visit her, and did not feel so persecuted by all the people around her.

For elderly and dependent mourners neither the short-term bereavement-focused therapy, nor more conventional psychotherapy, which aims at increasing insight, is appropriate. Their need is for a long supportive contact on a counseling or social work level. Once a trusting relationship has been securely established, other helpers may be included, and the agency may then become 'the good object'. This widening of the contact can help to avoid a degree of dependence which throws the mourner back into the original grief situation at the slightest threat of termination, or on any occasion when the individual helper is not available. Careful timing, however, is very important. In the case we have just discussed, the social worker brought his student along too early, and his client protested justifiably. She felt that this visit was not planned for her sake but as a learning experience for the student.

Not many bereaved show their need for acceptance and love in such a bizarre way. Yet many, perhaps all, feel at times that they have lost their own loving self with the loved (but also sometimes hated) person. Extreme ambivalence, the fear that the hate is greater than the love, makes it impossible to integrate the lost person and thus complete the mourning process. [. . .]

Although grief involves grave departures from the normal attitude to life, it never occurs to us to regard it as a morbid condition and hand the mourner over to medical treatment. We rest assured that after a lapse of time it will be overcome, and we look at any interference with it as inadvisable or even harmful.[5]

This was written in 1914, before the First World War. In Freud's Jewish middle-class world mourners were likely to be less isolated than they are in our time and place; death and grief were still acknowledged facts of life, and the mourners' emotional responses to bereavement were generally accepted. Also since Freud's time the practice of psychotherapy has become more flexible. Now many therapists see the human and supportive relationship as the most important element in the therapeutic situation. This is especially appropriate and helpful in work focused on bereavement.

In spite of all the changes since 1914, it is crucial that normal mourning should not be regarded or treated as an illness and that therapeutic intervention be considered only in exceptional situations.

Vamik Volkan calls such therapy 're-grief work'. Although I am not entirely happy with this term, I believe that his concepts of bereavement therapy are important. He writes:

The short-term psychotherapy of re-grief work helps a patient suffering from pathological grief to resolve the conflicts of separation—however distant in time this resolution may have spent itself. . . . The author has attempted to show that the clinical entity of pathological grief, with its predictable symptomatology and characteristic findings, lies between uncomplicated grief and those reactions to death which turn into depression or other identifiable neurotic, psychosomatic

or psychotic conditions. Only those patients who occupy middle ground are suitable for re-griefing . . . .[6] [. . .]

Through bereavement-focused therapy some bereaved become aware of previously unacknowledged conflicts and confusions with which they feel unable to cope without further help. Once the acute grief problem has been resolved, they may, explicitly or implicitly, make a new contract with the therapist in order to work on the wider problems.

In all therapy one of the major aims is to help people toward more satisfactory relationships in the broadest sense. In bereavement work this task is of paramount importance. The bereaved often feels that with his lost object he has lost all that is good in him. In this situation of self-doubt he is faced with the task of adjusting his ongoing relationships, and having sufficient trust to risk new attachments.

To offer help in this difficult task is implied in all types of work with the bereaved. Often it is expressed in encouragement to join clubs, attend evening classes, 'get out of the shell'. A frequent suggestion is to do some charitable work, for to have nobody to care for is one of the great deprivations of bereavement. Such advice is absolutely right and valid in uncomplicated grief situations. Often, however, such suggestions end in disappointment and frustration both for the well-meaning adviser and for the bereaved who may be too shut up inside himself to get out of his shell. Because he is struggling to deal with extremely intense feelings of guilt, anger, and agonizing regret, he may retreat into denial and unreality.

The difficulty in taking advice in emotional turmoil was shown by an elderly woman who had recently suffered multiple and very painful losses in situations for which she justifiably blamed others. She was a deeply religious person, who throughout her life had successfully coped with many problems, and was now profoundly disturbed by her depression and unabating grief. In talking to her it became clear that she found it impossible to tolerate her own hating feelings toward those whom she blamed for her losses. This woman was living alone in a huge, isolated house, which not only created many problems for her but also increased her depression. She was unable to take steps toward a move, however, nor could she make use of any advice given to her. She was convinced that because of her hatred and subsequent self-hatred, nobody could help her or would care for her, and that she would only be a burden and evoke negative feelings wherever she went. Only after she had understood and accepted her guilt about her hateful feelings, which she found irreconcilable with her religion, did she begin to consider plans to move and become able to perceive that relatives and friends were affectionately supporting her in them. She had to feel justified in having hating feelings, and be good enough in spite of them, before she could ask for and accept help from others.

The greatest obstacles in the way of making new relationships after bereavement and being able to live meaningfully again are ambivalent feelings about the deceased and the denial of one's own hating self. By denying his hate the mourner impairs his love, and with it the capacity to be in loving contact with other people.

In some cases, this aspect of therapeutic work can be done by a lay person who cares for and understands the bereaved and offers him the degree and quality of compassion and reliability which will enable him to regain hope. Only when this has been achieved can he risk a new attachment. This should not be an attempt to replace the lost one, but rather an expression of renewed confidence that life is still worth living and meaningful relationships are still possible.

New life-affirming attachments may take a wide variety of forms, according to the needs of the individual bereaved. It may be a job, an interest, a cause, or a child, perhaps a new grandchild. Or it may be a new committed relationship with a person of the same or the opposite sex with whom the bereaved can share his life, someone who will both give and accept care.

The majority of bereaved people will return to a new life without therapeutic help after they have mourned their dead in a way appropriate for them. A general climate of acceptance of the importance of mourning will support them. If that climate is lacking, the completion of the mourning process may be hindered or delayed, which will increase the mourner's anxieties that his responses are abnormal or childish and must be suppressed.

The task of mourning, and of returning to life with renewed strength, may take a long time—often much longer than the traditional year. It is important for the bereaved and for those around him to know and accept this, but also to know that the phase of mourning will pass.

REFERENCES

1. S. de Beauvoir, *A Very Easy Death*, Weidenfeld and Nicholson, 1966.
2. T.S. Eliot, 'Sweeney Agonistes', in *Collected Poems 1909–1962*, Faber and Faber, 1963.
3. C. Murray Parks, *Bereavement*, Tavistock Publications, 1972.
4. M. Stott, *Forgetting's No Excuse*, Faber and Faber, 1973.
5. J. Strachey (ed.), *The Complete Psychological Works of Sigmund Freud*, Vol. 14, Hogarth Press, 1953–66.
6. V. Volkan, 'Study of patient's re-grief work', *Psychiatric Quarterly*, **45**, 255–73 (1971).

Elderly people and drug-based therapy

BRUCE BURNS* and CHRIS PHILLIPSON†

Formerly Professor of Applied Social Studies, University of Keele
†*Formerly Consultant Psychiatrist, Hollymoor Hospital, Birmingham*

SOCIAL AND PHARMACOLOGICAL ISSUES

[. . .] Clearly, many drugs are capable of improving the quality of life experienced by elderly people, many of whom face debilitating physical and psychological illnesses. Unfortunately, even for those drugs that work, there are invariably costs, side effects or adverse reactions. This is particularly true with older people. Moreover, we must also be aware of failures at the level of drug promotion and medical practice; these failures have themselves contributed to illness and death in old age.

PRESCRIBING PATTERNS

In the United Kingdom, three-quarters of people aged 75 or over receive prescribed drugs of some kind. Two-thirds of this age group receive one to three drugs and one-third four to six drugs simultaneously (Williamson, 1978). As well as taking more medication per head, the number of prescriptions for elderly patients is increasing sharply, over and above the increasing numbers of older people in the population. In 1982 elderly people in the United Kingdom received 15.9 prescriptions per head compared with 5.2 for the non-elderly; their prescriptions were also for longer periods (Committee on Safety of Medicines, 1985). [. . .]

Repeat prescriptions are particularly common amongst older age groups (Bliss, 1981). Such prescriptions are often made out by ancillary staff, particularly if they are given over a long period (Parish, 1971).

From *Drugs, Ageing and Society—Social and Pharmacological Perspectives*, B. Burns and C. Phillipson, Croom Helm, 1986 (edited). Reproduced by permission of Croom Helm Limited.
© B. Burns and C. Phillipson.

Prescriptions written by ancillary staff are associated with a rise in errors of prescribing, a fall in early recognition of adverse drug reactions and of clinical change, and a rise in drug interactions (Sharpe and Kay, 1977).

Law and Chalmers (1976) reviewed the drug prescriptions of 151 patients over the age of 75 years living at home. 87 per cent were on regular drug treatment, with 34 per cent taking three to four drugs each per day. They were prescribed three times the number of drugs that were prescribed for the general population, and there were twice as many women as men on regular drug treatment. [. . .]

The Institute for Social Studies in Medical Care has carried out a number of surveys on the characteristics of drug prescribing. These indicate that men and women aged 55 and over are more likely than younger people to be taking psychotropic and cardiovascular drugs (Anderson, 1980a, 1980b). In addition the 1977 survey reported some interesting class as well as age differences. For example, working class people aged 55 plus were more likely to be taking drugs for rheumatism than middle class people of similar ages (13 per cent compared with 4 per cent); this probably reflects higher rates of chronic illness amongst working class people (see, for example, Townsend and Davidson, 1982). Anderson, (1980a, 1980b) confirmed the high prevalence of combination drug treatment in the elderly with chronic illness conditions, in particular the combination of psychotropic drugs (those acting primarily on the brain) and diuretics (drugs to promote water loss) and medicines for rheumatism. [. . .]

OVER-THE-COUNTER MEDICINES

There is increasing awareness of the large-scale nature of over-the-counter (OTC) drug use amongst the elderly and the inevitable increase in drug interactions (Kofoed, 1986). In Dunnell and Cartwright's (1972) UK survey two out of three old people were found to have taken an OTC drug in the fortnight immediately prior to being questioned. A study by Adams and Smith (1978) showed that 40 per cent of older people in their study practised self-medication during a 48 hour period, and about 80 per cent over a one year period. Much of this self-medication will be unknown to the GP (Taylor, 1983). The practice of self-medication appears to increase with advanced age and be more common amongst women. [. . .]

DRUG-INDUCED DISEASE IN THE ELDERLY

A simple definition of an adverse drug reaction is 'any unintended or undesired consequence of drug therapy' (Martys, 1979). Any drug may produce unwanted, unexpected adverse or unpleasant reactions. In other words, there are risks in all forms of drug therapy. It can be said that every individual's drug treatment is an experiement which needs close monitoring. This view is particularly important for those patients who are either very young or very old. Patients aged 60–70 have, in fact, double the rate of adverse reactions compared with those aged under 50. Only a minority of older patients are likely to be warned about the dangers of the drugs they are taking. Thus, a national pharmacy survey found that side effects were mentioned in only 25 per cent of prescriptions given to older people. In addition, 42.5 per cent of the older people surveyed reported that they would not know how to cope with adverse reactions if they occurred (Busson and Dunn, 1986).

Caird (1977) argues that the most important single cause of iatrogenic (doctor-induced) disorders in old age is the improper prescription and ingestion of drugs; and in similar vein Bliss (1981) sees older people today as the main 'victims' of modern drugs. He includes as the reasons for this, first, that many doctors lack training in prescribing for older people, and, secondly, the dual prescribing systems in hospitals and in general practice, which prevent doctors from being fully responsible for their own prescribing. [. . .]

All drugs tend to be more dangerous in older people because of misunderstandings of medical treatment

schedules, an increase in inter-current illness and impaired liver and kidney function. The elderly are two to three times more likely to suffer harm from medicines than younger people (George, 1981), and the mortality from this form of iatrogenic disease rises exponentially with age. There are many factors that contribute to this high incidence of adverse reactions to drugs. Amongst these we would include inadequate diagnosis, uncritical assessment of the need for treatment, excessive prescribing combined with a tendency for repeat prescriptions to replace clinical reassessment, altered drug handling and increased sensitivity to many drugs in old age. Problems for older people are further exacerbated by the biological changes which accompany the ageing process.

PHARMACOLOGICAL ISSUES AND OLDER PEOPLE

The use of drugs with older people is complicated by a number of factors. First, body tissues in older people undergo changes which mean that they handle and respond to drugs differently in comparison to younger people. Secondly, several major or minor physical diseases may be present at the same time. Thirdly, poor nutrition (a significant problem amongst some groups of older people) may contribute to adverse drug reactions. These problems have to be taken into account when prescribing, in order to reduce the high rate of undesired side effects. Undesirable effects are particularly common with certain groups of durgs. Amongst these we can include psychotropic drugs (minor and major tranquillisers and other drugs that have their primary site of action in the central nervous system); drugs acting on the cardio-vascular system, in particular those for high blood pressure; and analgesics, especially the non-steroidal anti-inflammatory drugs (NSAIDs) used for arthritis.

More research is required regarding altered drug handling (pharmacokinetics) in older people. Speaking very generally, though, a smaller dose of a drug will produce the same effect as the higher 'normal' dose for a younger person. Unfortunately, the situation is not straightforward. For example, it seems that different drugs — even those within the same general group — are handled differently as a factor of age.

Most detailed drug studies are made after single doses in young and usually healthy volunteers. This means that there are very few long-term large-scale studies amongst older people, particularly the frail elderly. There remains a shortage of basic information for the clinician on how their patients will handle many commonly used drugs (such as digoxin) should the patient be old, sick and poorly nourished. Therefore every time a different drug is prescribed for such patients it has to be seen as a unique experiment and monitored with the utmost clinical judgement.

Organ function slowly becomes impaired with age. However, this can be very variable, since the ageing process affects people in different ways. In general there is a decline, among people in their sixties and above, in the reserve capacity of organs such as the heart, liver and kidneys. For example, kidney function is reduced by about a half between 20 and 90 years of age, this decline in function being particularly rapid in very elderly people. Initially, the majority of drugs are broken down in the liver by enzymes to inactive substances. These substances in turn, and sometimes the active drug itself, are expelled from the body via the kidneys. Because of a decline in the capacity of the kidneys, there may be a narrowing of the safety margin between the therapeutic and toxic dose of many drugs. Therefore older people, despite wide variations, have a greater tendency to toxic reactions, overdosing and drug interactions. A 'normal' dose for the young could in an old person result in accumulation of the drug if given over a longer period; this may transform a well individual into one who is confused and perhaps incontinent. [. . .]

Older people and the drugs industry

[. . .] We have indicated the need for careful monitoring in the use of drugs, and for caution when new products are prescribed. Yet the reality is that these conditions are often not met and that, in consequence, older people have had often to face considerable problems when using drugs. These problems have been exacerbated by, first, a pharmaceutical industry anxious to increase its profits, secondly, weaknesses in controls from regulatory bodies and, thirdly, negative attitudes within the medical profession. A combination of these factors has helped to create a climate of risk and uncertainty for older people seeking medical care. [. . .]

Older people are, in an important sense, both products *and* victims of the rise of the modern drugs industry.

The application of modern pharmacology has undoubtedly stimulated improvements in mortality and morbidity. [. . .]

Many pensioners would undoubtedly be dead or, at the very least, extremely ill, were it not for some of the major post-war successes in the drugs field. However, the companies themselves would be substantially poorer without the massive market provided by older people. In many cases it has been the financial attraction of sales in this sector which has been a guiding influence for companies, the prospects of major financial gains blurring an appreciation of the dangers of pharmaceutical drugs to elderly consumers.

The market *is* an impressive one. In a single month, in Britain, over ten million prescriptions are likely to be made out to people of pensionable age, and older people receive twice as many prescriptions as the national average. But the protection for older people against adverse side effects is often inadequate. The Royal College of Physicians, in their report 'Medication for the elderly', commented that:

[. . .] clinical pharmacological studies with new drugs are usually conducted on young, healthy subjects and pre-marketing clinical trials rarely involve significant numbers of old and very old patients. Consequently, manufacturers' data sheet information on the safety and efficacy of new drugs in the elderly is often inadequate (Royal College of Physicians, 1984, p.6).

This statement was made 21 years after the formation of the Committee on Safety of Medicines (CSM), formed in the wake of the thalidomide scandal, and 13 years after the introduction of the Medicines Act which requires that all new drugs be scrutinised for safety, quality and efficacy. Unfortunately, these controls, which are weaker in Britain than in many other countries have proved vulnerable to various kinds of pressure exercised by drug companies. This pressure has become more intense as the companies have faced a squeeze on their profits. This has arisen for a variety of reasons: the cut-backs in government spending, the ending of patents on money-spinning drugs and the failure to find new super-drugs to boost sales. Reduced profits have led companie to increase the amount they spend on research an   opment, and to diversify the work they do ir   .]

The promotional activities of mar   st somewhat unfavourably with   when introducing new drugs   eed, in cases such as those illustrated by Opren (and other NSAIDs) the lucrative nature of the market often leads to premature and unjustifiable claims being made in relation to both safety and efficacy. This situation is further exacerbated by weaknesses in the professional care and support received by older people. In fact, it was the limitations of this support which was to give such a powerful presence to the drug companies in treatment strategies for older people. In the 1950s and 1960s the growth of the pharmaceutical companies went hand-in-hand with an ageing population. The enormous advances made by the pharmaceutical industry became influential in the determination of the medical construction of ageing—a development aided by the weaknesses in state controls and the limited influence of clinical pharmacology within primary care settings. [. . .]

Older people and the use of psychotropic drugs

The psychotropics are the main category of mood-altering drugs prescribed by doctors; they include sedatives, stimulants, tranquillisers and anti-depress-ant medications. Within the psychotropic group there is a bewildering multiplicity, many drugs having the same pharmacological actions. There is little clarification for the GP, at the sharp end of clinical practice, on the distinction between drugs and on their individual limitations. The GP is often confronted with a range of conflicting and exaggerated information from the drug companies; new drugs are introduced at a bewilderingly fast rate. Unfortunately, not only is the need for them uncertain, as many are very similar to products already on the market, but also the full spectrum of side effects has yet to be elucidated, and this may take at least 5–10 years for an individual drug. The vast variety of psychotropic drugs, the polished quality of the publicity for their use and the attendant creation of an unlimited market, amplifies the demand for drugs. It overwhelms the more critical scientific literature to which the doctor might become exposed, calling upon stamina, self-discipline and a background of thorough initial training to resist. How-ever, resistance is one thing, providing alternative methods of treatment and management is another.

Prevalence of psychotropic drug use

The issue of mass usage finds particular currency with the psychotropic drugs because of the ubiquitous nature of anxiety and bodily symptoms that stem from chronic degenerative diseases. The use of sedatives and minor tranquillisers has risen by two to three times in the last twenty years; this increase is especially marked in the case of older people. In a community survey of psychotropic drug use, Williams (1980) reported that 14 per cent of men and 22 per cent of women over the age of 65 years admitted to taking at least one psychotropic drug in the previous two weeks. In the age group 45–64, the figures were 9 per cent for men and 17 per cent for women. This is not just short-term but involves long-term use of drugs. [. . .]

It is now being realised that patients can become psychologically and physically dependent on benzodi-azepines (Peturrson and Lader, 1981; Tyrer, 1984), that this number is rising and that it is related to the duration of drug treatment. In turn the duration of treatment has been found to be age and sex-related (Parish, 1971; Williams, 1983).

Despite the fact that the efficacy of hypnotics such as the benzodiazepines may decline after 3–12 days and that treatment with the benzodiazepines should be short term (Committee for Review of Medicines, 1980), very little change in the number of prescriptions and none in the duration of supply has yet become apparent. Following scares concerning the value of diazepam (Valium) after reports of spontaneous outbursts of violent aggression (*British Medical Journal* leader, 1975), increasing anxiety (Parrott and Ken-tridge, 1982) and other problems such as insomnia (Kales *et al.*, 1983), restlessness, depression and suicidal ideation (Hall and Joffe, 1972), there has been a 20 per cent fall in diazepam prescriptions. Yet this fall has usually been made up by one or other of the nineteen other newer benzodiazepines rushed onto the UK market by the pharmaceutical companies. Some of these 20 drugs are marketed by different companies giving 32 trade preparations for the UK prescriber to choose from in 1984.

In a survey among six GPs, Williams (1983) studied the duration of drug treatment with psychotropic drugs generally and tranquillisers in particular, this either for the first time ever or for new episodes of disorder. He found that, in the main, treatment with psychotropic drugs was a short-term affair. A survival distribution curve showed that about half the patients had ceased treatment by the end of the first month. Subsequently, however, the rate at which treatment was stopped decreases sharply so that by the end of the follow-up period of six months, about one-fifth of the patients were found to have received drug treatment continuously. The presence of physical illness was not related to the duration of treatment, but older recipients of tranquillisers were likely to receive treatment for a longer period than younger recipients. There was no relationship between the patient requesting drug treatment and duration. He confirmed the marked differences between doctors in their prescribing habits, reiterating that there still was no universal agreement, let alone clear criteria, to enable a doctor to distinguish between 'necessary' and 'unnecessary' psychotropic drug treatment. The suggestion arises that some doctors interact with their patients in such a way as to encourage long-term use. Not all doctors are, it seems, prepared, or even able, to discuss with patients the medicines they prescribe, or possible alternatives to drugs. This situation is worsened with the elderly patient by problems of communication and by altered attitudes of doctors towards the elderly. [. . .]

IMPROVING PROFESSIONAL PRACTICE

[. . .] Not only is there a need for vigilance by health care workers to assess the cost/benefit ratio in individual elderly patients undergoing drug treatment, there should also be continuing attention to safety procedures in terms of drug monitoring, especially for new drugs.

In many instances, drugs now given to older people are not needed because they are ineffectual or because although effective their adverse effects are greater than the beneficial effects, that is they make the patient worse. [. . .]

Should drugs be prescribed when an individual is symptom-free, e.g. for raised blood pressure, she/he may in fact feel worse when given drugs. This must always be explained to the patient. In addition, if patients are dissatisfied with their treatment they should be free to discuss this with their doctor. The doctor in turn should seek to amend the treatment to remove the patient's dissatisfaction. The concept of 'blind compliance' with an apparently useless or unacceptable regime is inappropriate. In fact, non-compliance is more likely, the hoarding of drugs then follows, with the final scenario being the older person taking the drugs at random from their 'geriatric confectionery', thus making adverse reactions almost inevitable. [. . .] It is necessary to avoid the two extremes, namely drugs being the only treatment practice for the elderly, or the equal mistake of avoiding drug treatment at all costs. Our argument is, first, against excessive prescribing of multiple kinds of drugs of uncertain value; secondly, against drugs where the ratio of value to danger shifts towards the latter. We have to keep reminding ourselves, with regard to drugs, that growing old involves an increase in the diversity of impairments; these changes vary markedly from individual to individual and are often totally unpredictable in general clinical practice. [. . .]

Better prescribing

It is important to remember that many of the illnesses or symptoms from which older people suffer are doing the patient no immediate harm and do not require treatment. Certainly, there is no need to prescribe a different drug for each disease or symptom. The decision to prescribe should be made in the light of the drug's pharmacokinetics and pharmacodynamics and their potential to produce adverse effects in the elderly.

There is a very restricted need to continue drugs in the elderly indefinitely or to take many at the same time. Many old people admitted to hospital improve greatly when the particular regime of drugs that they have been taking is stopped. The need to discontinue medication in the old, especially when adding new drugs, cannot be over-emphasized. Much suffering of drug adverse reactions or interactions could be prevented, with considerable savings in money, with the regular review of the need for continued medication. [. . .]

The WHO (1981) report outlined a number of proposals for rational drug therapy for older people. It is worth while reiterating in brief some of the recommended strategies.

1. Drugs should not be used for longer than necessary and repeat prescriptions should be reviewed at periodic intervals.

2. Drug treatment should never be regarded as a substitute for time spent in helpful advice or in endeavouring to plan treatment by simple adjustment of the daily living of the elderly individual.
3. The margin between therapeutic effect and toxicity is so small in many cases that a drug which is indicated for a particular condition in younger patients may be unsuitable in an elderly patient with the same condition.
4. The fewest number of drugs that a patient needs should always be used. Drug regimes should be easy to follow.
5. Touch and colour vision are well preserved in the elderly, making the size, shape and colour of tablets very important components to correct drug compliance. Large tablets should be avoided as the elderly often have difficulty in swallowing. Liquid preparations are usually acceptable to older people.
6. Drugs should be specially packed and clearly labelled in containers that can be readily opened by disabled people.
7. The elderly patient should be taught to understand his or her drugs. Time should be spent on educating the patient on their use and administration. Clear instructions should also be made in writing. A calendar to record daily drug administration may also be required.
8. It may be necessary to involve a relative, friend or neighbour to supervise potent drugs, especially when the elderly person lives alone and has problems with memory.
9. There must be regular reviews of treatment. Drug regimes should be discontinued when no longer needed. [. . .]

Overcoming the problems affecting drug prescribing requires the collaboration of all the professional disciplines and caring agencies, in addition to central government. Little value can come from finding a single scapegoat like the doctor. Guidelines that lead to improved practice require co-operation and collaboration including that by older people themselves.

Polypharmacy

The indications for long-term polypharmacy in the elderly are few (Jones, 1976). Short-term polypharmacy is sometimes necessary and acceptable provided drug dosage is adjusted for age, the presence of renal and liver disease is considered and the combination of drugs is looked at for possible interactions. The disadvantages of the increased complexity of drug regimes for the elderly are considerable, and it is undoubtedly preferable to attempt to find the appropriate dose of a single drug rather than to combine the hazards of even two drugs.

If polypharmacy cannot be avoided particular care should be taken with certain groups of drugs. George (1980) lists digoxin, antihypertensives, hypoglycaemic agents, anticoagulants and anticonvulsants. There are, of course, others; those that depress the central nervous system (the psychotropic drugs) stand out as particularly important (Prescott, 1979).

Labels and drug containers

In the past, although most prescribed medicines for the elderly have been labelled, most have lacked explicit instructions about indications for taking the tablets, together with dispensing and expiry dates. Many labels have been found to be illegible and many others had the ubiquitous 'as directed' instructions (Law and Chalmers, 1976). With the introduction, in January 1984, of the British Pharmaceutical Society's requirements for large typed or machine printed labels, more older people can now actually read the instructions designed for them. Where drugs are not essential, further details should be on the label, e.g. 'One at night as required for sleep' or 'two tablets four times a day if necessary for pain'.

A container in which a day's supply can be laid out is useful especially for those taking three or more different drugs. Various types of dispenser have been designed that allow any helper to lay out the drugs for the patient and readily check that they have been taken. Opaque child-proof containers are a source of much error and consternation as many are 'granny-proof' (Law and Chalmers, 1976). For those who have particular difficulty with manual dexterity, large winged screw lids have proved useful. The shape and colour of tablets are important because older people retain discrimination in colour and shape. Confusion can arise if the doctor prescribes a different brand of the same drug. Treatment is facilitated when the patients bring all their drugs to the consultation and when careful records of repeat prescriptions are made.

Memory aids

Packaging devices have recently been introduced to act as memory aids, especially for those with complicated drug regimes or in those who have memory difficulties. Calendar packs similar to those used for oral contraceptives, 'Dial Pack', 'Dossett' and 'Medidos' trays, are examples. These devices are only standardising many patients' attempts to devise their own memory aids such as setting out doses for the day or week. The typical tray has 28 blisters in 4 rows of 7 to represent each day of the week. The pills for each day can be put into each blister by the patient, relative or home help and covered with one or four sliding clear plastic covers. Thus they can display up to a week's supply of tablets and capsules in a closed plastic container for four dose times per day.

An improvement in compliance with such devices in patients of all ages was illustrated by Linkewich et al. (1974), who found that the number of patients taking the correct number of tablets was increased from 28 per cent to 88.5 per cent by changing from plain labelled medicine bottles to a 'Dial Pack' together with an instruction card.

Written information

Many simple yet innovative devices have been introduced to help old people improve their ability and commitment to pursue a drug treatment regime. Treatment cards for the patient with simple clearly written drug lists, dosage and timing have been designed. A sample of each drug stuck down with sellotape and a brief comment of what it is for in language that can easily be understood have helped many older patients (e.g. 'water tablets', 'pain tablets' and 'breathing tablets'). These personal cards act as a ready check and reinforce verbal instructions that have been given earlier and which can be reinforced in the future. Written instructions increase drug compliance (Wandless and Davie, 1977) over and beyond verbal instructions. In some cases a calendar sheet listing the dose and time of each medicine, with spaces

for the patient to check off every dose, has proved useful and acceptable. However, rather than a single method a combined approach using visual and verbal reminders from doctors, pharmacists, community nurses and relatives is preferable.

Finally, information leaflets (Drury, 1984) have been devised for patients on long-term treatment for conditions such as hypertension (George, 1983) or depression (Myers and Calvert, 1978). Such material has been shown to increase the patient's knowledge of and satisfaction with their medication. Information booklets are now available to the patient on a range of medical topics (Sloan, 1984). Not to be outdone by their medical colleagues, pharmacists have also made recommendations on information leaflets for patients (Laekeman, 1984). In addition, as Taylor (1983) points out, the spread of information about drugs to the able and fit elderly majority may be facilitated by the general education of the younger population who may pass on their learning to older relatives in the course of their day-to-day contact.

The issuing of repeat prescriptions is a continuing problem for older people. In response to this, many surgeries are now devising improved safety measures on prescribing. With the appropriate filing card system or microcomputer, the primary care team and the patient could, for example, have instructions that their prescriptions could only be repeated on two occasions. In other words, after this point the prescription could not be re-issued until they saw their GP. Different medical practices have established their own monitoring procedures for repeat prescriptions. [. . .]

The hospital and the community

Many prescribing problems arise from the unnecessarily large gap between the GP and the hospital doctor in the ongoing care of older people. The links between primary care and secondary hospital care doctors should be shortened and made more secure. Part of the fault here is the separate administrative structure within the NHS of the two groups of doctors. Probably the principle that the GP is the arbiter and prescriber of drugs for older people in the community is as valid now as it ever was.

It is well recognized that after discharge from hospital some patients spontaneously resume the medication prescribed for them before their admission, often because the patient feels unclear as to what he should be taking after discharge. Parkin *et al.* (1976) reported on a follow-up of patients discharged from hospital and their actual drug-taking practices. They found that 66 of the 130 patients that they followed through deviated from their drug regime prescribed on discharge from hospital acute medical wards. Of the 66, 46 did not have a clear understanding of the regimes and the remaining 20 understood the regimes but did not follow instructions. They found that the failure to understand and the non-compliance related to the complexity of the drug regimes and the availability of medicines prescribed before admission to hospital. [. . .]

Treatment may be interrupted by episodes of what is intended to be short-term therapy initiated perhaps at several different out-patient clinics. In such a situation, it is vital that good communication is maintained between the GP and specialist clinics. A clear record of the treatment policy in the hospital notes would help. Further, this should be communicated to the GP, who is often embarrassed that he does not know what is happening when the patient visits him next.

Conditions that need long-term carefully monitored drug treatment, such as hypertension or refractory depression, present particular difficulty. Should these patients be programmed to have continuous monitoring at the hospital, this must be clearly stated to the GP, who has to maintain the patient's records in the most meaningful and up-to-date manner possible. Generally it is recommended that, except for very specific reasons, the bulk of patients should receive their long-term care from the GP. This means that, when the treatment is recommended to be continued for any length of time by the hospital, or if it is complicated, detailed information on the treatment policy and how it should be monitored (and when it should be stopped) must be conveyed to the GP.

The transition from hospital to community must be seen as part of a continuum of care and not as one agency relinquishing responsibility to another. An assessment of the elderly patient's needs should be identified and effectively organised before discharge. To ensure drug treatment compliance and long-term drug monitoring this will involve collaboration between different professional disciplines both in hospital and

in the community. Where necessary the patient's written information should be shared with the relative or key care worker.

These developments to improve continuity of care do not negate the need for the initial hospital discharge note, including the current drug treatment schedule. GPs say they need the note the day after discharge. Notes available at the time of discharge and delivered by hand best approach this goal (Dover and Low-Beer, 1984), and are thus available to the doctor who first sees the patient after discharge.

Drug treatment compliance

Lack of compliance with drug treatment is currently a major concern with therapists. The balance sheet on this equation does not just include stubborn, awkward, forgetful old people, but also includes lack of comprehension of the drug regime (which can in fact be very complicated) and a positive decision on the part of the older patient that they are better off without the drug. Should the patient make deliberate alterations of dosage him/herself, even after apparently understanding the instructions, there must be room for further on-going discussions on the drug regime. Only by doctor–patient collaboration can one negotiate drug use to obtain the necessary commitment by the patient to comply with an agreed drug schedule.

Therapeutic enthusiasm must be carefully measured. Some old people stop their drugs when they have discovered that the drug therapy appears to make no difference to their well-being, or makes them worse. It has been suggested that 'intelligent non-compliance' may be rational behaviour on the part of the patient. Initial concern that their patients fail to take their medicine has later led some doctors to become aware that they may have been wrong on occasions and that their instructions were best ignored.

Some common factors associated with non-compliance include:

1. Characteristics of the container
2. Labelling
3. Taste and colour of tablets or capsules
4. Size and shape
5. Number of tablets or capsules
6. Product-related reasons including side effects
7. Physical and mental disabilities

8. Lack of understanding
9. The patient's own beliefs

Drugs with sedative effects often confuse older people and impair their ability to comply. Large tablets cannot be swallowed and small ones may be difficult physically to handle. Many drugs are needlessly prescribed in divided doses when a single daily dose is possible (e.g. beta-blockers, diuretics and antidepressants as well as minor and major tranquillisers). [. . .]

The role of other health workers

The progress needed for safer, more effective prescribing amongst the elderly involves collaboration between doctors and other health workers, as well as relatives and the variety of care workers involved in looking after the frail elderly in the community. Regular home visiting by health visitors, district nurses, occupational therapists and related groups can assist the process of medical control (Baxendale *et al.*, 1978).

The introduction of a community psychiatric nursing service, especially for the elderly mentally ill, is being increasingly appreciated by general practitioners. A number of examples of good practice in this area can be found in the United Kingdom. One such is the community nursing services for the elderly mentally ill based at the General Hospital, Hereford. At this hospital, trained psychiatric nurses are available 24 hours a day to provide help and assistance to relatives in coping with elderly mentally ill people. To ensure quick response to calls the nurses are in radio contact with their base. Such schemes, apart from their general value, must increase the potential for safe prescribing in the community. [. . .]

The receptionist and the practice manager

The GP receptionist plays a critical role in the community health delivery service, not least as a liaison worker for the prescription of medicines. In-service training to improve and maintain a high standard of service would seem to have much to commend it. One such in-post training scheme is described by Moules (1984). There is a strong argument to introduce practice managers (as Moules was herself). A manager could, together with the rest of the primary care team, improve record-keeping practices and prescribing practices including standardising safe repeat prescription procedures. Drug prescribing policies could become more attuned to local experience and need. Information, including written information, could be repeatedly reinforced for patients and their families.

The pharmacist

Pharmacists are currently putting forward their own proposals for greater involvement in the prescribing process, as well as the dispensing and monitoring of drugs. Pharmacists claim that they are well trained and capable of much more than merely dispensing drugs that they can act as a check on adverse reactions and drug interactions, and that they can limit the extent of polypharmacy (Weedle and Parish, 1984). They also argue that they should be able to give patients some prescriptions. [. . .]

A welcome development in the pharmacist's participation in hospital out-patient clinics for the elderly has been described by Hackett and Moss-Barclay (1984). They provide drug medication profiles and a medication counselling service for patients and their relatives. In so doing they may identify side effects and drug interactions which otherwise might not be noticed. They also advise physicians on rational drug therapy and cost-effective prescribing and identify potential adverse drug reactions, interactions and inappropriate therapy. The detailed records of the patient's drug programmes were included in the notes and welcomed by the doctor for quick and easy reference. They put forward evidence that counselling and the providing of written information significantly increases compliance. In addition they provide a pharmacokinetic service, which, for example, offered drug level monitoring to out-patients for drugs such as digoxin. This in turn allows for a much more sophisticated drug dose adjustment and hence scope for optimum drug treatment.

Community pharmacists in their turn have not been slow in putting up detailed propositions for treatment schedules and cards for each patient in the community. These cards are essential for any elderly person on regular drug treatment, especially where multiple drug schedules are involved. With regular procedures of updating the cards, compliance and safety must improve. Shulman and Shulman (1980) reported on the operation of a two-card medication record system in a general practice pharmacy, which they found of particular value for older patients and those on multiple drug therapy. Patients were advised to carry their card with them at all times. The pharmacy cards had additional data about histories of adverse drug reactions and chronic illness in the patient. Drugs regularly purchased without prescriptions were also noted as well as special cautions such as diabetes or special allergies. Before a new dose or strength was entered on the card the patient was consulted to check that the change was intentional. Shulman and Shulman found that most of those patients over 60 years regularly returned with their cards when they had a new prescription. They reported that the number of potential adverse reactions or interactions detected in a year amounted to about one per 250 items recorded on the cards, most of which could not have been detected without the card system. They also found that the reaction of the doctors to their system was positive and appreciative. [. . .]

Drug education programmes

Developing innovative drug education programmes is one important task for the future. In Britain, such work is still in its early stages; in America, however, some important projects have been developed by health and social work professionals. The Seniors' Health Program, launched in 1975 by the Chicago-based Augustana Hospital and Health Care Center, is one such example. Under the direction of two half-time geriatric social workers, the programme aims to meet the drug education needs of older people in the Chicago area. This is achieved through group health education, local and out-of-state conferences for health care personnel, health fairs, individual counselling and research. The project works through presentations in sites where older people congregate, through community social agencies, and through drug awareness conferences. [. . .]

Drug monitoring

Any policy for controlling drugs must include reforms of drug trials and post-marketing surveillance. The CSM and CRM, together with other national bodies, have a pressing need to devise new methods of surveillance, not least because of the very limited success of the yellow card system. Recent developments to improve monitoring include the request that doctors be particularly alert to adverse reactions when specific drugs are used (the black triangle system). The symbol denotes that a new drug is in use where it is even more important to report anything unexpected both by the doctor and the patient. In addition, a free telephone facility has been made available for doctors to communicate immediately with the CSM concerning possible untoward drug reactions.

The Drugs Surveillance Research Unit at Southampton University provides another avenue for monitoring drugs. The unit invites participation from doctors nationally who have been identified by the Prescribing Pricing Authority as having patients receiving the drug under study. The prescribers are asked to provide retrospective details of all clinical events following administration of the drug in all their recipients. There are no controls in this method, but there is the potential for earlier detection of toxicity. [. . .]

Clinical studies of elderly patients are now required for product licence applications for new chemical entities, or novel formulations which may be used in the elderly, if any of the factors listed by the CSM give cause for concern about the product. [. . .]

Drug advertising

Finally, rational prescribing will also be helped through reforming the advertising and promotion of drugs. Here, we support Shulman's view that new rules are needed for the acceptance of advertisements for drugs in medical journals. These rules should prevent: 'the trivialisation of side effects, the printing of misleading statements or supply of insufficient information'. In addition: 'Important information on dosage, side effects, contra-indications and drug inter-actions (should be) in a print size at least as prominent as the rest of the advertisement' (Shulman, 1983, p.10). However, we would go further than this in two major respects. First, we would question whether the language and presentation used in drug adverts should be identical to that which is used for advertising all kinds of commodities. It is difficult to envisage how even new rules can be successful if advertising retains its present form, with its focus on dramatic visual imagery in preference to clearly designed displays of relevant prescribing information.

Secondly, a balance must be struck between advertising drug products and educating health care workers about other approaches to achieving health in old age. At a practical level, we think that medical journals would be much improved if there was an equal number of health education adverts to those provided by the pharmaceutical industry. Moreover, we suggest that the financing of these advertisements should be derived from the industry's own promotional budget. So, for example, for every polished advert extolling the virtue of a new anti-arthritic preparation, the industry should pay for an equally glossy presentation, focusing upon complementary approaches in areas such as diet, exercise, self-help and counselling. This would ensure that drug education and health education at least competed on fairer and more equal terms.

REFERENCES

Adams, K.A., and Smith, D.L. (1978). 'Non-prescription drugs and the elderly patient'. *Canadian Pharmaceutical Journal*, **111**, 80–3.

Anderson, R.M. (1980a). 'Prescribing medicine: who takes what?', *Journal of Epidemiology and Community Health*, **34**, 299–304.

Anderson, R.M. (1980b). 'The use of repeatedly prescribed medicines', *Journal of the Royal College of General Practitioners*, **30**, 609–13.

Baxendale, C., Gourlay, M., Gibson, I.I.J.M. (1978). 'A self medication re-training programme'. *British Medical Journal*, **ii**, 1278–9.

Bliss, M.R. (1981). 'Prescribing for the elderly'. *British Medical Journal*, **283**, 203–6.

British Medical Journal leader (1975), 'Tranquillizers causing aggression', **i**, 113–4.

Busson, M., and Dunn, A. (1986). 'Patients' knowledge about prescribed medicines', *The Pharmaceutical Journal*, **236**, 624–6.

Caird, F.I. (1977). 'Prescribing for the elderly', *British Journal of Hospital Medicine*, **17**, 610–13.

Committee for the Review of Medicines (1980). 'Systematic review of the benzodiazepines', *British Medical Journal*, **285**, 910–12.

Committee on Safety of Medicines (1985). 'Update: drugs and the elderly'. *British Medical Journal*, **290**, 1345.

Dover, S.B., and Low-Beer, T.S. (1984). 'The initial hospital discharge note: send out with the patient or post?'. *Health Trends*, **16**, 48.

Drury, V.W.M. (1984). 'Patient information leaflets', *British Medical Journal*, **288**, 427–8.

Dunnell, K., and Cartwright, A. (1972). *Medicine Takers, Prescribers and Hoarders*, Routledge and Kegan Paul, London.

George, C.F. (1980). 'Can adverse reactions be prevented?', *Adverse Drug Reaction Bulletin*, **80**, 288–90.

George, C. (1981). 'The effect of age on drug metabolism', *MIMS Magazine*, 1 March, 55–59.

George, C.F., and Hall, M.R.P. (1981). 'Drugs for dementia', *Prescribers Journal*, **21**, 272–7.

George, I.M.S.F. (1983). 'Patient education leaflets for hypertension: a controlled study', *Journal of the Royal College of General Practitioners*, **33**, 508–10.

Hackett, K., and Moss-Barclay, C. (1984). 'Pharmacist participation in a geriatric out-patient clinic', *British Journal of Pharmaceutical Practice*, December **1984**, 375–6.

Hall, R.C.W., and Joffe, J.R. (1972). 'Aberrant response to diazepam: a new syndrome'. *American Journal of Psychiatry*, **129**, 738–42.

Jones, C.R. (1976). 'Polypharmacy in the elderly', *Geriatric Medicine Update*, October **1976**, 845–9.

Kales, A., Soldates, C.R., Bixler, E.O., and Kales, J.D. (1983). 'Early morning insomnia', *Science*, **220**, 95–7.

Kofoed, L.L. (1986). 'OTC drugs: a third of the elderly are at risk', *Geriatric Medicine*, February **1986**, 37–41.

Laekeman, G.M. (1984). 'Drug information leaflets for patients', *Pharmacy International*, April **1984**, 103–6.

Law, R., and Chalmers, C. (1976). 'Medicines and elderly people: a general practice survey', *British Medical Journal*, **i**, 565–8.

Linkewich, J.A., Catalano, R.B., and Flock, H.L. (1974). 'The effect of packaging and instruction on outpatient compliance with medication regimes', *Drug Intelligence and Clinical Pharmacy*, **8**, 10–15.

Martys, C.R. (1979). 'Adverse reactions to drugs in general practice', *British Medical Journal*, **ii**, 1194–7.

Moules, G. (1984). 'Tune in to better reception', *World Medicine*, September **1984**, 36.

Myers, E.D., and Calvert, E.J. (1978). 'Knowledge of side effects and perseverence with medication', *British Journal of Psychiatry*, **132**, 526–7.

Parish, P. (1971). 'The prescribing of psychotropic drugs in general practice', *Journal of the Royal College of General Practitioners*, **21**, supplement 4, 1–77.

Parkin, D.M., Henney, C.R., Quirk, J., and Crooks, J. (1976). 'Deviation from prescribed treatment after discharge from hospital', *British Medical Journal*, **ii**, 686–8.

Parrott, A.C., and Kentridge, R. (1982). 'Personal constructs of anxiety under the 1,5-benzodiazepine clobazam related to trait-anxiety levels of the personality', *Psychopharmacology*, **78**, 353–7.

Peturrson, H., and Lader, M.H. (1981). 'Benzodiazepine dependence', *British Journal of Addiction*, **76**, 133–45.

Prescott, L. (1979). 'Factors predisposing of adverse drug reactions', *Adverse Drug Reaction Bulletin*, **78**, 280–3.

Royal College of Physicians (1984). 'Medication for the elderly, *Journal of the Royal College of Physicians of London*, **18**, 7–17.

Sharpe, D., and Kay, M. (1977). 'Worrying trends in prescribing', *Modern Geriatrics*, **7**, 32–6.

Shulman, J. (1983). 'Prevention of adverse drug reactions', *Update*, 15 October **1983**, 1127–1126.

Shulman, S., and Shulman, J.I. (1980). 'Operating a two-card medication record system in general practice pharmacy', *Practitioner*, **224**, 989–92.

Sloan, P.J.M. (1984). 'Survey of patient information booklets', *British Medical Journal*, *288*, 915–19.

Taylor, D. (1983). 'Medicine for the elderly', *Journal of the Market Research Society*, **25**, 263–74.

Townsend, P. and Davidson, N. (eds.) (1982). *Inequalities in Health*, Pelican Books, London.

Tyrer, P. (1984). 'Benzodiazepines on trial', *British Medical Journal*, **288**, 1101–2.

Wandless, I., and Davie, J.W.L. (1977). 'Can drug compliance in the elderly be improved?', *British Medical Journal*, **i**. 359–61.

Weedle, P., and Parish, P. (1984 and 1985). 'Pharmaceutical care of the elderly', *British Journal of Pharmaceutical Practice*, November and subsequent issues to June.

Williams, P. (1980). 'Recent trends in the prescribing of psychotropic drugs', *Health Trends*, **12**, 6–7.

Williams, P. (1983). 'Factors influencing the duration of treatment with psychotropic drugs in general practice: survival analysis approach'. *Psychological Medicine*, **13**, 623–33.

Williamson, J. (1978). 'Prescribing problems in the elderly', *Practitioner*, **220**, 749–55.

World Health Organisation (1981). *The Control of Drugs for the Elderly*, WHO Report, WHO, Copenhagen.

The ethics of compulsory removal

J.A. MUIR GRAY

Community Physician, Radcliffe Infirmary, Oxford

In recent years there has been considerable debate about the compulsory removal from their homes of people who are mentally ill. The debate has focused on a number of different issues: how mental illness should be defined, who should be responsible for removal, and what safeguards should exist for the protection of the individual. With the exception, however, of a very few radicals such as Thomas Szasz,[1] there is general acceptance of the need for such powers, because it is generally accepted that there is a condition of mind, still most usefully defined by the old-fashioned term 'insanity', which ethically justifies paternalistic interventions such as the compulsory removal of someone from his home. There is, though, another piece of legislation in the United Kingdom which has received much less attention in recent years, although it is ethically far more contentious. This is Section 47 of the National Assistance Act which allows for the removal of individuals who are not insane and for their compulsory detention in institutions.

Section 47 of the 1948 National Assistance Act gave the Medical Officer of Health the power to apply to a magistrate for the compulsory removal of persons who

(a) are suffering from grave chronic disease or, being aged, infirm or physically incapacitated, are living in insanitary conditions, and (b) are unable to devote to themselves, and are not receiving from other persons, proper care and attention.

Section 47 also allows the Medical Officer of Health to use these powers to remove a person to prevent 'injury to the health of, or serious nuisance to, other persons'. To obtain an order for removal the Medical Officer of Health had to give seven days' notice to a

Court of Summary Jurisdiction which could authorize a person's 'detention' for a period not exceeding three months in a 'suitable hospital or other place'.

In 1951 this Act was amended to allow for the immediate removal of individuals who could not be left for seven days. The legislation was amended because of the fate of one woman who lay on her kitchen floor for the seven-day period of notice required by the 1948 Act and who during that time developed a pressure sore which became infected with tetanus bacteria, with the result that she died of tetanus. The powers of immediate removal were obviously open to abuse because the legislation allowed for a Justice of the Peace to grant an order in his own home and did not require the Medical Officer of Health to approach a court. To safeguard the rights of the individual the Medical Officer of Health was required to obtain the support of another registered medical practitioner and was allowed to apply for removal only for a period of three weeks' detention.

With the reorganization of the National Health Service in 1974, the responsibility for the execution of these powers passed from the Medical Officer of Health to the community physician. The legal power is still invested in the District Council, which is also responsible for environmental health, but the community physician acts as the 'Proper Officer' to the District Council.

These powers are infrequently used. Only about 200 people are removed annually. In most cases the powers of immediate removal are employed and the great majority of individuals removed are elderly. These 200 cases are, however, only the tip of the iceberg. Many more are referred to community physicians and are not removed; and there are many more old people who are either at risk or who are neglecting themselves who are not referred and who are either left at home at risk or in a state of dirt and disorder, or whose admission is effected by one means or another. The elderly person may, for example, be coerced into accepting hospitalization by the unremitting pressure of her relatives and professional advisers. She may be deceived by being told that she is only 'going for a holiday' when she is in fact being admitted permanently to a home or her resistance may be overcome by tranquillizing drugs. In one case in which Section 47 was not used the general practitioner simply added a powerful tranquillizer to the old person's tea.

SELF-NEGLECT

It is common for people to take less care of their appearance as they grow older, for example to buy fewer new clothes or to go to the hairdresser less frequently. For the majority of people this trend simply reflects the fact that income usually declines on retirement and the fact that many people become less vain about their appearance as they grow older.

There is, however, a small proportion of people who seriously neglect themselves and their dwellings. The common pattern is for the individual to wear old clothes and to live in a cluttered and dirty house surrounded by an unkempt garden. The precise pattern differs from individual to individual. (Personally, I tend to divide such cases into those with cats, and those without.) Some maintain personal cleanliness; while others become dirty and begin to smell. Some simply wear old clothes, whereas others wear torn and filthy ones. Some simply preserve newspapers, books, and papers; others have piles of mouldering food and rows of unwashed milk bottles. Some seek medical attention when they become unwell; others fail to do so.

It has been suggested that all individuals who neglect themselves are suffering from the 'Diogenes Syndrome';[2] but this term is a reflection more of the desire of the medical profession to classify individuals, than of the objective existence of any such condition. Individuals who neglect themselves and their environment have only this feature in common; they are no more likely to be similar in other respects than are any two individuals selected at random.

OLD PEOPLE AT RISK

Elderly people who neglect themselves are often at risk: risk of hypothermia, risk of falling, or risk of fire. But there are other individuals who do not neglect themselves in any way other than in failing to take appropriate steps to reduce the risks they run, for example the clean and well-dressed elderly person who lives in a neat and tidy house but who refuses to use more than one electric fire in the winter, even though he has previously been admitted to hospital suffering from hypothermia.

Old people who are deemed to be 'at risk' are the subject of considerable public and professional concern. They, like elderly people who neglect themselves, are frequently referred to consultants in geriatric medicine or psychiatrists or to community physicians. Referrals to the latter are often accompanied by requests for compulsory removal.

REFUSAL OF HELP

The fact that an elderly person is at risk or neglecting herself does not by itself constitute an ethical problem. There are two things that make it a problem: first, the old person's refusal of offers of help, and secondly the beliefs and attitudes of other people, which determine the ethical context in which the professional has to work and make his decisions.

The beliefs of elderly people help to influence their attitudes towards and decisions about help and treatment. Some elderly people believe that all their problems are caused by the ageing process and are *ipso facto* untreatable. Alternatively, the elderly person may accept that his problem was at one time treatable, but believes that it is now 'too late' or even—a commonly expressed view—that the health and social services should not waste their resources on elderly people: as one old woman who was refusing help put it, 'Help those handicapped children who are in much greater need than I am'.

It is important to appreciate the strength of these beliefs and not simply to see them as a form of ignorance. In many cases the elderly person has a very solid foundation for his or her beliefs.

Miss R. was house-bound and immobilized by Parkinson's disease and arthritis. She was referred to the community physician because she consistently refused to heat her house other than by one storage heater. The community physician visited her on a cold frosty February morning. The window of the room in which the old person was sitting was open and cold fog was drifting into the room. All the community physician's arguments about why the old person should be using more heating were politely received but obviously made no impact. As he was on the point of leaving, the old lady said 'I used to work for your predecessor, the Medical Officer of Health'. When questioned she revealed that she had been a schoolteacher in the school for delicate children forty years previously, working in an era in which the medical profession advocated cold fresh air as a vitally important prophylactic and therapeutic measure.

Yet another reason why many elderly people say 'What else can you expect at my age?' is that at some time or other some doctor has said to them 'What else can you expect at your age?'[3]

Religious beliefs are also important. Some elderly people are fatalistic, believing that their problem has been sent by God or that God has let it happen; that it is a manifestation of God's will. Fortunately this does not usually lead to a refusal of offers of help and treatment, because they too are seen as manifestations of God's will. Of greater importance is the fact that some older people interpret their suffering as a punishment for some past sin, basing their belief on the Prayer for the Sick in the *Book of Common Prayer*. On occasion, an elderly person becomes preoccupied with her guilt and for this reason is not interested in offers of help.

In some cases shame at the condition into which she has drifted leads an old person to bar her house to those who would help her. Miss N. was the only surviving sister of three who had once lived in a large house. She now lived in the basement of the house and had consistently refused offers of help when these were suggested by a neighbour who did all her cooking and shopping. One December evening the neighbour felt unable to continue her support and asked the general practitioner to visit. He found Miss N. sitting on the floor of her basement, her face and hands dirty, she was cold and blue, showed signs of early hypothermia and congestive cardiac failure, and her left foot was lying in an awkward position suggesting a fractured neck of femur. She refused the offer of hospital admission and the community physician had her compulsorily removed from her cold and filthy basement. She sobbed as she was removed, the tears coursing through the dirt that was thick on her cheeks.

An hour after admission, after she had been bathed and changed, she smiled and waved at the community physician and said that the reason she had been unwilling to accept help was that she had become ashamed of the condition into which she had allowed herself to slip.

Self-neglect may of course be a sign of depression, with the elderly person feeling himself worthless and useless and perhaps wishing to die. There are, however, elderly people who want to die who cannot be said to be depressed; for example, elderly disabled people who find their lives intolerable or pointless and who wish to be released. Such people rarely actively refuse offers of treatment, though. Usually they accept passively the help that is given, often expressing the wish that they would die and cease to be a burden on those who help them.

INCOMPETENT OLD PEOPLE

If an old person is neglecting herself or allowing herself to be at risk because she is suffering from a severe degree of dementia, or a severe degree of depression, she can be considered to be insane and the Mental Health Act can be used to remove her from her home to a hospital. But what about the very many elderly people who have either a milder degree of dementia or some other disease that causes intellectual impairment, for example alcoholism? These people cannot be removed using the Mental Health Act, for when interviewed they are quite obviously not severely mentally ill and would not, in the opinion of a reasonable person, be considered to be insane; but nor would they be considered by the man on the Clapham omnibus to be completely normal. Individuals such as this may be considered to be incompetent.

The concept of incompetence is, like the concept of insanity, a legal concept. But unlike the latter is does not refer to the individual's mind as a whole but only to the individual's ability to use his mind in certain specific situations. As Beauchamp and Childress put it,

Some persons who are legally incompetent may be competent to conduct most of their personal affairs, and vice versa. The same person's ability to make decisions may vary over time, and the person may at a single time be competent to make certain practical decisions but incompetent to make others. For example, a person judged incompetent to drive an automobile may not be incompetent to decide to participate in medical research, or may be able to handle simple affairs easily, while faltering before complex ones.[4] [. . .]

Determining incompetence is relevant both in situations in which the individual is deemed to be at risk and in situations in which he is either neglecting himself or refusing the offer of effective treatment. Numerous referrals are made to the health and social services concerning elderly people who are deemed to be at risk of setting fire to their dwellings; and indeed it is true that the mortality rate from fire is higher in old age, increasing from 3 deaths per 100,000 per annum in the age group 65–74 to 15 deaths per 100,000 per annum in people aged over 85. Requests for the compulsory removal of individuals who are refusing admission to hospital for treatment are common, in spite of the fact that Section 47 does not give doctors the power of treatment, but only the power of removal. Even if a person were to be removed using Section 47, the doctor in hospital who treated that person against his will could still be charged with assault. This is less of a problem in practice, however, than it is in theory. I have admitted six people compulsorily to hospital, all of whom have required treatment of one sort or another, and all accepted the treatment without explicit refusal. This was either because they ceased their opposition to hospital treatment once hospital admission had been effected, or because they simply complied with the expectations of firm, polite, and busy hospital staff who were in many cases unaware of the difficulties that preceded admission. Hospital staff do not, after all, ask the patient for his consent every time they have to perform a test or give treatment: compliance is assumed once the person has been admitted to hospital.

THE ATTITUDES AND BELIEFS OF OTHER PEOPLE

The attitudes and beliefs of other people influence the behaviour of the old person, the timing and nature of the referral, and the behaviour of the professionals involved. In these attitudes and beliefs, genuine care and concern are typically combined with an underestimation of the ability of elderly people to assess the risks they are running. Hence there is a general assumption that elderly people should be protected from the consequences of their actions. [. . .]

The greatest pressure on the old person and the attending professionals often comes from neighbours and relatives who feel guilty. For the person who feels guilty as a result of the condition in which he sees one of his elders and wants to alleviate his guilt, the choice is simple: either he must provide practical assistance for the old person, or else he must attempt to have the old person removed from his sight to be 'looked after' or 'cared for', thus removing the object of his guilt. Some people still feel morally outraged if a person is neglecting himself, because they feel that this neglect is tantamount to suicide by an act of omission, and as such is as wrong, morally, as suicide by an act of commission. In this context, it is important to remember that when the legislation which became Section 47 (Section 56 of the Bradford Corporation Act of 1925) was first drafted, suicide was a crime, and was still regarded by many people as a grave sin.

Similarly, calls for the removal of elderly people, which were articulated first at the end of the nineteenth century and in the majority and minority reports of the Poor Law Commission in 1909, reflected not only concern about the individual but also a general concern about the effects of dirt and disorder on society as a whole. [. . .] Societies depend on a degree of order if they are to survive. And dirt is merely one form of physical disorder. Our reactions to the old person who is living in filthy conditions may in part reflect the fear, at some deep level of our psyche, that disorder may engulf us. [. . .]

I would suggest, at any rate as an historical matter, that Section 47 has had, as one implicit objective, that of imposing order and cleanliness, not merely as a way of protecting others from some palpable threat, such as that of disease, but for its own sake: because deviance in these respects offends and disturbs us. [. . .]

At any event, one still encounters strong feelings about elderly people who are living in a state of dirt and disorder. Sympathy for the elderly person is mixed with fear, on the part of the neighbours who are worried about fire, and with the anger of those who feel that the old person could do more to help himself if he tried:

Miss S. had lived all her life in a small village. She was now nearly seventy and lived in a small almshouse, the door of which faced that of a neighbouring almshouse, a mere four feet away. The floors of her dwelling were two feet thick in hard-packed dirt; and for light she relied on paraffin which she kept by her front door in open containers. Her clothes and her person were dirty and in the summer both she and her house stank.

It was decided not to remove her from her house, but to dig out the dirt. In order to facilitate this, her furniture was temporarily removed and stored in the village hall. The result was that the hall keeper and several members of the hall committee resigned in protest; and it became clear that although a number of villagers thought it wrong that help had not been offered this lady earlier, others in the village, while conceding that she was of limited intelligence, felt that it was wrong to use public money to help her at all. This in view of the fact that she was, for example, still able to take the bus to a neighbouring town to play bingo, and indeed occasionally won. [. . .]

People are uncertain where neighbourly help stops and professional help starts. Members of the public see social problems in their society and maintain that professionals should do the caring but feel guilty that they themselves are not caring, just as in seventeenth-century England—with one difference. The accusations are no longer directed at the poor elderly people themselves but at the professionals; the term 'witch-hunt', used to describe the search for professional culprits when an old person is found dead or a child in care is killed, symbolizes this attitude dramatically and clearly. The public do not wish the old people punished, in the sense in which that word is used today, but many people do want them 'put away', or in their terms 'cared for', to alleviate guilt and reduce anxiety.

THE COMMUNITY PHYSICIAN'S DILEMMA

These are the factors that the community physician has to bear in mind. But his basic dilemma is relatively simple: should he, or should he not, apply for an order for removal?

The first step is to decide whether or not removal is necessary, for in many cases it is possible to find a technical alternative to removal, thus freeing one from the ethical dilemma. If the problem is primarily environmental, with the old person living in 'insanitary conditions' or in conditions which are likely to cause an 'injury to the health of, or serious nuisance to, other persons', it is not necessary to remove the old person from his environment. In all the cases in which I have been involved it has been possible to improve the environment in which the old person is living. For the Public Health Act gives the community physician power, in co-operation with his colleagues in environmental health, to deal with flea-invested cats and dogs, clear accumulations of animal excreta, destroy soiled clothing and bedding, clean up filthy conditions in which rats are breeding, unblock toilets that are overflowing, clear blocked sewers, and remove accumulations of rubbish or rotting food. Sometimes the old person is very distressed by this type of intervention, and it is not one that is undertaken lightly. But if the old person is putting other people at risk then the ethical issue is clear-cut; the law can be invoked to fulfil its traditional purpose, namely the protection of the individual from harm by others, in this case harm from the old person who is living in insanitary conditions. [. . .]

Secondly, it is essential to consider whether the old person can benefit only if he is removed from his dwelling or whether it is possible to provide a similar, or even greater, benefit by intervening in his own home. One's options are, of course, limited if the old person is not only refusing admission to hospital but also refuses to have domiciliary services such as home help or district nursing:

Miss P. lived alone in a semi-detached house and kept herself to herself. She visited the GP from time to time but had insisted that she was not in need of any help from the domiciliary services. The general practitioner was called to see her late one night in December and saw her lying in bed unable to open the door and obviously in need of some care and attention, for the house was very cold. It might have been possible to keep her in her own home by organizing district nursing and home help, but she adamantly refused to discuss the possiblity of care in her own home. She was therefore compulsorily admitted to hospital, in spite of the fact that she did not require any treatment that could not have been given her in her own home.

If the person is willing to accept domiciliary care and if she has the type of problem that allows her to be dealt with at home, the community physician may face a different dilemma. For the extent to which it is possible to care for someone in their own home is a function not only of the nature of their problem; it is a function also of the resources that are available. If one were able to provide an old person suffering from pneumonia with one or two nurses right round the clock, then care at home would frequently be feasible. Given that resources are limited, however, and have to be spread thinly, it is not possible in practice to provide a person with two skilled nurses round the clock in their own home. In any case, the community physician knows full well that even if he were to press very hard for this level of domiciliary service and succeed in getting it, it would not be the ratepayers and taxpayers that paid for it; it would be other elderly people, whose services would have to be reduced to provide intensive care for this one individual. This would inevitably mean that other elderly people would have to go into institutional care sooner than would otherwise have been necessary, had not this one very assertive elderly person (or elderly person championed by a very assertive community physician) successfully demanded the intensive care in her own home instead of going into hospital when she had reached the conventional limits of domiciliary care. The community physician has, therefore, like all other professionals, to act as a rationer of resources; and when he tells an elderly person that it is not possible for her to be looked after in her own home, what he often means is that it is not possible to look after her in her own home with the amount of resources that are currently available, without creating inequities: without, that is, being unfair to his other clients.

Even if the old person cannot be looked after in her own home, the decision to apply for an order for compulsory removal is still a difficult one to take. The decision that admission is necessary is usually based on the need for specialist treatment; but, as I emphasized above, the order for compulsory removal does not confer the right to treat if the elderly person withholds her consent after admission. This has not been a common problem in practice, but a more difficult problem arises from the fact that the relocation of an elderly person itself carries an element of risk.

In 1976 the *British Medical Journal* published an article with the provocative title, 'Slow euthanasia or—"she will be better off in hospital" ',[5] which received considerable publicity. There are, in fact, a number of detailed studies demonstrating the adverse effects of relocation.[6] It has been shown that both morbidity and mortality may be increased by uprooting elderly people from one environment and placing them in another that is supposedly more beneficial. Just how likely it is that removal will have an adverse effect depends on a number of factors. But it is known that physical illness, depression, and feelings of hopelessness are all associated with a higher probability that harmful consequences will follow if an old person is moved against her will; whereas these, ironically, are the very factors which usually give rise to the request for compulsory removal. The community physician therefore has to bear in mind not only the possible benefits of a move but also the possible harm that such a move may entail.

THE QUESTION OF COMPETENCE

Where the community physician judges that an elderly person is incompetent, what he must try to do is act in a way that the person would herself, in her competent state, have approved of—would indeed approve of if, as lawyers sometimes say, she were to be granted a 'moment of lucidity'. This may be very difficult, if the community physician is given no information about her beliefs and attitudes before confusion set in.

Mrs I. had been widowed for many years. She lived in a flat above a church hall and for a number of years had been a conscientious caretaker, able both to look after herself and to help others. She developed both dementia and physical illness and after one admission to hospital her intellectual impairment became markedly worse. She was discharged to her flat, where she spent most of her time sitting in the kitchen neither eating the meals on wheels that were brought to her nor even drinking the tea that was poured out and left by her side. She was not completely immobile, however; for she used to go outside and wander in the road, looking for a cat that had been dead for three years. This behaviour continued until cold weather set in.

She was obviously at serious risk, because she was found at two in the morning during a freezing night, wandering about dressed only in blouse and skirt calling for her cat. She was compulsorily admitted to hospital and then transferred to an old-people's home. She said that she would like to go back home; but the church, on the advice of the health and social services, stated that they required her flat for other workers in the church. This was true, but to spare her feelings they omitted to say that they were afraid of her setting fire to her flat, the church hall, or the vicarage. She therefore continued to live in the old-people's home.

This woman had dementia, but the psychiatrist had decided that she could not be considered insane and therefore could not be removed using the Mental Health Act. The community physician therefore ruled her incompetent and obtained an order for her removal using the National Assistance Act.

The community physician is faced with a different problem if the person is not so obviously incompetent. Let us consider the case of Mr T.

Mr T. had recently retired. He lived alone in a room near the city centre and spent his days walking in the streets, sitting in the public library, and seeing friends. He was admitted to hospital for a bleeding ulcer, had an operation, and was then discharged, weak and anaemic. Unfortunately, he fell and twisted his knee and therefore became confined to his bed in his room. Because the meals-on-wheels service was unable to get into the multi-occupied house in which he lived, nobody knew that he was unable to get up until his landlord called his GP three weeks later, by which time his mattress and bedding were soaked with three weeks' accumulated urine and faeces.

His soiled bedding was then destroyed, he was washed and fed and made much more comfortable in bed; but his knee failed to improve, and he was obviously developing pneumonia in one lung. He said he did not want to die and that his wish was to get fit enough to walk about town again, but he still refused to go into hospital.

This man did not show any evidence of dementia, nor did he show any evidence of being confused as a result of his physical illness. Should a man like this be considered to be competent but misguided and therefore be removed by the community physician because he is making a wrong decision? Or should he be considered to be incompetent by virtue of the fact that he is making an illogical decision in wishing to remain active but refusing to go to hospital, which

is the only means that would enable him to regain his previous level of activity? I was unable to work out the precise reasons for my action on that hot Sunday afternoon in his small cramped room; but I decided to remove him compulsorily. He told me that he did not think it was right. I replied that it might or might not be right, but that I considered it to be legal. He was admitted to hospital, made a good recovery, and was discharged to a hostel where he occupied a pleasant single room. When interviewed after discharge he was asked why he had kept refusing admission. He replied that he had simply kept telling himself that things could be worse.

The dilemma is even more dramatic when the person has a life-threatening illness, is incompetent by virtue of confusion or unconsciousness, and where there is a treatment for that illness that can be given only in hospital. In such cases the community physician has to decide whether the person's illness should be accepted as being a terminal illness or whether it should be considered to be a treatable or potentially curable disorder. This type of case is particularly difficult when the life-threatening illness is itself responsible for the confusion, a common occurrence in old age, when diseases such as pneumonia and congestive cardiac failure frequently cause confusion in addition to their physical signs and symptoms. In such cases the doctor has to rely on the reports of other people regarding the person's previous wishes and preferences; and it is sometimes very difficult to get an accurate account of the individual's beliefs and attitudes before the onset of the illness. Where the individual is known to have a severe degree of dementia, the problems of the professionals are obvious; for it is rare in this country for the elderly person to leave instructions that can help the professionals attending her when she develops dementia and an acute severe illness. In the United States, however, it has become common for elderly people to write 'living wills' setting out their views about the most appropriate way to manage severe life-threatening illness should they be incompetent to make a decision themselves. These living wills have been interpreted differently from State to State. In some States the medical profession has been strongly advised that it cannot assume that a living will could be taken as a legal instruction in a court of law if, for example, relatives were to sue a doctor who had omitted to treat an old person with pneumonia because she had said in her living will that she did not want to be given life-saving treatment were she to have developed dementia in the interim.

In the United Kingdom few people have taken this formal step. Perhaps because the population is less prone to litigation than in the United States, doctors intervene less in old age. In this country many doctors will not use antibiotics in the treatment of pneumonia, if the patient has dementia, although they and their nursing colleagues will take steps to ensure that the patient is well cared for, for example by being given adequate fluid The doctor in this situation is making his decision within the ethical context defined by the values and attitudes of the society in which he is working.

Similar problems arise when the old person is known to have been opposed to any form of intervention before the onset of the disease that caused her confusional state. In such cases the community physician has to weigh up a number of factors, most notably the expressed wishes of the old person, her behaviour in the past when help was offered her, the likely course of events if her disorder is not treated, and the potential benefits of treatment.

THE FUTURE OF SECTION 47

There is a case for amending Section 47 if it is to remain an effective means of protecting individual elderly people from paternalistic relatives and professionals, and not to become merely a tool for the latter; its use should be more clearly monitored than it is at present. Unlike the compulsory removals made using the powers of the Mental Health Act, there is no requirement to notify the Department of Health and Social Security of the number of times the powers granted by Section 47 are used; thus there are no means of comparing the use made of the powers in different parts of the country. Similarly, no mechanism exists for scrutinizing the effects of compulsory removal. It seems to me that a system of review would provide the best safeguard against abuse. The decision to remove or not to remove has to be left to the discretion of the individual magistrate, guided by the professionals involved, and it would not be feasible to attempt to draw up a set of guidelines or conditions to cover all the varied circumstances that one encounters. Nevertheless it is highly desirable that doctor and magistrate should be made subject to the kind of accountability that a system of review would introduce.

REFERENCES

1. Thomas S. Szasz, 'Involuntary mental hospitalization: a crime against humanity'. In Tom L. Beauchamp and L. Walters (eds.), *Contemporary Issues in Bioethics*, Wadsworth, Encino, California, 1978, pp.551–7.
2. E.N. Clark and I. Grey, 'The Diogenes syndrome', *Lancet* 1975, 366–8 (1975).
3. See G.K. Wilcock, J.A.M. Gray and P.M.M. Pritchard, *Geriatric Problems in General Practice*, Oxford University Press, Oxford, 1982.
4. Tom L. Beauchamp and James F. Childress, *Principles of Biomedical Ethics*, Oxford University Press, New York and Oxford, 1979, pp.67–70.
5. A.A. Baker, 'Slow euthanasia or—"she will be better off in hospital"', *British Medical Journal*, **2**, 571–7 (1976).
6. M.A. Lieberman, V.N. Prock and S.S. Tobin, 'Psychological effects of institutionalisation', *Journal of Gerontology*, **23**, 343–53 (1968).

Index